CW00519916

DISRAELI'S JEWISHNESS

Parkes-Wiener Series on Jewish Studies
Series Editors: David Cesarani and Tony Kushner
ISSN 1368-5449

The field of Jewish Studies is one of the youngest, but fastest growing and most exciting areas of scholarship in the academic world today. Named after James Parkes and Alfred Wiener, this series aims to publish new research in the field and student materials for use in the seminar room, to disseminate the latest work of established scholars and to re-issue classic studies which are currently out of print.

The selection of publications reflects the international character and diversity of Jewish Studies; it ranges over Jewish history from Abraham to modern Zionism, and Jewish culture from Moses to post-modernism. The series also reflects the inter-disciplinary approach inherent in Jewish Studies and at the cutting edge of contemporary scholarship, and provides an outlet for innovative work on the interface between Judaism and ethnicity, popular culture, gender, class, space and memory.

Other Books in the Series

DISRAELI'S JEWISHNESS

Edited by
TODD M. ENDELMAN
and
TONY KUSHNER

VALLENTINE MITCHELL
LONDON • PORTLAND, OR

First published in 2002 in Great Britain by
VALLENTINE MITCHELL
Crown House, 47 Chase Side
Southgate, London N14 5BP

and in the United States of America by
VALLENTINE MITCHELL
c/o ISBS, 5824 N. E. Hassalo Street
Portland, Oregon 97213-3644

Website: www.vmbooks.com

Copyright of collection © 2002 Vallentine Mitchell
Copyright of chapters © 2002 contributors

British Library Cataloguing in Publication Data

Disraeli's Jewishness. – (Parkes-Wiener series on Jewish studies)
1. Disraeli, Benjamin, 1804–1881 2. Prime ministers – Great
Britain 3. Jews – Great Britain 4. Great Britain – Politics
and government – 1837–1901 5. Great Britain – Race relations
– Political aspects
I. Endelman, Todd M. II. Kushner, Tony
941'.081'092

ISBN 0-85303-366-8 (cloth)
ISBN 0-85303-373-0 (paper)
ISSN 1368-5449

Library of Congress Cataloguing-in-Publication Data
A catalog record for this book is available from the
Library of Congress

*All rights reserved. No part of this publication may be reproduced, stored in or
introduced into a retrieval system or transmitted in any form or by any means,
electronic, mechanical, photocopying, recording or
otherwise, without the prior written permission of the publisher of this book.*

Typeset in Janson 11/13pt by Cambridge Photosetting Services, Cambridge
Printed in Great Britain by MPG Books Ltd, Bodmin, Cornwall

CONTENTS

Part 3: Afterlife

ILLUSTRATIONS

(on pages 110 to 138)

NOTES ON CONTRIBUTORS

Richard W. Davis is Professor of History and Director of the Center for the History of Freedom at Washington University. He is the editor and author of many books and articles on the eighteenth and nineteenth century including *Disraeli* (1976) and *The English Rothschilds* (1983).

Todd M. Endelman is William Haber Professor of Modern Jewish History at the University of Michigan. He is the author of *The Jews of Georgian England, 1714–1830: Tradition and Change in a Liberal Society* (1979; 2nd edn, 1999), *Radical Assimilation in English Jewish History, 1656–1945* (1990) and *The Jews of Britain, 1656–2000* (2002).

Edgar Feuchtwanger has written several books on British politics in the later Victorian period, including biographies of Disraeli (2000) and Gladstone (2nd edn, 1989) and a book on the Conservative party of that period, *Disraeli, Democracy and the Tory Party* (1968). He has also published books and articles on modern German history.

Tony Kushner is Marcus Sieff Professor in the Department of History and Head of the Parkes Institute for the Study of Jewish/non-Jewish Relations at the University of Southampton. His books include *The Holocaust and the Liberal Imagination: A Social and Cultural History* (1994) and, with Katharine Knox, *Refugees in an Age of Genocide: Global, National and Local Perspectives during the Twentieth Century* (1999).

Daniel R. Schwarz is Professor and Stephen H. Weiss Presidential Fellow in the English Department, Cornell University. He has written many books including *Disraeli's Fiction* (1979) and most recently *Imagining the Holocaust* (1999) and *Rereading Conrad* (2001).

Nadia Valman is Lecturer in the English Department and Research Fellow in the AHRB Parkes Centre for the Study of Jewish/non-Jewish Relations at the University of Southampton. She has published a number of articles on Victorian Anglo-Jewish literature, is co- editor of *Remembering Cable Street: Fascism and Anti-Fascism in British Society* (1999) and editor of the journal *Jewish Culture and History*.

Tony Wohl has just retired after 38 years teaching at Vassar College. He is the author of *The Eternal Slum: Housing and Social Policy in Victorian London* (1977) and *Endangered Lives: Public Health in Victorian and Edwardian England* (1983). He has edited key texts and essay collections on Victorian England and is currently working on a book dealing with representations of Disraeli in Victorian periodical, pamphlet and pictorial literature.

ACKNOWLEDGEMENTS

This volume grew out of a conference held under the auspices of the Parkes Centre for the Study of Jewish/non-Jewish Relations at the University of Southampton in 1994. One 'excuse' for the conference was to mark the one hundred and fiftieth anniversary of the publication of Disraeli's novel *Coningsby*. More important, however, was a recognition of the growing interest in Disraeli's Jewishness in the academic world, work that was particularly exciting because of its multi- and inter-disciplinary nature incorporating approaches from history, literary studies, politics, gender studies, cultural studies, racial and ethnic studies, and Jewish studies. It was felt, quite rightly, that a conference on the topic by bringing these international scholars together would be timely and fruitful. A selection of the papers from the conference was published in a special issue of the journal *Jewish History* (Fall 1996). These have been amended and extended and new essays introduced to form this more inclusive volume.

We should like to take this opportunity of thanking all the speakers and delegates for making the conference so successful, Professor Paul Smith for his advice in planning the conference, Dr Chris Woolgar, Director of the Hartley Institute at the University of Southampton, whose support enabled the conference to happen and the Department of History for further financial support. We should like to acknowledge the contribution of Kenneth Stow, editor of *Jewish History*, the assistance of Melanie Aspey, archivist at the Rothschild Archive, and, for granting permissions, the Earl of Rosebery, the staff at the National Portrait Gallery, London, and the British Library Reproductions Department. Finally, we should like to thank Dr Joanna Newman, who was the conference administrator, Dr Jo Reilly for her extensive support in the editing process, Sybil Lunn for providing the index and the staff at Frank Cass Publishers, especially Sally Green, and Frank Cass himself for his enthusiasm for this project.

INTRODUCTION

Todd M. Endelman and Tony Kushner

Born a Jew, Benjamin Disraeli became a Christian at age 12 when his father decided that he and his siblings would have more opportunities in life as Christians than Jews. There was nothing unusual about this. Many Sephardim in late-Georgian England who were indifferent to religion made the same decision and broke with the Spanish and Portuguese synagogue in Bevis Marks. Disraeli remained a Christian, with unorthodox views to be sure, for the rest of his life. He was not, however, fervent in his faith or pious in his devotions and some would claim was as much a sceptic as his deistic father, noting that on his deathbed he rejected the suggestion of his doctor that he summon a clergyman. Nonetheless, his romantic-organic conservatism led him to value the social function of religion and in particular an established church. Like other respectable Victorians he attended church, acknowledged Jesus as messiah and redeemer and voiced the classical supercessionist view that Christianity completed Judaism. At his death he was buried as a Christian, not a Jew, in the churchyard at Hughenden, down the hill from the country house he had owned since 1848.

Despite his conversion and his more than nominal attachment to Christianity Disraeli remained a Jew in the eyes of his Jewish contemporaries and was never regarded as a traitor or renegade, as was often the case with converts at the time. In 1844, an English Jew wrote to him to say how much he esteemed his genius and how much the Jewish nation was indebted to him for his work on its behalf. Four decades later, the American Jewish poet Emma Lazarus asked in the *Century Magazine*, 'Was the Earl of Beaconsfield a Representative Jew?', a question she answered in the affirmative. Disraeli's perseverance in the face of hostility was emblematic of the Jewish struggle for survival. He embodied what was for her 'the most characteristic feature of the Jew', a trait 'developed to perfection by ages of persecution': 'the faculty which enables this people, not only to perceive and make the most of every advantage of their situation and temperament, but also, with marvellous adroitness, to transform their very disabilities into new instruments of power'. Louise de Rothschild, the youngest child of the founder of the English branch of the banking clan, wrote that when she heard Disraeli speak she could not help feeling 'a sort of pride in the thought that he belongs to us – that he is one of Israel's sons'. When her niece Lady Battersea, daughter of Sir Anthony de Rothschild, heard of Disraeli's death she wrote to her husband that their late friend had always been loyal 'to the race from which he sprung' and added that 'his racial instincts were his religion and he was true to that religion until he drew his last breath'. Even Jewish assimilationists considered him a 'representative' Jew. The Danish critic Georg Brandes who deplored Disraeli's racial chauvinism and his 'wearisome' lists of great Jews, nonetheless cited his energy, perseverance, quickness, wit, love of pomp and ambition as 'typical' Jewish traits.[1] Comments like these were in no sense unusual; with few exceptions, Disraeli's Jewish contemporaries saw him as one of their own.

In the decades after his death Jews everywhere, not just in Britain, continued to view Disraeli as a 'representative' Jew, a credit to his people. The preface to the *Jewish Encyclopaedia*, published in New York between 1901 and 1906, noted that in modern times 'the genius of the Jews' had asserted 'its claims to intellectual leadership through men like Mendelssohn, Heine, Lassalle, and Disraeli'. That Heine and Disraeli were Christians was not a problem for the editors. Since they viewed the Jews as a race they did not 'exclude those Jews who were of that race, whatever their religious affiliations may have been'. The German-language *Encyclopaedia Judaica*, issued in Berlin between 1928 and 1934 (when, having reached the letter L, it ceased publication), also did not hesitate to enrol Disraeli in the ranks of the Jews, nor did the English-language *Encyclopaedia Judaica*, published in Jerusalem in 1972. The introduction to the latter work noted that anyone born a Jew qualified for inclusion, even if he later converted or disassociated himself from Jewish life. As a rule when European Jews thought of Jews in politics Disraeli came to mind; he was their point of reference, the Jewish politician *par excellence*. Thus, when the geneticist R. N. Salaman ran for a seat on the Hertfordshire County Council in 1910 and was attacked for being a foreigner (his ancestors had been in England since the mid-eighteenth century), he reminded his opponents that Disraeli was a Jew and that if he could govern the empire then he (Salaman) was capable of looking after their footpaths. The critic George Steiner, recalling that his Viennese father was fascinated with Disraeli, told an interviewer: 'For the eastern and central European Jewish intelligentsia, the career of Disraeli had assumed a mythical, talismanic aura.'[2]

The willingness of Jews in Britain and elsewhere to include Disraeli within the tribal fold was not an isolated example. Most converts who made their mark in Christian society were 'reclaimed' in this way. This was in part because popular Jewish notions of who was a Jew were much broader than those that communal leaders articulated when defending Jewish interests.[3] It is often asserted that in the age of emancipation Jews traded a national or ethnic definition of Jewishness for one based on religion, since this definition of Jewishness, and only this definition, would allow their integration into the modern nation state. In public discourse, this tended to be true. When western Jewish leaders spoke in public forums they talked about German or French citizens of the Jewish faith. In apologetic and defence literature they insisted that Jews differed from their fellow citizens only in regard to their religious beliefs and customs. In truth, however, popular sentiment was at odds with the public statements of communal officials. Emancipation and acculturation did not erase the collective social character of western Jews, most of whom continued to think of themselves as part of a centuries-old social unit regardless of their beliefs or level of ritual observance.

Moreover, the nature of Jewish conversions in the modern period encouraged the popular perception that baptised Jews remained Jews.[4] Most conversions lacked a spiritual dimension. They were conversions of convenience, not conviction, designed to improve the social and material fortunes of those taking the step while protecting them from humiliation and stigmatisation. Most Jews who converted did not want to be Christians. What drove them to convert was the desire to escape the disadvantages associated with being Jews. Conversion meant that Jews who had absented themselves from the synagogue became Christians who did not attend church, except where bourgeois respectability demanded it, as in Victorian Britain. Because they were indifferent to the claims of the Christian religion, few of them followed in the footsteps of their medieval and early modern predecessors who became rabid Jew-baiters, intent on establishing their bona fides and silencing any lingering doubts they may have had.[5] Many converts maintained amicable social ties with Jews, including family members who remained members of the Jewish community. Disraeli himself was a close friend of the Rothschilds and a frequent guest in their homes from the mid-1840s.[6] These patterns were consistent with and, in turn, reinforced a broad, inclusive, ethnic definition of who was a Jew.

Jewish humour shared this widespread perception that baptism was a charade that did not change the fundamental or essential identity of the convert. Collections of eastern and central European Jewish humour that were published in the interwar period (but contain material from before the First World War) include dozens of jokes that make this point. Typical is the following. A Catholic priest converted a Jew on a Thursday. The next day – a Friday, when Catholics were forbidden to eat meat – he found him eating roast goose. The convert looked at the priest and, seeing that he was furious, said, 'Don't worry, dear priest, this is fish.' This made the priest even angrier. 'It's not enough that you are a transgressor but you are also a liar.' The convert replied: 'God forbid, dear priest. I have simply done as you have done. You threw pure water on me and said, "Until now you were a goose; from now on, you are a fish."' The same point is made in a story about the banker Otto Kahn that the Vienna-born psychoanalyst Theodor Reik used as an illustration in his study *Jewish Wit*. Kahn, the story goes, was strolling along Fifth Avenue in New York City with the humorist Marshall Wilder, who was a hunchback. Pointing to a church, Kahn said, 'Marshall, that's the church I belong to. Did you know that I once was a Jew?' Wilder answered, 'Yes, Otto, and once I was a hunchback.' Or, in the words of one witticism, 'In three places water is useless – in the ocean, in wine and in the baptism of Jews.'[7]

From the late nineteenth to the mid-twentieth century the most enthusiastic Jewish admirers of Disraeli were Zionist publicists and historians. Because their definition of Jewishness was national rather than religious his baptism into the Church of England posed no obstacle to thinking of him as a Jew. The basis of their attraction to him was threefold. First, he was a Jew who won and exercised political power. Second, despite his success, he never repudiated or ignored his Jewish background, as did many ambitious western Jews in the nineteenth century.[8] Indeed, he embraced his origins with gusto, as the essays in this collection make clear, championing the racial virtues of the Jews, highlighting their role as recipients of God's word and harping on Christian indebtedness to them. In Nahum Sokolow's view, 'There never was a Jew who wrote in more glowing terms of the greatness of the Jewish race.'[9] Hebrew writers like Sokolow delighted in Disraeli's unabashed pride in his people. For them, his uncompromising, in-your-face attitude was the antithesis of assimilationist 'timidity' and 'shame'. Third, they saw in Disraeli's Eastern policies – Britain's purchase of the Khedive's Suez Canal shares in 1875, which led to its occupation of Egypt in 1881, and its acquisition of Cyprus in 1878 – the beginnings of a diplomatic trajectory that ended with the issuance of the Balfour Declaration in 1917, in which the government pledged to create a Jewish homeland in Palestine.

Disraeli's initiatives in the Levant, along with his publicly expressed fascination with the 'Land of Israel' in his novels *Alroy* and *Tancred*, led some early Zionist historians to include him in the ranks of Zionism's precursors, that is, Jews who envisioned the recreation of a national home in the Land of Israel before the advent of political Zionism in the late nineteenth century. In his encyclopaedic history of proto-Zionism Sokolow devoted a full chapter to Disraeli, claiming him as 'one of the greatest representatives' of the movement.[10] N. M. Gelber went even further, claiming that Disraeli cherished hope of the restoration of the Jews throughout his life and that he urged the creation of a Jewish state under British protection prior to the Congress of Berlin in 1877.[11] In a slim volume published in Tel Aviv in 1947 Gelber argued that Disraeli was the author of an obscure, 16-page pamphlet *Die jüdische Frage in der orientalischen Frage*, published anonymously in Vienna in 1877, which urged the excision of Palestine from the Ottoman Empire and the establishment there of a British protectorate, which, in the future, would become an independent Jewish state. In the meantime, Britain's occupation of Palestine would strengthen its hold on Egypt and the Suez Canal – the lifeline to India, the jewel in the imperial crown. According to Gelber, whose evidence for Disraeli's authorship is suggestive but not compelling, Disraeli wrote the pamphlet prior to the Congress of Berlin, convinced that the dismemberment of the Ottoman Empire was at hand. Gelber suggested that Disraeli sent the text of the pamphlet to the British embassy in Vienna, where it was translated into German and published. However, he surmised, when Disraeli learned of Bismarck's opposition to the creation of an independent Jewish state, he halted its distribution – hence, the rarity of the pamphlet. Whatever the truth of Gelber's claim Zionists remained enamoured of Disraeli. In their view he was a prophet of Jewish national rebirth, not a renegade from Judaism, and they paid him the compliment of naming a street in his honour in Jerusalem.

It is ironic that Disraeli became a hero to the Jewish world in the decades after his death. As Edgar Feuchtwanger and Richard Davis show in their contributions to this volume, both the claim that he championed Jewish rights and the claim that he promoted Jewish nationalism lack substance. To be sure, Disraeli was proud of being a Jew. No scholar denies that he celebrated the virtues and contributions of the Jews, their history, perseverance and survival, in the most fulsome, even extravagant, terms. However, praising Jews is not the same thing as promoting their well-being. When Disraeli *acted* in the political and diplomatic arenas, he reined in his imagination and Jewish fantasies.

Edgar Feuchtwanger explains that long-standing Conservative concerns about blocking Russian expansion and stabilising the ailing Ottoman Empire determined Disraeli's actions in the Balkans and the Near East in the 1870s. British imperial interests, rather than Jewish national sentiments, were decisive, even if his enemies, including W. E. Gladstone, thought otherwise and represented his policy as an anti-Christian, anti-English, 'Hebraic' policy, a theme that both Feuchtwanger and Anthony Wohl address at length in their essays.

In fact, there were few, if any, occasions in Disraeli's long political career when he used his position or influence to promote Jewish interests, either at home or abroad. His intervention in the mid-century emancipation debate was belated, erratic and idiosyncratic.[12] Above all, it was of no practical use to the Jewish community, since his reasoning did not invoke liberal notions of toleration but his own eccentric religious and racial views, especially his belief that Jews were an aristocratic, conservative people and that Christians were indebted to them for their own faith. His argument that Christians must revere, rather than damn, Jews for their part in the crucifixion, since Jesus' death made possible the Atonement, did nothing to advance the Jewish cause. It is not irrelevant that the communal leaders who managed the emancipation campaign did not consult with Disraeli nor ask for his assistance. Indeed, the *Jewish Chronicle*'s editor, Abraham Benisch, was a bitter critic of his silent votes, his opposition to Liberal measures in 1850 and 1854 and his bizarre views.[13] His friends the Rothschilds were also critical of his behaviour. As Richard Davis notes in this volume, in 1858, toward the end of his long fight to take his seat in the Commons, Lionel de Rothschild wrote to his wife about their friend, 'But you know what a humbug he is: he talked of what is customary without promising anything'.

Disraeli was just as inactive in British Jewish efforts to improve the lot of Jews in eastern Europe, the Middle East and North Africa. Moses Montefiore never requested Disraeli's help with his missions to relieve Jewish suffering in foreign lands, nor did the Board of Deputies.[14] Disraeli's intervention on behalf of Rumanian Jewry at the Congress of Berlin in 1878 was also less important than it has been made out to be. The German Chancellor, Otto Bismarck, and the French Foreign Minister, W. H. Waddington – urged on, respectively, by Gerson von Bleichröder (Bismarck's banker and confidant) and Adolphe Crémieux (president of the Alliance Israélite Universelle) – took the lead in forcing Rumania to grant equal rights to its Jewish population in exchange for international recognition of its independence.[15] Disraeli went along with them but, because he was Jewish and championed the Jews in his writing, the man in the street, as well as some historians, assumed that he was responsible for pressuring Rumania. The truth is that in Berlin, as earlier in London, Disraeli's Jewishness was more a state of mind than a commitment to action.[16] Sokolow's appraisal – that 'no one could have used more persuasive arguments, or adopted wiser measures to remove restrictions from which the Jews were suffering' – is nonsense.[17]

Although Disraeli was no champion of the Jews when it came to the actual conduct of foreign affairs, his critics were convinced, nonetheless, that his Jewishness was a key element in his behaviour. In their view, his motives, sentiments and policies were 'Jewish' or 'Hebraic', linked to an essential Jewishness at the very core of his character. Using the evidence of political cartoons, Anthony Wohl shows in his contribution to this volume how prominent Disraeli's Jewishness was in the Victorian imagination, not only during his early years as an aspiring politician, struggling to make a place for himself, but even more during his second ministry, from 1874 to 1880. Indeed, Wohl argues that Disraeli's background assumed greater significance in political life in this period than at any time earlier. Edgar Feuchtwanger's contribution takes up this theme in regard to Disraeli's management of the Eastern Crisis from 1875 to 1878. He describes the anti-Jewish character of Liberal attacks on his policy, exposing how they drew on the arsenal of classic antisemitism, and then explains the traditional political and diplomatic considerations that, in fact, guided Disraeli's conduct of British policy during the crisis – that is, the desire to maintain Britain's prestige and strengthen its imperial position. Interestingly, in the decades immediately after his death even friends and admirers tended to highlight his Jewishness in assessing his character and legacy. We have already quoted Lady Battersea's comment in 1881 that her friend's racial instincts were his religion and that he was true to his religion until his death. A generation later, Israel Zangwill, who included the 'Primrose Sphinx' in his *Dreamers of the Ghetto* (1898), described Disraeli as 'the Ghetto parvenu', 'a Heine of action', 'a successful Lassalle', 'a Dreamer of the Ghetto' and 'a Semitic Sphinx', who brought to English politics 'the Jew's unifying sweep of idea'. More sober, but just as telling, was the assessment of G. E. Buckle, a former editor of *The Times*, who completed the six-volume authorised *Life of Benjamin Disraeli* (1910–20) after the death of W. F. Monypenny. In summing up Disraeli's character in the final volume he declared that 'the fundamental fact' about him was that 'he was a Jew' and that throughout his life he seemed 'never to be quite of the nation which he loved, served, and governed' but always remained, rather, 'a little detached when in the act of leading; always … the spectator, almost the critic, as well as the principal performer'.[18]

In contrast to these early treatments of Disraeli twentieth-century British writers, with a few exceptions, took little interest in the Jewish dimensions of Disraeli's career. They ignored or minimised both his racial preoccupations and the antisemitism that dogged his political career from start to finish. The *Encyclopaedia Britannica* reduced the theme to two sentences. It noted, first, that he was 'always strongly conscious of the Jewish antecedents of his religion' and, second, that 'his unfailing pride in his own Jewish ancestry' owed something to his voyage to the Levant in 1830–31. The *Dictionary of National Biography* (1885–1901) was just as reticent. It indicated that Disraeli was baptised but not that he or his parents were Jews by birth! It also wondered, *en passant*, whether 'the instincts of his race' contributed to his belief in a strong monarch and noted, briefly, that in *Coningsby* the author offered 'an eloquent vindication of the Jewish race' that reflected honour on himself. The most widely read twentieth-century biography of Disraeli, Robert Blake's much-praised 700-page account, dismissed the importance of Disraeli's Jewish origins and fantasies, arguing instead that, if national or racial traits were to be introduced at all, it was the Italian 'streak' in his character that was dominant. In his view Disraeli's pride, vanity, flamboyance, generosity, emotionalism, quarrelsomeness, extravagance, theatricality, addiction to conspiracy and fondness for intrigue were Mediterranean traits. British writers were even reluctant to assess the Jewish themes in Disraeli's fiction, which is remarkable, given their prominence in *Alroy*, *Coningsby* and *Tancred*. Thom Braun's *Disraeli the Novelist* (1981), for example, avoided the subject altogether, even though Isaiah Berlin's seminal essay on Disraeli's Jewishness appeared a decade earlier. And when the Labour Party leader Michael Foot reviewed a work of American scholarship, Daniel R. Schwarz's *Disraeli's Fiction* (1980), that unselfconsciously foregrounded the Jewish themes in the novels, Foot remained silent about them.[19]

This reticence, which stands in such stark contrast to Victorian interest in the subject, requires comment. Certainly, one reason for the disappearance of Disraeli's Jewishness is the connection between earlier treatments and unambiguous expressions of antisemitism. This made the topic suspect and one best avoided, especially in the wake of the destruction of European Jewry in the Second World War. In addition, most Victorian accounts of Disraeli, whether sympathetic or hostile, assumed that there were timeless and essential Jewish traits – traits that Disraeli inherited at birth by virtue of his 'racial' descent. While this kind of thinking – what Bryan Cheyette calls 'semitic discourse'[20] – did not disappear in the twentieth century, it became increasingly less respectable. There was more at work than this, however. For the disreputability of racial thinking does not explain the indifference or blindness of English writers to the extent to which Disraeli was the target of antisemitic attacks, a topic that interested them no more than the influence of his background on his self-image and thinking, as Tony Kushner demonstrates in his contribution to this volume. It would seem that the banishing of Disraeli's Jewishness was symptomatic of a much broader tendency in *bien pensant* circles to ignore the presence of Jews and Jewish issues in English literature and history, a topic that Todd Endelman has discussed at length elsewhere.[21] Here it is sufficient to note that there was a sense of awkwardness, perhaps embarrassment, in recognising the Jewishness of Jews who figured in British history and literature and assigning this Jewishness, however defined, an active or causative role. To be too concerned with Jews was not good form.

Jewish writers, whether in Britain, the United States or Israel, were not subject to this reticence. As Todd Endelman explains in his contribution, they developed what is now the accepted view of Disraeli's Jewish obsessions – that they constituted a bold, if unusual, strategy to combat his own sense of social inferiority as an outsider in aristocratic Tory circles. The seminal figures in the 'rediscovery' of his Jewishness were Hannah Arendt, who discussed his racial ideas and their function in *The Origins of Totalitarianism* (1951), and Isaiah Berlin, whose frequently reprinted landmark essay – 'Benjamin Disraeli, Karl Marx and the Search for Identity' (1970) – won a large readership. In the late twentieth century, their perspective, which other Jewish writers, including Harold Fisch, Daniel Schwarz, Benjamin Jaffe, Abraham Gilam, Stanley Weintraub, and Todd Endelman,[22] meanwhile elaborated, began to influence mainstream historiographical circles in England. The pioneer in the English re-evaluation of Disraeli (one of the exceptions alluded to above) was Paul Smith, who insisted on the central importance of Disraeli's Jewish concerns as early as 1986, in a lecture to the Royal Historical Society, and foregrounded them ten years later in his brief life of Disraeli.[23] By the last decade of the century Disraeli's Jewishness was again integral to English accounts of his life and fiction, although not, of course, in the crude way it had been in the Victorian period. One only has to compare Blake's biography with work published in the 1990s – John Vincent's volume in the Past Master series, Jane Ridley's *Young Disraeli*, and the essays in Charles Richmond's and Paul Smith's *The Self-Fashioning of Disraeli*[24] – to appreciate the shift that occurred.

If historians of Victorian Britain were indifferent to Disraeli's Jewishness (at least until recently), they were also unwilling to weigh and assess the hostility his Jewishness aroused. In 1994, David Feldman concluded in his *Englishmen and Jews* that 'antipathy to Jews and censure of Judaism' were 'a much stronger presence in mid-Victorian political culture than has been acknowledged'. Indeed, he suggested that hostility to Disraeli's Jewishness in the late 1870s was blatant 'Judaeo-phobia'. Feldman's claim was a response to widely respected histories of the Bulgarian atrocities agitation that minimised their anti-Jewish dimension. Richard Shannon, for example, concluded 20 years earlier that the 'anti-Semitic aspect of the atrocities agitation was prominent but superficial', adding that it lacked 'the substantial bulk of prejudice which in France produced the Dreyfus Affair'. Shannon's remarks were representative of a much broader historical consensus regarding British antisemitism. Thus, in discussing Disraeli's early political career Blake also dismissed its strength and influence: 'England at the beginning of the nineteenth century was a tolerant place, and its Jewish inhabitants were far below the figure at which, sociologists tell us, an alien minority risks becoming the object of hatred to their fellow citizens.'[25]

Two fundamental assumptions shaped assessments like these. First, historians like Blake and Shannon saw antisemitism as a continental problem, one which manifested itself most obviously in Nazi Germany but also, as Shannon suggested, in *fin-de-siècle* France as well. Second, they linked antisemitism to numbers – the more Jews, the more anti-semitism – finding in tsarist Russia's treatment of Jews confirmation of their belief. (Not coincidentally they wrote at a time, the 1960s, when both the Labour and Tory parties supported immigration controls, believing that good 'race relations' depended on minimising non-white immigration. Historians and politicians alike, it seemed, wanted to 'blame the victim' or find a 'rational basis' for racial hostility.)[26] In the past these assumptions hindered attempts to explain the function and significance of antisemitism in British history, in general, and in Disraeli's career, in particular. For example, Smith, in his otherwise sophisticated overview of Disraeli's life, repeated Blake's comment about the small size of the Jewish community, while John Vincent, in his brief biography, hinted that Disraeli deserved whatever hostility came his way in the 1870s: 'The question is whether anti-Semitism stood in his way, or whether his character and conduct created anti-Semitism.' In a similar vein, Albert Lindemann, who grounded his provocative history of modern antisemitism on the principle that 'Jews have been as capable as any other group of provoking hostility', remarked that Disraeli was 'the kind of man who might have been an anti-Semite, had he been a German or a Russian' and that it was 'not surprising that so many anti-Semites cited him to bolster their own beliefs about Jews'.[27] It is difficult, in other words, to separate historical accounts of antisemitic attacks on Disraeli from the often ideological or politicised understandings of intolerance of those who wrote them.

In the conclusion to his biography of Disraeli Blake noted how the Disraeli-Gladstone rivalry generated passions that 'have been carried far beyond the grave', adding that it was 'only fairly recently that people have at least been able to praise one of the great rivals without feeling obliged to damn the other'. With praising Gladstone often inseparable from damning Disraeli, the fact of the latter's Jewishness meant that much more was at stake than questions of loyalty to Gladstone and Liberalism. As Feldman argued, 'In defining and casti- gating Disraeli as a Jew his critics also affirmed the Christian principles which the Prime Minister's actions and speeches seemed to challenge.'[28] Early historical scholarship on Gladstone reflected this linkage. When G. W. E. Russell's biography, first published in 1913, took up the Eastern Question, it highlighted how

> Mr Disraeli, with a strange frankness of cynical brutality, sneered at the rumour [of atrocities] as 'coffee house babble', and made odious jokes about the oriental way of executing malefactors. But Christian England was not to be pacified with these Asiatic pleasantries, and in the autumn of 1876 the country rose in passionate indignation against what were known as 'the Bulgarian atrocities'.[29]

But the dominant tendency of Gladstone's biographers, from John Morley at the beginning of the twentieth century to Richard Shannon at the end, was to gloss over the antisemitism generated by the Eastern Question, generally noting Gladstone's comments about 'Dizzy's crypto-Judaism' without comment or analysis.[30]

Evidence of anti-Jewish hostility to Disraeli was never hidden from view, buried in unpublished correspondence or obscure journals. The failure of British historians to treat it critically was due, rather, to their interpretive assumptions, as Tony Kushner explains in his essay in this volume. Liberals, like Goldwin Smith, E. A. Freeman and T. P. O'Connor, insisted that Disraeli *was* pursuing racially inspired Judaic policies that conflicted with Britain's Christian mission, so for them there could be no question of irrational antisemitism. Conservatives, including Disraeli's earliest biographers, also acknowledged his alien character – often as much as did his Liberal critics – but they did so in order to claim that this was what enabled him to be a true patriot. They emphasised the antisemitism that he faced, especially early in his life, in order to highlight his essential difference. The young Disraeli, Walter Sichel wrote in 1904, 'felt that he was not as others ... his family were sometimes eyed askance as foreigners'. In an earlier biography, Harold Gorst suggested that, in his battle with Sir Robert Peel, Disraeli was the 'political master of men who despised and hated him, and who called him "Jew" and "adventurer" behind his back'. In the 1920s in particular, when the Conservative Party, faced with a mass electorate and the challenge of the Labour Party, wanted to emphasise its inclusiveness, it utilised Disraeli's memory to promote 'One Nation' Toryism, celebrating his triumph over his origins.[31]

There were some, however, who saw Victorian hostility to Disraeli in the context of a more worrying European-wide, even global problem. G. F. Abbott's *Israel in Europe* (1907), one of the first comprehensive histories of antisemitism, treated the Eastern Question in 1870s Britain at length. Abbott recognised that Disraeli's Jewishness loomed large in the public debate: 'Disraeli was opposed to Russia's ambition, and Disraeli was a Jew. What could be easier than to connect the two things?' Deeply concerned about anti-Jewish violence and the politicisation of antisemitism on the continent, Abbot advocated an assimilationist solution to the 'Jewish Question'. If the Jews were treated kindly they would lose their separateness, the source of antipathy toward them, within 200 years. In particular, he felt that western Europe should set a good example in order to show eastern Europe what was possible. For this reason Abbott highlighted attacks on Disraeli by Goldwin Smith and other writers, arguing that they were counterproductive, strengthening rather than weakening Jewish 'clannishness'. Moreover, because such attacks originated in a liberal, tolerant society, they helped to legitimate the 'backward' antisemitism of the continent.

The Anglo-Jewish historian, journalist and communal 'foreign secretary' Lucien Wolf was also eager to highlight the antisemitism associated with the Eastern crisis of 1876 to 1878 but for different reasons. Wolf believed that antisemitism in Great Britain was essentially an import from abroad. In his path-breaking entry on 'Anti-Semitism' in the eleventh edition of the *Encyclopaedia Britannica* (1910), he wrote: 'While the main activity of anti-Semitism has manifested itself in Germany, Rumania, Austria-Hungary and France, its vibratory influences have been felt in other countries when conditions favourable to its extension have presented themselves.' The premiership of Lord Beaconsfield provided one such opportunity 'to acclimatize the doctrines of Marr and Treitschke'. In particular Wolf emphasised the role of Goldwin Smith, who, he believed, 'sought to synthesize the growing anti-Jewish feeling by adopting the nationalist theories of the German anti-Semites'. Here was an opportune moment for Wolf, who had been defending Anglo-Jewry since the 1880s, to counter the charge that not just Disraeli but British Jewry as a whole was unpatriotic. Instead, Wolf argued that anti-Jewish attacks were rare, constructing antisemitism as fundamentally un-English, just as the *Jewish Chronicle* regularly did. Even though the agitation against Disraeli in the late 1870s 'did not fail to find an equivocal response in the speeches of some of the leading Liberal statesmen', he concluded that 'on the country generally it produced no effect'.[32]

Popular portrayals of Disraeli in the 1910s and 1920s, especially on stage and in film, also stressed the animosity he experienced because of his Jewish ancestry. They did so to show that Disraeli, despite his background, was a better patriot than the antisemitic aristocrats who mocked him. Still, the historiographical refusal to take British anti-semitism seriously persisted in the interwar period, along with the inclination to view Disraeli in racial terms. The result was confusion and contradiction when historians tried to account for the prejudice he faced, as in R. W. Seton-Watson's history of the Eastern Question, published in 1935.

Seton-Watson's Disraeli owed much to contemporary 'semitic discourse' even if it was invoked to explain his positive traits, such as his 'restless energy and still more vivid imagination'. These, he argued, Disraeli 'unquestionably owed to his Jewish blood, from which only too often spiteful deductions have been made, but whose significance can scarcely be exaggerated'. Rather than analysing Disraeli's Jewishness as socially constructed, Seton-Watson saw it as racially given. Thus, when Lord Derby complained that Disraeli sought prestige 'as all foreigners do', Seton-Watson commented that the remark showed 'the breach to be final between this typical English aristocrat and his enigmatic and brilliant, but *essentially* [our emphasis] un-English chief'. Seton-Watson also invoked the language of race to contrast Disraeli and Gladstone: 'If Disraeli possessed the oriental imagination and resource of his ancient race, Gladstone had all the *"perfervidum ingenium Scotorum"* and a certain Celtic vision, tempered by a Viking's fire.' Similarly, he attributed the sense of private and public honour of Lords Salisbury and Derby to 'their English nature [which] cried out against Disraeli's ornate cynicism'. Yet at the same time Seton-Watson condemned attacks like Freeman's as 'outrageous', seeing his comment about Queen Victoria 'going ostentatiously to eat with Disraeli in his ghetto' as 'unnecessary bad form'.[33] Seton-Watson was able to condemn the racialised attacks of Disraeli's contemporaries but unable to query the racial constructs that informed his own work.

During the Second World War and the years leading to it popular and scholarly representations of Disraeli tended to suppress mention of his Jewishness, fearing its exploitation by Nazis and other antisemites. This, of course, further hindered attempts to understand the hostility he faced throughout his life. For example, unlike the 1929 film *Disraeli*, Warner Brothers' 1941 motion picture *The Prime Minister* made no mention of antisemitism – perhaps not surprisingly in a film that was designed to strengthen national identity in wartime rather than query its exclusive nature.[34] It is significant, however, that in both films, despite their sympathetic objectives, the actors playing Disraeli, George Arliss and John Gielgud, played him as Fagin and Shylock respectively, a tribute to the strength of 'semitic discourse' at the time.

Even though Hannah Arendt pioneered a non-essentialist approach to Disraeli in the 1950s, showing that he constructed his Jewishness as a response to antisemitism, her work exerted little influence on British historians, who were either unfamiliar with it or unsympathetic to its approach. Blake failed in his monumental biography of 1966 to incorporate her insights, as did the American scholar Richard Millman in the following decade in his authoritative account of Britain and the Eastern Question. Millman was clearly shocked by Freeman's hysterical attacks, which he regarded as 'blatantly anti-Semitic' and 'despicable'. Yet, when it came to understanding the meaning of the attacks, Millman, following in Shannon's footsteps, concluded (in an endnote) that the antisemitism of the campaign was superficial.[35] Significantly, only in 1979, the year that Millman's account appeared, did a history of antisemitism in modern Britain become available, with the publication of Colin Holmes's landmark *Anti-Semitism in British Society, 1876–1939*. Before this date, there was little scholarship on antisemitism in Britain, scholarship that would have stimulated historians to contextualise the antisemitism that Disraeli faced in the 1870s.

A social historian and pioneer of minority studies in Britain, Holmes charted a tradition of ethnocentrism native to the United Kingdom, beginning his account with the campaign against Disraeli, the strength of which he attributed to the threat of war. He emphasised in particular the role of key figures in the agitation, especially Goldwin Smith and his 'personal anti-semitism'. David Feldman criticised Holmes for seeing the agitation as 'a brief and narrowly based episode in the history of anti-Semitism'. Yet, without the foundation of Holmes's pioneering work subsequent scholarship would not have been possible. Feldman, quite rightly, argued that the 'reappearance [after emancipation] of the Jewish question [between 1876 and 1880] reveals a fierce debate over the meaning of patriotism between contending doctrines of national identity'. Yet, to be fair to Holmes he also suggested, without elaborating, that the collective and individual antisemitism at the time of the Bulgarian crisis revealed 'how tenuous the threads of toleration could be and how the wisdom of Jewish toleration could be questioned'.[36] Holmes paved the way for subsequent, more sophisticated work by scholars on both sides of the Atlantic concerned with constructions of Jewishness and Englishness. Their work, however, has yet to exert much influence on historical scholarship in the British academy, which seems reluctant to acknowledge that racism was a feature of the British past.

The essays in this volume, which originated at a conference at the University of Southampton in 1994 marking the 150th anniversary of the publication of *Coningsby*, do more than restore the Jewish dimension to Disraeli's life and work. They also explore aspects of this dimension that have been ignored in earlier reappraisals. Nadia Valman reveals the intense gender concerns that were intertwined with Disraeli's Jewish concerns in his fiction, showing how he constructed a myth of Jewish virility to counter the myth of feminised Jewishness. Seeking to place Disraeli's representations of Jews, Judaism and Jewish history in a wider context, Valman argues that these representations were conditioned by the aesthetics of contemporary political debate, 'which imagined the future of England in terms of a chivalric renewal of national masculinity'. Yet the power of contemporary discourse was such that Disraeli was still being represented as an exotically dressed, lisping dandy 40 years after he had abandoned this persona. Indeed, as Anthony Wohl reveals, he was sometimes represented, quite unambiguously, as a woman. (Disraeli continued to be represented as effeminate in twentieth-century films. The British government regarded John Gielgud's portrayal of Disraeli in *The Prime Minister* (1941) as unmanly, while Anthony Sher's Disraeli in *Mrs Brown* (1997) was a comic, foppish stage Jew who lacked the masculinity of the film's hero.)[37] Daniel Schwarz situates Disraeli's 'Jewish' novels firmly in the context of romanticism and the history of nineteenth-century taste. Todd Endelman takes up a hitherto unexplored theme in Disraeli's self-identity – the myth of Sephardi superiority – and traces the origins of the myth and suggests how it reached Disraeli, who, in general, was not in touch with cultural and intellectual currents in Jewish life. Richard Davis asks why Disraeli was the target of such virulent antisemitic abuse while his friends Lionel and Mayer Rothschild received much better treatment and, in answering this intriguing question, illuminates notions of Victorian gentility, masculinity and toleration. Anthony Wohl and Edgar Feuchtwanger, as mentioned earlier, discuss the antisemitism that swirled around Disraeli's conduct of foreign policy during his second ministry, exposing its links to hoary anti-Jewish myths. In his extended epilogue, Tony Kushner explores how Disraeli's Jewishness was constructed and contested during the twentieth century on both sides of the Atlantic. He focuses, in particular, on debates inside and outside the Jewish community about where or to whom Disraeli belonged, and he shows how these debates became politicised and how they reveal more about those who participated in them than about Disraeli himself. Together these essays illuminate Disraeli's inner and outer life in all its complexity. At the same time, they also expose the passions, preoccupations and priorities of those who both damned and feted their 'un-English', 'Hebraic' premier.

NOTES

1. Benjamin Joffe, *Ha-meimad ha-yehudi shel Disraeli: emdot ve-teguvot be britanyah* [The Jewish Dimension of Disraeli: Positions and Reactions in Britain] (Ph.D. diss., Bar-Ilan University, 1986), p. 77; Emma Lazarus, 'Was the Earl of Beaconsfield a Representative Jew?', *Century Magazine*, new ser., Vol. 1 (1881–82), pp. 939–42; Louise de Rothschild, journals, 11 February 1850, quoted in Richard Davis, *The English Rothschilds* (Chapel Hill, NC, 1983), pp. 90–1; Battersea Papers, Add MSS 47910/5, British Library, London; Georg Brandes, *Lord Beaconsfield: A Study*, trans. Mrs George Sturge (1880; reprint, New York, 1966), p. 229.
2. *Hertfordshire and Cambridgeshire Reporter*, 11 March 1910; interview with Jason Cowley, *The Times*, 22 September 1997.
3. For a discussion of this point, see Todd M. Endelman, 'Making Jews Modern: Some Jewish and Gentile Misunderstandings in the Age of Emancipation' in Marc Lee Raphael (ed.), *What is Modern about the Modern Jewish Experience?* (Williamsburg, VA, 1997), pp. 17–31.
4. Todd M. Endelman, 'Conversion as a Response to Antisemitism in Modern

Jewish History' in Jehuda Reinharz (ed.), *Living with Antisemitism* (Hanover, NH, 1987), pp. 60–84; *idem*, 'The Social and Political Context of Conversion in Germany and England, 1870–1914' in Todd M. Endelman (ed.), *Jewish Apostasy in the Modern World* (New York, 1987), pp. 83–107.

5. The Russian Jewish experience was a notable exception to this rule. Todd M. Endelman, 'Memories of Jewishness: Jewish Converts and Their Jewish Pasts' in Elisheva Carlebach, John Efron and David Myers (eds), *Jewish History and Jewish Memory: Essays Honoring Yosef Hayim Yerushalmi* (Hanover, NH, 1998), pp. 322–3.

6. See Davis, *The English Rothschilds*, pp. 86–91.

7. Abraham Alter Druyanov, *Sefer ha-bedihah ve-ha-hidud* [The Book of Jokes and Wit], 3 vols (Tel Aviv, 1980), Vol. 2, No. 138; Theodor Reik, *Jewish Wit* (New York, 1962), p. 90; Salcia Landmann, *Der Jüdische Witz: Soziologie und Sammlung* (Olten and Freiburg im Breisgau, 1960), p. 439.

8. On the evolution of Disraeli's Jewish self-consciousness, see Todd M. Endelman, '"A Hebrew to the End": The Emergence of Disraeli's Jewishness' in Charles Richmond and Paul Smith (eds), *The Self-Fashioning of Disraeli, 1818–1851* (Cambridge, 1999), pp. 106–30.

9. Nahum Sokolow, *History of Zionism, 1600–1918*, 2 Vols (London, 1919), Vol. 1, p. 143.

10. Ibid.

11. N. M. Gelber, *Tokhnit ha-medinah ha-yehudit le-Lord Beaconsfield* [Lord Beaconsfield's Program for a Jewish State] (Tel Aviv, 1947). Mark Wischnitzer endorsed Gelber's conclusion in *Tokhnit ha-medinah ha-yehudit le-Beaconsfield* [Beaconsfield's Program for a Jewish State] in *Bitsaron*, November/December 1947, pp. 163–72, while Cecil Roth expressed scepticism in *Benjamin Disraeli: Earl of Beaconsfield* (New York, 1952), pp. 159–62. Interestingly, in the introduction to the above-cited edition of Brandes's *Lord Beaconsfield*, Salo Baron seemed to endorse the idea that Disraeli was the author, but he did not cite new evidence to substantiate Gelber's claim.

12. Abraham Gilam, *The Emancipation of the Jews in England, 1830–1860* (New York, 1982), appendix, 'Benjamin Disraeli and the Emancipation of the Jews'.

13. Abraham Gilam, 'Anglo-Jewish Attitudes Toward Benjamin Disraeli During the Era of Emancipation', *Jewish Social Studies*, Vol. 42 (1980), pp. 313–22.

14. Sonia and V. D. Lipman (eds), *The Century of Moses Montefiore* (Oxford, 1985); Moshe Samet, *Moshe Montefiore: metsiyut ve-aggadah* [Moses Montefiore: Reality and Legend] (Jerusalem, 1989); Charles H. L. Emanuel, *A Century and a Half of Jewish History Extracted from the Minute Books of the London Committee of Deputies of the British Jews* (London, 1910).

15. Fritz Stern, *Gold and Iron: Bismarck, Bleichröder, and the Building of the German Empire* (New York, 1977), ch. 14; Jaffe, *Ha-meimad ha-yehudi shel Disraeli*, p. 175.

16. Endelman develops this point in '"A Hebrew to the End"'.

17. Sokolow, *History of Zionism*, p. 143.

18. Israel Zangwill, *Dreamers of the Ghetto* (1898; reprint, Philadelphia, 1948), pp. 424–9; W. F. Monypenny and G. E. Buckle, *The Life of Benjamin Disraeli, Earl of Beaconsfield*, 6 Vols (London, 1910–20), Vol. 6, pp. 633–4.

19. Robert Blake, *Disraeli* (Garden City, NY, 1968), p. 47; Thom Braun, *Disraeli the Novelist* (London, 1981); Michael Foot, 'The Tory as Hero' (review of Daniel R. Schwarz, *Disraeli's Fiction*), *Times Literary Supplement*, 18 April 1980.

20. Bryan Cheyette, *Constructions of 'the Jew' in English Literature and Society: Racial Representations, 1875–1945* (Cambridge, 1993).

21. Todd M. Endelman, 'Writing English Jewish History', *Albion*, Vol. 27, No. 4 (Winter 1995), pp. 628–30. See also Michael Ragussis, 'The "Secret" of English

Anti-Semitism: Anglo-Jewish Studies and Victorian Studies', *Victorian Studies*, Vol. 40 (Winter 1997), pp. 295–307.

22. Harold Fisch, 'Disraeli's Hebraic Compulsions' in H. S. Zimmels, J. Rabbinowitz and I. Finestein (eds), *Essays Presented to Chief Rabbi Israel Brodie on the Occasion of His Seventieth Birthday* (London, 1967), pp. 81–94; Schwarz, *Disraeli's Fiction*; Abraham Gilam, 'Disraeli in Jewish Historiography', *Midstream*, Vol. 26, No. 3 (March 1980), pp. 24–9; *idem*, 'Benjamin Disraeli and Jewish Identity', *The Wiener Library Bulletin*, new ser., Vol. 33, Nos 51–2 (1980), pp. 2–8; *idem*, 'Anglo-Jewish Attitudes toward Benjamin Disraeli during the Era of Emancipation', *Jewish Social Studies*, Vol. 42 (1980), pp. 313–22; *idem*, 'Benjamin Disraeli and the Emancipation of the Jews', *Disraeli Project Newsletter*, Vol. 5, No. 1 (1980), pp. 26–46; Benjamin Jaffee, 'A Reassessment of Benjamin Disraeli's Jewish Aspects', *Transactions of the Jewish Historical Society of England*, Vol. 27 (1982), pp. 115–23; Stanley Weintraub, *Disraeli: A Biography* (New York, 1993); Todd M. Endelman, 'Disraeli's Jewishness Reconsidered', *Modern Judaism*, Vol. 5 (1985), pp. 109–23.

23. Paul Smith, 'Disraeli's Politics', *Transactions of the Royal Historical Society*, 5th ser. Vol. 37 (1987), pp. 65–85; *idem*, *Disraeli* (Cambridge, 1996).

24. John Vincent, *Disraeli* (Oxford, 1990); Jane Ridley, *Young Disraeli, 1804–1846* (London, 1995); Charles Richmond and Paul Smith (eds), *The Self-Fashioning of Disraeli, 1818–1851* (Cambridge, 1999).

25. David Feldman, *Englishmen and Jews: Social Relations and Political Culture, 1840–1914* (New Haven, 1994), p. 120; R. T. Shannon, *Gladstone and the Bulgarian Agitation, 1876* (London, 1963), pp. 200–1; Blake, *Disraeli*, p. 10.

26. Kathleen Paul, *Whitewashing Britain: Race and Citizenship in the Postwar Era* (Ithaca, 1997), ch. 5; Bryan Cheyette, 'Hilaire Belloc and the "Marconi Scandal", 1900–1914: A Reassessment of the Interactionist Model of Racial Hatred' in Tony Kushner and Kenneth Lunn (eds), *The Politics of Marginality: Race, the Radical Right and Minorities in Twentieth Century Britain* (London, 1990), pp. 131–2.

27. Smith, *Disraeli*, p. 46; Vincent, *Disraeli*, p. 13; Albert Lindemann, *Esau's Tears: Modern Anti-Semitism and the Role of the Jews* (Cambridge, 1997), pp. xvii, 248.

28. Blake, *Disraeli*, p. 761; Feldman, *Englishmen and Jews*, p. 102.

29. G. W. E. Russell, *William Ewart Gladstone* (London, 1913), p. 242.

30. John Morley, *The Life of William Ewart Gladstone* (London, 1903), Vol. 2, *1859–1880*, pp. 552 and 558, Vol. 3, *1880–1898*, p. 475; Philip Magnus, *Gladstone: A Biography* (London, 1954), pp. 243–5; H. C. G. Matthew, *Gladstone, 1875–1898* (Oxford, 1995), p. 34; E. J. Feuchtwanger, *Gladstone* (London, 1977), p. 181 (but see the comments on p. 185); Richard Shannon, *Gladstone: Heroic Minister, 1865–1898* (London, 1999), p. 183, which, while mentioning the pro-Turkish sympathies of British Jews, also refers to 'a distinct anti-Semitic tinge' to the agitation and does not totally distance Gladstone from it.

31. Walter Sichel, *Disraeli: A Study in Personality and Ideas* (London, 1904), p. 322; Harold Gorst, *The Earl of Beaconsfield* (London, 1900), p. 39; Edward Clarke, *Benjamin Disraeli: The Romance of a Great Career, 1804–1881* (London, 1926), p. 4.

32. *Encyclopaedia Britannica*, 11th ed., s.v. 'Anti-Semitism'; David Cesarani, *Reporting Anti-Semitism: The Jewish Chronicle, 1879–1979* (Cambridge, 1993). The entry on 'Anti-Semitism' in the New York-based *Jewish Encyclopedia* (1901) drew on Wolf's work on Goldwin Smith but introduced the section 'Other Countries' with the statement that 'Anti-Semitism as such does not exist either in England or in the United States'.

33. R. W. Seton-Watson, *Disraeli, Gladstone and the Eastern Question: A Study in Diplomacy and Party Politics* (1935; reprint, London, 1962), pp. 3, 113, 248–9, 309, 561, 562. Seton-Watson taught in the School of Slavonic and East European Studies at the University of London.

34. *Disraeli* (dir. Alfred E. Green, 1929); *The Prime Minister* (dir. Thorold Dickinson, 1941).
35. Richard Millman, *Britain and the Eastern Question, 1875–1878* (Oxford, 1979), pp. 181, 524 n. 63.
36. Colin Holmes, *Anti-Semitism in British Society, 1876–1939* (London, 1979), pp. 11–12; *idem*, 'Goldwin Smith (1823–1910): A "Liberal" Antisemite', *Patterns of Prejudice*, Vol. 6, No. 5 (September/October 1972), pp. 25–30; Feldman, *Englishmen and Jews*, p. 94.
37. *Mrs Brown* (dir. John Madden, 1997).

PART 1:

SELF-CONSTRUCTIONS

BENJAMIN DISRAELI AND THE MYTH OF SEPHARDI SUPERIORITY

Todd M. Endelman

On the day following Benjamin Disraeli's death, Lady Battersea (1843–1931), daughter of Sir Anthony de Rothschild (1810–76), wrote to her husband that their late friend had been 'not only loyal to his Queen and country, but also to the race from which he sprung', adding that 'his racial instincts were his religion and he was true to that religion until he drew his last breath'.[1] Lady Battersea's observation – that Disraeli's ideas about race were central to his self-definition – was consistent with contemporary interpretations of his character and beliefs. Friend and foe alike routinely linked his political behaviour and thinking to his ethnic background, to what Lady Battersea called 'his racial instincts'. In the century following his death, however, his biographers, as well as historians and political scientists, hesitated to view his racial concerns as central to his identity and career, preferring to ignore them or at least minimise their importance. In his biographical triptych *Burke, Disraeli, and Churchill* (1961), Stephen Graubard, for example, though prepared to acknowledge Disraeli's interest in race, confessed to not knowing what to make of it. 'It is difficult to understand', he admitted, 'why Disraeli charged Sidonia with another teaching mission – to instruct Coningsby in the greatness of the Jewish race.' With less hesitation, his biographer Robert Blake dismissed Disraeli's Jewishness in favour of the Italian 'streak' in his character. If national or racial stereotypes were to be introduced at all, Blake believed, then the traits associated with the 'Mediterranean character' were more dominant: pride, vanity, flamboyance, generosity, emotionalism, quarrelsomeness, extravagance, theatricality, an addiction to conspiracy, and a fondness for intrigue. Indeed, in Blake's view, Disraeli's financial ineptitude demonstrated the weakness of the Jewish element in his makeup.[2]

The first historian or political scientist in this century to accord Disraeli's racial ideas their due was Hannah Arendt, who, over five decades ago in *The Origins of Totalitarianism* (1951), suggested that Disraeli's declaration of Jewish racial 'chosenness' was a strategy to combat his own sense of social inferiority. In her view, he was acutely sensitive of his status as an outsider in upper-class Tory circles and, to compensate, invented a myth of Jewish racial superiority.[3]

It was not Hannah Arendt, however, but Isaiah Berlin who re-established for historical scholarship the central place of racial thinking in Disraeli's sense of self. In his presidential address to the Jewish Historical Society of England in 1967, in which he compared the links between ideology and identity in Disraeli and Marx, Berlin offered what is still the most elegant and authoritative exposition of this interpretation. Published in at least three different forums in English and translated into several other languages as well, his lecture described how Disraeli overcame a serious obstacle to his career – his Jewish background – by inflating it into a claim to noble birth. Disraeli 'needed to do this', Berlin explained, 'in order to feel that he was dealing on equal terms with the leaders of his family's adopted country, which he so profoundly venerated'.[4] As a result, in part, of the diffusion of this interpretation, there is now a consensus that Disraeli's racial ideas cannot be dismissed as irrelevant. Paul Smith's lecture to the Royal Historical Society on Disraeli's politics (1986), John Vincent's short account of Disraeli's thought in the Oxford Past Masters series (1990), Stanley Weintraub's full biographical treatment (1993) and Smith's brief life (1996) are testimony to the reintegration of Disraeli's Jewish chauvinism into evaluations of his life and work.[5] Reviewers of Weintraub's biography, while critical at times of his treatment of Victorian politics, have not balked at his restoration of Disraeli's Jewish concerns to centre stage.[6]

In these and other accounts of Disraeli's Jewishness,[7] one curious current remains unexplored – his use of the long-lived myth of Sephardi superiority, a myth that originated in medieval Spain and later migrated to western and northern Europe with the expansion of the Sephardi diaspora. The core of the myth, which remained more or less constant over the centuries despite changes in its external details, was the belief that Jews from the Iberian peninsula were different in kind from other Jews, that they were superior by virtue of their culture, learning, wealth, descent, manners or, indeed, even blood. Illuminating this theme in Disraeli's racial thought and viewing it in a broad historical context brings his construction of Jewishness into clearer focus. But, even more so, it makes his chauvinism seem less curious. It suggests that what can be viewed – and dismissed – as personal and aberrant was, instead, a reworking of a well established Sephardi tradition.

As is well known, Disraeli was not, in a strict sense, a Spanish or Portuguese Jew. His four grandparents or their parents were Italian-born. However, his grandmothers, Sarah Shiprut de Gabay Villa Real D'Israeli (1743–1825) and Rebecca Rieti Basevi (d. 1798), came from Iberian families that had settled in Italy in the late fifteenth century or thereafter. Thus, of his eight great-grandparents, three had Spanish or Portuguese antecedents; the other five were from native Italian stock or from Ashkenazi families that migrated there in the late-medieval period.[8] But since there were too few Italian Jews in London to sustain their own congregation, his relations who settled there associated with the well-established Spanish and Portuguese synagogue in Bevis Marks. This, rather than knowledge about his grandmothers' families, facilitated his romantic identification with Iberian Jewry.

In Disraeli's telling of his family history, as recorded in a memoir of his father for a new edition of *The Curiosities of Literature* (1849), his ancestors fled from Spain at the end of the fifteenth century and settled in Venice. There they flourished as merchants for two centuries, before his great-grandfather Disraeli, impressed by the commercial dynamism and religious tolerance of Hanoverian England, sent his youngest son to London in the mid-eighteenth century. In this con-struction of his family background, which was as much fiction as fact, Disraeli enhanced both the grandeur and demographic strength of the London Sephardim at the time. According to his account, the Jewish families then settled there were 'all of them Sephardim' who had been driven 'from their pleasant residences and rich estates in Arragon [*sic*], and Andalusia, and Portugal'. Ashkenazim, who, in fact, outnumbered Sephardim by the 1720s, were, in Disraeli's account, 'then only occa-sionally stealing into England'. Coming from 'an inferior caste', they were kept at arm's length by the wealthy Sephardim.[9]

In conversation and correspondence as well, Disraeli identified himself with Spanish and Portuguese Jews and emphasised their superi-ority. Walking at Lord Carrington's park one cold day in January 1851 with Edward Stanley, eldest son of the Earl of Derby, he remarked that the one obstacle to the return of the Jews to the Land of Israel was 'the existence of two races among the Hebrews, of whom one, those who settled along the shores of the Mediterranean, look down on the other, refusing even to associate with them'. He called 'the superior race', Stanley noted in his diary, 'Sephardim'.[10] In letters to Sarah Brydges Willyams (ca. 1780–1863), the childless widow of Sephardi ancestry whose fortune he inherited, he wrote often of their shared background, of their common descent from the aristocratic Laras, of 'the mysterious sympathy' that bound them together.[11] And in 1844 he wrote to his fellow Tory MP Richard Monckton Milnes, then visiting Berlin, that although German Jews were 'now the most intelligent of the tribes' they did not 'rank high in blood', not being Sephardim.[12]

That Disraeli bestowed Sephardi origins on the international banker Sidonia in his Young England novels *Coningsby* (1844) and *Tancred* (1847) was no accident. 'Descended from a very ancient and noble family of Arragon [*sic*], that, in the course of ages, had given to the state many distinguished citizens',[13] the multi-talented Sidonia acts as spokesman for Disraeli's racial and Jewish fantasies and as representative of those traits – worldliness, intellect, natural grace, social knowledge, wealth – with which Disraeli longed to be identified. When Sidonia makes an entrance at Lord Monmouth's country home for dinner, with but ten minutes to spare, 'there was a stir in the chamber ... a general pause in the room'. Even the magnificent, haughty Marquess of Beaumanoir 'seemed a little moved' in the presence of this 'gentleman of distinguished air'.[14] Would it be far-fetched to suggest that Disraeli himself would have liked to make such an entrance? Furthermore, Disraeli's choice of an Iberian background for Sidonia meant that he had to ignore what would have been obvious to a keen social observer like himself: a well-connected, cosmopolitan Sephardi banker was a socio-economic anachronism in Victorian Britain. The heyday of Sephardi influence and opulence was long past. In the 1840s, when Disraeli was writing *Coningsby* and *Tancred*, Spanish and Portuguese Jews were absent from the front ranks of City firms engaged in international finance. Sidonia was a ghost from the previous century, brought back to life to meet Disraeli's own needs. Most of the important Jewish houses – the Rothschilds chief among them – traced their origins to the Frankfurt ghetto, not the courts and estates of Castile and Aragon. Moreover, in its broad outlines, Sidonia's rise to financial pre-eminence after his arrival in England parallels that of the outstanding Ashkenazi banker of the period, Nathan Rothschild (1777–1836). In fact, Disraeli attributed Sidonia's success to having, like Rothschild, 'a brother, or near relative, in whom he could confide, in most of the principal capitals' of Europe.[15]

In invoking the myth of Sephardi superiority, Disraeli tended to avoid explicit comparisons between Spanish and Portuguese Jews, on the one hand, and Polish and German Jews, on the other.[16] The mere evocation of Sephardi grandeur was sufficient to indicate that an implicit and invidious comparison was being made, given the oft-remarked ties of London's Ashkenazim to low-status street trades. However, on at least two occasions, Disraeli went further. One was in the above-mentioned memoir of his father. The other was a longer passage, in *Tancred*, in which he contrasted the Sephardim of the sunny Mediterranean with the Ashkenazim of the bleak north, in Houndsditch and the Minories in London and the *Judengassen* of Hamburg and Frankfurt. Here he noted how the Sephardim, 'in their beautiful Asian cities or in their Moorish and Arabian gardens', more easily celebrated and identified with the agricultural festivals of Judaism and their nature-based rites, like the building of *sukkot* (booths), than the Ashkenazim in their squalid quarters in the icy climes of northern towns. Although he expressed admiration for the latter's steadfast devotion to 'Oriental customs in the heart of our Saxon and Sclavonian cities', he described the typical Ashkenazi Jew as 'an object ... of prejudice, dislike, disgust, perhaps hatred'. Imagine, he asked his readers,

> ... a being ... born to hereditary insult, without any education, apparently without a circumstance that can develop the slightest taste, or cherish the least sentiment for the beautiful, living amid fogs and filth, never treated with kindness, seldom with justice, occupied with the meanest, if not the vilest, toil, bargaining for frippery, speculating in usury, existing for ever under the concurrent influence of degrading causes.[17]

In addition, Disraeli knew and used, in private at least, an epithet-like term to refer to Ashkenazim. In a letter to his father in December 1835, he wrote that the merchant banker Isaac Lyon Goldsmid (1778–1859), whom he had just met, was 'not an ass in business, but a sharp Tedesco'.[18] This is, however, the sole occasion in his voluminous correspondence on which he used this pejorative term (which is not to say, of course, that he did not use it more often in conversation with family members). But for the most part Disraeli tended to praise Sephardim rather than disparage their northern counterparts, an understandable strategy in that he staked his claim to aristocratic status on the basis of the nobility of the Jewish race in general rather than one small part of it. In fact, at the end of the above-quoted passage in *Tancred* contrasting Sephardim and Ashkenazim, he praised the spiritual nobility of the latter in their attachment to ancient customs.

Although blessed with a fertile imagination, Disraeli neither created nor even much embellished the myth of Sephardi noble lineage. Rather, he made use of a well-established tradition, whose history has yet to receive the attention it merits. The oldest expression of the myth can be traced back to Muslim Spain, centuries before the expulsion, when it took the benign form of the genealogical claim that the Jews of Spain were *galut yerushalayim asher be-sefarad* – descendants of the royal tribe of Judah, of the inhabitants of Jerusalem whom Nebuchadnezzar carried off to Babylonia at the end of the sixth century BCE. The emergence of a Jewish courtier elite, who served Spain's monarchs as tax-farmers, physicians, diplomats, astronomers and political advisers, was seen as confirmation of their own noble origins.[19] Although the theme of Judaean descent was later incorporated into versions of the myth, full-blown claims of superiority arose only in the last century of open Jewish life on the peninsula, in response to Iberian racial antisemitism. The mass conversions sparked by the pogroms of 1391 and the disputation of Tortosa in 1413–14 created the basis for the entry of thousands of New Christians into offices of the church, the military, the universities, the royal courts and the municipalities. Their rapid upward mobility provoked a backlash in Old Christian society, which at mid-century exploded in racial polemics against the New Christians. The Jewish religion having ceased to define difference in former Jews and their offspring, Old Christians came to believe that it was New Christian racial descent, their blood, their unalterable, baptism-proof essence, that constituted the source of their evil traits and explained, as well, their social and economic success. The introduction of the statutes of *limpieza de sangre* (purity of blood), beginning in 1449 and continuing through the mid-sixteenth century, represented the insti-tutionalisation of the spreading belief that there were profound differ-ences between the noble blood of Old Christians and the tainted blood of New Christians.[20]

One response was to counter Hispanic claims of descent with Jewish claims. On the principle that nobility derives from antiquity, Spanish Jews, including some converts, claimed that they were the noblest of all peoples, since they were able to trace their ancestry to Judaea and Jerusalem. The family of Pablo de Santa Maria (né Solomon Halevi), bishop of Burgos, who had converted in 1391, claimed descent from the family of Mary, mother of Jesus, while a *converso* family that had settled in Brazil claimed to possess a deed of nobility proving its descent from the Maccabees![21] Jews who went into exile in 1492 and never donned New Christian masks celebrated their descent as well. They also tended to idealise their own immediate past, a natural response to dislocation, recounting with pride (and exaggeration) the learning, wealth, wisdom and influence of their ancestors, especially the courtier class. In this idealisation of their former life, the Jewish communities of Spain, it was claimed, surpassed all other diaspora communities whatever the criteria.[22] The rapid rise of the exiles to dominance in the Jewish communities of North Africa and the Balkans where they found refuge confirmed their sense of superiority – as did the subsequent 'sephardicisation' of these communities, that is, their adoption of the Sephardi *minhag* (liturgical rite).

Conversos who returned to Judaism in northern and western Europe in the seventeenth and eighteenth centuries brought with them the Iberian discourse of noble lineage and racial separateness, as did, to a lesser extent, those few Sephardim from Italy and North Africa whose ancestors had fled in 1492 and who now migrated northward.[23] As former New Christians worked to create new Jewish identities for themselves, they used these notions to help establish boundaries, to mark off who they were in relation to Christians in general, the Spanish and Portuguese in particular and Jews from other lands, as well. Their sense of ethnic separateness was nourished even more by their face-to-face encounter, beginning in the seventeenth century, with Polish and German Jews, especially in Hamburg, London and Amsterdam. Most Ashkenazim who reached these cities were poor and unskilled, with little prior exposure to western education, culture and manners. A large number were *Betteljuden* – vagabonds and *schnorrers*, the flotsam and jetsam of the Ashkenazi world, persons without resources or fixed residence who wandered from community to community, begging, stealing and in general living by their wits.

This encounter, between two groups of Jews whose historical experiences differed profoundly one from the other, bred contempt among Iberian Jews for their northern brethren and, at the same time, strengthened their obsession with lineage, descent and blood and their desire to hold themselves aloof. In Amsterdam, the centre of the western Sephardi diaspora, social ties between the two groups failed to develop; with a few exceptions, contacts remained at the instrumental level, between givers and receivers of relief or between masters and mistresses and their servants.[24] The caste pride of the Amsterdam Sephardim manifested itself in discriminatory measures against Jews of non-Iberian origin from the mid-seventeenth century on. In 1654, for example, the Amsterdam *mahamad* (communal board) forbade Ashkenazi women (in effect, servants) from attending services in the Sephardi synagogue; in 1657, it banned non-Sephardim from studying in its communal school; in 1671, it prohibited Ashkenazim who married Sephardi women, as well as their offspring, from becoming *yehidim* (privileged members) or being buried in the Sephardi cemetery; in 1697, it revoked the membership of Sephardim who took non-Sephardi wives. Moreover, in 1632, in the hope of discouraging penniless Ashkenazim from settling in Amsterdam, the Spanish and Portuguese leadership prohibited its members from giving charity to beggars at their doors or the gate of the synagogue. In the mid-1630s, it also began repatriating German and Polish Jews.[25] (The practice of sending the poorest members of the community to distant lands was first used against indigent Sephardim.) Not surprisingly, few mixed Ashkenazi-Sephardi marriages took place in Amsterdam, even as late as the mid-nineteenth century.[26]

In London, where contact between the two groups was greater, the Bevis Marks authorities imposed humiliating conditions on the celebration of Ashkenazi-Sephardi unions to express their displeasure. In 1745, when Jacob Israel Bernal (d. ca. 1766) asked permission to be married to an Ashkenazi woman, the elders consented but stipulated that no member of the *bet din* (rabbinic court) or *hazzan* (cantor) was to officiate, that the groom was not to be called to the Torah, that no *mi-she-berakhs* (special prayers) were to be made in his honour and that no celebration of any kind was to be held in the synagogue. In other cases, permission to marry was denied or, when given, the name of the bride omitted from the marriage register, where she was listed as merely 'Tudesca'. The revised *ascamot* (communal laws) of 1784 prohibited the *hakham* (chief rabbi) from officiating at mixed marriages and barred Sephardim who married non-Sephardim or even the Sephardi widows of non-Sephardim from receiving communal relief.[27]

In the seventeenth century, Sephardi motives for distinguishing and segregating themselves from other Jews were internal: the emotional need to forge a new, non-*converso* group identity and the practical need to reduce the burden of caring for destitute newcomers from central and eastern Europe. In the eighteenth century, external motives as well came into play. Eager to advance their social integration and improve their legal status, Sephardi polemicists and apologists from the mid-eighteenth century on displayed a lively concern with their public image. In particular, they tried to disassociate themselves from destitute German and Polish Jews then migrating westward in increasing numbers, whom, they believed, blackened the name of all Jews.

The most famous example of this strategy is found in the reply of the political economist Isaac de Pinto (1717–87) to Voltaire's vulgar remarks about Jews in his *Dictionnaire Philosophique*.[28] Pinto charged

Voltaire with failing to distinguish between Spanish and Portuguese Jews and '*la foule des autres enfants de Jacob*'. The former, he told Voltaire, were descendants of the tribe of Judah who migrated to Spain at the time of the Babylonian captivity. They scrupulously avoided mixing with and marrying other Jews and, though they shared the same religion, observed it differently, maintaining separate synagogues. Moreover, the manners and habits of the Portuguese were different. They did not have beards or distinctive dress, while the rich among them cultivated learning, elegance and pomp to the same extent as other European nations. The gap between the Sephardim and other Jews was so great, he reported, that, if a Portuguese Jew in Holland or England were to wed a German Jewess, he would lose his communal privileges: he would lose his membership in the synagogue; he would be denied all religious honours; he would be cut off from the body of the nation; he would be refused burial among his Portuguese brethren. German and Polish Jews, on the other hand, were degraded, having been deprived of the advantages of social contact, treated with contempt, persecuted, humiliated and insulted through the ages. A Portuguese Jew from Bordeaux and a German Jew from Metz were '*deux êtres absolument différents*'.[29]

When Jewish status was debated in France in the last years of the *ancien régime* and during the revolutionary and Napoleonic period, spokesmen for the Sephardi communities in southwestern France invoked this distinction repeatedly. For example, in a *mémoire* to the government in June 1788, Abraham Furtado (1756–1817) and Solomon Lopes-Dubec emphasised, as Pinto had earlier, the ease with which Sephardim assimilated to their adopted homes in northern and western Europe:

> A Portuguese Jew is English in England and French in France, but a German Jew is German everywhere because of his customs from which he deviates rarely; thus one can look at the English and the Germans as brothers who, although sharing the same mother, have nevertheless developed characteristics which are absolutely different, nay even incompatible.[30]

In August 1806, when the so-called Napoleonic Sanhedrin in Paris composed its replies to 12 questions about Judaism's relationship to French citizenship, the first draft of its answer to question four – did Jews consider Frenchmen as brothers or strangers? – established a difference between Portuguese and German Jews.[31] This strategy of differentiation bore fruit in the end: when Napoleon, disappointed by the failure of French Jews to 'regenerate' themselves following emancipation, imposed new restrictions on Jewish commerce, conscription and residence, he exempted the Sephardim.[32]

   There is both indirect and direct evidence that Isaac D'Israeli (1766–1848) was not only familiar with but embraced the myth of Sephardi superiority. Even if an infrequent visitor to the synagogue in Bevis Marks, he was not a stranger to Sephardi society. His own father was an immigrant to England, like others in his family circle, and was in touch with social and cultural currents that flowed strongly in Sephardi communities abroad. As a teenager, he was sent to live in Amsterdam, with his father's agent there. It can also be inferred that he used the term 'tudesco' – with all its negative associations. After all, from whom else did his son learn the term? In addition, a public debate about Jewish poverty and criminality took place in London in 1802 during which the Sephardi community disassociated itself from the rest of London's Jews. Following publication of a work critical of the Jewish poor, influential Ashkenazim proposed to Parliament the establishment of a Jewish relief board with the authority to tax Jewish rate payers, centralise the distribution of charity and jail and deport undesirable aliens. The Spanish and Portuguese community fought inclusion in the scheme, instructing their attorney to see that their name was not connected with it.[33] In a document prepared for a Member of Parliament who was assisting them, they emphasised that the Portuguese and the Germans formed 'two distinct (not religious, but) political bodies', that they 'always considered each other (as they actually are) separate and distinct bodies'.[34] There is no reason to doubt that Isaac D'Israeli, who had written about the reform of Jewish culture in a biographical sketch of Moses Mendelssohn in the *Monthly Magazine* in 1798, was aware of this debate. A few years later, when the Parisian Sanhedrin convened, he followed its proceedings, publishing two articles about the assembly, again in the *Monthly Magazine*.[35]

   The most compelling evidence that Isaac was the conduit through which the Sephardi myth reached Benjamin is in Isaac's anonymous treatise *The Genius of Judaism* (1833). Using similes, rhetorical devices and illustrations lifted, without acknowledgement, from Isaac de Pinto's *Apologie*, D'Israeli restated the claim that the Jews were not one but several nations, each, like the chameleon, reflecting the colour of the spot they rested on.[36] (The simile was Pinto's.) Thus: 'After a few generations, the Hebrews assimilate with the character, and are actu-

ated by the feelings, of the nation where they become natives.' The
first Jews to settle in England, he told his readers, were Spanish and
Portuguese Jews – 'noblemen, officers, learned physicians, and opulent
merchants' – who brought with them 'their national characteristic ...
their haughtiness, their high sense of honour, and their stately manners'.
Subsequent Jewish immigrants from Germany and Poland were 'a
race in every respect of an inferior rank'.

> The Portuguese Grandees shrunk from their contact; they
> looked on those lees of the people in bitter scorn, and through
> a long century the contumely was never forgiven. In every
> respect these differing races moved in contrast. The one
> opulent and high-minded; the other humiliated by indigence,
> and pursuing the meanest, and not seldom the most disrep-
> utable, crafts. The one indolent, polished, and luxurious; the
> other, with offensive habits, active and penurious, hardy in
> frame, and shrewd in intellect. The one splendid in dress and
> equipage, while the abject Polander still retained the beard
> commanded by Moses with the gabardine.

Between the two groups, mutual hatred flourished. D'Israeli even
claimed that 'the haughty Lusitanian Jew would have returned to the
fires of Lisbon, ere he condescended to an intermarriage with the Jew
of Alsace or Warsaw'.[37] If, as widely acknowledged, Isaac's Tory and
royalist sympathies influenced his son's interpretation of English history
it is also probable that his Jewish prejudices left their mark as well. It
is no coincidence that Benjamin Disraeli used images and terms
similar to those his father used in describing the cultural and social
gulf between the two communities.

In tracing this tradition from late-medieval Spain to Victorian
England, I do not intend to suggest that it, rather than some other
influence, is the hitherto unknown key to Disraeli's racial thinking.
Multiple cultural and intellectual currents, especially those of a romantic
hue, oversaw its genesis. Disraeli belonged to a broad stream of conservative, romantic, organic thought in Britain that hated Benthamite
utilitarianism, free market economics, and liberal doctrines of progress.
His ideological bedfellows included Walter Scott, Robert Southey,
A. W. N. Pugin, Thomas Carlyle and, to a lesser extent, collectors of
old armour, builders of battlemented, asymmetrical, picturesque castles
and enthusiasts of the chivalric revival. Moreover, while full-blown
deterministic racial theories were rare when Disraeli's outlook was

taking shape, inchoate notions of racial hierarchy were not. The discourse of Anglo-Saxonism was widely diffused in the first half of the nineteenth century.[38] The author of *The English and Their Origins*, writing in 1866, noted that there were few educated Englishmen who had not been taught as children that 'the English nation is a nation of almost pure Teutonic blood', that its constitution, customs, wealth and empire were the necessary result of 'the arrival, in three vessels, of certain German warriors' centuries earlier.[39] Isaac D'Israeli's close friend Sharon Turner, who convinced him to make his children Christians and afterward took them to St Andrew's, Holborn, to be baptised, was author of a best-selling multi-volume *History of the Anglo-Saxons* (1799–1805) that was shot through with a racial reading of English history.[40]

If racial ideas were 'in the air', it also must be recalled that Disraeli's own needs prepared him to absorb them. Driven by ambition but unable to shake his Jewish origins (like the *conversos* before him), he discovered that the idea of race, when given a novel, 'Jewish' twist, allowed him to counter the hereditary claims of the great English landed families. His ancestral community's obsession with descent helped to determine his novel response, while infusing it at the same time with an Iberian flavour. Without reference to this myth and its history, the Sephardi component of his Jewish chauvinism is inexplicable.

Disraeli's reaction to the prejudice that he continued to encounter after his baptism was unusual. No other Victorian Jew, baptised or otherwise, opted for such a strategy. Jews in Britain (and elsewhere, as well) who desired entrée to Christian circles hid, minimised or, at most, did not call attention to their Jewishness, even when it was thrown in their faces. To paraphrase Heine, Jewish chauvinism was not their ticket of admission into European society. Their hopes for inclusion rested, instead, on non-biological, liberal theories of social behaviour and historical development that stressed nurture over nature, the malleability of manners, traits and character and, in particular, the similarity of Jews to other persons in all spheres of human activity other than religion.

Given the eccentric character of Disraeli's response, one is tempted to discount its historical importance, to consider it a bizarre, though entertaining, footnote to the main text of English Jewish history. After all, if his use of the idea of race was unrepresentative – which, indeed, it was – then what is its larger historical relevance, its connection to broader historical themes? Of course, one could argue that Disraeli's solution, however peculiar, is one more telling example of how difficult it was for even well acculturated Jews to avoid antisemitic obstacles on the road to integration. And this is fair enough. But there is another, more important, historiographical dimension to Disraeli's Jewish chauvinism that comes into focus when his use of the myth of Sephardi superiority is emphasised. For while his racial ideas were untypical, his invocation of the Sephardi myth was not.

From the late eighteenth century, Sephardim throughout western Europe, as well as Ashkenazim, deployed the myth to promote their own cultural, political and social agendas. As we saw, Sephardi spokesmen used it repeatedly to disassociate themselves from Jews who, in their view, threatened their own status. In the German states, the pioneers of *Wissenschaft des Judentums* and the leaders of the Reform movement constructed an image of Sephardi Judaism that stressed its cultural openness, philosophical rationalism and aesthetic sensibilities in order to criticise what they disliked in their own tradition, that is, its backwardness, insularity, aversion to secular studies. In France, Austria, Germany, Hungary and the United States, communal and congregational boards erected imposing synagogues of so-called Moorish design, assertive symbols of their break with the 'unenlightened' Ashkenazi past. Jewish poets and novelists who were Disraeli's contemporaries – Heinrich Heine (1797–56), the brothers Phöbus (1807–70) and Ludwig (1811–89) Philippson, Berthold Auerbach (1812–82) and Grace Aguilar (1816–47) – were fascinated with the Iberian experience and drew on it for themes and subjects, with the result that their work further augmented its mystique.[41]

Before the end of the century, the myth of Sephardi superiority was widely disseminated and available for appropriation by Jews and their enemies alike. In his attack on the Jewish historian Heinrich Graetz (1817–91) in 1881, the German nationalist historian Heinrich von Treitschke (1834–96) maintained that the Spanish and Portuguese Jews were closer to the German people than were the Jews of Poland and Germany because their history was prouder and more distinguished than that of the latter, who had been scarred by centuries of Christian tyranny. In their battle against racial myths about Jewish deformities, Jewish anthropologists drew on the Sephardi mystique to create a counter-myth of their own – that of the well-bred, aesthetically attractive, physically graceful Sephardi, a model of racial nobility and virility. In their work, John Efron notes, 'the Sephardi served as the equivalent of the Jewish "Aryan" ... the physical counterpart to the ignoble Jew of Central and Eastern Europe'. For some acculturated Ashkenazim who wished to distance themselves from impoverished east European Jews and their alleged defects, fantasies of Sephardi descent became a strategy for enhancing their own self-image. Theodor Herzl (1860–1904), whose attitudes toward Jews vacillated between pride and disdain, claimed Iberian roots for his family. He told the early English Zionist Jacob de Haas (1872–1937) that his paternal grandfather was a Spanish Jew who had been forced to convert to Christianity and had later fled to Constantinople, where he re-embraced Judaism. In a different version, told to the Hebrew and Yiddish writer Reuben Brainin (1862–1939) in 1904, he traced his descent to a high-ranking *converso* monk who returned to Judaism while abroad on a mission.[42]

In a structural sense as well, Disraeli's use of the Iberian Jewish mystique resembled other assimilationist strategies in the age of emancipation. Westernised, upper-middle-class Jews unsure of their social status routinely made public declarations that Jews fell into two categories, 'good' Jews and 'bad' Jews. In England, native-born Jews in the period of mass migration struggled to distance themselves from impoverished, Yiddish-speaking, foreign-born newcomers, while Bayswater and Mayfair Jews poured scorn on their less cultured co-religionists in Maida Vale. These distinctions, conveyed in novels, tracts, newspapers, lectures and other public forums, were intended to convince the gentile world that their authors, 'good' Jews, were nothing like 'bad' Jews and thus merited political rights, social acceptance, exemption from contempt or whatever was on the agenda at the time.[43] In this sense, the Disraelian strategy was all too representative.

NOTES

I should like to thank my colleagues Zvi Gitelman and Miriam Bodian for their comments and advice on an earlier version of this article.

1. Battersea Papers, Add MSS 47910/5, British Library, London.
2. Stephen R. Graubard, *Burke, Disraeli, and Churchill: The Politics of Perseverance* (Cambridge, MA, 1961), p. 123; Robert Blake, *Disraeli* (Garden City, NY, Doubleday Anchor edn, 1968), p. 47. Blake's observation reveals more about him than it does about Disraeli.
3. Hannah Arendt, *The Origins of Totalitarianism*, Part 1, 'Antisemitism' (New York, Harvest Book edn, 1968), pp. 72–5.
4. Isaiah Berlin's 'Benjamin Disraeli, Karl Marx and the Search for Identity' appeared initially in the *Transactions of the Jewish Historical Society of England*, Vol. 22 (1970), pp. 1–20. It was reprinted in *Midstream*, Vol. 16, No. 7 (August/September 1970), pp. 24–49, and in a collection of Berlin's essays, Henry Hardy (ed.), *Against the Current: Essays in the History of Ideas* (New York, 1979), pp. 252–86. Translations have appeared in French, German and Spanish.
5. Paul Smith, 'Disraeli's Politics', *Transactions of the Royal Historical Society*, 5th ser., Vol. 37 (1987), pp. 65–85; John Vincent, *Disraeli*, Past Masters series (Oxford,

1990); Stanley Weintraub, *Disraeli: A Biography* (New York, 1993); Paul Smith, *Disraeli: A Brief Life* (Cambridge, 1996).

6. See, for example, Richard Shannon, 'The Cult of the Prophet', *Times Literary Supplement*, 29 November 1993, pp. 3–4.

7. See also Abraham Gilam, 'Disraeli in Jewish Historiography', *Midstream*, Vol. 26, No. 3 (March 1980), pp. 24–9; *idem*, 'Benjamin Disraeli and Jewish Identity', *The Wiener Library Bulletin*, new ser., Vol. 33, Nos 51–2 (1980), pp. 2–8; Benjamin Jaffee, 'A Reassessment of Benjamin Disraeli's Jewish Aspects', *Transactions of the Jewish Historical Society of England*, Vol. 27 (1982), pp. 115–23; M. C. N. Salbstein, *The Emancipation of the Jews in Britain: The Question of the Admission of the Jews to Parliament, 1828–1860* (Rutherford, NJ, 1982), ch. 5 ('Benjamin Disraeli, Marrano Englishman'); Todd M. Endelman, 'Disraeli's Jewishness Reconsidered', *Modern Judaism*, Vol. 5 (1985), pp. 109–23. Salbstein alone mentions Disraeli's invocation of alleged Sephardi superiority.

8. The most reliable account of Disraeli's ancestry is Cecil Roth, *Benjamin Disraeli, Earl of Beaconsfield* (New York, 1952), ch. 1. See also Michael Selzer, 'Benjamin Disraeli's Knowledge of his Ancestry', *Disraeli Project Newsletter*, Vol. 1, No. 2 (1976), pp. 8–17.

9. Benjamin Disraeli, 'On the Life and Writings of Mr. Disraeli', in Isaac D'Israeli, *The Curiosities of Literature*, new edition, 3 vols (London, 1858), Vol. 1, pp. viii–ix.

10. John Vincent (ed.), *Disraeli, Derby and the Conservative Party: Journals and Memoirs of Edward Henry, Lord Stanley, 1849–1869* (Hassocks, Sussex, 1978), p. 32.

11. Quoted in Weintraub, *Disraeli*, p. 377.

12. M. G. Wiebe *et al.* (eds), *Benjamin Disraeli Letters*, Vol. 4, *1842–1847* (Toronto, 1989), p. 153.

13. Benjamin Disraeli, *Coningsby, or, The New Generation*, Bk IV, ch. x.

14. *Idem*, IV, ch. ix.

15. Ibid.

16. John Vincent comments that as a rule 'Disraeli said little about the lower races; his object was to praise, not disparage'. *Disraeli*, p. 27.

17. Benjamin Disraeli, *Tancred, or, The New Crusade*, Bk X, ch. vi.

18. J. A. Gunn *et al.* (eds), *Benjamin Disraeli Letters*, Vol. 2, *1835–1837* (Toronto, 1982), p. 109. The word 'tudesco' (to use the more common Sephardi orthography) is an Iberianised form of the Italian word 'tedesco' (German), used by western Sephardim to refer to Jews from Germany and Poland. Although at first non-pejorative, it became, by the eighteenth century at the latest, a term of contempt, expressing disdain for persons considered to be of low, even disreputable, rank. I am grateful to Miriam Bodian, whose own research and writing focus on the Sephardi diaspora, for clarifying this for me.

19. Haim Hillel Ben Sasson, 'Dor golei sefarad al atsmo' [The Generation of Spanish Exiles on its Fate], *Zion*, Vol. 26, No. 1 (1961), p. 23.

20. Yosef Hayim Yerushalmi, *Assimilation and Racial Anti-Semitism: The Iberian and the German Models*, Leo Baeck Memorial Lecture No. 26 (New York, 1982).

21. Miriam Bodian, '"Men of the Nation": The Shaping of *Converso* Identity in Early Modern Europe', *Past & Present*, No. 143 (May 1994), p. 62.

22. Ben Sasson, 'Dor golei sefarad', pp. 23–9.

23. On the Iberian legacy of caste pride among western Sephardim, see Yosef Kaplan, *Mi-natsrut le-yahadut: hayyav u-fealo shel ha-anus Yitshak Orobio de Castro* [From Christianity to Judaism: The Life and Work of Isaac Orobio de Castro] (Jerusalem, 1982), pp. 269–74; *idem*, 'Political Concepts in the World of the Portuguese Jews of Amsterdam during the Seventeenth Century: The Problem of Exclusion and the Boundaries of Self-Identity' in Yosef Kaplan, Henry

Méchoulan and Richard H. Popkin (eds), *Menasseh ben Israel and His World* (Leiden, 1989), pp. 45–62.

24. Yosef Kaplan, 'Yahasam shel ha-yehudim ha-sefaradim ve-ha-portugalim li-yehudim ha-ashkenazim be-amsterdam be-meah ha-17' [The Relationship of Spanish and Portuguese Jews to Ashkenazi Jews in Amsterdam in the Seventeenth Century] in Shmuel Almog *et al.* (eds), *Temurot ha-historiyah ha-yehudit ha-hadashah: kovets maamarim shay le-Shmuel Ettinger* [Transformations in Modern Jewish History: Essays Presented to Shmuel Ettinger] (Jerusalem, 1987), p. 399.

25. Kaplan, 'Yahasam', pp. 403–6; *idem*, 'The Portuguese Community in 17th-Century Amsterdam and the Ashkenazi World' in Jozeph Michman (ed.), *Dutch Jewish History*, Vol. 2 (Jerusalem, 1989), pp. 33–4, 43–4.

26. Jozeph Michman, 'Beyn sefaradim ve-ashkenazim be-amsterdam' [Between Ashkenazim and Sephardim in Amsterdam] in Issachar Ben Ami (ed.), *Moreshet yehudei sefarad ve-ha-mizrah* [The Sephardic and Oriental Jewish Heritage] (Jerusalem, 1982), pp. 136–7.

27. Albert M. Hyamson, *The Sephardim of England: A History of the Spanish and Portuguese Jewish Community* (London, 1951), pp. 170–1, 190, 228. Hyamson claims that the authorities' motivation was a concern 'lest the numbers of these individuals [non-Sephardim] should become too large so as perhaps to threaten the preservation of their Community as a Sephardi one' (p. 170).

28. Isaac de Pinto, *Apologie pour la nation juive, ou, réflexions critiques sur le premier chapitre du VII. tome des oeuvres de monsieur de Voltaire au suject des Juifs* (Amsterdam, 1762). On Pinto's work in general and the genesis of his apology in particular, see Arthur Hertzberg, *The French Enlightenment and the Jews* (New York, 1968), pp. 142–53, 180–3, 269–70.

29. Pinto, *Apologie*, pp. 12–16.

30. Quoted in Frances Malino, *The Sephardic Jews of Bordeaux: Assimilation and Emancipation in Revolutionary and Napoleonic France* (University, AL, 1978), p. 32.

31. Diogene Tama (ed.), *Transactions of the Parisian Sanhedrim*, trans. F. D. Kirwan, mimeographed edn (Cincinnati, 1956), p. 19.

32. The campaign of the Sephardim to secure exemption is described in Malino, *Sephardic Jews of Bordeaux*, pp. 95–109.

33. Todd M. Endelman, *The Jews of Georgian England, 1714–1830: Tradition and Change in a Liberal Society* (Philadelphia, 1979), pp. 231–6.

34. The document is reproduced in full in Charles H. L. Emanuel (ed.), *A Century and a Half of Jewish History Extracted from the Minute Books of the London Committee of Deputies of the British Jews* (London, 1910), pp. 10–12.

35. [Isaac D'Israeli], 'A Biographical Sketch of the Jewish Socrates', *Monthly Magazine*, Vol. 6, Pt 2 (1798), pp. 38–44; 'On the Late Installation of a Great Sanhedrim of the Jews in Paris', ibid., Vol. 24, Pt 2 (1807), pp. 34–8; 'Acts of the Great Sanhedrim at Paris', ibid., pp. 134–6, 243–8.

36. It is impossible to know whether Isaac D'Israeli owned a copy of the Pinto work. In the Rothschild Archive in London, there is a list of books from the library of Benjamin Disraeli that his heirs sold in 1881 (Lord Rothschild was executor of his will), DFamE(1)/9A. The list contains 54 entries, most on Jewish themes. Given the large number of eighteenth-century publications, it seems reasonable to conclude that many belonged to Isaac initially. The Pinto work is not among them. However, this does not prove that Isaac did not own a copy, since it was a pamphlet, not a book, and the Jewish tracts in the collection, covering the years 1747 to 1794, were bound together into two volumes and identified only with the words 'various authors' and 'various publishers'. I am grateful to Melanie

Aspey, archivist at the Rothschild Archive, for providing me with a photocopy of the list.

37. [Isaac D'Israeli], *The Genius of Judaism* (London, 1833), pp. 237–8, 244–8.

38. Hugh A. MacDougall, *Racial Myth in English History: Trojans, Teutons, and Anglo-Saxons* (Montreal, Hanover, NH and London, 1982), ch. 5; Leon Poliakov, *The Aryan Myth: A History of Racist and Nationalist Ideas in Europe*, trans. Edmund Howard (New York, 1977), pp. 50–2.

39. Luke Owen Pike, *The English and Their Origins* (London, 1866), p. 15.

40. MacDougall, *Racial Myth in English History*, p. 94.

41. Ismar Schorsch, 'The Myth of Sephardi Supremacy', *Leo Baeck Institute Year Book*, Vol. 34 (1989), pp. 47–66; Ivan Marcus, 'Beyond the Sephardi Mystique', *Orim: A Jewish Journal at Yale*, Vol. 1, No. 1 (1985), pp. 35–53.

42. Walter Boehlich (ed.), *Der Berliner Antisemitismusstreit* (Frankfurt a.M., 1965), pp. 37–8; John M. Efron, 'Scientific Racism and the Mystique of Sephardi Racial Superiority', *Leo Baeck Institute Year Book*, Vol. 38 (1993), pp. 75–96; Jacques Kornberg, *Theodor Herzl: From Assimilation to Zionism* (Bloomington, IN, 1993), pp. 76–7.

43. See, for example, Todd M. Endelman, 'The Frankaus of London, 1837–1967: A Study in Radical Assimilation', *Jewish History/Historiyyah Yehudit*, Vol. 8, Nos 1–2 (1994), pp. 1–38.

'MENE, MENE, TEKEL, UPHARSIN': JEWISH PERSPECTIVES IN DISRAELI'S FICTION

Daniel R. Schwarz

In the book of Daniel there is a famous scene in which the Babylonian king Belshazzar is feasting and drinking from sacred vessels which his father, Nebuchadnezzar, had plundered from the Temple in Jerusalem; suddenly a hand unattached to a body appears and writes mysterious words on the wall: *'Mene, Mene, Tekel, Upharsin'*. Neither Belshazzar nor his followers can understand the words, which seem to belong to an unknown tongue. So, desperate to know their meaning, Belshazzar summons Daniel, who has a reputation for wisdom. Daniel can read the words, which are in Aramaic. Literally, Daniel explains, the words mean 'numbered, numbered, weighed, and divided'. But Daniel then offers an ethical interpretation, foretelling the destruction of Belshazzar and his kingdom. Daniel's reading is a prophecy: 'God hath numbered thy [Belshazzar's] kingdom, and brought it to an end; thou art weighed in the balances, and found wanting. Thy kingdom is divided, and given to the Medes and the Persians.'

The mysterious words that appear to Belshazzar and require an interpretation may serve us as a parable of what Disraeli felt he must do. For Disraeli the so-called Glorious Revolution was an event in which a Nebuchadnezzar had come and destroyed the Holy Temple of the English constitution. Those who deposed James II in the name of civil and religious liberty were the very Whig families who formed the Venetian party and who, as he puts it in *Sybil*, 'in one century plundered the church to gain the property of the people and in another century changed the dynasty to gain the power of the crown'.[1] When Daniel's prophecy comes true, is it because Daniel knows and speaks God's will or because he is lucky? Texts – and our life experiences – cry out for interpretation even as they resist our understanding. For Disraeli, the text of English history needed to be interpreted, and he – in temperament as rabbinical as he was English – sought to do so. Since,

Disraeli understood, we cannot call upon Daniel, we have to be our own Daniel and do the work ourselves. For Disraeli believed in his own genius and believed we must interpret our words and experiences according to our own perspective and trust in our own intelligence, imagination and ethics. Disraeli would be the Daniel of his culture, the seer who would interpret his culture – its politics, history and values. He sees himself as a figure who understands that if his advice is not followed, England's days will be 'numbered, numbered, weighed, and divided'.

Disraeli's presentations of Jews relate to his quest of self-definition, his desire to differentiate himself from his fellows and the concomitant need to capitalise on his difference, on his *otherness*, in the face of antisemitism. But it is well to remember that Disraeli and his contemporaries believed in the possibility of a homogeneous European culture, even as it sought to propose diverse and contradictory alternatives. For Disraeli, as John Elderfield puts it, 'history was not always thought to be quite possibly a species of fiction but once comprised a form of order, and might still'.[2] One might recall James Clifford's comment that in 1900 '"Culture" referred to a single evolutionary process. The European bourgeois ideal of autonomous individuality was widely believed to be the natural outcome of a long development, a process that, although threatened by various disruptions, was assumed to be the basic, progressive movement of humanity.'[3]

In this essay, I propose to discuss how Disraeli's Jewishness appears in his novels. My use of the term 'novel' – not text, not site – will signal, I trust, that I am a traditional humanist who believes literature is written by human authors about human characters for human readers. I am also an Aristotelian who believes that the aesthetic, ethical and political are inextricably related and that novels unfold in time as they propose, modify, transform, discard and reformulate patterns of meaning. So much for what in the United States is called truth in labelling or what medieval scholastics called the problem of nominalism. I think cultural studies need to address the special ontology of events that constitutes the unique individuality of the artist – what might be called the idioverse in which the artist lives.

EARLY FICTION

Disraeli's literary career spans over a half a century, from 1826 to 1880. He published the first volumes of *Vivian Grey* when Scott, Blake, Wordsworth and Coleridge were still alive and before any of the major

Victorians, excepting Carlyle, were published. He concluded his career in 1880 – Dickens and Thackeray were long dead, George Eliot was to die that year, and Thomas Hardy had by then published *Far From the Madding Crowd* and *The Return of the Native*.

Disraeli's novels tell us something about the history of taste in the nineteenth century. His early novels – *Vivian Grey* (1826–27), *The Young Duke* (1831), *Contarini Fleming* (1832) – met the middle-class desire for revelations of aristocratic life, for romances about bizarre characters in strange lands and for extreme behaviour on the part of wilful egoists posing as latter-day Byrons. Indeed, as an outsider, as a man who savoured his own feelings and sought unusual sensations, the youthful Disraeli saw himself as an heir to Byron and Shelley. But in the later 1830s, Disraeli, like Dickens, began responding to audiences who wanted sentiment and sweetness; in *Henrietta Temple* Disraeli wrote about love between virginal young women and idealistic young men whose motives are temporarily misunderstood because of circumstances beyond their control. Even when he wrote of Byron and Shelley in *Venetia*, he threw the mantle of Victorian respectability over them in spite of his empathy with their unconventionality. In the mid-1840s, in the Young England trilogy, he met the demand for serious novels that addressed themselves to major moral and political ideas. In *Lothair* (1870) he drew upon the public's fascination – rekindled by the conversion of the Marquess of Bute – with the journey from Anglicanism to Roman Catholicism, while in *Endymion* (1880) he responded to the interest in character psychology created by Browning, Eliot and Hardy, which was in effect part of an inward turning and questioning as the Victorian era passed its high tide of confidence. Throughout his career his fiction fulfilled the nineteenth-century fascination with heroic men; in an age of uncertainty this fascination reflected a need for larger-than-life personalities.

Describing the process of writing *Death in Venice*, Thomas Mann recalled,

> Originally the tale was to be brief and modest. But things or whatever better word there may be for the conception *organic* have a will of their own, and shape themselves accordingly ... The truth is that every piece of work is a realization, fragmentary but complete in itself, of our individuality; and this kind of realization is the sole and painful way we have of getting the particular experience – no wonder, then, that the process is attended by surprises.[4]

Mann reminds us that the author both creates a text and discovers an aspect of his or her self during its creation. In Disraeli's first four novels – *Vivian Grey*, *The Young Duke*, *Contarini Fleming* and *The Wondrous Tale of Alroy* – he 'realised' aspects of his individuality. Not only did he create imagined worlds in his novels but the novels played a crucial role in creating his character and personality. In discussing Disraeli's first four novels, we need to understand this symbiotic relationship between author and text as an essential condition to appreciating his art. An 1833 entry in Disraeli's so-called 'mutilated diary' shows that the novels compensate for his failure to excel even as they protest against accepted English conventions and manners:

> The world calls me 'conceited' – the world is in error. I trace all the blunders of my life to sacrificing my own opinion to that of others. When I was considered very conceited *indeed*, I was nervous, and had self-confidence only by fits. I intend in future to act entirely from my own impulse. I have an unerring instinct. I can read characters at a glance; few men can deceive me. My mind is a continental mind. It is a revolutionary mind. I am only truly great in action. If ever I am placed in a truly eminent position I shall prove this. I could rule the House of Commons, although there would be a great prejudice against me at first. It is the most jealous assembly in the world. The fine character of our English society, the consequences of our aristocratic institutions, renders a *career* difficult.[5]

Here is the myth of a strong, confident, gifted 'continental' personality functioning in a larger world than the English one that Disraeli felt stifled his creativity and ignored his genius. Disraeli used his travels to define the heroic and spiritual self that he believed he needed to discover in order to make himself the political visionary he sought to be. The subsequent passage in the diary makes it clear that literature is a compensation for the frustration he feels at not being given the opportunity to play a major role in public events: 'Poetry is the safety valve of my passions – but I wish to act what I write. My works are the embodification of my feelings. In *Vivian Grey* I have portrayed my active and real ambition: in *Alroy* my ideal ambition: [*Contarini Fleming: A Psychological Romance*] is a development of my poetic character. This trilogy is the secret history of my feelings – I shall write no more about myself.'

One aspect of Contarini's travels requires further mention. Contarini, whose father was a Saxon, expresses a characteristic Disraeli theme when he speaks disparagingly of the Franks. He stresses their comparatively recent history as a civilised people and depicts them as visitors to the lands in which they are not the majority. His protagonists, from Contarini to Tancred to Lothair, are always more at home in the East than are other Europeans and find there a spiritual equilibrium that they lack in their own culture. As we know, Disraeli took great pride in his Jewish heritage. He empathised with those who had a non-European heritage and resented the pretensions of those who thought that the Europeans were the fathers of civilisation. This reflected, no doubt, his own frustration at being patronised by Anglo-Saxons whom he regarded as only a few centuries removed from barbarism in contrast to the Semitic peoples' substantial contribution to Western civilisation. At this stage in his career, the glorification of the Arabs was Disraeli's metaphor for illustrating the importance of the Jewish race. We must recall that in the 1830s Arab and Jew more or less peacefully co-existed in the Middle East, or so Disraeli thought. Since Disraeli regarded the Arabs as brothers of the Jews, his glorification of them disguised similar claims for the Jews. That the desert Bedouins approximate a utopia more than any other people will be clearer if we recall that Disraeli spoke of the Jews as a Bedouin race. The Bedouins, he wrote, 'combined primitive simplicity of habits with the refined feelings of civilisation, and ... in a great degree, appeared to me to offer an evidence of that community of property and that equality of condition, which have hitherto proved the despair of European sages, and fed only the visions of their fanciful Utopias'.[6]

Alroy is Disraeli's ultimate heroic fantasy. He uses the figure of the twelfth-century Jewish prince Alroy as the basis for a tale of Jewish conquest and empire. Disraeli found the medieval world in which Alroy lived an apt model for some of his own values. He saw in that world an emphasis on imagination, emotion and tradition; respect for political and social hierarchies; and a vital spiritual life. Alroy anticipates Disraeli's attraction for the Middle Ages in Young England. Writing of the flowering of medieval Jewry under Alroy enabled him to express his opposition to rationalism and utilitarianism. In fact, the 'historic' Alroy was a self-appointed messiah in twelfth-century Kurdistan who asserted mythical and magic powers and who was finally executed and disgraced.

Since completing *Vivian Grey*, Disraeli had been fascinated by Alroy, the Jew who had achieved power and prominence during Jewish captivity. But perhaps he needed the inspiration of his 1830 trip to Jerusalem to finish *Alroy*. On a journey with William Meredith that lasted almost 15 months, Disraeli visited Gibraltar, Malta, Corfu, Constantinople, Cairo, Alexandria and Jerusalem, a city that was to be vital to his definition of his spiritual identity as a Jewish hero possessing a particular spiritual insight. At his several stops, his behaviour and dress were flamboyant, a studied effort to impress his various hosts with his energy, wit and confidence; the experience was to stand him in good stead later on in his political career, for as Blake puts it, 'the world will take a man at his own valuation'.[7] In Greece he thought of himself as an heir to Odysseus: 'Five years of my life have been already wasted and sometimes I think my pilgrimage may be as long as that of Ulysses.'[8] His tone also reveals a kind of Romantic listlessness that sometimes interrupts the hyperactive mood of his letters from his Grand Tour.

Disraeli wrote in the preface to *The Revolutionary Epick* (1834) that the purpose of *Alroy* was 'the celebration of a gorgeous incident in the annals of that sacred and romantic people from whom I derive my blood and name'.[9] Undoubtedly the tale of a Jew becoming the most powerful man in an alien land appealed to Disraeli, who at the age of 29 had still to make his political mark or artistic reputation. Indeed, David Alroy's first name evokes visions of the David and Goliath legend, which embodies another victory for a Jewish underdog. Disraeli uses the factual Alroy as a basis for his romance, but extends Alroy's power and prowess and introduces supernatural machinery and ersatz kabbalistic lore and ritual.

The fictional editor's notes, interweaving personal recollections of the East with abstruse knowledge of Jewish lore, mediate between the text and the audience. *Alroy* fuses the myths of the Chosen People, of return to the homeland and of the long-awaited messiah. As is appropriate in Judaic tradition, Alroy turns out to be a heroic man, but not without human limitations. His demise may be Disrael's unconscious affirmation of the Jewish belief that the Messiah has not yet come to redeem mankind. When Jabaster, a wisdom figure who anticipates Sidonia, rebukes him for not following his mission ('you may be King of Bagdad, but you cannot, at the same time, be a Jew'), a spirit shrieks, 'MENE, MENE, TEKEL, UPHARSIN', the words upon the wall that Daniel interprets to mean that God had weighed Belshazzar and his kingdom and found them wanting.[10] Significantly, Alroy regains the Jewish title Prince of Captivity after he is overthrown as Caliph. In his final suffering and humility, he has achieved the stature that the Jewish exiled prince, Disraeli's metaphor for himself, deserves.

The Wondrous Tale of Alroy indicates Disraeli's commitment to his Jewish background. Alroy represents Disraeli's own dreams of personal heroism and political power in the alien British culture. *Alroy* embodies not only his concept of himself as a potential leader, but his notion that the nation requires strong, visionary leaders who are true to its traditional manners and customs.

Disraeli wanted to establish the authenticity of his wondrous tale. For that reason he created as his editor-speaker a Jewish historian and scholar – the kind of bibliophile his father Isaac was. But he must have known that very few readers would discover that he had taken liberties with the Alroy legend and really knew only scattered bits and snips of kabbalah. One wonders whether the notes are in part an elaborate joke at the expense of readers apt to take the editor and themselves too seriously and accept as serious scholarship what is often mumbo jumbo. Is there not a note of deadpan humour in the following from the 1845 preface: 'With regard to the supernatural machinery of this romance, it is Cabalistical and correct'?

In *Alroy*, finally, the Jewish desire for a messiah is not fulfilled, but Alroy has significance for others, and particularly other Jews, as an historical figure. His sister Miriam's epitaph suggests Carlyle's notion of the value of an heroic figure: 'Great deeds are great legacies, and work with wondrous usury. By what Man has done, we learn what Man can do; and gauge the power and prospects of our race …The memory of great actions never dies.'[11] Disraeli the imaginative poet is the heir to Alroy the imaginative man. Perhaps, by telling his story of the Jew who rose to prominence in a foreign land, it became more plausible to imagine himself as a political leader. But if Alroy is an objectification of Disraeli's ambition, does he not also reflect Disraeli's anxieties and doubts, specifically his fear of his own sensual weakness and a certain paranoia about betrayal? Perhaps he wondered whether, like Alroy, he would be found somewhat wanting when his opportunity came.

Yet *Alroy* indicated Disraeli's commitment to his Jewish origins. His surrogate, the narrator, glories in the Jewish victories and in the triumph of the Prince of Captivity over his oppressors and regrets his fall due to pride and worldliness. Disraeli's notes, which are a fundamental part of reading *Alroy*, show not only his knowledge of Jewish customs, but his wide reading in matters Jewish. They are there not only to demonstrate to both *himself* and his readers that he has the intellectual and racial credentials to narrate Jewish history and legend, but they give us the perspective of a Jewish scholar who is trying to provide an authoritative edition of the Alroy legend.

Like Oscar Wilde, another flamboyant outsider, Disraeli used his literary creations as masks to disguise his wounded sensibilities and as devices to objectify aspects of himself that society would not tolerate. In his fiction, he freed himself from conventions and traditions, from priggishness and condescension, and found room for his fantasies. He discovered an alternative to the turmoil of his personal life in the act of creating the imagined worlds of his novels. But Disraeli's early novels are more than the creations of an egoistic, ambitious but frustrated young man who found a temporary outlet for his imagination in the fictions he created. For the roles one imagines are as indicative of one's real self as supposedly 'sincere' moments, intense personal relationships or daily routines. In the early novels the title character and the narrator represent the two sides of Disraeli. While the title character embodies Byronic fantasies of passionate love, heroism and rebellion against society's values, the narrator judges him according to standards that represent traditional values and the community's interest. In the first four books of *Vivian Grey* and in *The Young Duke*, the narrator represents the political and social health of England; in *Alroy* the narrator speaks for the interests of the Jews even after Alroy has betrayed them. In *Contarini* and in the later books of *Vivian Grey*, Disraeli speaks for a commitment to public life based on ideals rather than cynical self-interest.

Disraeli's first four novels mime his psyche. His emotions, fantasies, aspirations and anxieties become fictional names, personalities and actions. These novels are moral parables told by himself for himself about ambitious egoists. He dramatises the political rise and setback of an unscrupulous young man; the moral malaise and subsequent enlightenment of a young English duke; the flamboyant career of a young count who is torn between politics and poetry as well as between feeling and intellect; and finally the biography of Alroy, a Jewish prince who conquers much of Asia only to lose his kingdom and his life as he compromises his principles.

Disraeli uses his early novels, in particular *Alroy* and *Contarini*, as a means of controlling himself, of understanding himself and of exorcising flamboyant postures and forbidden emotions. For example, *Alroy* reflects Disraeli's fantasies of conquest and his will to power. In his early novels, the distinction between external events and the interior visions of the title character is blurred. The reason is that both are reflections of the author's subjective life and both are dramatisations of his evolving imagination. In *Alroy*, both the divine machinery and the title character's adventures are metaphorical vehicles for Disraeli's attitudes and states of mind, and have as little to do with the phenomenal world as do William Blake's prophecies.

Disraeli's career as artist and politician should be seen in the context of the Romantic movement. His imaginative use of travel followed in the footsteps of the Romantics, especially Byron, who regarded the continent, and in particular Italy and Greece, as exotic, passionate, impulsive and liberated from sexual restraints. As Harold Fisch has remarked,

> Insofar as his novels are the expression of his personal life, his feelings, his scarcely avowed hidden ideals, he achieves an appropriately resonant statement. His novels have the subtle egoism of all true romantics, of Shelley, of Wordsworth, of Milton. His subject is himself: he is Coningsby; he is Contarini Fleming; he is Alroy; he is Tancred; and he is the Wandering Jew, Sidonia. From these varied characters we are able to reconstruct the inner vision of Disraeli, the rich landscape of his dreams, his irrepressible vision of grandeur, of power, but power used for glorious and elevating ends ... Disraeli is certainly an egoist, but if that means that he is impelled by a sense of personal dedication, of election, of being favoured and gifted to an almost unlimited degree, and of being charged with grand tasks and opportunities, then it is the sort of egoism which finds its parallel in the lives of the great romantic poets and dreamers, of Milton, Wordsworth and Shelley.[12]

In the early novels, he could be the Romantic figure that so tantalised his imagination without sacrificing the public image that he wished to cultivate. To be sure, he might dress unconventionally and play the dandy, but that kind of socially sanctioned rebelliousness was different in kind rather than degree from the imagined social outlawry of Vivian Grey, Alroy and Contarini.

Contarini Fleming and *Alroy* are meant as visions rather than restatements of known truths. Disraeli tries to extend into prose the fusion of politics and philosophy – as well as the range and imaginative energy – of the Miltonic epic and Romantic masterworks such as Blake's prophecies, *The Prelude, Prometheus Unbound* and *Don Juan*. While Disraeli's works at times seem bathetic when viewed in the context of this tradition, there can be no doubt that he saw himself in the line of Romantic visionaries as described by M. H. Abrams:

> The Romantics, then, often spoke confidently as elected members of what Harold Bloom calls 'The Visionary

Company', the inspired line of singers from the prophets of the Old and New Testament, through Dante, Spenser, and above all Milton ... Whatever the form, the Romantic Bard is one 'who present, past and future sees'; so that in dealing with current affairs his procedure is often panoramic, his stage cosmic, his agents quasi-mythological, and logic of events apocalyptic. Typically this mode of Romantic vision fuses history, politics, philosophy and religion into one grand design, by asserting Providence – or some form of natural teleology – to operate in seeming chaos of human history so as to effect from present evil a greater good.[13]

THE YOUNG ENGLAND NOVELS

Disraeli's Young England novels – *Coningsby; or the New Generation* (1844); *Sybil; or The Two Nations* (1845); and *Tancred; or The New Crusade* (1847) – are a radical departure from his earlier fiction. Politics were more than a vocation for Disraeli. In the 1840s, his political life seemed to fulfil for him what George Eliot speaks of as 'that idea of duty, that recognition of something to be lived for beyond that mere satisfaction of self'.[14] For the first time since the beginning of his parliamentary career in 1837, he returned to fiction because he understood the potential of presenting his ideas in an imaginative framework.

Disraeli's trilogy presents both a political geography and an historical survey of England and simultaneously suggests how England could experience a political and moral rebirth. One function of the trilogy is to establish the importance of Judaism to western civilisation. He created Sidonia – in the line of the earlier larger-than-life figures Contarini and Alroy – as a mouthpiece to argue in *Coningsby* and in the first two books of *Tancred* for the historical significance of the Jewish people. Tancred's pilgrimage to Jerusalem in search of Semitic spirituality – a pilgrimage undertaken at the urging of Sidonia – and his discovery of the Hebraic basis of Christianity dramatise Disraeli's intense personal need to reconcile his Jewish origins with the Christian religion. He believed that Christianity was completed Judaism, although he may have unconsciously taken his position because of his need to justify his own conversion. He argued in *Lord George Bentinck* (1852) that the Jew converted to Christianity professes the 'whole Jewish religion and believes in Calvary as well as Sinai'.[15] In his study of Disraeli's Jewish aspect, Cecil Roth writes:

> But it seems as though the Christianity which he professed,
> quite sincerely, in his own mind was not that of the established
> Church, but a Judaic ethical monotheism, of which the Jew
> Jesus was the last and greatest exponent. As he put it, Chris-
> tianity was developed Judaism and Judaism a preparation for
> Christianity. Jesus was the ideal scion of Jewish people ... in
> whose teachings the Mosaic faith received its culmination, the
> New Testament being the perfection, and climax of the Old.[16]

Disraeli's self-confidence in part depended upon his belief that the
Jews deserved esteem as an especially gifted race. Often, and with
considerable justification, Disraeli is accused of political expedience
and intellectual legerdemain. But the defence of Jews was, for him, an
article of faith. Disraeli risked his chances for leadership when, in 1847,
he insisted that his friend Lionel de Rothschild be allowed to take his
seat in parliament without taking the required oath 'on the true faith
of a Christian'. On that occasion, he invoked arguments similar to
those that appeared in both *Tancred* and later in *Lord George Bentinck*
to support Rothschild's position.

If, in the end, the Young England trilogy does not always hold
together as an aesthetic entity or as a coherent polemical statement,
it does have substantial aesthetic and intellectual continuities. And
where it lacks continuity this is not entirely a fault. For the differences
among the novels give the reader multiple perspectives on England's
moral and political controversies in the period from the Reform Bill
to the late 1840s. The changes in form and theme from novel to novel
prevent the reader from taking a complacent one-dimensional view of
complex political and religious problems. That Disraeli shifts attention from character to public issues and back to character as he moves
from *Coningsby* to *Sybil* and then to *Tancred*, and that within each novel
he focuses alternatively on politics and on the individual's moral life,
emphasises a major theme in the trilogy, namely how the individual's
life is woven into the web of the community.

In each novel of the Young England trilogy, Disraeli's persona
speaks not only as a member of parliament, but also as an enlightened
and perceptive aristocrat. One implicit premise of the trilogy is that a
prophetic voice could arouse the sensibilities of his fellow aristocrats
to the spiritual and economic plight of the people and to the need for
restoring the monarchy and the church to their former dignity. The
comprehensive political consciousness of the speaker is the intellectual and moral position toward which the hero of each volume of the

trilogy finally develops. The narrator empathetically traces the quest of the potential hero (Egremont, Coningsby and Tancred) to discover the appropriate values by which he can order his own life and fulfil the prominent public role that he feels himself obliged to play. (The complete absence of irony toward the protagonist occasionally has the negative effect of neutralising Disraeli's wit and vivacity.)

In many significant ways, however, the three novels are separate and distinct. In the Young England novels, Disraeli used three different genres of fiction. *Coningsby* is a *Bildungsroman* concerned with the intellectual and moral development of the potential leader. *Sybil*, heavily borrowing from Blue Book material, is a polemical novel that primarily focuses on socio-economic conditions that need to be remedied. And *Tancred* is an imaginary voyage in the tradition of *Gulliver's Travels*, *Robinson Crusoe* and Disraeli's own neglected *Popanilla*. In terms of his career *Coningsby* may have been the most important novel that Disraeli wrote. In *Coningsby* he not only defined his political philosophy at a crucial time in his career, but in Coningsby and Sidonia he created two important fictional models for himself. Coningsby, the man who is elected to parliament in his early twenties and who seems destined for leadership, enacted a fantasy that sustained Disraeli.

Coningsby's growth is measured by a kind of intellectual barometer: his acceptance of the views held by Sidonia (which generally echo the narrator's) is the index of his development. He discovered anew his potential to be a political leader by imagining himself as Coningsby, who overcomes apparent loss of wealth and position by means of diligence, self-confidence and extraordinary ability. For Disraeli, imagining that merit was acknowledged and setbacks overcome played an essential if indeterminate role in fortifying his self-confidence. We understand that his fantasy figure does not have the burden of Disraeli's past notoriety, his Jewish ancestry and his debts, or that at the age of 40 it was no longer possible for Disraeli to achieve pre-eminence at a precocious age. As he wrote as spokesman for and leader of Young England, he embraced the romance of Coningsby's heroism; this explains *Coningsby*'s oscillation between *Bildungsroman* and novel of purpose.

As ones reads *Coningsby*, one senses Disraeli groping for the appropriate form for the political novel. He knows that he must maintain a delicate balance between public issues and historical context on the one hand and, on the other, the gradual development of young men who might set things right. He also understood the danger of allowing the characters through whom he expresses his ideas to become wooden. Not only Coningsby, but even Sidonia is a more complex psychological figure than has generally been realised. While at first it might seem that Disraeli has trouble focusing on his title character, the truth is otherwise. For Disraeli understood how novels unfold to readers. He realised that the process of reading about England's political turmoil would be the best way to interest his readers in the development of Coningsby from adolescent to young adult and make them appreciate his qualities of courage, integrity, boldness and 'high ambition'. Ambition for Disraeli was a positive value in a culture where ostentatious ambition was often equated by others with arrogance. He knew he had to establish the need for a new generation of leaders by discrediting the recent past of both Tories and Whigs and showing that idealistic younger men, untarnished by political intrigue, were emerging to govern England. Thus, he contended that since the Congress of Vienna material advance had been accompanied by 'no proportionate advance in our moral civilization'.[17] Writing of those in positions of responsibility in 1834, Disraeli remarks: 'It was this perplexed, ill-informed, jaded, shallow generation, repeating cries which they did not comprehend, and wearied with the endless ebullitions of their own barren conceit, that Sir Robert Peel was summoned to govern.'[18] Perhaps Disraeli best expresses the novel's aesthetic and political creed when he says: 'Man is never so manly as when he feels deeply, acts boldly, and expresses himself with frankness and with fervour.'[19]

If Disraeli, the man of action, imagines himself as Coningsby, Disraeli the artist views himself as Sidonia, the Jewish polymath who sees more profoundly than his fellows. If Coningsby embodies the romance of youthful political success, Sidonia is the romance of the Jewish outsider who, despite having no position in government, is one of the most important, sophisticated and knowledgeable figures in all Europe. His is a role that Disraeli enjoys imagining. Brilliant, worldly and influential, he becomes Coningsby's intellectual guide.

Sidonia is Disraeli's Daniel, a man of rabbinic wisdom, a figure whose gentle interventions suggest for Jews a cultural ideal. Sidonia articulates Disraeli's creed; Coningsby evolves into the man who will carry it out. Often Coningsby articulates ideas that he has learned directly from Sidonia; in turn, they become the thoughts of Coningsby's friends and followers. Sidonia enables Disraeli to dramatise Coningsby's education within the novel's action, for Coningsby is profoundly affected by his conversations with a man who not only knows the history of civilisation but is familiar with the intricacies and secrets of every

European government. Moreover, Sidonia enables Disraeli to make provocative statements without fully committing himself to them. Not every Tory member, including those who might be sympathetic to Young England on some issues, would have been pleased to read Sidonia's assertion: 'The tendency of advanced civilisation is in truth to pure Monarchy ... Your House of Commons, that had absorbed all other powers in the State, will in all probability fall more directly than it rose.'[20]

Through Sidonia he not only establishes the position of Jews, but acknowledges his own Jewish heritage. His readers would have recognised immediately that the first three letters of Sidonia's name reversed were the author's and that Sidonia, like his creator, had a three-syllable name with the accent on the second syllable.[21] Disraeli describes Sidonia the way he himself might have been described by one who was favourably disposed to him: 'He was ... of a distinguished air and figure; pale, with an impressive brow, and dark eyes of great intelligence ... He spoke in a voice of remarkable clearness; and his manner, though easy, was touched by a degree of dignity that was engaging.'[22] Sidonia instils in Coningsby the belief that a young man can be a great leader and that heroism and greatness are possibilities for him. Like Winter in *Contarini* or Jabaster in *Alroy*, he delivers advice in shibboleths and abstractions, such as 'Nurture your mind with great thoughts. To believe in the heroic makes heroes'.[23] Do we not hear Disraeli speaking to Disraeli in an act of self-uniting and self-making?

As to Sidonia's psychologically complex character, because he is excluded from participation in the political processes, he can only be, as he puts it, 'a dreamer of dreams'.[24] He regrets that he cannot be part of the life of action. Given the quality of English political institutions in the novel, the nation can certainly not afford to exclude a man of Sidonia's calibre. Disraeli illustrates the potential loss to England of excluding Jews; he knows that, had he not been baptised, he would not have been permitted to take his seat in parliament.

Sidonia deserves sympathy for another reason. He cannot find love and intimacy, partly because he will not compromise his racial purity. But Disraeli gives Sidonia a more serious problem, what E. M. Forster might have called the problem of an underdeveloped heart: 'He was a man without affections. It would be harsh to say he had no heart, for he was susceptible of deep emotions, but not for individuals ... Woman was to him a toy, man a machine.'[25] In fact, his subsequent behaviour to Lucretia and his friendship to Coningsby belie this generalisation. While he does withhold himself from the rituals of courtship and avoids the kind of zealous pursuit of heterosexual love that motivates Coningsby or Egremont, his departure from Lucretia makes us realise that Disraeli's analyses do not always do justice to Sidonia's psychosexual complexity. In a melancholy scene, Sidonia asserts to Lucretia that his life is 'useless'.

If *Coningsby* were written, as Disraeli claimed, simply 'to vindicate the just claims of the Tory Party to be the popular political confederation of the country', it would be, at best, only partially successful. Yet *Coningsby* is a novel that improves with each reading and when read in conjunction with *Sybil*, it is a splendid work. In a sense, *Sybil* 'completes' *Coningsby*; by illustrating the discontent and deprivation of the common people, the later novel implies the need for new leadership. Our minds revert to Coningsby and his friends who are gradually developing their potential for leadership during the 1837–41 period and who, we realise, represent the hope of England far more than the transitory 'three good harvests' with which *Sybil* ends. Despite its great caricatures and its incisive analyses of characters and politics, *Coningsby* is less effectual than *Sybil* because its intellectual and moral abstractions at times lack dramatic correlatives. Sidonia tells Coningsby that England's 'character as a community' has declined and that the contemporary period is 'an age of social disorganization' when 'the various classes of this country are arrayed against each other'.[26] But these ideas, like so many of Sidonia's oracular comments, are not illustrated within the narrative of *Coningsby*. Disraeli tells rather than shows. It remains for *Sybil* to illustrate how men lacking adequate political and spiritual leaders may totemise their own worst instincts in the form of a savage chieftain like the Wodgate Bishop; how Chartism appeals to men who feel a void in their lives; and how church has become virtually a hollow anachronism. Egremont perceives rural poverty for himself in the town of Marney and sees the effect of urban industrialisation on craftsmen such as Warner. While Egremont is able to empathise with the plight of the common people as he becomes aware of their economic deprivation and while he takes a superb stand in parliamentary debate, he lacks the magnetism and ambition to lead.

Tancred is a fictional version of the Victorian spiritual autobiography, epitomised by Newman's *Apologia*, Carlyle's *Sartor Resartus* and Tennyson's *In Memoriam*. Along with *Tancred*, several examples of the genre were published within a few years, including Charles Kingsley's *Yeast* (1848), James Anthony Froude's *Shadows in the Clouds* (1847) and Newman's *Loss and Gain* (1848). Mimesis in *Tancred* is based on entirely different assumptions from the rest of the trilogy. As in *Popanilla* and

Alroy, verisimilitude of time and space is virtually absent. *Tancred* reflects Disraeli's continued admiration for romance plots. Like Byron's heroes, Childe Harold and Don Juan, or Scott's heroes in his historical romances, Tancred inhabits an imagined world where diurnal details rarely intrude into his quest. An imaginary voyage, *Tancred* is loosely held together by the hero's physical journey which introduces him to incredible people and fantastic places. The novel begins in the present tense in England, but Tancred's crusade is virtually a journey backward in time; he discovers remote cultures which have religious beliefs and political customs that in 1847 Christian England were regarded condescendingly: Judaism, pagan worship of the Greek gods and feudalism.

Let us turn to Tancred's epiphany. That the angel's revelation is not tested as a viable system is a failure of *Tancred* that severely affects the argument of the entire trilogy. The novel does not explore the meaning of the angel's message as a plausible alternative to political intrigue in Asia or to the decline of the monarchy and the church in England. Disraeli's dramatisation of Tancred's communion with the angel reflects the urge to experience the presence of a higher being which permeated the Victorian period. It should be noted that Tancred's quest is not as bizarre as it seems. As Elie Halévy notes, when writing about religious questions in the 1840s, 'The belief was beginning to spread in British Protestant circles that the Second Advent of Jesus to judge the living and the dead must be preceded by a return of the Jews to Jerusalem and the rebuilding of Solomon's Temple, that on the very spot where the Saviour had been crucified they might be confuted, converted and pardoned.'[27] Disraeli's readers would have thought it was particularly appropriate that Tancred discovers the Jewish origins of Christianity in Jerusalem. But the shibboleth of theocratic equality does not justify the angel's appearance, and the angel's words are vague, if not bathetic:

> The equality of man can only be accomplished by the sovereignty of God. The longing for fraternity can never be satisfied but under the sway of a common father. The relations between Jehovah and his creatures can be neither too numerous nor too near. In the increased distance between God and man have grown up all those developments that have made life mournful. Cease, then, to seek in a vain philosophy the solution of a social problem that perplexes you. Announce the sublime and solacing doctrine of theocratic equality.[28]

Tancred becomes a ludicrous parody of, rather than – as Disraeli intended – an heir to, those biblical heroes to whom God and his angels spoke. Does not the book's ending imply Disraeli's failure to integrate a spiritual vision into his political ideology as well as a dwindling away or at least a deflection from his imaginative goals?

Lothair (1870) may have been Disraeli's reaction to *Culture and Anarchy* (1869). Disraeli would have rejected Arnold's association of Hebraism with 'firm obedience' as apposed to 'clear intelligence':

> As Hellenism speaks of thinking clearly, seeing things in their essence and beauty, as a grand and precious feat for man to achieve, so Hebraism speaks of becoming conscious of sin, of awakening to a sense of sin ... To get rid of one's ignorance, to see things as they are, and by seeing them as they are to see them in their beauty, is the simple and attractive ideal which Hellenism holds out before human nature; and from the simplicity and charm of this ideal, Hellenism, and human life in the hands of Hellenism, is invested with a kind of aerial ease, clearness, and radiancy; they are full of what we call sweetness and light.[29]

Responding to his father's antisemitism, M. Arnold in *Culture and Anarchy* proposed an idea of a transforming culture, which as Bryan Cheyette puts it, 'Jews, newly assimilated into the nation-state, exemplify the Enlightenment virtues of tolerance, justice and equality.'[30] For Arnold, as Cheyette notes, Hebraism is 'both an alien "semitic growth"' and, at the same time, a metonym for the English Puritan tradition.[31] As Cheyette makes clear in his shrewd discussion of *Culture and Anarchy*, 'The acculturated "Jew", in terms of this ambivalent Arnoldian liberalism, is an extreme example of those that may draw closer to "grace" and "beauty" by surpassing an unaesthetic, worldly Hebraism.'[32]

By contrast in *Lord George Bentinck: A Political Biography*, a remarkable book that is often as much a disguised autobiography as it is a biography of its subject, Disraeli writes: 'The Jews represent the Semitic principle: all that is spiritual in nature. They are the trustees of tradition, and the conservators of the religious element. They are a living and the most striking evidence of the falsity of that pernicious doctrine of modern times, the natural equality of man.'[33] Disraeli argued in *Lord George Bentinck* not only that Judaism was the source of Christianity's truth, but also that the Hebrew race was the inspiration for the arts in modern Europe, particularly music: 'We hesitate not to say that there is no race at this present, and following in this only the example of a long period, that so much delights, and fascinates, and elevates, and ennobles Europe, as the Jewish.'[34] Disraeli would not have accepted Arnold's cultural archetypes because they directly contradicted his own racial and historical ones. He still believed, as he argued in *Lord George Bentinck*, that the Greeks were an exhausted race, while the Jews were the source of both the creative and the moral, both the intellectual and the spiritual. For Disraeli the Jew represented 'the spiritual nature of man', 'religion, property, and natural aristocracy'.[35]

THE ART OF CREATING LIFE

Disraeli's ultimate aesthetic triumph was his political career. Before he was elected to parliament, he spoke of the day when he would become Prime Minister. His career was predicated on his ability to imagine himself in a position and then to find the resources to attain that position. By position, I mean not only a post but a political attitude, stance or policy. Disraeli instinctively adopted the role necessary to further his political career. As Robert Blake has remarked, 'He knew that he had to preserve an iron control over his voice and countenance if he was to avoid revealing the passion and ambition which seethed in his mind. Hence his assumption of that magniloquent half-ironic half-serious manner which so disconcerted those who had expected the ordinary self-deprecatory candour of the English upper class.'[36]

Disraeli's career tells us something about the continuities between life and art. Disraeli used his novels not only to create the political figure he became but also to define his essential character and personality. His first six novels – *Vivian Grey*, *The Young Duke*, *Contarini Fleming*, *Alroy*, *Henrietta Temple*, *Venetia* – were outlets for his fantasies, fears, hopes and doubts. The novels provided him with the sense that he could impose an order on the recalcitrant flow of events. Were it not for his first six novels – his romances about young heroes – written prior to his election to parliament, he would not have discovered the self he wanted to be. Indulging his fantasy in heroic exploits and passionate love affairs provided a necessary outlet for his frustrated energies. Moreover, he objectified in his protagonists parts of himself that he wanted to exorcise, while creating in his more mature narrator the balance, judgement and character he required to fulfil his political and social ambitions.

The early novels compensated for the disappointment at not achieving prominence. In the late 1820s and 1830s, he felt that, although he had aristocratic blood and deserved to be esteemed on the grounds of birth as well as merit, his heritage and accomplishments were patronised. Dandyism was another kind of self-dramatisation for Disraeli; it fulfilled his need for public attention at the same time as it enabled him to show himself that he was unique. His arrogance, self-assertiveness and flamboyance made him unpopular; yet his novels and his behaviour show that he needed to have love and companionship. When Disraeli created characters within fiction, he created, tested and often discarded tentative models for the various selves which he brought to the disparate social and private roles he was called upon to play.

Disraeli's compulsion for self-dramatisation, extravagance and hyperbole found an outlet in his political career. When, after he was first elected to parliament in 1837, he required a forum to articulate his social, political and spiritual principles, he returned to fiction and wrote the Young England trilogy as a testing ground for his political and moral philosophy. Young England itself was another of Disraeli's fictions, and, like his novels, enabled him to voice extravagant aspects of his complex and often contradictory political views. As the climax to the trilogy, *Tancred* emphasises the need to discover faith and mystery as the bases for political health and proposes a theocracy as the way to reunite man with God and to make government 'again divine'. But *Tancred* is a fairy tale; even in the trilogy, except for most of *Sybil*, Disraeli is still using his novels as escapes from the frustrating world of responsibilities.

When he actually achieved power, he ignored the romantic, visionary nostalgic tenets of Young England. While in office he was conservative but practical and did not oppose reasonable compromise. John Manners may have understood the tentative nature of Disraeli's beliefs when he wrote of Disraeli in his journal: 'His historical views are quite mine, but does he believe them?'[37] Disraeli tested an idea or an attitude by committing himself to it fully, by making it his own and living it. This, much more than expedience and hypocrisy, explains his notable political flip-flop on the Corn Laws or his change from Radical to Tory. Disraeli changed his attitudes in response to his experience, as when he condemned Catholicism in *Lothair* because he felt it had become a divisive force in English life. Disraeli published no fiction for 23 years between *Tancred* and *Lothair* because his imagination and creativity found an outlet in politics. He wrote *Lothair* and more than half of

Endymion while he was out of office from 1868–74 and completed *Endymion* after his second term as Prime Minister. Even in these final novels, his personality looms larger than those created in all his novels' characters, who often play roles, adopt disguises and undergo radical transformations of status and personality. His novels, like his public career, are about the art of creating life.

To conclude, rather than blame Disraeli for introducing racial discourse, one should understand him as taking up a defensive position to ward off those who would exclude Jews from parliament and who would denigrate his qualifications because of his heirs. The attention on the Jew in England in the later years of the nineteenth century owes much to Disraeli's overwhelming presence. Cheyette quotes a famous letter of Goldwin Smith: 'The secret of Lord Beaconsfield's life lies in his Jewish blood ... Certainly a century and a quarter of residence in England on the part of his ancestors and himself has left little trace on the mind and character of Lord Beaconsfield. He is almost in every essential ... a Jew.'[38] Certainly much of the nineteenth- and early-twentieth-century British response to Jews, including that of Joyce, depends on understanding Disraeli's Jewishness. One wonders if the family and personal values of Leopold Bloom was Joyce's response to Sidonia's isolation and detachment. Joyce felt that what made Jews different in part was their domestic patriarchal and family values and that Jews were better fathers, sons and husbands. Perhaps we should regard Bloom – based, among other things, on the Hasidic legend of the Lamed-Vov, the 36 just men – as a rewriting of Disraeli's view of Jewish heroism in public and romantic terms.

Disraeli's encounter with the dominant culture teaches us that culture is dynamic and heteroglossic – a dialogue of diverse thoughts, feelings, goals and values. According to Isaiah Berlin, 'Cultures – the sense of what the world meant to societies, of men's and women's collective sense of themselves in relation to others and the environment, that which affects particular forms of thought, feeling, behaviour, action – ... cultures differ.'[39] Disraeli's fiction is a kind of distinguished autobiography, a place where the mysteries of self are revealed to a perspicacious reader of coded texts. Disraeli's fiction and life fulfil the words of Clifford Geertz – words which themselves take up where Berlin left off: 'The problem of integration of cultural life becomes one of making it possible for people inhabiting different worlds to have a genuine, and reciprocal, impact upon one another.'[40] It was this problem that for Disraeli was a constant throughout his career.

NOTES

1. *Sybil*, Bk I, ch. iii, p. 14. Page references throughout the notes refer to the readily accessible Hughenden Edition (London, 1882). Book and chapter number, indicated respectively by upper and lower case Roman numerals, are standard for every edition.
2. John Elderfield, *Matisse in Morocco* (Washington, DC, 1990), p. 203.
3. James Clifford, *The Predicament of Culture: Twentieth-Century Ethnography, Literature and Art* (Cambridge, 1988), p. 93.
4. Thomas Mann, *A Sketch of My Life*, trans. H. T. Lowe-Porter (New York, 1930, 1st American edn, repr., 1960), pp. 43–4.
5. 'Mutilated Diary', Hughenden Papers, A/III/C.
6. *Contarini Fleming*, Bk VI, ch. iii, p. 350.
7. Robert Blake, *Disraeli* (London, 1966), p. 61.
8. Quoted in Blake, *Disraeli*, p. 65.
9. Quoted in William F. Monypenny and George E. Buckle, *The Life of Benjamin Disraeli, Earl of Beaconsfield*, 6 vols (London, 1910–20), Vol. 1, p. 198.
10. *Alroy*, Bk VIII, ch. vi, pp. 156–7.
11. Ibid., Bk X, ch. xix, p. 241.
12. Harold Fisch, 'Disraeli's Hebraic Compulsions' in H. S. Zimmels, J. Rabbinowitz and I. Finestein (eds), *Essays Presented to Chief Rabbi Israel Brodie on the Occasion of His Seventieth Birthday* (London, 1967), p. 91.
13. M. H. Abrams, 'English Romanticism: The Spirit of the Age' in Harold Bloom (ed.), *Romanticism and Consciousness* (New York, 1970), pp. 102–3.
14. George Eliot, *Scenes of Clerical Life*, Cabinet edn (Edinburgh, n.d.), pp. 162–3.
15. *Lord George Bentinck* (London, Archibald Constable edn, 1905), p. 324.
16. Cecil Roth, *Benjamin Disraeli* (New York, 1952), p. 79.
17. *Coningsby*, Bk II, ch. i, p. 69.
18. Ibid., Bk II, ch. iv, p. 98.
19. Ibid., Bk VII, ch. ii, p. 350.
20. Ibid., Bk V, ch. viii, p. 303.
21. Ibid., Bk III, ch. i, p. 114.
22. Ibid., Bk III, ch. i, p. 120.
23. Ibid.
24. Ibid., Bk IV, ch. x, p. 217.
25. Preface to 1849 edn, reprinted as Note D in Bernard N. Langdon-Davis (ed.), *Coningsby; or The New Generation* (New York, 1961), p. 587.
26. *Coningsby*, Bk IV, ch. xiii, pp. 237–8.
27. Elie Halévy, *Victorian Years, 1841–1895*, trans. E. I. Watkins (New York, 1951), p. 62.
28. *Tancred*, Bk IV, ch. vii, p. 291.
29. Matthew Arnold, *Culture and Anarchy*, Ian Gregor (ed.) (New York, 1951), pp. 111–13. Most of *Culture and Anarchy* was originally published as magazine articles in *Cornhill Magazine* between July 1867 and August 1868. See Gregor, xxxvi.
30. Bryan Cheyette, *Constructions of 'The Jew' in English Literature and Society: Racial Representations, 1875–1945* (Cambridge, 1993), p. 5.
31. Ibid., p. 20.
32. Ibid., p. 5.
33. Ibid., p. 59.
34. *Lord George Bentinck*, p. 320.
35. Ibid., p. 55.
36. Blake, *Disraeli*, p. 175.

37. Charles Whibley, *Lord John Manners and his Friends*, 2 vols, Vol. 1, pp. 148–9, quoted in Blake, *Disraeli*, p. 175.
38. Cheyette, *Constructions of 'The Jew'*, p. 15.
39. Isaiah Berlin, 'Philosophy and Life and Interview', *New York Review of Books* (28 May 1992), p. 51.
40. Clifford Geertz, *Local Knowledge: Further Essays in Interpractice Anthropology* (New York, 1983), p. 161.

MANLY JEWS: DISRAELI, JEWISHNESS AND GENDER

Nadia Valman

Recent work in Jewish cultural history has shown increasing interest in the figuring of gender and sexuality in representations of Jewish identity.[1] Daniel Boyarin, for example, contends that 'psychoanalysis and Zionism were two specifically Jewish cultural answers to the rise of heterosexuality at the fin de siècle'.[2] Paul Breines also views the rhetoric of Jewish nationalism from the perspective of gender, describing the genesis of Jewish national consciousness as 'the historic break with the culture of Jewish meekness and gentleness and the beginnings of a tough Jewish counterculture'.[3] For Breines, 'the emergence of a tough Jewish imagery at the turn of the century' must be seen as 'an extension of the Jewish nationalist awakening of the period [and] ... a logical outcome of the larger nationalist dynamic' sweeping contemporary Europe. He argues that such imagery derives from a reaction against, as well as a reflection of, European nationalisms:

> [T]he racial and bodily dimension of much of turn-of-the-century nationalist anti-Semitism was a decisive factor in the emergence of Jewish ideals of toughness, courage and physicality. Modern, postreligious, racial anti-Semitism presented a double image of the Jew: first, as the wielder of immense economic power ... and second, as physically weak, repulsive, and cowardly.[4]

Boyarin and Breines both locate the invention of a masculinised Jewish body within the context of new visions of the body politic in late-nineteenth-century Europe. But such concerns, I will argue, are also evident in earlier debates about national identity – in England during the social crises of the 1840s. This chapter will consider the writings of Benjamin Disraeli in the 1830s and 1840s and, in particular, his representations of 'tough Jews', in order to discuss the connections between masculinity, Jewishness and nationalism in early Victorian England.

NATION AND MISCEGENATION

Disraeli's association with the Young England faction of the Tory party
resulted in a series of novels published in quick succession in the 1840s:
Coningsby; or The New Generation (1844), *Sybil; or The Two Nations* (1845)
and *Tancred; or The New Crusade* (1847), later known collectively as the
'political trilogy'. The novels articulate a Conservative response to the
new power of the manufacturing class, the grievances of the Chartists,
and the contemporary crisis of faith in the English national church.
They assert a renewed commitment to the ancient institutions of church
and monarchy but also seek a direct engagement with the modern
problems of a nation irrevocably altered by constitutional change,
industrialisation and capitalism.

The trilogy presents a manifesto for Young England's radical version
of Toryism. In particular, Disraeli demands an alternative to what he
terms the 'Venetian republic', the long tradition of government by a
self-interested Whig elite sustained only through 'the subordination
of the sovereign and the degradation of the multitude'.[5] In diagnosing
the present crisis Disraeli also reassesses England's past. He dismisses
the Radical notion that the class conflicts of early Victorian England
derive from the racial persecution of Saxons by Normans following
the Conquest.[6] In Disraeli's alternative account, the division of the
modern nation is the inevitable result of Henry VIII's dissolution of the
monasteries and creation of a bogus, Whig aristocracy, whose hegemony
was consolidated by their support for William of Orange and his
'system of Dutch finance ... to mortgage industry in order to protect
property' through the national debt.[7] Disraeli thus also radically challenges the Whig argument that English history shows no evidence of
progress. The narrator in *Tancred* continually asks: 'Progress to what,
and from whence?'[8] The Reformation, according to Disraeli, was not
progressive since it disenfranchised the people, whose interest the
church originally represented, and broke the bond between the aristocracy and the organic body of feudal society. In *Tancred's* view,
modern England is in crisis because 'the people of this country have
ceased to be a nation'.[9]

The crisis of the nation is embodied in the novels' heroes, Coningsby,
Egremont and Tancred, young aristocrats ill-equipped for social duty.
Products of an 'age of infidelity' and political 'latitudinarianism', they
find no models for personal or national idealism in the generation of
their parents, who are equally complacent and selfish, whether Whigs
or Tories.[10] Tancred tells his father despairingly,

> I cannot find that it is part of my duty to maintain the order
> of things, for I will not call it system, which at present prevails
> in our country ... In nothing, whether it be religion, or govern-
> ment, or manners, sacred or political or social life, do I find
> faith; and if there be no faith, how can there be duty?[11]

Disraeli's ruling-class families are notably dysfunctional, as if the
malaise of the nation were reflected in its domestic infrastructure.
Class conflict and aristocratic irresponsibility have left their mark on
the younger generation: Coningsby, a 'solitary orphan', is denied his
mother's love when she dies young, cast out from her husband's family
for being of a lower social class. For Egremont, the pampered younger
son of a Whig noble, 'enjoyment, not ambition, seemed the principle
of his existence'.[12] Brought up in a world of privilege and empty sophis-
tication where 'to do nothing and get something, formed a boy's idea
of a manly career', Egremont enters adulthood with a sense of ener-
vation: 'he wanted an object'.[13] And in *Tancred* the sins of a decadent
and profligate noble are visited upon two generations, forever weakened because 'at a certain period of youth, the formation of character
requires a masculine impulse, and that was wanting'.[14] The degeneration of the aristocracy is thus explicitly linked to gender dysfunction:
sons of the old régime, Disraeli's heroes lack direction and conviction;
they are aimless and emasculated.

Instead, England's potential for political regeneration is embodied
in the heroines of the trilogy. Edith Millbank the manufacturer's
daughter, Sybil Gerard the Chartist's daughter and Eva Besso the Jew's
daughter are non-aristocratic women, and yet they incarnate the noble
qualities so lacking in English youth. In Sybil this nobility is evident
to the eye and ear: 'the daughter of the lowly, yet proud of her birth.
Not a noble lady in the land who could boast a mien more complete,
and none of them thus gifted, who possessed withal the fascinating
simplicity that pervaded every gesture and accent of the daughter of
Gerard.'[15] The contradiction between Sybil's demeanour and her class
status strikingly symbolises Disraeli's argument that England's last
hope lies in the traditions and principles of its 'national character' and
that such resources are found only in those excluded from political
representation.[16] Edith Millbank and her family similarly exemplify
the virtues of a class misguidedly excluded from power. In Edith, the
daughter of a manufacturer, Disraeli presents a heroine who maintains
direct contact with the world of labour and instinctively resists the
corrupting influence of the sophisticated society made accessible by her

father's wealth: 'though by no means insensible to homage, her heart was free; was strongly attached to her family; and notwithstanding all the splendour of Rome, and the brilliancy of Paris, her thoughts were often in her Saxon valley, amid the green hills and busy factories of Millbank'.[17] Edith, Sybil and Eva are frequently described in terms of a close connection with their native landscapes; the national soil is the source of their vitality. In fact, it is the daughter of a manufacturer and of the 'Saxon' lower class who teaches the urbane Norman noble the true value of English pastoral, of 'an existence to be passed amid woods and waterfalls with a fair hand locked in his'.[18] But Disraeli's heroines are emblems of the modern nation as well as symbols of its past traditions: Edith leads the way in redefining the future England as both a factory and a garden.

As representatives of national sources of vigour, the women of the political trilogy offer inspiration to the heroes. In this way Disraeli employs the romance form to carry his ideological message. Only Sybil and her Chartist father can tell the decadent, aimless Egremont who he is and what it means to be English, a revelation which is political as well as erotic:

> It seemed to Egremont that, from the day he met these persons in the Abbey ruins, the horizon of his experience had insensibly expanded; more than that, there were streaks of light breaking in the distance, which already gave a new aspect to much that was known, and which perhaps was ultimately destined to reveal much that was now utterly obscure. He could not resist the conviction that from the time in question, his sympathies had become more lively and more extended; that a masculine impulse had been given to his mind; that he was inclined to view public questions in a tone very different to that in which he had surveyed them a few weeks back, when on the hustings of his borough.[19]

Through his struggle to love a woman of the working class, a woman whom he meets among the relics of feudal England and whose order is excluded from the political nation, Egremont begins to reshape his own political and masculine identity.[20]

Eva Besso, *Tancred*'s Jewish heroine, has a similarly striking impact on the novel's diffident protagonist. When he is taken captive in the desert, it is she who rides to his rescue, personifying the virile imperiousness to which he himself aspires: 'To Tancred, with her inspired

brow, her cheek slightly flushed, her undulating figure, her eye proud
of its dominion over the beautiful animal which moved its head with
haughty satisfaction at its destiny, Eva seemed the impersonation of
some young classic hero going forth to conquer a world.'[21] The aristocratic women of Tancred's milieu have exerted only a 'disturbing influence' over him, distracting him from youthful idealism.[22] But Eva
reinspires him, awakening the imperial aspirations which will, in the
course of the novel, transform his sense of English identity:

> That face presented the perfection of oriental beauty ... it was
> in the eye and its overspreading arch that all the Orient spake,
> and you read at once of the starry vaults of Araby and the
> splendour of Chaldean skies. Dark, brilliant, with pupil of great
> size and prominent from its socket, its expression and effect,
> notwithstanding the long eyelash of the Desert, would have
> been those of a terrible fascination, had not the depth of the
> curve in which it reposed softened the spell and modified irre-
> sistible power by ineffable tenderness.[23]

Eva's physiognomy, described in terms of the oriental landscape,
provokes in Tancred a simultaneous desire for both the body and the
territory of which it speaks. At the same time her feminine 'tender-
ness' implicitly reassures him that the desert will not itself overpower
him. Tancred's response to Eva's beauty is a metonym for his vision of
the Orient, which he sees as both thrilling and malleable. This description looks forward to the structure of the novel (and the trilogy) as
a whole, in which aristocratic English boys learn how to be heroes
through their encounter with heroines from outside their own class and
culture. Emphasising the inspirational power of transgressive desire,
Disraeli's trilogy advocates miscegenation as the heroic challenge
which both the protagonist and the population as a whole must
embrace.

AN UNMIXED RACE

At the same time, Jews and Jewish history are also instrumental in the
political education of Disraeli's heroes. In *Sybil* the English working
class (unlike the aristocracy) is linked, through the bibliocentricity of
its dissenting Protestantism, to the Jews, with whom they share the
same signs of disinheritance:

little plain buildings of pale brick with the names painted on them, of Sion, Bethel, Bethesda; names of a distant land, and the language of a persecuted and ancient race; yet, such is the mysterious power of their divine quality, breathing consolation in the nineteenth century to the harassed forms and the harrowed souls of a Saxon peasantry.[24]

Using the same biblical language, Oswald Millbank hails Coningsby as a new King David to deliver the oppressed nation.[25]

In *Coningsby* and *Tancred* the protagonists engage with the significance of Jewish history more directly through their encounters with the Jewish financier Sidonia. For Tancred this meeting facilitates his journey to the Holy Land in the footsteps of his crusader ancestor Tancred de Montacute. It becomes a journey to the origin of Tancred's own culture, as he discovers that 'he had a connexion with these regions; they had a hold upon him ... for this English youth, words had been uttered and things done, more than thirty centuries ago, in this stony wilderness, which influenced his opinions and regulated his conduct every day of his life in that distant and seagirt home'.[26] In Jerusalem the meaning of Jewish history is revealed to the reader as a story not of tragedy and disinheritance but of tenacity: 'Titus destroyed the temple. The religion of Judæa has in turn subverted the fanes which were raised to his father and to himself in their imperial capital: and the God of Abraham, of Isaac, and of Jacob is now worshipped before every altar in Rome.'[27] Using a typically loose definition of 'the religion of Judæa' to include its theological descendants, Disraeli thus views Titus' destruction of the temple from a positive perspective. In Disraeli's view, the ruins of Jerusalem speak the same message as the chapels of industrial, northern England: in the Hebrew roots of British Protestantism is the key to national survival.

In recasting the meaning of Jewish history in terms of survival, cultural influence and 'mysterious power', Disraeli contests a number of contemporary stereotypes. In a similar way he attempts a complex transformation of the literary image of the Jew through the figure of Sidonia. Disraeli's Jew is no less than a model of ideal masculinity and a mentor for aristocratic English youth, but his character is constructed through a revaluation of traits stereotypically associated with Jews in Victorian culture. Thus, on the one hand, Sidonia suffers the emasculation of the unemancipated Jew: 'His religion walled him out from the pursuits of a citizen; his riches deprived him of the stimulating anxieties of a man.'[28] Yet, for Disraeli, Sidonia's exclusion from political and financial responsibility also guarantees an important freedom: he is 'independent of creed, independent of country, independent even of character'.[29] If Jews were considered incapable of allegiance, in Sidonia's case this is a strength. Far from the lecherous stereotype of antisemitic representation, he is passionless: 'the individual never touched him'.[30] Sidonia's cold intellectuality is impervious even to the manipulative Princess Lucretia Colonna who finds herself defeated in a struggle to engage his attention: 'She could not contend with that intelligent, yet inscrutable, eye; with that manner so full of interest and respect, and yet so tranquil.'[31] In this detachment, Sidonia sets an example for the young heroes in danger of being distracted from political ambition by female sexuality. Disraeli sees even his obstinacy as a racial trait rather than a religious habit – a temperament 'peculiar to the East', a psychological manifestation of its 'barren' desert landscape but one which 'befits conquerors and legislators'.[32]

Moreover, for Sidonia, sprung from a family of international capitalists, inheriting the culture of cosmopolitanism without the taint of trade, statelessness is no disadvantage but an aid to universal wisdom. Sidonia is 'master of the learning of every nation, of all tongues dead or living, of every literature, Western and Oriental': in this formulation Disraeli recasts the wandering Jew as Victorian polymath.[33] Sidonia's toughness is a result of his diasporic identity: solidarity with 'all the clever outcasts of the world' gives him access to 'knowledge of strange and hidden things'.[34] Whereas Protestant conversionists commonly characterised Jews as 'prejudiced' in resisting Christianity, Disraeli presents Sidonia's 'absolute freedom from prejudice, which was the compensatory possession of a man without a country' as a political virtue.[35] His only pleasure lies in this, his ability to deconstruct the world, 'to contrast the hidden motive, with the public pretext, of transactions'.[36] Here Disraeli draws on the image of the Wandering Jew of gothic literature, whose penetrating gaze he subtly refigures as a diplomatic skill.[37]

In a place and time when political culture has become impossibly corrupted by factional interests, Disraeli insists, only the outsider is fit for the role of mentor to the new generation. Only Sidonia can see beyond the surface of party politics and prophesy that 'England should think more of the community and less of the government'.[38] His statement to the admiring young Coningsby, 'Action is not for me ... I am of that faith that the Apostles professed before they followed their Master', epitomises Disraeli's purpose: in Sidonia he constructs a role of significant status for the man compelled to inaction.[39] He employs what Paul Smith calls his 'technique of radical inversion', the reversal of stereotype which he used to reposition the public image of the Tory party in the late 1830s.[40] In Disraeli's writing the figure of the un-emancipated Jew is also radically inverted: far from being politically impotent, he is the man behind politics, the 'dreamer of dreams'.[41] With his tough, yet unheroic Jew, then, Disraeli engages in a complex way with contemporary Jewish stereotyping to produce a figure whose attributes address perfectly the needs of crisis-ridden England in the 1840s.

Sidonia's presence in the texts also provides the occasion for a long meditation on the significance of Jewish history and the Jewish diaspora. In the chapter on Sidonia's Iberian ancestry in *Coningsby*, Disraeli evokes the possibility of productive symbiosis between Jews and the nations with whom they share territory and culture. He sees the effect of the Catholic Inquisition on the Jews of Aragon as a tragic and misplaced severing of the relationship between a people and the culture which was its creation and therefore its rightful heritage, 'the delightful land wherein they had lived for centuries, the beautiful cities they had raised, the universities from which Christendom drew for ages its most precious lore'.[42] But Disraeli also uses the unique circumstances of Spanish Jewry to tell the story of Jews who were not helpless victims but retained their identity as crypto-Jews (New Christians) whilst rising to 'great offices' in the state and church.[43] This version of Jewish history emphasises the benefits to Christian Spain of incorporating the Jews into cultural and political life. Generations later Sidonia's father becomes 'lord and master of the money-market of the world' but looks forward to direct-ing 'his energies to great objects of public benefit'.[44] In Sidonia's ances-tral history, then, the Jews' privately practised religion has never com-promised their national loyalty; Sidonia himself is 'an Englishman, and taught from his cradle to be proud of being an Englishman'.[45]

But if the narrative voice appears to be operating in this passage with a religious definition of Jewishness, it quickly shifts to racial terms. Moving seamlessly from the narrative of Iberian-Jewish history to a more 'scientific' analysis of its meaning, the chapter concludes with a flight into racial theory in order to explain Jewish survival in adversity:

> Sidonia and his brethren could claim a distinction which the Saxon and the Greek, and the rest of the Caucasian nations, have forfeited. The Hebrew is an unmixed race ... An unmixed race of a firstrate organisation are the aristocracy of Nature. Such excellence is a positive fact; not an imagination,

a ceremony, coined by poets, blazoned by cozening heralds, but perceptible in its physical advantages, and in the vigour of its unsullied idiosyncrasy.

... To the unpolluted current of their Caucasian structure, and to the segregating genius of their great Lawgiver, Sidonia ascribed the fact that they had not been long ago absorbed among those mixed races, who presume to persecute them, but who periodically wear away and disappear, while their victims still flourish, in all the primeval vigour of the pure Asian breed.[46]

Although this theory is supposed to provide inspiration for the young Coningsby, it is difficult to see precisely how. The significance of the Jewish 'race' in world history bears as little relevance to a novel about the changing political culture of contemporary Britain as it does to Disraeli's later biography of Lord George Bentinck, where it makes a gratuitous reappearance.[47] Furthermore, Sidonia's insistence on the importance of the 'unmixed race' in ensuring historical survival disturbs the closure of the novels, which emphasise conversely, as I argued in the previous section, the regenerative power of miscegenation. Many critics have drawn attention to a similar 'failure of logic' within the novels' plots.[48] Each narrative appears to end with the symbolic reunification of divided classes and cultures, but finally these divisions are revealed to be ambiguous if not illusory. Coningsby discovers that his own mother nearly married Edith's manufacturer father, Egremont finds that Sybil is heiress to the estate adjacent to his own family's and Tancred realises his 'connexion' with Eva's land and culture. Daniel Bivona identifies here an ambivalent desire, 'the tension between the imperative to incorporate the alien – the exogamous necessity – and the contrary demand for racial and class purity – the endogamous ideal', which fissures the texts.[49]

One explanation for this anomaly might be that the discourse on Jewish racial purity in Disraeli's writings is there for personal rather than ideological reasons. Certainly, such sentiments constituted an audacious provocation to the Anglican establishment Disraeli was seeking to join at this time.[50] But from a different perspective they can also be seen as part of the strategy through which Disraeli, in his first decade as a Member of Parliament, was able to redefine the significance of his own Jewish birth, now a potential weapon in the hands of his political enemies. Concentrating on Spanish history enables Disraeli to reconstruct a narrative of Jewishness which stresses the Jews' 'very

ancient and noble' pedigree, central role in national culture and loyal
service to the state.[51] Paul Smith reads the trilogy in these terms, arguing that Disraeli's novels are essentially about himself. Their goal is
'the integration of Disraeli's fully realised genius into its inexorably
given surroundings, by asserting its supereminent role in confronting
the great national tasks the nature of which only its superior vision
can define and the accomplishment of which only its superior inspiration can guide'.[52] Most critics see Disraeli's novels as an arena for
his own self-fashioning, in which the notion of race is a response to his
particular strategic needs.[53]

Even so, Disraeli's needs were complex. Although Sidonia's story
appears to hark back to a golden age of Jewish prosperity in a Christian
state, it is not an argument for Jewish civil rights. On the contrary,
Disraeli's idiosyncratic representation of Jews and Jewish history in
Coningsby also reinforced his own strategic position within a party
which was firmly opposed to the political emancipation of British
Jewry.[54] Disraeli's Jews require no favours from the British government. Sidonia finds his political restrictions 'absurd', but they do not
prevent him from exercising power nationally and internationally.[55]
The pattern of his family history in Spain provides a model in which
Jewish ascendancy is not dependent on political rights but on racial
advantage. 'Race' is thus the key to Disraeli's avoidance of the question
of Jewish emancipation in England. By redefining the Jews as a racial
elite, unharmed by the march of progress and the decay of civilisations,
an 'aristocracy of Nature', Disraeli was able both to assert his own
qualification for greatness and to concur implicitly with his party's
opposition to emancipation.[56]

The 'contrary demands' which fissure Disraeli's trilogy can, then,
be seen as an effect of his own uncomfortable position as a baptised
Jew, which became particularly acute in the mid-1840s. As Smith has
put it, 'the relation of his Jewish home to his English was the question
which his political advance compelled him to face', and his struggle
with it can be seen in the novels as an unresolved conflict between
Jewish integration and Jewish separatism.[57] However, as I will argue
in the remainder of this chapter, the rhetoric of Disraeli's trilogy is
not simply a strategy to defend his own problematic position as a 'Jew'
within the Tory party. Both the dialectical design of the narratives
and the discourse of racial separatism which seems to disrupt them are
part of a discussion of the relationships between nation, heroism and
masculinity which Disraeli was developing in the 1840s. In this he
was not only revising the stereotype of Jewish manhood but was

contributing to a wider contemporary debate about masculinity and British political culture.

A RELIGION OF CONQUEST?

Disraeli had attempted to find a usable past for himself several years before his election to Parliament in *The Wondrous Tale of Alroy* (1833), an epic tale of tragic heroism. The legend of Jewish liberation fighters on which *Alroy* is based offers an unconventionally tough image of mediaeval Jews, but the novel is nevertheless ambivalent about the possibility of Jewish national autonomy it raises. *Alroy* is set in twelfth-century Hamadan, where the Jews, dispossessed of national sovereignty, live as a tributary people under Seljuk rule. Alroy, descendant of the house of David, the messianic line, and heir to the title of 'Prince of the Captivity', is a Hebrew Hamlet, galled at the weakness of the Jews and his own inability to take action against the humiliation of diaspora existence. Inspired by the kabbalist Jabaster, he embarks on a journey to Jerusalem, whose ruins are 'like the last gladiator in an amphitheatre of desolation'.[58] But Alroy experiences a vision of a transfigured Jerusalem and a godlike figure, which he believes to be a confirmation of his own mystical election as messiah. He unites the 'singular and scattered people' of the diaspora into a nation and leads them to liberation, conquest and empire.[59] As the new 'master of the East', he turns the Turks from rulers into ruled but only to become their tyrant in his turn.[60]

   Although *Alroy* is at one level a fable of the folly of romantic individualism – the hero finally realises that 'he who places implicit confidence in his genius, will find himself some day utterly defeated and deserted' – it is also a complex discussion of relationships between race, religion and national identity which anticipates in interesting ways Disraeli's later writing.[61] Published in the year in which the first major debates about Jewish emancipation and the limits of the Protestant state were dividing the British Parliament, Disraeli's novel uses the story of Jewish national liberation to consider universalist and particularist definitions of the nation. Disraeli satirises the old rabbis in Jerusalem, 'the forlorn remnant of Israel, captives in their own city' but bound by religious pedantry to perpetuate their own disenfranchisement.[62] In contrast, the text's poetic diction valorises the romantic nationalism which inspires Alroy as he looks upon a ruined city of the East:

All was silent: alone the Hebrew Prince stood amid the regal creation of the Macedonian captains. Empires and dynasties flourish and pass away; the proud metropolis becomes a solitude, the conquering kingdom even a desert; but Israel still remains, still a descendant of the most ancient kings breathed amid these royal ruins, and still the eternal sun could never rise without gilding the towers of living Jerusalem. A word, a deed, a single day, a single man, and we might be a nation.[63]

Shifting in and out of past and present, evoking the present thoughts of the hero and an unspecific, eternal present, the 'we' of Alroy's people and the 'we' of *Alroy*'s readers, the narrative identifies the reader with the project of national liberation and suggests the dynamic power of the nation embodied in a charismatic hero.

However, in the course of the novel Alroy comes to temper this mystical nostalgia with a modernising politics and to shift his rootedness in place and past towards a concept of the nation expanding indefinitely in time and territory. Eventually Jabaster's vision of a particularist national existence based on a fixed history and religious affiliation is rejected by Alroy: 'Jerusalem, Jerusalem – ever harping on Jerusalem. With all his lore, he is a narrow-minded zealot, whose dreaming memory would fondly make a future like the past.'[64] Instead he favours an imperial, inclusive and expansionist notion of the nation, embracing both Jews and non-Jews. Alroy's inclusive conception of Judaism appropriates Christianity's traditional claim to universalism (as Disraeli himself was to do in a later parliamentary debate). Moreover, this universalism is the source of Alroy's military success. In his view the only way of attaining permanent political empowerment is to renounce the narrow religious definition of Judaism for a national and tolerant one:

> Universal empire must not be founded on sectarian prejudices and exclusive rights. Jabaster would massacre the Moslemin like Amalek [the archetypal enemy of the Jews]; the Moslemin, the vast majority, and most valuable portion, of my subjects. He would depopulate my empire, that it might not be said that Ishmael shared the heritage of Israel. Fanatic! ... We must conciliate. Something must be done to bind the conquered to our conquering fortunes.[65]

Here, Alroy is seeking to redefine the Jews as a nation in precisely the terms that Disraeli employs to discuss the future of England in the political trilogy of the 1840s, where he suggests that racial, social and religious divisions can be transcended in the name of a perceived common political ideal. Indeed the novel shows this to be a successful strategy: in the Jewish army 'the greater part were Hebrews, but many Arabs, wearied of the Turkish yoke, and many gallant adventurers from the Caspian, easily converted from a vague idolatry to a religion of conquest, swelled the ranks of the army of the "Lord of Hosts" '.[66]

Yet in *Alroy*, in contrast to the later trilogy, this universalist nationalism, or imperialism, is unsustainable. As Alroy's tolerance increasingly earns him the resentment of his generals, the novel's movement towards tragedy is underscored by pessimism about the possibility of a permanent Jewish national existence. Jabaster warns: 'We must exist alone. To preserve that loneliness, is the great end and essence of our law ... Sire, you may be King of Bagdad, but you cannot, at the same time, be a Jew.'[67] In making the Jews conquerors, Alroy has universalised Judaism and destroyed the particularist motivation of many of his fighters. Loss of military unity is a reflection of Alroy's own loss of masculine identity in his luxurious marriage to the Muslim princess Schirene. Alroy's tolerance, his failure to preserve Jewish 'loneliness', is associated with his feminisation: 'Egypt and Syria, even farthest Ind, send forth their messengers to greet Alroy, the great, the proud, the invincible. And where is he? In a soft Paradise of girls and eunuchs, crowned with flowers, listening to melting lays, and the wild trilling of the amorous lute.'[68] Jews, it seems, cannot be conquerors.

Schirene's eventual betrayal of Alroy is a final confirmation of the novel's mistrust of miscegenation. Indeed, it is only by reasserting his Jewish identity in martyrdom at the end of the novel that Alroy regains his heroic stature, reaffirming that '... my people stand apart from other nations, and ever will despite of suffering'.[69] In this final rejection of luxury for physical pain, Alroy reverses the identification with Schirene and re-establishes his masculine and Jewish 'loneliness'. Yet it is only within christological terms that Disraeli is able to figure Alroy's fall as triumphant. As the novel moves into its final phase, in which Alroy is captured and humiliated, the style shifts, using shorter, simpler sentences and explicit references to the life of Jesus:

> A tear stole down his cheek; the bitter drop stole to his parched lips, he asked the nearest horseman for water. The guard gave him a wetted sponge, with which, with difficulty, he contrived to wipe his lips, and then he let it fall to the ground. The Karasmian struck him.

> They arrived at the river. The prisoner was taken from the camel and placed in a covered boat. After some hours, they stopped and disembarked at a small village. Alroy was placed upon a donkey with his back to its head. His clothes were soiled and tattered. The children pelted him with mud. An old woman, with a fanatic curse, placed a crown of paper on his brow. With difficulty his brutal guards prevented their victim from being torn to pieces. And in such fashion, towards noon of the fourteenth day, David Alroy again entered Bagdad.[70]

This dramatic use of intertext suggests that Disraeli, in searching for a narrative within whose terms Jewish suffering can be refigured as heroic, finds only the Christian Passion.

If the novel is unable to conceive of Jewish toughness except in christological terms, it is also unable to maintain a notion of Jewish authenticity except in domestic terms. Only Alroy's sister Miriam, a figure of domestic but not erotic love, succeeds in sustaining a Jewish identity uncompromised by ambition or bigotry. Unlike other definitions of Jewishness in the text, hers requires no political expression. National liberation means nothing to her: 'For Miriam, exalted station had brought neither cares nor crimes. It had, as it were, only rendered her charity universal, and her benevolence omnipotent.'[71] In this text Disraeli represents feminine virtue as transcendent, independent of political status, unaffected by either oppression or autonomy. Disraeli's eulogistic language (the novel was dedicated to his own sister) suggests that it is Miriam who alone maintains an authentic Jewish identity. The contrast with the corruption of Alroy is striking. The feminised, domesticated definition of Jewishness, which the Anglo-Jewish writer Grace Aguilar was to exploit so successfully during the 1840s, is here presented as a pragmatic and more enduring alternative to the romantic, militant and ultimately tragic political nationalism of Alroy.[72] Meanwhile, Disraeli's own writings of the 1840s show a crucial reworking of *Alroy*'s concerns with the relationships between Jewishness, masculinity and national identity.

DISRAELI, GENDER AND POLITICAL ARGUMENT

If martyrdom and domesticity, 'feminised' constructions of Jewishness, had a certain appeal for Disraeli in *Alroy*, the association of Jewishness and femininity was more commonly invoked pejoratively. Disraeli's preoccupation with Jewish toughness in the 'political trilogy', I believe, must be read in the context of contemporary ideas about gender and Jewishness that were constantly projected onto his writing. Despite his obvious adoption of the language and thematics of political debate in the 1840s, reviewers continued to refer to the dandy style he had paraded 20 years previously, which they found inseparable from his Jewishness. In 1841, for example, *Punch* mockingly described him as 'the Hebrew Adonis'.[73] Thackeray deliberately linked *Coningsby* with the decadence of Disraeli's first publication, the 'dandy' novel *Vivian Grey* (1826), and affected not to notice any political content:

> *Coningsby* possesses all the happy elements of popularity. It is personal, it is witty, it is sentimental, it is outrageously fashionable, charmingly malicious, exquisitely novel, seemingly very deep, but in reality very easy of comprehension, and admirably absurd; for you do not only laugh at the personages whom the author holds up to ridicule, but you laugh at the author too, whose coxcombries are incessantly amusing. They are quite unlike the vapid cool coxcombries of an English dandy; they are picturesque, wild, and outrageous; and as the bodily Disraeli used to be seen some years ago about town, arrayed in green inexpressibles with a gold stripe down the seams, an ivory cane, and, for what we know, a peacock's feather in his hat – Disraeli the writer in like manner assumes a magnificence never thought of by our rigid northern dandies, and astonishes by a luxury of conceit which is quite oriental.[74]

Thackeray uses the associations of dandyism and oriental luxury to denigrate Disraeli's realism; the satire in *Coningsby* is thus 'amusing' rather than coherent political critique. George Henry Lewes, for whom the publication of the fifth edition of *Coningsby* in 1849 was an occasion to attack Disraeli's ability as both writer and statesman, drew implicit parallels between the two spheres: 'It is all a show "got up" for the occasion; and the showman having no belief in his marionnettes, you have no belief in them.' Lewes also questioned Disraeli's capacity for literary realism, detecting 'a want of truthfulness' because 'he does not work from *inwards*, but contents himself with externals'. This literary style, however, could be explained by Disraeli's 'race': 'His writings abound with ... instances of tawdry falsehood. They are thrown in probably out of that love of ornament, which is characteristic of his race: they are the mosaic chains and rings with which the young "gentlemen of the Hebrew persuasion" adorn their persons, to give a *faux air de gentilhomme* to that which no adornment can disguise.'[75] In this account, the Jew decorates his body in an effort to pass for a gentleman but only succeeds in accentuating his effeminacy. Both Lewes and Thackeray link Jewishness with inauthentic representation by questioning the Jew's essential masculinity.[76]

The 'feminised' model of Jewishness was also used by Jews themselves and by their supporters during the debates about the remission of parliamentary disabilities which extended through the 1830s and 1840s.[77] Disraeli's contemporary Grace Aguilar, whose best-selling historical romances and domestic novels for Jewish and non-Jewish women avoid the language of political theory, nevertheless responded and contributed indirectly to the debate about the political status of contemporary British Jews.[78] Whereas Disraeli remythologised the Jews as a racial elite and thus assimilated them to an aristocratic ideology, Aguilar, by using the terms of bourgeois domestic writing, refigured the Jews as pious and respectable middle-class citizens. Aguilar's desexualised Jewesses and Disraeli's asexual Sidonia are similar responses to contemporary literary stereotypes which endorsed the political and social exclusion of Jews by suggesting that they posed a sexual threat. In Aguilar's *The Vale of Cedars, or, The Martyr* (1850) – a literary appeal for toleration – the virtuous heroine evokes sympathy and pity for her persecution, in contrast to the disturbing sexuality of Walter Scott's Jewish heroine Rebecca.[79] Aguilar's 'apologetic' account of contemporary Judaism diminished its difference from the Anglican majority culture and presented its toleration as unthreatening.[80]

The language of the emancipation debate in Parliament was itself gendered. If what was at stake in the controversy was the Protestant character of the state, opinion was divided broadly between the brave men who thought they ought to 'rally round the Cross' and the tender souls who insisted that Christianity enjoined 'love and charity'.[81] The representation of the Jews within the debates also had a gendered dimension. Many supporters of emancipation mirrored Grace Aguilar's approach and emphasised the 'peaceful' nature of the Jews, who, far from presenting a political or religious threat to the nation, were exemplary in their homely virtues:

> this peculiar people were distinguished by their veneration for the domestic and social relations of life. Instances of the violation of the duties of husband and wife – of parent and child – were rare amongst them ... From drunkenness which,

beyond any other vice called for the most anxious and urgent correction of the Legislature, and which was more and more infecting and demoralizing the whole of the lower classes, and had become a great national calamity, they were happily, and beyond others, exempted.[82]

This argument, however, had its limitations, since it opened the way to the charge that the Jews' unmanliness disqualified them from citizenship. In 1834, Lord Malmesbury opposed emancipation on principle and, echoing William Cobbett's earlier accusations, contended that 'the Jews never laboured. They had in them no principle of bodily industry. They were never seen wielding the flail, or mounting the ladder with the hod.'[83] Macaulay, on the other hand, took a different tack. For him it was crucial to establish the contingent nature of what was referred to as 'Jewish character'. Jewish vices, he argued, were a reflection of the Jews' persecutors: 'they prevented the Jews from possessing an acre of land, and they now complained that the Jews devoted themselves entirely to trade.'[84] But biblical history provided ample evidence for the virility and civic pride that Jews could manifest when circumstances allowed them:

> In the earliest ages of civilization ... this despised nation had made large conquests, carried on an extensive commerce, had erected splendid temples and palaces, and boasted of eminent statesmen, warriors, philosophers, historians, and poets. What nation had ever more manfully exerted itself in the cause of civil and religious liberty? What nation in the last agonies of its dissolution, had given greater proofs of what might be accomplished by a brave despair?[85]

For Macaulay it was precisely the fundamental manliness of the Jews, rather than their 'peacefulness', that qualified them for full citizenship in modern England.

It is in this context that I want to examine Disraeli's eventual intervention in the debate on Jewish emancipation. Although Disraeli located 'the Jews' at the centre of his political thought in the 1830s and 1840s, he showed little interest in the civil disabilities of British Jews. In fact, as Abraham Gilam has commented, despite the energetic discussion of the history of the Jews in Disraeli's novels, 'the enthusiasm displayed in his rhetoric was not matched by his actions' as a Member of Parliament.[86] However, in December 1847, in response to the bill proposed by the Whig Prime Minister Lord John Russell enabling Lionel de Rothschild to take up the seat to which he had been elected by the City of London, Disraeli defied his party to declare support for Jewish emancipation. Even on this occasion his language was oxymoronic and his terms were those of his own literary fantasy, recalling Sidonia's eulogies to Jewish power: 'Has not the Church of Christ – the Christian Church, whether Roman Catholic or Protestant – made the history of the Jews the most celebrated history in the world? On every sacred day, you read to the people the exploits of Jewish heroes, the proofs of Jewish devotion, the brilliant annals of past Jewish magnificence.'[87] Disraeli's account of the manly heritage of British Jews, then, recalled Macaulay's emphasis on Jewish virtue as ancient and heroic rather than modern and domestic.

The same argument constitutes the narrative of *Tancred*, which was published only a few months before Disraeli's pro-emancipation speech. The hero's journey from England to Jerusalem enacts his return to the Jewish roots of his Christian culture and in these terms critiques the status of contemporary British Jews:

> The life and property of England are protected by the laws of Sinai. The hard-working people of England are secured in every seven days a day of rest by the laws of Sinai. And yet they persecute the Jews, and hold up to odium the race to whom they are indebted for the sublime legislation which alleviates the inevitable lot of the labouring multitude.[88]

The Hebrew Bible is seen as the origin not only of Christian legislation but of British political culture itself. Turning the Whig language of English liberties against itself, Disraeli claims that those very liberties were defined by Jewish culture: 'Vast as the obligations of the whole human family are to the Hebrew race, there is no portion of the modern populations so much indebted to them as the British people. It was "the sword of the Lord and of Gideon" that won the boasted liberties of England; chanting the same canticles that cheered the heart of Judah amid their glens, the Scotch, upon their hill-sides, achieved their religious freedom.'[89]

However, Disraeli's more impressive achievement in this debate was to displace the language of religious liberties from the question of Jewish civil rights altogether and thus to turn the 1847 debate on the Jews into another opportunity to demonstrate his loyalty to the Tory party. The Tory opposition to the measure was based on a belief in the necessity of preserving the Christian nature of the legislature, whereas Jews had become 'natural supporters of those Whiggish and other reforming groups within parliaments which, under the guidance of such politicians as Fox and Canning, moved to espouse the cause of civil and religious liberty'.[90] Disraeli's argument in favour of emancipation, however, eschewed the language of liberalism and replaced it with terms recognisably Tory. The Jews should not be excluded from the legislature, he argued, because their religion was the basis of the Christian state. The legislature should indeed remain exclusively Christian, but it should be recognised that Jews were always already included in this elite.[91]

Insisting on the common ground between Jews and Christians, Disraeli drew out the political implications of the theology of Evangelicalism. Evangelical Protestantism, which had been enjoying a renewed popularity in the 1830s and 1840s, sought to establish a new closeness with both Judaism and Jews.[92] The Evangelical periodical *The Jewish Herald* declared in 1847 that 'to the fullest extent we admit the divinity of Judaism. Christianity is founded on that admission ... What lover of his race can think without emotion of the service done to humanity and religion by the great men who were produced, nourished and cultivated by Judaism?'[93] The Evangelical conversionist organisation the London Society for Promoting Christianity amongst the Jews saw Disraeli as exemplary for his philosemitic Christianity: 'Though a Christian, he was proud of his Jewish origin, and ever upheld the traditions of his race.'[94] Support for Jewish emancipation in the parliamentary debates had frequently come not only from liberals but also from Evangelicals, who saw the relief of Jewish disabilities as a step towards the mass conversion of the Jews.[95] By mobilising Evangelical arguments, Disraeli was able to articulate a form of support for Jewish emancipation that did not rely on liberal arguments about the privacy of religious belief.

Hence, the strategy was useful for Disraeli personally: while replacing his uncomfortable silence on the question of Jewish rights, it also reiterated his public commitment to traditional Tory values – the Church, established institutions and exclusive nation. He declared: 'I am prepared to lay down the broadest principles as to the importance of maintaining a Christian character in this House and in this country; and yet it is on this very ground you will found and find the best argument for the admission of the Jews.'[96] Contrary to the fears of anti-emancipationists in his party, Disraeli argued, Jewish emancipation would reinforce rather than undermine the Christian state.[97]

At the same time, Disraeli's sudden public espousal of Jewish emancipation allowed the articulation of a new kind of Toryism. Abraham
Gilam suggests that Disraeli's change of heart at this stage was expedi-
ent for the Tory party as it facilitated their own necessary adjustment
of strategy on Jewish emancipation. Following the passage of relief
acts for Protestant Dissenters and Catholics in the 1820s and 1830s,
the party's continued commitment to the exclusion of Jews became
increasingly anachronistic.[98] But Disraeli was able to frame this adjustment of strategy not as a concession to religious liberalisation but in
terms of a new vision of the nation.[99] In *Coningsby* and *Sybil* Disraeli had
demonstrated that the ideology of Young England would address both
middle- and working-class concerns. Similarly, in his racial representations in *Tancred* and his parliamentary speech of the same year,
Disraeli was displaying the flexibility of a new Toryism which could
incorporate previously excluded groups within an inclusive concept of
the nation. In this sense, Disraeli's idealised Hebrews are just as much
part of the 'condition of England' debate as his righteous Chartist and
responsible manufacturer; all are part of Disraeli's challenge to the
Tory party over the changing boundaries of English national identity.
His answer to both the social and the religious questions of the 1840s,
as Egremont had argued in *Sybil*, is both conservative and radical: 'the
future principle of English politics will not be a levelling principle; not
a principle adverse to privileges, but favourable to their extension'.[100]

By claiming that 'the sword of the Lord and of Gideon' and 'the
exploits of Jewish heroes' were the force behind English political and
religious culture, moreover, Disraeli was doing more than extending
the Tory definition of Englishness to include the Jews. He was also
seeking to alter the terms of the debate. Disraeli's argument for Jewish
emancipation in 1847 was part of the attempt begun in *Alroy* to rewrite
Jewish historiography, transforming it into a virile political myth.

One sign of this transformation is the new relationship between
Jewishness and femininity which emerges in the later texts. In *Tancred*,
Disraeli satirises the Laurella sisters, daughters of a Syrian merchant
who 'were ashamed of their race'. Sophonisbe, who preaches toleration,
modesty and an unquestioning belief in the progress of civilisation,

> felt persuaded that the Jews would not be so much disliked if
> they were better known; that all they had to do was to imitate
> as closely as possible the habits and customs of the nation
> among whom they chanced to live; and she really did believe
> that eventually, such was the progressive spirit of the age, a

difference in religion would cease to be regarded, and that a respectable Hebrew, particularly if well dressed and well mannered, might be able to pass through society without being discovered, or at least noticed.[101]

In this passage, Disraeli characterises the 'apologetic approach' to Jewish identity as feminised – a mincing mimicry, a demeaning passivity that provokes his undisguised disdain. And he is equally resistant to the other contemporary image of Jewish female passivity, the persecuted martyr. *Tancred*'s Jewish heroine Eva bears a closer resemblance to the other heroines of the 'political trilogy' than to the more familiar figure of the suffering Jewess like Alroy's sister Miriam or Aguilar's Marie Morales. Her sexuality manifests itself in racial pride, which is inflamed rather than wounded by insult: 'Tancred looked at her with deep interest as her eye flashed fire, and her beautiful cheek was for a moment suffused with the crimson cloud of indignant passion.'[102] Because in Disraeli's historiography the Jews are central rather than marginal to Christian civilisation, he does not need the Jewess to function as a symbol of their tragic marginalisation. The liberal rhetoric of emancipation, which used the figure of feminine weakness to argue for toleration, is replaced by a strikingly tough image of the Jewess.

Disraeli's resistance to the image of the victimised Jewess is, then, part of his refusal of the liberal ideology of Jewish passivity with which it was associated. In his novels and in the 1847 debate, Disraeli displaced liberalism's passive construction of the Jews with a virile rhetoric of Jewishness. He eschewed both the apologetic argument for toleration and the plea for justice and civil rights; by publicly arguing instead that the Jews are 'unquestionably those to whom you are indebted for no inconsiderable portion of your known religion, and for the whole of your divine knowledge', he reversed the power relationship between Jews and the Christian parliament which had been accepted by both pro- and anti-emancipationists.[103] Disraeli's intervention in the 1847 debate was immediately seen as a confirmation of his personal integrity, even if, as Gilam suggests, its effect was actually shrewdly calculated: 'The results of this strategy were profitable; even his enemies admired his courageous and determined vindication of Jewish emancipation.'[104] Disraeli's unapologetic assertion of Jewish identity was interpreted as an endorsement of his own manliness.

MANLINESS IN VICTORIAN ENGLAND

George L. Mosse has contended that 'the history of racism and anti-semitism has, up to now, all but ignored the important part modern manliness played in the patterns of prejudice'. For the construction of modern masculinity, he argues, took place 'in concert with the rise of a new national consciousness'.[105] Indeed, the language of the Jewish emancipation debate suggests the important ways in which political definitions of the nation were being contested through the terms of gender in the 1830s and 1840s. If the representation of a virile Jewish-ness in Disraeli's trilogy of novels and 1847 speech was a strategic means of legitimising his own position within the Tory party, it was also an entry for him into a critical contemporary debate about the relationship between religion, nation and masculinity.

Discussions about the politics of ethnicity in the 1860s, as Catherine Hall has shown, were informed by conflicting concepts of proper man-hood.[106] These were famously articulated as responses to the controversy surrounding Governor Eyre's brutal repression of the Morant Bay riot in Jamaica in 1865, in which opposing positions were taken by Thomas Carlyle and John Stuart Mill. For Mill, the Jamaican Negroes, like all other British colonial and domestic subjects, were entitled to justice. For Carlyle the Negroes were of an inferior race and therefore not subject to the same laws as whites. But their arguments were under-pinned by a conflict over the politics of masculinity. Mill insisted that with education all humans could achieve the independent selfhood he associated with manhood, whereas for Carlyle masculine dignity could only be attained in an hierarchical society in which both master and man recognised their common duty of work, an order that had been violated in Jamaica.

In some respects, their arguments bear a striking resemblance to those articulated during the 1840s in the parliamentary debate about Jewish disabilities, which was also fought over opposed conceptions of political authority and English tradition. As David Feldman has pointed out, 'the defence of Jewish disabilities expressed an hierarchical as well as a religious vision of political authority'; the opponents of emanci-pation, who believed in an intrinsic link between Christianity and Englishness, saw Jews as 'subjects' to whom privileges might be granted. In contrast the Jews' supporters saw them as 'fellow-citizens' entitled to equal rights within a constitution which was not fixed but con-tinually developing.[107] In Hall's analysis, the arguments of Carlyle and Mill also spoke to 'different conceptions of authority and power

associated with masculinity. While Carlyle clung to a notion of hierarchy and order, with white Englishmen as the ultimate arbiters in the
interests of all, Mill dreamed of a more egalitarian society in the future
in which all individuals, whether black or white, male or female, would
have achieved "civilization".'[108] Questions of gender and 'race', then,
were clearly linked in expressions of different notions of political
authority, and it is this debate which Disraeli's novels reflect and to
which they contribute.

The gendering of political debate is evident in many texts from the
1830s onwards. David Rosen has suggested that 'writers like Carlyle
and Crabbe became preoccupied with the issue of what constituted
masculinity, a re-examination prompted by the growing displacement
of rural laborers to factory settings and non-agricultural occupations'.[109]
Working men 'expressed increasing impatience with problems they
conceptualized in terms of gender'; in *Sybil*, this is echoed when a
hand-loom weaver displaced to the city describes social and economic
changes as a loss of masculine identity:

> Why am I, and six hundred thousand subjects of the Queen,
> honest, loyal, and industrious, why are we, after manfully
> struggling for years, and each year sinking lower in the scale,
> why are we driven from our innocent and happy homes, our
> country cottages that we loved, first to bide in close towns
> without comforts, and gradually to crouch into cellars, or find
> a squalid lair like this ...? It is that the Capitalist has found a
> slave that has supplanted the labour and ingenuity of man.
> Once he was an artizan: at the best, he now only watches
> machines; and even that occupation slips from his grasp, to
> the woman and the child.[110]

Meanwhile, during the power struggle between the aristocracy,
gentry and middle classes over the Reform Bill, 'the debate over who
should rule often devolved into a debate over who belonged to that
privileged group called "men"'.[111] *Fraser's Magazine*, in which Carlyle's
work appeared, had been engaged since the 1830s in a forceful critique
of what it saw as a decline in masculine virtue in the English ruling
class. It attacked fashionable literature for contributing to the culture
of feminisation: 'What noble faculties are addressed in such works?
Are they calculated to make readers in general better or wiser? – to brace
up manly energy, and promote heroic virtue? Or rather, have they not
an evident tendency to effeminate and enfeeble the mind ...?'[112] Ideas

about true English manhood in the post-reform period, like those underlying the *Fraser's* campaign, were deeply influenced by Kenelm Henry Digby's widely read eulogy to chivalry *The Broad Stone of Honour*, first published in the 1820s and expanded during the next 20 years. Digby did not see history as tending towards progress but as fluctuating continually between good and evil. The mediaeval chivalric period represented an heroic age and modernity a time of advancing evil, whose only salvation lay in a revival of the permanently valid code of chivalry. Like *Fraser's*, Digby was writing partly in reaction to the dominance of Utilitarian ideas in the 1820s. He condemned the belief that society could be organised on a rational basis and argued for absolute ethical values perceived through the imagination.[113]

In this text, Digby attributed masculine virtue not to learning, intellect or verbal skill but to 'faith', 'honour', independence and physical vigour. A man's knightliness depended on his demonstrated values rather than his blood, and among the lower orders there might be found the 'natural aristocrat', who despite his low birth 'combines natural nobility with ardour and great ability' and should be encouraged to rise in society. However, Digby believed that democracy was anathema to chivalry and hierarchical government was the best and most natural means of ordering society.[114] For Carlyle as well as for Digby, a particular concept of masculinity was linked to a hierarchical notion of political authority. In *Past and Present*, his meditation on heroism and labour in the twelfth and nineteenth centuries, Carlyle wrote of masculinity as both hierarchical and combative: 'Man is born to fight; he is perhaps best of all definable as a born soldier; his life "a battle and a march", under the right General.'[115] Carlyle saw the concept of 'Work' as analogous to chivalric battle, for this was where masculine virtue was enacted: 'there is a perennial nobleness, and even sacredness, in Work. Were he never so benighted, forgetful of his high calling, there is always hope in a man that actually and earnestly works'. Both work and battle made possible the transformation of chaos into order, not through rationality but through violence.[116]

Carlyle's emphasis on manual labour is in the same tradition as William Cobbett's anti-capitalist nostalgia in the 1820s and 1830s for a pre-industrial, rural England. For Cobbett, modernity was epitomised by the rise to power of the Jews, who, he insisted, did not *work*. In 1833, in one of his many vociferous attacks on the principle of the Jewish emancipation bill, Cobbett challenged a fellow Member of Parliament as to 'whether he could produce a Jew who ever dug, who went to plough, or who ever made his own coat or his own shoes, or who did anything at all, except get all the money he could from the pockets of the people'.[117] Carlyle's antisemitism posited the same opposition between Jewishness and toughness, drawing on a similar romanticisation of manual labour. According to him, the political virtue of the nation was intrinsically linked to its masculine vigour: 'Show me a People energetically busy; heaving, struggling, all shoulders at the wheel; their heart pulsing, every muscle swelling, with man's energy and will; – I will show you a People of whom great good is already predictable; to whom all manner of good is yet certain, if their energy endure.'[118] Ideas about individual and national potential, then, were linked through the language and imagery of chivalric masculinity.

The elision between moral, political and physical toughness became particularly pronounced in the 'muscular Christianity' movement which emerged in the late 1840s to articulate a specifically Christian, Carlylean and counter-revolutionary response to the social unrest of the preceding years. Charles Kingsley, one of the leading figures of the movement, wrote in 1849: 'This is a puling, quill-driving, soft-handed age', advocating instead a militantly combative approach to atheism and revolutionary agitation, by addressing their causes.[119] His novels *Yeast* (serialised in *Fraser's* in 1848), about agricultural workers, and *Alton Locke* (1850), about sweated tailoring, were part of his campaign to improve conditions for working people and to generate mutual respect rather than enmity between social classes. In the 1850s, Kingsley became preoccupied with physical toughness as a means of self-improvement. He also advocated 'manliness' in writing and condemned Shelley as 'girlish' and Browning as 'effeminate'.[120] Kingsley and other Christian Socialists welcomed the Crimean War in 1854 and later the Volunteer movement in the 1860s as opportunities for the nation to prove its manliness, and their novels of the 1850s glorified the muscular male body and the noble heroism of war. In the 1860s, Kingsley became a champion of the destiny of the 'Teutonic' English race, which he considered 'the strategy of providence', so that 'the welfare of the Teutonic race is the welfare of the world'.[121] He lost Hughes' friendship by his support for Governor Eyre, whom he probably saw as embodying his ideas about heroism. In Kingsley's work in particular, English masculinity is explicitly defined in terms of the reassertion of Protestantism and the restriction of femininity; it also became associated closely with racial supremacy and imperial warfare.

DISRAELI'S ROMANCES OF MANLINESS

Between the 1830s and the 1860s, then, political definitions of English-ness were frequently expressed in terms of ideas about masculinity. It is with this context in mind that I wish to return to Disraeli's political trilogy, which is suffused with the language of manliness. The Young England movement of the early 1840s took debates which had been circulating since Carlyle's *Signs of the Times* in 1829 to the sphere of parliamentary politics. Young England's leading light, Lord John Manners, and his fellow young Tory MPs were deeply influenced by *The Broad Stone of Honour.* Although Digby's book had been written as a guide for the behaviour of the modern gentleman, the Young England movement took his precepts seriously as the basis for a new political philosophy. They sought a revival of feudalism and the ordered society, arguing that the increased power of the church and a respon-sible aristocracy would improve the condition of the working classes and thus unite the nation.

Disraeli, whose 1820s and 1830s novels had been part of the 'fash-ionable literature' so notoriously representative of an irresponsible ruling class, now became part of the reaction against it. His 1840s novels, in articulating the ideology of Young England, reflect the terms and ideas of contemporary debate. Sidonia, like Carlyle, believes in a 'naturally' hierarchical society; he tells Coningsby that 'Man is made to adore and to obey'.[122] Echoing many Victorian mediaevalists, he declares that the philosophy of utilitarianism has failed because human life and its ethical questions cannot be subjected to reason but must be ruled by the instinct of honourable men: 'We are not indebted to the Reason of man for any of the great achievements which are the landmarks of human action and human progress ... Man is only truly great when he acts from the passions; never irresistible but when he appeals to the Imagination.'[123] In the trilogy, Disraeli demonstrates a more bombastic confidence in the kind of romantic heroism which framed Alroy's vision of national rebirth, since by the 1840s these terms had much wider currency.

For political critique, like so many of his contemporaries, Disraeli employs the language of gender. Contemporary political life lacks heroism, the Tory party 'yields' to public opinion that is, to a feminis-ing democracy, a politics of effeminacy.[124] The narrator complains that contemporary politicians 'have no conception that public reputation is a motive power, and with many men the greatest. They have as much idea of fame or celebrity, even of the masculine impulse of an honourable pride, as eunuchs of manly joys.'[125] *Punch's* vulgarised version of the same metaphor described Disraeli's own struggle in the Tory party with Robert Peel as a boxing match between 'Pawky Bob' and the 'Shrewsbury Slasher', acknowledging the machismo of Disraeli's rhetoric.[126] The 'New Generation' in Disraeli's novels also spend their time in excited discussion of their roles as heroic leaders of the nation. As Mary Poovey has interestingly commented, 'the homoerotics of manly conversation constitute Disraeli's version of a reformed political domain'.[127] The New Generation are distinguished by their vigorous masculinity: Oswald Millbank looks forward with enthusiasm to a revival of mediaeval militancy, when the Church 'that struggled against the brute forces of the dark ages, against tyrannical monarchs and barbarous barons, will struggle again in opposition to influences of a different form, but of a similar tendency, equally selfish, equally insensible, equally barbarous'.[128] The true mission of the Tory party, Disraeli argues, is to uphold the influence of Church and aristocracy, whose role as 'the ancient champions of the people against arbitrary courts and rapacious parliaments' is essentially combative.[129]

The rhetoric of mediaevalism and chivalry which structures Disraeli's vision of national regeneration is drawn from Carlyle. Like Carlyle, Disraeli showed sympathy for the Chartist cause and nostalgia for the social role of the mediaeval monastery in *Sybil*. He suggested that the new feudalism was an answer to the problem posed abstractly by Sidonia, when he comments that 'England should think more of the community and less of the government'.[130] In *Tancred* Disraeli is full of enthusiasm for the liberties of the peoples of Lebanon, whose 'feudal' combination of religion and militarism is the breeding ground for the 'Young Syria' movement of the 1840s.[131] In the British context, Mr Millbank, an enlightened industrialist and 'Disciple of Progress', uses his wealth to create a model village, promoting health and education for his workers while proving that the spirit of ancient feudalism, even if practised by the modern middle class, can redeem capitalism.[132] Similarly, Trafford, the philanthropic mill-owner in *Sybil*, is a man of 'old English feelings', who has 'a correct conception of the relations which should subsist between the employer and the employed. He felt that between them there should be other ties than the payment and the receipt of wages', an attitude described by Walter Gerard as 'just and manly'.[133] Manliness in Disraeli's trilogy is associated with an aspiration towards neo-feudal social organisation.

Furthermore, whereas both Cobbett and Carlyle included a violent Jew-hatred in their evocation of mediaeval England, Disraeli, drawing on the imagery of *Alroy*, incorporates the Jews into an endorsement of chivalric values.[134] It is Carlyle's insistent link between political idealism and imagery of the tough masculine mind and body that shapes Disraeli's representation of the Jew. If Disraeli's Sidonia is not a man of action, he is nevertheless far from being alienated from English life. On the contrary, his mental energy gives him an alternative kind of toughness: 'The somewhat hard and literal character of English life suited one who shrank from sensibility, and often took refuge in sarcasm. Its masculine vigour and active intelligence occupied and interested his mind.'[135] Sidonia's identification with English life even extends to the means by which he disciplines his own vigour, through a 'devotion to field sports, which was the safety-valve of his energy'.[136] In the figure of Sidonia, Disraeli contests the exclusiveness of the rhetoric of Victorian masculinity, demonstrating its malleability.

Young England's myth of national regeneration through the renewal of masculinity is inscribed not only in the vocabulary but in the romance form of Disraeli's novels. The narratives indicate that the heroes' education in principles of national vision and purpose is the key to the restoration of their masculine identity. Egremont's awakening to his political mission through a growing awareness of the social condition of England replaces his dandyism with a new 'masculine impulse'.[137] Coningsby finally realises that his transgressive love for Edith is inseparable from his political idealism. While erotic engagement initially threatens to distract him from political ambitions, the trial to which it is put in the course of the novel transforms it into a test of his heroism. When he refuses to become his grandfather's candidate for parliament because it would mean standing against Edith's father, Mr Millbank, one of his own political mentors, Coningsby risks disinheritance for the sake of his principles. At this point the novel's political and romance narratives intersect and Coningsby begins to understand the link between his public and private lives, 'that the conduct which would violate the affections of the heart, or the dictates of the conscience, however it may lead to immediate success, is a fatal error'.[138] By remaining loyal to both 'conscience' and 'heart' for the sake of Young England and 'a maiden fair enough to revive chivalry', Coningsby is able to redeem the political errors of the past through a marriage for the future.[139] In marrying the manufacturer's daughter Edith, he re-establishes the middle-class connection suppressed by his own family and redresses the wrong done to his mother by an earlier generation of aristocrats, who cast her out for her middle-class birth. By thus reviving chivalry, Coningsby demonstrates his fitness for the political career which is his final reward. The novel, like the rest of the trilogy, reverses *Alroy*'s pessimism about the link among national unity, miscegenation and masculine identity.

The structure of the novels also reinforces this narrative of masculine ascendancy. In all three stories the heroine, initially the source of inspiration, finally submits to the guidance and protection of the newly invigorated hero. Sybil, initially the agent of Egremont's moral and political education, soon becomes the subject of his campaign to persuade her to renounce the 'prejudice' of her proudly-guarded class identity. He wishes her to learn instead that to see him as 'a Norman, a noble, an oppressor of the people, a plunderer of the church – all the characters and capacities that Sybil had been bred up to look upon with fear and aversion, and to recognise as the authors of the degradation of her race' constitutes a misreading of English history.[140] For Egremont argues that this history is being rewritten:

> You look upon me as an enemy, as a natural foe, because I am born among the privileged. I am a man, Sybil, as well as a noble ... And can I not feel for men, my fellows, whatever be their lot? ... You deem you are in darkness, and I see a dawn. The new generation of the aristocracy of England are not tyrants, not oppressors, Sybil, as you persist in believing. Their intelligence, better than that, their hearts are open to the responsibility of their position.[141]

Egremont contests the racial historiography espoused by the Gerards and their Chartist comrades. Instead of Norman oppressors and Saxon victims, he evokes a vision of national unity which transcends race and history, a unity whose basis is instinctive rather than rational and closely connected to a new understanding of manhood.

Sybil's eventual enlightenment is also accounted for as a function of her gender. During a riot at the climax of the novel she is protected from a mob of angry working-class men by the aristocratic women of Mowbray Castle, 'sympathising with womanly softness with her distress'. Sybil is obliged to abandon her belief in the fixity of class division as the women demonstrate a new kind of unity: 'It touched Sybil much, and she regretted the harsh thoughts that irresistible circumstances had forced her to cherish respecting persons, who, now that she saw them in their domestic and unaffected hour, had apparently many qualities to conciliate and to charm.'[142] But female solidarity here displaces another form of 'feminine' politics. *Sybil*'s depiction of the struggle between 'moral force' Chartism and 'physical force' Chartism becomes in the final phase of the novel a gendered opposition. Sybil's belief in 'the irresistible influence of their moral power' links Chartists with women, who in terms of Victorian domestic ideology were deemed to hold a similar ability to achieve change without action.[143] *Sybil* thus casts conflicting versions of Chartism as an opposition between the rhetoric of feminine influence and Walter Gerard's growing critique of this rhetoric as 'womanish weakness'.[144] Finally, Sybil is forced to confront the naïveté of her belief that 'irresistible influence' could effect social change. With the failure of the Charter and the eruption of the riot, she finds her faith betrayed and turns away from feminine politics to the ideology of Young England and the arms of Egremont.

In *Sybil*, the relationship between hero and heroine has important political resonance. It is linked metonymically to the new relationship between social classes which the novel promotes. When Sybil reflects that Egremont 'was what man should be to woman ever, gentle and yet a guide', she is also implicitly acknowledging that his model for social relations is correct.[145] Thus, as Mowbray Castle burns, and Sybil, no longer protected by feminine sympathy, is set upon by a 'band of drunken ruffians', it is left to Egremont, the lover she had previously rejected as a 'natural foe', to complete her conversion.[146] His chivalric rescue of Sybil in her moment of helplessness metonymically enacts his earlier warning: 'The People are not strong; the People never can be strong ... The new generation of the aristocracy of England ... are the natural leaders of the People.'[147]

In *Tancred* these relations between classes are mapped onto the imperial sphere. In an infatuation with the Englishman Tancred, the Young Syrian Fakredeen 'recognized ... the stedfast and commanding spirit, whose control, he felt conscious, was often required by his quick but whimsical temperament'.[148] While Fakredeen inspires Tancred to imperial endeavours in Syria, he also finds himself irresistibly mastered by Tancred's 'virtue in an heroic form, lofty principle, and sovereign duty' to which he can only aspire.[149] In Disraeli's romances, erotic desire mirrors political desire; in Sidonia's words, 'Man is made to adore and to obey.' In *Tancred*, like the earlier novels of the 1840s, the hero's regeneration is enacted not only through the inspiration of the exotic woman or man but by their domination. As much as the narratives insist on the necessity for mixing races and classes in a new inclusive nation, they are equally insistent that the new nation must be hierarchical in structure.

At the same time, the marriages which end the novels, symbolically uniting different classes and religions, also herald a recovery of original racial purity, the 'primeval vigour' advocated by Sidonia as the only guarantee of national survival. Egremont's fitness to rule is confirmed only with his marriage to Sybil, who it turns out is the true proprietor of the soil while Tancred looks for his own salvation through a blood tie with the 'daughter of my Redeemer's race'.[150] Disraeli's heroes, the sons of the decadent upper class, require racial redemption through the heroines. The symbolic marriage, apparently an act of miscegenation, is revealed by the novels' final plot-twists to be an act of racial purification.

The novels' resolutions in a recovery of purity and mastery reinforce Disraeli's theory of race. In this essay, I have argued that Disraeli's racial theory was not simply a self-justifying strategy but represented his engagement with discourses about manliness in the 1840s. Like Carlyle, Kingsley and the 'muscular Christians', Disraeli linked the chivalric masculine ideal with a theory of English racial destiny. Digby's account of chivalry had included the notion of 'natural aristocrats', men of the lower orders whose faith, integrity and unconscious adherence to knightly values enabled them to transcend their social class. But Disraeli rewrote Digby's notion of natural aristocracy in terms of race, using it as 'proof' that the hierarchical ordering of society was a 'law of nature'.[151]

He illustrated this theory with the paradigm of the Jews. According to Sidonia, the Tory model of social order is itself based on the 'physiological fact' of racial hierarchy. Sidonia's lecture on Jewish emancipation is thus less irrelevant than it might seem for the young Coningsby, who is seeking to revitalise Conservative values. Sidonia begins with what looks like an argument for the Tory party to take on the Jewish cause – 'the Jews, Coningsby, are essentially Tories'. But he continues with an explanation of the link between political and ethnographic organisation: 'Toryism indeed is but copied from the mighty prototype which has fashioned Europe.'[152] Thus Toryism, according to Sidonia, has its basis in the 'law of nature'. Again, in his digression on 'The Jewish Question' in *Lord George Bentinck: A Political Biography* (1852), Disraeli argues that the Jews 'are a living and the most striking evidence of the falsity of that pernicious doctrine of modern times, the natural equality of man'.[153] Disraeli's racial theory, then, is a metaphor by means of which he naturalises an aristocratic notion of political authority.

The language of race also gave Disraeli the means to remasculinise the Jewish body. In the face of the tall, handsome Jerusalem banker

Adam Besso, Disraeli's narrator sees 'the archetype of manly beauty, the tradition of those races who have wandered the least from Paradise'.[154] In a similar way, Sidonia's 'scientific' theory of race is based on explaining Jewish toughness in the face of persecution: 'You must study physiology, my dear child. Pure races of Caucasus may be persecuted, but they cannot be despised, except by the brutal ignorance of some mongrel breed, that brandishes faggots and howls exterminations, but is itself exterminated without persecutions, by that irresistible law of nature which is fatal to curs.'[155] For Sidonia, considering the 'primeval vigour' of the Jewish body is inseparable from accounting for its place in a political hierarchy and historical destiny.[156] And by the same token, the imperial ascendancy of England is assured, not on the basis of its advancing 'civilisation' but on the basis of its essential, unchanging racial character. Sidonia asserts that 'a Saxon race, protected by an insular position, has stamped its diligent and methodic character on the century. And when a superior race, with a superior idea to Work and Order, advances, its state will be progressive ... All is race; there is no other truth.'[157] Disraeli's theory of racial destiny was not only designed to augment the status of his own Jewishness; it also reflected the English racial thinking of Carlyle and his later Victorian heirs.

Despite Carlyle's antipathy for Disraeli as a person and as a symbol, they shared a language and set of ideas about race and nation which formed part of the emergent discourse of racial theory.[158] The coherence of racial theory was less important than its striking romanticism: here as elsewhere Disraeli realised, as Paul Smith has argued, that an appeal to the public 'depended partly on the ability to touch their imaginations in a manner that called for the artistic orchestration of images rather than the logical exposition of arguments'.[159] Its incoherence was also a reflection of the competition between monogenist and polygenist paradigms, neither of which had primacy in racial thought of the 1840s.[160] But for both Carlyle and Disraeli ideas about race were also clearly connected to ideas about manliness. If Disraeli used the conjunction of race and masculinity as a defence for the Jews against their European persecutors, Carlyle could also invoke it as an argument against slave emancipation, and the muscular Christians could link it to the manliness of imperial struggle. They all used a language of virile masculinity and of racial election in order to endorse a hierarchical notion of political authority as a 'law of nature'.

In the early twentieth century, the physician and Zionist ideologue Max Nordau coined the term 'Muscular Judaism' (*Muskeljudentum*) to express his aspirations for a new Jewish physique 'against the background of the regnant imagery of Jewish frailty, timidity and gentleness'. At the same time, as Paul Breines argues, the phrase evokes Theodor Herzl's preoccupation 'with the style and image of manliness ... tastes and impulses conditioned by Herzl's immersion in the pageantry and heraldry of late-nineteenth-century European nationalism'.[161] Disraeli's representations of Jews, Judaism and Jewish history are conditioned by similar stereotypes of Jewish weakness and effeminacy in mid-nineteenth-century England, but also by the aesthetics of contemporary political debate, which imagined the future of England in terms of a chivalric renewal of national masculinity. By creating 'manly Jews' and a virile Jewish history and by arguing that both were intrinsically linked to the destiny of England, Disraeli also reinforced these definitions of national identity.

NOTES

Some of the material in this article appeared in my 'Muscular Jews: Gender and Jewishness in Disraeli's "Political Trilogy"', *Jewish History*, Vol. 10, No. 2 (Fall 1996), pp. 57–88). I am grateful to Todd Endelman, Bryan Cheyette, David Feldman and Ken Stow for comments on the earlier version.

1. See Sander L. Gilman, *The Jew's Body* (London, 1991) and *Freud, Race and Gender* (Princeton, 1993); David Biale, 'Zionism as an Erotic Revolution' in Howard Eilberg-Schwartz (ed.), *People of the Body: Jews and Judaism from an Embodied Perspective* (New York, 1992), pp. 283–307; Daniel Boyarin, *Unheroic Conduct: The Rise of Heterosexuality and the Invention of the Jewish Man* (Berkeley, 1997); Paul Breines, *Tough Jews: Political Fantasies and the Moral Dilemma of American Jewry* (New York, 1990); Jacob Press, 'Same-Sex Unions in Modern Europe: *Daniel Deronda*, *Altneuland* and the Homoerotics of Jewish Nationalism' in Eve Kosofsky Sedwick (ed.), *Novel Gazing: Queer Readings in Fiction* (Durham and London, 1997), pp. 299–329.
2. Boyarin, *Unheroic Conduct*, p. 28.
3. Breines, *Tough Jews*, p. 30.
4. Ibid., pp. 12, 126.
5. Benjamin Disraeli, *Sybil; or, The Two Nations* (London, 1845), Bk 1, p. 86.
6. For a discussion of the 'Norman yoke' theory in Victorian England see Asa Briggs, 'Saxons, Normans and Victorians' in *The Collected Essays of Asa Briggs*, Vol. 2, *Images, Problems, Standpoints, Forecasts* (Brighton, 1985), pp. 215–35.
7. *Sybil*, Bk 1, p. 44.
8. Benjamin Disraeli, *Tancred; or, the New Crusade* (London, 1847), Bk 2, p. 119. For a fuller account of Disraeli's theory of English history see, in particular, *Coningsby*, Bk 7, chs ii and iv, and *Sybil*, Bk 1, ch. iii.
9. *Tancred*, Bk 1, p. 102.
10. Benjamin Disraeli, *Coningsby; or, the New Generation* (London, 1844), Bk 1, pp. 262, 266.
11. *Tancred*, Bk 1, pp. 98–9.
12. *Coningsby*, Bk 1, p. 237; *Sybil*, Bk 1, p. 66.

13. *Sybil*, Bk 1, p. 79.
14. *Tancred*, Bk 1, p. 21.
15. *Sybil*, Bk 1, p. 301.
16. *Coningsby*, Bk 3, p. 100.
17. Ibid., Bk 3, p. 35.
18. Ibid., Bk 3, p. 133.
19. *Sybil*, Bk 1, p. 303.
20. C. J. W-L. Wee, discussing Charles Kingsley's narratives of national renewal through the recovery of manly vigour, calls this 're-racination'. See 'Christian Manliness and National Identity: The Problematic Construction of a Racially "Pure" Nation' in Donald E. Hall (ed.), *Muscular Christianity: Embodying the Victorian Age* (Cambridge, 1994), p. 82.
21. *Tancred*, Bk 2, p. 289.
22. Ibid., Bk 1, p. 220.
23. Ibid., Bk 2, pp. 41–2.
24. *Sybil*, Bk 1, p. 122.
25. *Coningsby*, Bk 3, p. 112.
26. *Tancred*, Bk 3, p. 194.
27. Ibid., Bk 2, p. 3.
28. *Coningsby*, Bk 2, p. 133.
29. Ibid.
30. Ibid., Bk 2, pp. 133–4. In eighteenth-century England there was a 'common prejudicial notion that Jews were exceptionally lustful and that their wealth, when put at the service of their sexual longings, was a threat to English womanhood'. See Todd M. Endelman, *The Jews of Georgian England, 1714–1830: Tradition and Change in a Liberal Society* (Philadelphia, 1979), p. 130. See also Frank Felsenstein, *Anti-Semitic Stereotypes: A Paradigm of Otherness in English Popular Culture, 1660–1830* (Baltimore and London, 1995), p. 55.
31. *Coningsby*, Bk 2, p. 169.
32. Ibid., Bk 2, pp. 134–5.
33. Ibid., Bk 2, p. 131.
34. Ibid., Bk 2, pp. 136, 137.
35. Ibid., Bk 2, p. 132. Joseph Ben Joseph's review in the conversionist periodical *The Jewish Herald* of 'Faith Strengthened', a defence of Judaism translated by Moses Mocatta, uses a typical formulation: 'May the Lord "take away the stony heart" of bigotry and prejudice from our Jewish brethren.' See *The Jewish Herald*, No. 7 (1852), p. 133.
36. *Coningsby*, Bk 2, p. 137.
37. Matthew Lewis's Wandering Jew in *The Monk* (1796), for example, is described in these terms: 'He was a man of majestic presence; his countenance was strongly marked, and his eyes were large, black, and sparkling; yet there was something in his look which, the moment that I saw him, inspired me with a secret awe, not to say horror.' The Jew's evil eye had been part of folkloric myth since the Middle Ages, but was particularly invoked by Romantic writers using the Wandering Jew as a figure of awe and horror. For further discussion of this trope see Edgar Rosenberg, *From Shylock to Svengali: Jewish Stereotypes in English Fiction* (London, 1960), p. 214.
38. *Coningsby*, Bk 2, p. 176.
39. Ibid., Bk 1, pp. 256–7. According to Boyarin's analysis, ascribing high status to the man of inaction is not simply 'the desperate product of an abnormal situation' but 'an assertive historical product of Jewish culture'. See Boyarin, *Unheroic Conduct*, pp. 23–4.
40. In the terms which later became the rhetorical framework for the political trilogy,

Disraeli claimed that it was the Tory party, rather than the Whigs, who stood for the defence of popular liberties. See Paul Smith, *Disraeli: A Brief Life* (Cambridge, 1996), pp. 48–9.

41. *Coningsby*, Bk 1, p. 254.
42. Ibid., Bk 2, p. 123.
43. Ibid., Bk 2, p. 124.
44. Ibid., Bk 2, pp. 126, 127.
45. Ibid., Bk 2, p. 128.
46. Ibid., Bk 2, pp. 138–40.
47. See *Lord George Bentinck: A Political Biography* (1852), ch. 24, 'The Jewish Question', which similarly interrupts the narrative.
48. The phrase is Patrick Brantlinger's, in *The Spirit of Reform: British Literature and Politics, 1832–1867* (Cambridge, MA, 1977), p. 99. See his chapter, 'Two Responses to Chartism: Dickens and Disraeli' in the same volume, pp. 81–107, and Daniel Bivona, *Desire and Contradiction: Imperial Visions and Domestic Debates in Victorian Literature* (Manchester and New York, 1990), ch. 1.
49. Bivona, *Desire*, p. 16. In *Tancred*, in particular, this tension is left unresolved at the end of the novel. In this chapter, Bivona convincingly links the three novels in terms of their common project of 'colonising' the alien, domestic or foreign, and sees the novels' contradictions as 'the literary expression of an ambivalent imperial desire' (p. 24). For another discussion of the relationship between race and nation in the trilogy see Patrick Brantlinger, 'Nations and Novels: Disraeli, George Eliot, and Orientalism', *Victorian Studies*, Vol. 35 (1991–92), pp. 255–73.
50. Smith, *Disraeli*, pp. 85–6. Disraeli's racial theory about the Jews is expressed with most extravagance in *Tancred*, which was published in March 1847 just as Disraeli was being bought up by the Protectionists as the most articulate parliamentary speaker. Smith suggests that the novel should be read with precisely this context in mind, and that its Jewish chauvinism functioned 'as an oblique definition of the terms on which he was prepared to take service on the front bench'.
51. *Coningsby*, Bk 2, p. 117.
52. Smith, *Disraeli*, p. 60.
53. See, for example, Daniel R. Schwarz, *Disraeli's Fiction* (London, 1979) and Todd M. Endelman, 'Benjamin Disraeli and the Myth of Sephardi Superiority', in this volume.
54. In 1837, the first year of his election to Parliament, Disraeli voted against a petition on behalf of the relief of Jewish disabilities. He remained uninvolved in the debates about Jewish relief in the 1830s and 1840s, despite key debates in 1841 and 1845. See Abraham Gilam, 'Benjamin Disraeli and the Emancipation of the Jews' in Abraham Gilam, *The Emancipation of the Jews in England, 1830–1860* (New York and London, 1982), p. 155.
55. *Coningsby*, Bk 2, p. 198.
56. Todd M. Endelman suggests that Disraeli's 'enthusiasm for illiberal ideas reflected his distance from mainstream Anglo-Jewry, which was then struggling to gain full political emancipation and had pinned its hopes for success on the triumph of liberalism'. See Todd M. Endelman, 'The Frankaus of London, 1837–1967: A Study in Radical Assimilation', *Jewish History*, Vol. 8, Nos 1–2 (1994), p. 25. Indeed, Disraeli often sought to emphasise his distance from contemporary Anglo-Jews; in a letter to his sister Sarah in 1850, for example, he wrote satirically of

> a banquet at the Antony Rothschild's, given in honour of the impending fate of a brother-in-law, Montefiore, and a daughter of Baron de Goldsmid. The Hebrew aristocracy assembled in great force and

> numbers, mitigated by the Dowager of Morley, Charles Viliers, Abel
> Smiths, and Thackeray! I think he will sketch them in the last number
> of Pendennis.

See Benjamin Disraeli, letter, 26 April 1850, in *Lord Beaconfield's Correspondence
with his Sister, 1832–1852* (London, 2nd edn, 1886), p. 244. The reference to
wealthy London Jews as the 'Hebrew aristocracy' and the 'impending fate' of
their marriage, is here clearly ironic; Disraeli identifies himself more closely with
Thackeray, who would produce a similarly satirical 'sketch'. The 'Hebrew aristocracy' of Victorian London and the 'aristocracy of Nature' of Disraeli's rhetoric
are distinctly different; indeed, I would argue, embracing 'illiberal' concepts
like the 'aristocracy of Nature' enabled Disraeli to 'distance' himself from the
'Hebrew aristocracy'.

57. Smith, *Disraeli*, p. 93.
58. Benjamin Disraeli, *The Wondrous Tale of Alroy* (London, 1833), Bk 1, p. 195.
59. Ibid., Bk 2, p. 41.
60. Ibid., Bk 2, p. 66.
61. Ibid., Bk 3, p. 34.
62. Ibid., Bk 1, p. 213.
63. Ibid., Bk 1, pp. 110–11.
64. Ibid., Bk 2, p. 61.
65. Ibid., Bk 2, pp. 100–1.
66. Ibid., Bk 2, pp. 46–7.
67. Ibid., Bk 2, p. 140.
68. Ibid., Bk 2, pp. 174–5.
69. Ibid., Bk 3, p. 92.
70. Ibid., Bk 3, pp. 24–5.
71. Ibid., Bk 3, p. 69.
72. Grace Aguilar's novels and stories were mostly written in the 1830s but published
     only in the 1840s. See Nadia Valman, 'Jews and Gender in British Literature,
     1815–1865' (unpublished Ph.D. diss., London University, 1996); Michael
     Galchinsky, *The Origin of the Modern Jewish Woman Writer: Romance and Reform
     in Victorian England* (Detroit, 1996); Michael Ragussis, *Figures of Conversion: 'The
     Jewish Question' and English National Identity* (Durham and London, 1995).
73. Mary S. Millar and M. G. Wiebe, '"This power so vast ... & so generally mis-
     understood": Disraeli and the Press in the 1840s', *Victorian Periodicals Review*
     (Summer 1992), p. 84.
74. W. M. Thackeray, review in *Pictorial Times*, 25 May 1844, quoted by S. S. Prawer,
     Israel at Vanity Fair: Jews and Judaism in the Writings of W. M. Thackeray (Leiden,
     1992), p. 140.
75. G. H. Lewes, *British Quarterly Review*, Vol. 10 (August 1849), pp. 118–38, included
     in R. W. Stewart (ed.), *Disraeli's Novels Reviewed, 1826–1968* (Metuchen, 1975),
     pp. 194–8.
76. For extended discussion of the nineteenth-century perception of the male Jew
     as 'feminised' see Gilman, *The Jew's Body*, and Boyarin, *Unheroic Conduct*.
77. For full accounts of these debates see M. C. N. Salbstein, *The Emancipation of
     the Jews in Britain: The Question of the Admission of the Jews to Parliament, 1828–
     1860* (Rutherford, Madison, London and Toronto, 1982); David Feldman,
     Englishmen and Jews: Social Relations and Political Culture, 1840–1914 (New
     Haven, 1994) and Gilam, *Emancipation of the Jews*.
78. See n. 72 above.
79. Scott's Rebecca of York in *Ivanhoe* (1819) was the most famous beautiful
     and dangerous Jewess of the first half of the nineteenth century. The lecherous

Jewish male was also a common stereotype from the eighteenth-century (see n. 30 above).

80. See Bryan Cheyette, 'From Apology to Revolt: Benjamin Farjeon, Amy Levy and the Post-emancipation Anglo-Jewish Novel, 1880–1900', *Transactions of the Jewish Historical Society of England*, Vol. 24 (1982–86), pp. 253–65.
81. *Hansard*, Third ser. 16 (1 March–1 April 1833) and 17 (2 April–20 May 1833), col. 242.
82. Poulter, *Hansard*, Third ser. 17 (2 April–20 May 1833), col. 241.
83. Earl of Malmesbury, *Hansard*, Third ser. 24 (2 June–9 July 1834), col. 722.
84. Macaulay, *Hansard*, Third ser. 17 (2 April–20 May 1833), col. 236.
85. Ibid., p. 237.
86. Gilam, *Emancipation of the Jews*, p. 162.
87. *Hansard*, Third ser. 95 (18 November–20 December 1847), col. 1328.
88. *Tancred*, Bk 2, pp. 194–5.
89. Ibid., Bk 2, p. 196.
90. Salbstein, *Emancipation of the Jews in Britain*, p. 36.
91. *Hansard*, Third ser. 95 (18 November–20 December 1847), cols 1323–6. In response to the suggestion that admitting the Jews to Parliament as fellow-subjects would be the first step to admitting Muslims, Hindus, pagans and other subjects of the British empire, Disraeli argued 'a Christian senate and community are placed, in reference to the Jews, in a position quite different, and must not for a moment be confounded with what their position would be in reference to a follower of Mahomet or a Pagan' (1326). He was thus able to stress Judaism's closeness to Christianity by distancing it from other 'oriental' religions.
92. For a full account of Evangelical philosemitism, see Mel Scult, *Millennial Expectations and Jewish Liberties: A Study of the Efforts to Convert the Jews in Britain, up to the Mid Nineteenth Century* (Leiden, 1978).
93. Unsigned review of 'The Spirit of Judaism' by Grace Aguilar, *The Jewish Herald*, Vol. 2 (February 1847), pp. 29, 30, 31.
94. Rev. W. T. Gidney, *The History of the London Society for Promoting Christianity amongst the Jews from 1809 to 1908* (London, 1908), p. 408.
95. See, for example, Mr Poulter's comments, *Hansard*, Third ser. 17 (2 April–20 May 1833), col. 242.
96. *Hansard*, Third ser. 95 (18 November–20 December 1847), cols 1325–6.
97. See Feldman, *Englishmen and Jews*, pp. 32–6.
98. Gilam, *Emancipation of the Jews*, pp. 160–1.
99. See Feldman, *Englishmen and Jews*, pp. 36–8. Feldman argues that the distinction between the Whig pro-emancipationist position and Tory anti-emancipationist arguments should not be seen only as the battle of modern liberalism against anachronistic prejudice. In fact both are based on a similar concern with national identity, which each defines differently according to a distinctive historiography. Whereas Tory opposition to emancipation cited a fundamental link between Christianity, the nation and political authority, Whigs like Russell and Macaulay argued for emancipation as a civil right, although

> this argument was interwoven with an equally significant concern with the nature of the collectivity to which the individuals belonged ... Because the Englishness of English history was bound to the idea of individual liberties protected by the law, the language of rights, the argument for Jewish emancipation, constituted an argument about the nation as well as the individual. (pp. 43–5)

100. *Sybil*, Bk 3, pp. 33–4.

101. *Tancred*, Bk 3, pp. 85–6.

102 Ibid., Bk 2, p. 51.

103. *Hansard*, Third ser. 95 (18 November–20 December 1847), col. 1323. Disraeli also suggested in *Coningsby* that the Jews were not in fact in the subservient position implied by most of the debate. In the course of a discussion with Coningsby about the future of English politics, Sidonia warns that the continued exclusion of the Jews from political participation is 'impolitic'. Borrowing Macaulay's argument in favour of emancipation, Sidonia says that Jews already possess the means of power – property. Therefore it is not only inconsistent but dangerous to the stability of the state to alienate such a powerful section of the population, which at the moment has no choice but to join 'the same ranks as the leveller and the latitudinarian, and [be] prepared to support the policy which may even endanger his life and property, rather than tamely continue under a system which seeks to degrade him' (*Coningsby*, Bk 2, p. 199). These observations are clearly linked to the larger argument of *Coningsby* in favour of the incorporation of the materially powerful and hence potentially dangerous bourgeoisie into the Tory idea of a ruling class.

104. Gilam, *Emancipation of the Jews*, p. 162.

105. George L. Mosse, *The Image of Man: The Creation of Modern Masculinity* (New York, 1996), pp. 12, 52.

106. Catherine Hall, 'Competing Masculinities: Thomas Carlyle, John Stuart Mill and the Case of Governor Eyre' in Catherine Hall, *White, Male and Middle Class: Explorations in Feminism and History* (Cambridge, 1992), pp. 255–95.

107. Feldman, *Englishmen and Jews*, p. 33.

108. Hall, *White, Male and Middle Class*, p. 288.

109. David Rosen, 'The Volcano and the Cathedral: Muscular Christianity and the Origins of Primal Manliness' in Hall, *Muscular Christianity*, p. 20.

110. *Sybil*, Bk 1, pp. 263–4.

111. Rosen, 'The Volcano and the Cathedral', p. 21.

112. Cited in Ellen Moers, *The Dandy: Brummell to Beerbohm* (London, 1960), p. 171.

113. See Mark Girouard, *The Return to Camelot: Chivalry and the English Gentleman* (New Haven, 1981), pp. 60–1.

114. Ibid., pp. 61–5.

115. Thomas Carlyle, *Past and Present* (London: Chapman and Hall, n.d. (first pub. 1843)), Bk 3, ch. x, pp. 163–4.

116. Ibid., Bk 3, ch. xi, pp. 168–9. See also Norma Clarke's excellent discussion of Carlyle's attempt 'to reconcile two contradictory models of a masculine future: that represented by his father, a working peasant; and that represented by the lettered classes amongst whom he had found a place by virtue of his intellectual abilities' through the myth of the hero, in 'Strenuous Idleness: Thomas Carlyle and the Man of Letters as Hero' in Michael Roper and John Tosh (eds), *Manful Assertions: Masculinities in Britain since 1800* (London, 1991), pp. 25–43.

117. Cited by Salbstein, *Emancipation of the Jews in Britain*, pp. 67–8.

118. Carlyle, *Past and Present*, Bk 3, ch. xii, p. 178.

119. Charles Kingsley, letter to Mr Ludlow (editor of *The Christian Socialist*), cited in Thomas Hughes, 'Prefatory Memoir' to *Alton Locke, Tailor and Poet: An Autobiography* (London and New York, 1887), p. xxi.

120. Girouard, *The Return to Camelot*, pp. 132–6. C. J. W-L. Wee's account of Kingsley's novels *Alton Locke* (1850) and *Westward Ho!* (1855) suggests that Kingsley's

> muscular Christianity ... offered a number of ways out of England's effete and fragmented condition. A primitive vigor and character could be recovered from non-European lands – from someone else's

culture – where manly energy was unconstrained by modern life, or
from English historical precedents, where a united nation existed.

See Wee, 'Christian Manliness and National Identity: The Problematic Construction of a Racially "Pure" Nation', p. 68. Kingsley's narratives of national
regeneration thus clearly echo Disraeli's in the 'political trilogy'; Disraeli similarly argues that the only sources for the renewal of masculine vigour are the
disenfranchised middle and working classes, and the imperial sphere. For an
extensive discussion of Kingsley's relationship with manliness see Norman
Vance, *The Sinews of the Spirit: The Ideal of Christian Manliness in Victorian
Literature and Religious Thought* (Cambridge, 1985). Vance notes Kingsley's and
Disraeli's common concern with social crisis, but not their equally common
concern with the relationship between social crisis and manliness (p. 81).
121. See Hugh A. MacDougall, *Racial Myth in English History: Trojans, Teutons and
Anglo-Saxons* (Montreal, Hanover, NH and London, 1982), p. 98.
122. *Coningsby*, Bk 2, p. 181.
123. Ibid., Bk 2, pp. 180–1.
124. Ibid., Bk 3, p. 97.
125. Ibid., Bk 2, p. 225.
126. Millar and Wiebe, 'This power so vast', p. 84.
127. Mary Poovey discusses the homoeroticism that results from Disraeli's attempt
to fuse the romance form with analysis of the masculine sphere of politics in
'Homosociality and the Psychological: Disraeli, Gaskell, and the Condition-of-
England Debate' in *Making a Social Body: British Cultural Formation, 1830–1864*
(Chicago, 1995), pp. 132–43.
128. *Coningsby*, Bk 3, pp. 110–11.
129. *Sybil*, Bk 2, p. 312.
130. *Coningsby*, Bk 2, p. 176.
131. *Tancred*, Bk 2, p. 336; Bk 3, p. 16.
132. *Coningsby*, Bk 2, p. 41.
133. *Sybil*, Bk 2, p. 97; Bk 3, p. 270.
134. Carlyle's semitic representations included his attack on mediaeval Jewish usurers
in *Past and Present* (1843), his call in *Latter-Day Pamphlets* on 'Jesuitism' (1850)
for a conflagration of 'Jew old-clothes' (using the stereotype of Jewish old-
clothes sellers to refer to what he saw as the redundancy of Hebraic religion),
and personal attacks on Disraeli which stressed his Jewishness. For a detailed
discussion see T. Peter Park, 'Thomas Carlyle and the Jews', *Journal of European
Studies*, Vol. 20 (1990), pp. 1–21. For Cobbett's use of the image of the Jew see
Salbstein, *Emancipation of the Jews in Britain*, pp. 67–9.
135. *Coningsby*, Bk 2, p. 140.
136. Ibid., Bk 2, p. 141.
137. *Sybil*, Bk 1, p. 303.
138. *Coningsby*, Bk 3, pp. 227–8.
139. Ibid., Bk 3, p. 153.
140. *Sybil*, Bk 2, pp. 316, 315.
141. Ibid., Bk 2, pp. 317–18.
142. Ibid., Bk 3, pp. 285–6.
143. Ibid., Bk 3, p. 31. For more on 'the religious power of the woman' to influence
the morality of the nation, see Catherine Hall, 'The Early Formation of Victorian
Domestic Ideology' in Hall, *White, Male and Middle Class*, p. 86.
144. *Sybil*, Bk 3, p. 39.
145. Ibid., Bk 3, p. 48.
146. Ibid., Bk 3, p. 314; Bk 2, p. 317.

147. Ibid., Bk 2, pp. 317–18.
148. *Tancred*, Bk 2, pp. 176–7. For an account of this masochistic 'servility' in later imperialist literature, see Rana Kabbani, *Imperial Fictions: Europe's Myths of Orient* (London, rev. and exp. edn, 1994), p. 9.
149. *Tancred*, Bk 3, p. 64.
150. Ibid., Bk 3, p. 296.
151. *Coningsby*, Bk 2, p. 204.
152. Ibid., Bk 2, p. 200.
153. Benjamin Disraeli, *Lord George Bentinck: A Political Biography* (London, 1905 (first pub. 1852)), p. 323.
154. *Tancred*, Bk 2, p. 14.
155. *Coningsby*, Bk 2, p. 204.
156. Ibid., Bk 2, p. 140.
157. *Tancred*, Bk 1, p. 303.
158. Racial theory had increasing currency by the 1850s, particularly after the publication of Robert Knox's *The Races of Man: A Philosophical Enquiry into the Influence of Race over the Destinies of Nations* (1850/1862). See Christine Bolt, *Victorian Attitudes to Race* (London, 1971). Knox strikingly echoed Disraeli in his formulation 'Race is everything: literature, science, art – in a word, civilization depends on it' although he also dismissed Disraeli's account of Jewish racial difference (*The Races of Man: A Fragment* (London, 1862), p. v).
159. Smith, *Disraeli*, p. 75.
160. See Bivona, *Desire and Contradiction*, pp. 26–8, and Nancy Stepan, *The Idea of Race in Science: Great Britain, 1800–1960* (London and Basingstoke, 1982), chs 1 and 2.
161. Breines, *Tough Jews*, pp. 147, 141.

PART 2:

RESPONSES TO DISRAELI'S JEWISHNESS

'BEN JUJU': REPRESENTATIONS OF DISRAELI'S JEWISHNESS IN THE VICTORIAN POLITICAL CARTOON[1]

Anthony S. Wohl

Both biographies of Disraeli and the small but impressive body of literature on his Jewishness suggest that the Victorian public's interest in his ethnicity faded once he had climbed to the top of the greasy pole. Most studies of Disraeli give the impression that the prejudices he experienced as a schoolboy and as an aspiring politician, confounded perhaps by Jewish emancipation in 1858 and by his stature within the Tory party and the country at large, evaporated, or at least went underground, during his great ministry of 1874 to 1880.[2] Recently, however, Stanley Weintraub, in his evocative and intimate biography *Disraeli*, David Feldman, in his fine chapter on Disraeli in his *Englishmen and Jews*, and Michael Ragussis, in his superb *Figures of Conversion: The 'Jewish Question' and English National Identity*, have re-evaluated responses to the ageing Disraeli's Jewishness. This present volume also reflects a response to the comparative neglect, certainly the underestimation, of the question of Disraeli's Jewishness after 1874.[3]

In this essay I will argue that Disraeli's Jewishness assumed far greater political and social significance during his second ministry than at any previous stage in his career.[4] Indeed, for many it became *the* most critical aspect of the Prime Minister and his government. For example, E. A. Freeman, the future Regius Professor of Modern History at Oxford, seldom referred to Disraeli by name in his private correspondence. Disraeli was reduced, rather, to the basic, most significant element in Freeman's eyes – he was simply, time and again, 'the Jew' while to others he was the 'Jew Earl, Philo-Turkish Jew and Jew Premier', the 'traitorous Jew', the 'veritable Jew', the 'haughty Jew' and the 'abominable Jew'.[5] To the author of a political tract published in the year Disraeli died, he was a 'lump of dirt', a 'Fagin'.[6] Poems and broadsides in Gladstone's library at Harwarden refer to Disraeli as 'Judas', 'Jewish Dizzy', the 'Jewish chief', 'Sir Benjamin de Judah' and 'Chief Rabbi Benjamin'; to his cabinet as 'the government of the circumcision'; and to his title of earl as 'a Jewish brazen coronet'.[7] This new emphasis on Disraeli's Jewishness, though often couched in crude jibes, strikes me as deadly serious, fervent, even obsessive, rather than good-humoured, random or 'unthinking' (as John Plumb had characterised the antisemitism of early Victorian England).[8]

It is only natural that there would be a re-awakened interest in Disraeli's origins once he became Prime Minister, and perhaps Disraeli himself, having published in 1870 a new edition of his novels with their extravagant claims for Jewish genius and a special place in history for Jews, must take some responsibility for the renewed curiosity about his Jewishness. It is highly unlikely, however, that if Disraeli had refrained from harping on his Jewish origins, others would have forgotten them. In any case, Disraeli's use of racial language was very different from that employed by the majority of those who now emphasised his Jewishness. The latter, full of hatreds, fear and stereotyping, suggests that there was, just beneath the surface of liberal England, a large reservoir of inherited, long-standing prejudices and images to reinforce them. These prejudices cannot be explained away, or discounted, as simply a barrage of cheap and nasty shots directed at a political opponent or the seizing of any political edge to embarrass the government. Disraeli was now no longer a somewhat risible 'mere Jew-boy' (to quote the Duke of Argyll).[9] He was portrayed as the archetypical or paradigmatic Jew, widely stereotyped and caricatured as the personification of, the icon for, the allegedly sinister and alien qualities of international Jewry.

For example, the author of a three-part series in 1878 in the *Fortnightly Review* on 'The Political Adventures of Lord Beaconsfield' argued that Disraeli's 'Jewish blood' might possibly be the key to unlocking the enigma of his personality and policies:

> If Lord Beaconsfield's political adventures could be truly narrated without any reference to his Jewish blood and to the inherited qualities which are deeply stamped upon his nature, physical and moral, we should be very glad to keep the things apart. But ... the secret of Lord Beaconsfield's life lies in his Jewish blood ... it is not a matter for disparagement and contempt ... It is a simple question of fact and natural history.[10]

But what does being Jewish, this 'simple question of fact and natural history' mean? Though 'not a matter for disparagement and contempt', the author was clear: Jews could hardly be expected to be 'morally the better for the experience' of 'nineteen centuries of bondage'. As for Disraeli:

> The circumstances of his birth ... the inherited qualities of a race whose habits of mind and character have been formed by nearly two thousand years of persecution and social slight, have hindered Lord Beaconsfield from cultivating that subordination of mere personal greed, whether of fame, or wealth, or power, to the well-being of a sect, a party, a class, a nation, without which genuine community is impossible.[11]

Thus, call it inherited nature or centuries of nurture, the mere fact of his Jewishness put Disraeli beyond the pale of correct political conduct, the Victorian 'moralised polity' and its 'Christian morality' and was therefore a cause for alarm.[12] When Captain Richard Burton (of *Arabian Nights* fame) called Disraeli 'in nature as in name, a very Hebrew of Hebrews', it was as much a warning as an ethnic designation.[13]

Disraeli, 'a very Moses in the House of Lords', was widely portrayed as a man whose 'craftiness of race' was 'emblematic'.[14] *Emblematic*. It is this aspect of Disraeli's Jewishness, the way it was viewed emblematically, that this essay will examine through an analysis of the political cartoons of the popular illustrated comic journals, especially the Liberal journal *Fun*.[15] These journals enjoyed a wide circulation. In the 1870s, *Fun* (which so closely aped *Punch* that W. M. Thackeray called it '*Funch*'), at one penny, sold some 20,000 copies; *Punch*, at three pence, 40,000 copies; and *Funny Folks*, at one penny, 60,000. These are weekly circulation figures. By comparison, the *Fortnightly Review* had a monthly circulation of only 2,500.[16]

In the theoretical literature on the psychological and sociological significance of cartoons and caricatures, there are two broad concepts that are of particular relevance to the way Disraeli was represented. First, comic invention, whether in the form of cartoons or ethnic jokes, encourages stereotyping and so permits the expression of prejudice with an easy conscience (Don't be so po-faced! It is, after all, just a joke!). To Ernst Kris, the cartoon weakens the hold of the super-ego over our libidinal or aggressive tendencies and enables us both to 'satisfy instinctual demands' and to 'avoid censorship both from the external and internal world'.[17] Thus cartoons provide the 'expressibility' that social psychologists find so important to the growth of prejudice.[18] Richard Godfrey, in his *English Caricature: 1620 to the Present*, cautions us to remember that caricature is often designed to amuse; however, he rightly emphasises that 'it is also a blunt instrument for the expression of prejudice'.[19] In the liberal society of late-Victorian England, which prided itself on its openness and toleration, cartoons offered a release and a vehicle for the public expression of prejudices.

The second concept is that a caricature is more than just an exaggeration of a prominent or easily recognised feature. It is, either overtly or latently, aggressive, for, as Ernst Kris argued, it destroys natural harmony and balance and, most importantly, it both degrades and unmasks the individual.[20] In the case of Disraeli, the cartoons discussed below offered powerful symbolic representations of Disraeli's Jewishness, and in so doing they claimed to unmask or reveal the inner, motivating forces behind his outward actions.[21] They thus turned Disraeli's Jewishness from what it had been hitherto – just one characteristic of the man – into something far more ominous, the whole characteristic, the dominant and decisive fact, the key to decoding his allegedly devious policies and unmasking his ultimate designs.

The unmasking process also replaced Disraeli's own conception of racial Jewishness (elevated, romantic, pure, cultural, worldly-wise, conservative, in harmony with English ideals and interests and proto-Christian), spelled out earlier in *Coningsby*, *Tancred*, *Alroy* and *Lord George Bentinck: A Political Biography*, with one that was now imposed on him and presented to the nation – the Jew as materialistic, uncultured, superstitious, conspiratorial, so clannish that he could never be patriotic and bitterly hostile to Christianity. It was a radical shift from images that stressed the positive qualities in Judaism, qualities that Disraeli and others held would promote assimilation to Christianity and acculturation to English society, to images that stressed its negative and alien qualities, its pathogenic 'deviation from the norm'.[22]

To a society well-versed in the history of the Spanish Inquisition and the *conversos*, members of a secret race, clinging to their faith, all outward signs to the contrary, the notion of Disraeli being a crypto-Jew, despite his baptism at the age of 12, was not so far-fetched.[23] After all, his own earlier writings attested to his pride in his origins, and his assertion that Judaism was but incomplete Christianity was hardly reassuring to those who suspected the sincerity of his belief in his adopted religion. To Malcolm MacColl, later Canon of Ripon, it was plain from a reading of *Coningsby* 'that Lord Beaconsfield would think himself perfectly justified in conforming to the Christian Church of

England and receiving her Sacraments without pledging his conscience to a full acceptance of the dogmas of the Christian Creed'.[24] As we shall see, Disraeli's foreign policy, once he was in power, heightened these fears.[25] Gladstone did not, of course, challenge or criticise the growing suspicion that Disraeli was a crypto-Jew and in fact added to those suspicions by drawing attention to what he described as Disraeli's 'Judaic feelings' and commenting that 'though he has been baptised, his Jew feelings are the most radical and the most real, and so far respectable, portion of his profoundly falsified nature'. Indeed, Gladstone categorically stated that England's foreign policy was now under the influence of what he called 'Dizzy's crypto-Judaism'.[26] Doubtless there were many who were of like mind with Arthur Sketchley's immensely popular and opinionated 'character', Mrs Brown, who, in referring to 'Disreely', proclaimed herself 'one as don't believe in converted Jews'.[27] Cartoons played a major role in unmasking Disraeli's Jewishness and the allegedly secret machinations of the 'converted Jew'.

Cognitive psychologists point out that line drawings and cartoons have a remarkably quick 'perception time' and so an immediate impact.[28] Their graphic force is heightened by the elements of ridicule and distortion. Ridicule, it is argued, can serve as a form of 'rhetoric' that 'prepares the way for action', and Max Beerbohm was right to stress that one soon forgets that caricatures are distortions – they quickly become realities.[29] Hence the significance of the little girl's remark on meeting Disraeli: '"I know you", she said, "I've seen you in *Punch*."'[30]

There is, however, a danger of over-extrapolating, of reading into the cartoons far more than the cartoonist consciously intended. Given, for example, Disraeli's Jewish origins and the frequency with which Victorian political cartoonists found inspiration in Shakespeare, was it particularly antisemitic to portray Disraeli as Shylock? I believe we would think not from the 1867 *Fun* cartoon, 'The Westminster Play' (Figure 1), for while Antonio (John Bright) and Bassanio (Gladstone) look upon Shylock's (Disraeli's) advocacy of reform (the Second Reform Act) with suspicion, and while Disraeli's posture might suggest deviousness and hypocritical unctuousness, the cartoon, nevertheless, portrays Shylock in the posture of the pleading Jew, cringing perhaps (especially when compared to the 'manly' forms of Gladstone and Bright), yet basically passive, weak and harmless.[31] The representation of Disraeli as Shylock in the same journal some 13 weeks later is, however, very different. In the 1880 cartoon, 'Shylock and his "Pound of

1. 'The Westminster Play'   2. 'Shylock and his "Pound of Flesh"'

Flesh"' (Figure 2), Disraeli's 'semitic' features are exaggerated, and the whole attitude of his body is one of volatile menace. The contrast between the two cartoons is startling and demands analysis.[32] How are we to explain this transition from so benign to so savage and sinister a representation of Disraeli's Jewishness?

As with antisemitism in any period, the antisemitism directed against Disraeli during his ministry of 1874–80 was an amalgam of complex forces, psychological, social, political, economic and religious.[33] It would be simplistic to think otherwise, and if space permitted, we would have to explore a wide variety of forces – among them, the criticism that, following emancipation, Anglo-Jewry was coming on 'too fast' in too many areas; the resentment that Jews were ungrateful (that is, that they were deserting the Liberal party, which had worked so hard to achieve Jewish emancipation); the accusation that they were dominating the press, English and Continental; the renewed charge that they were parasites and not producers; the enmity that their exclusiveness, 'clannishness' and resistance to conversion provoked, on the one hand, and, on the other, the fear aroused by the apparently assimilated Jew who, through conversion and marriage, infiltrated and undermined English society. Also we would need to consider whether the Jew served as a scapegoat in a society not completely at ease with its capitalist ethos and development.[34] Viscount Bryce's analysis of antisemitism in the classical world held true also for Victorian England: 'The Jews were disliked ... on grounds which were rather creditable to them than otherwise. They were active and pushing; they held together and helped one another. Because they kept aloof and refused to acknowledge the gods of the heathen they were accused of hurting the human race.'[35] But the portrayal of Disraeli and Anglo-Jewry in general in the 1870s went beyond these stereotypical denunciations and took on some of the qualities of a more virulent, menacing form of antisemitism – mythic or chimerical qualities purporting to explain major developments or global events.[36]

This form of antisemitism feeds off, and in turn contributes to, a highly charged emotional atmosphere, and that atmosphere was produced in England by the Eastern Question and Disraeli's handling of that international crisis. It is in the context of this atmosphere that the following cartoons and caricatures need to be read.[37] In June 1876, the *Daily News* published a series of alarming exposés of the brutal repression by Turkey of an uprising in its dependency of Bulgaria. Against all evidence, Disraeli first denied and then dismissed (with a typically cynical *bon mot*) Turkey's suppression of the Bulgarian uprising.[38] Aroused, the Nonconformist conscience stimulated one of those periodic Victorian outpourings of national moral indignation. Gladstone reacted to the public agitation and further fuelled it with his famous pamphlet *The Bulgarian Horrors and the Question of the East*. Published in late 1876, it sold 40,000 copies in just three or four days and 200,000 in its first month.[39] When told he had started what amounted to a revolution, Gladstone readily agreed: 'That is just the word for it. But my conscience has nothing to upbraid me with, for it is pre-eminently a Christian revolution.'[40] W. T. Stead, the evangelical pioneer of the new journalism, and John Morley, Gladstone's close associate, rejoiced that the spirit which had once been the driving force behind Cromwellian puritanism was again directing English public opinion.[41] 'Righteous anger struck fire from the heart of England' was how one Liberal described it.[42]

In April 1877, Russia declared war on Turkey. Disraeli's much-divided cabinet formulated a policy based on several considerations: the fall of Turkey would pose a great danger to the Suez Canal and India; the Russian advance threatened the balance of power in Europe; for all its weaknesses, Turkey was capable of reform and could still serve as a viable buffer against Russian aggression. Turkey, therefore, must be maintained and Russia contained. As many historians have stressed, these considerations were diplomatically sound and had considerable tradition behind them.[43] That was the line the Queen and the Tory journal *Judy* (Figure 3, 'Shall It Ever Come to This?') took and it was

3. 'Shall It Ever Come to This?'

one with which *Punch* and many Liberals were in considerable
sympathy.[44] Disraeli's policy unleashed, however, perhaps the most
vituperative attack upon any nineteenth-century Prime Minister,
much of it focusing on his ethnicity.

Nonconformist liberalism faced a two-fold crisis in the 1870s: its
defeat by Disraelian Conservatism before it could attempt the dis-
establishment of the Church of England, and the Eastern Question
which stimulated a great burst of jingoism (a term that entered the
vocabulary during these years) and cast in an unpatriotic light the
pacifism and Little England-ism with which Nonconformity and
radical liberalism were associated. Defeated and disunited, Liberals
and Nonconformists now found a rallying point in an aroused, militant
Christianity passionately opposed to Islamic Turkey. 'This war', thun-
dered the Rev. T. Ashcroft, 'is undoubtedly and emphatically a conflict
of creeds – of Mahomedan and Christian beliefs; a war between the
crescent of Constantinople and the Cross of Calvary – the sword of
Mahomed and the sceptre of the Messiah. Which shall win?'[45] (Figure
4, 'The Shadow on the Cross').[46]

Judging from the language of the pamphlet and periodical literature of the day, many Liberals and Nonconformists were driven by a
fierce hatred of everything Islam and Turkey represented.[47] To give

4. 'The Shadow on the Cross'

just a few examples, Islam was 'a blot on civilization' and so 'it is the duty of all true Liberals to tame, or obliterate [it]';[48] '… as a nation having ruling power [Turkey] should be utterly wiped out from the face of the earth'.[49] For Goldwin Smith, former Regius Professor of Modern History at Oxford and one of the leading publicists of the day, 'Islam … is essentially anti-human'.[50] In short, there were many who agreed with one speaker at a protest meeting in London that 'these Turks must no longer pollute with their filthy and bloody feet this Christian Europe of ours'.[51]

The Bulgarian atrocities unleashed a militant, uncompromising liberalism, which, in the name of moral purity, religious truth and 'civilisation', unselfconsciously denounced another culture as polluted and barbaric.[52] Ethnic and religious prejudices, stereotyping and passionate hatreds now permeated the political vocabulary of Victorian Liberalism. Most ominously, a political atmosphere had been created in which England's identity and self-esteem as a great Christian power were presented in Manichaean terms – a struggle between Christianity and Islam, purity and corruption, progress and stagnation, absolute Good and absolute Evil.[53]

It is in this highly charged setting that we should place late-Victorian perceptions of Disraeli's Jewishness. Why was England supporting Turkey, the mass murderer of Christians and contemplating war with Russia, the protector of Christianity in the Balkans? One answer was that England's foreign policy was being directed and controlled by interests deeply hostile to Christianity. To the *Spectator*, pro-Turkish sentiment, or, as it called it, 'English Mahommedanism', was motivated by a 'deep-seated, subtle, vehement ... hatred of Christianity'.[54]

In his *Portrait of the Anti-Semite*, Sartre argued that 'since the anti-Semite has chosen hatred, we are forced to conclude that it is the state of being in a passion which he cherishes', and he drew attention to the role passionate Manichaeism played in antisemitism.[55] That state of passion, with its hatred of Islam and its Manichaean world view, so evident in the England of the mid-1870s, created an atmosphere potentially very dangerous for Anglo-Jewry, for, as social psychologists have emphasised, prejudice can quickly transfer itself from one 'out group' to another.[56] The transfer of prejudice from Islam, which was seen as an anti-Christian international force, to Jewry, also seen as anti-Christian and international, was facilitated by the widely held conception of the Jew as 'Oriental' or 'Asian'. To the *Echo*, the English Jew, despite his long sojourn in England, 'still remains an Asiatic with a morality which is not that of the West', while to the *Spectator* it was obvious that 'the Jews prefer the East to the West'.[57] It has been argued that medieval antisemitism was closely associated with Christian anti-Islamic sentiment: certainly the anti-Turkish passions unleashed by the Eastern Question now created, or brought to the surface, anti-semitic sentiments.[58]

Thus for Sir J. G. Tollemache Sinclair, MP for Caithness, the motives behind the government's Balkans policy were clear. The pro-Turkish party was 'the anti-Christian party', he wrote, noting that 'it is quite evident that the nucleus of the Turkophile party and its most rabid element consists of the race of Shylock'. The Jews wanted war with Russia, he declared, 'to avenge the real or fancied injuries of the Jewish race'.[59] Repeatedly during the Eastern Crisis Christian charity was contrasted to the Jewish–Oriental lust for revenge. Had England been drawn into the Russo-Turkish conflict, Goldwin Smith argued, 'it would have been in some measure a Jewish war, a war waged with British blood to uphold the objects of Jewish sympathy, or to avenge Jewish wrongs'.[60]

This vision of Disraeli, the archetypical but now empowered Jew, bent on a historic mission of bloody revenge for centuries of persecution, dominated the 1879 biography of Disraeli written by T. P. O'Connor, a popular journalist and MP. Disraeli 'viewed this whole Eastern controversy from the Jew's standpoint', he wrote, 'from the standpoint of the enemy and not the friend of Christians.' The struggle between Islam and Christianity in the Balkans afforded Disraeli an opportunity for revenge on an epic, Old Testament scale, which, of course, he seized:

> And mark the magnificent prospect which unfolded itself before the eyes of Lord Beaconsfield in this controversy! Here he was – the ruler of a great Christian empire – to some extent the arbiter of the destinies of all the Christian countries of Europe! Would not the shame of Israel be indeed blotted out, and its glory reach a sublimer height than it had ever touched even in its stupendous past, if in the nineteenth century of Christendom – this nineteenth century of Jewish persecution, Jewish degradation, Jewish humiliation by Christians – a single Jew could mould the whole policy of Christendom to Jewish aims, could make it friendly to the friends and hostile to the foes of Judaea! And would not this magnificent triumph be the sublimer to the mind of Lord Beaconsfield if it could be carried out under the guise of serving the interest of the Christians themselves?[61]

The Eastern Question, O'Connor argued, enabled Disraeli to practise the deceit and implement the policies for which his entire career was preparation. 'To deceive mankind' was the 'sublime good which he [Disraeli] set for himself in his youth. And thus his position as English Premier in this Russo-Turkish war offered to him an opportunity for attaining a more sublime triumph for his sympathies and antipathies as a Jew, and his longings as a man, than had ever yet presented itself.'[62]

O'Connor's almost apocalyptic vision of Disraeli's historic mission and hidden plans and his anger and frustration at Disraeli's skilful deceit in presenting them as English, not Jewish, policy, thus hoodwinking an honest if naïve nation, drove him to a pitch of frenzy. It reached its height when he contemplated the enthusiasm of the London crowd on Disraeli's return from the Congress of Berlin and Disraeli's boast that he had achieved 'Peace with Honour'. His anger was expressed in the staccato of hatred. Disraeli's policy, he wrote, 'represented the triumph, not of England, not of an English policy, not of an Englishman. It was a triumph of Judaea, a Jewish policy, a Jew. The Hebrew who drove through those crowds to Downing Street, was dragging the whole of Christendom behind the Juggernaut car over the rights of the Turkish Christians, of which he was the charioteer.' It was this type of imagery, this surrender, by a Liberal, of reason and measured analysis to emotion and prejudice, this eagerness to see in the Jew only the wrathful Shylock driven by revenge and a hatred of Christianity, that made the atmosphere of the time so tense for Anglo-Jewry. (Of course O'Connor claimed that he had no patience with 'vulgar bigotry myself nor any desire to excite it in others'.)[63]

Disraeli's *Realpolitik*, in combination with his well-known love of the East, helped to fuel the Manichaean thinking and paranoia of radical Liberals and Nonconformists, encouraging them to place a new emphasis on Disraeli as an alien and a Jew. It was an emphasis on, and an interpretation of, his Jewishness that cast him as unpatriotic and disloyal, as a man driven by tribal interests, rather than by the interests of the nation. To E. A. Freeman, writing in the *Contemporary Review*: 'The whole talk of Lord Beaconsfield, the slandering of Servia, the bragging against Russia, is the talk of an Asiatic. Throughout the East the Jew and the Turk are banded together against the European, and Lord Beaconsfield, as a man of the East, naturally takes the Asiatic side.' Freeman stressed that 'Jewish influence, as a rule, means Turkish influence'.[64] It was a warning he drove home with even greater force in his *Ottoman Power in Europe* (1877). In considerable agitation, Freeman wrote that 'we cannot sacrifice our people, the people of Aryan and Christian Europe, to the [that is, Disraeli's] most genuine belief in an Asian mystery'. Furthermore, he observed, 'We cannot have England nor Europe governed by a Hebrew policy'. Since 'blood is stronger than water ... Hebrew rule is sure to lead to Hebrew policy. Throughout Europe ... the Jew is the friend of the Turk and the enemy of the Christian.'[65] Freeman's linear logic could hardly be missed for it had the clarity of a scientific formula: Disraeli was a Jew. Therefore his policy was Jewish. Therefore his policy was anti-Christian. It was a formula that relied on stereotypes of ancient, ineradicable, tribal grudges and it placed the Jew well outside the boundaries of acceptable or patriotic nonconformity.

It was a formula that became something of a Liberal mantra in these years. 'Certainly as long as Lord Beaconsfield is Prime Minister we are not safe', wrote Henry Parry Liddon, Canon of St Paul's and

Gladstone's close associate. 'His one positive passion is that of upholding Asiatics against Europeans – non-Christian Asiatics', he emphasised, 'against Christian Europeans.'[66] Similarly the *Church Times* reduced Disraeli's foreign policy to the same formulaic simplicity: 'The Jew Premier sympathizes with the Turks because they are neither Europeans nor Christians.'[67] And W. T. Stead declared in his *Northern Echo*, 'The policy of Lord Beaconsfield in the East has practically amounted to a declaration of "Death to the Christians"'.[68] To the author of *The Beaconsfield Policy: An Address* (1878), that policy had a simple explanation: 'England's Prime Minister is a Jew; and his mind is *infected* with the ideas of his race.'[69] With one stroke Disraeli's foreign policy was damned as both pathological and pathogenic. The broad support within the Tory party (and indeed among a wide spectrum of Liberals) for Disraeli's foreign policy, to say nothing of the support from the Throne, could thus be brushed aside, although, as we shall see, reasons for that support were given.[70] A classic scapegoat situation had been created. This type of reasoning and the heated passions and equally heated rhetoric of the age must be kept in mind when examining the pictorial representations of Disraeli's Jewishness at the height of his ministry.

Throughout his long career Disraeli had been characterised, and sometimes condemned, as foreign or exotic and not by his enemies alone. In addition, his own writings and romance with the East, as well as his appearance, lent credence to the characterisation. But it was not an aspect of Disraeli that Liberals had taken great pains to exploit. Indeed, before he became Prime Minister in 1874, the opposition press apparently found it quite appropriate to represent him as the quintessential Englishman. In *Fun*, for example, he was portrayed (and in a straightforward rather than satirical manner) as a gamekeeper, stalwart working-man and cricketer (Figure 5, 'Conservative Hopes'; Figure 6, 'The New Friend of the Working-Man'; Figure 7, 'Conservative Bowlers').[71] With rare exceptions Disraeli's Jewishness was not a major issue in the cartoon literature prior to 1874. If portrayed at all, it was implied rather than categorically stated. His dark curly hair and 'exotic' looks could just as easily pass in most of the cartoons as vaguely Byronic or 'Mediterranean' as explicitly Jewish, and so they meshed nicely with Disraeli's own romantic view of himself.[72]

This pictorial image of Disraeli as the archetypical Englishman was carefully maintained by the Tory journal *Judy* throughout the 1870s. The opposition press, however, tended to strip him of authentic English characteristics and now explicitly represented him as an alien Jew.[73] A

5. 'Conservative Hopes'   6. 'The New Friend of the Working-
                                                          Man'

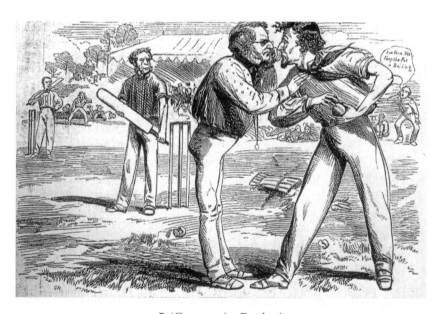

7. 'Conservative Bowlers'

common graphic symbol of the Jew in the nineteenth century was the old clothes man wearing three hats (see Figure 8, 'The Jew'; Figure 9, 'Mrs. London and Her Little Family of Suburbs taking a Holiday'). It instantly identified the Jew as a street pedlar, a foreigner with

8. 'The Jew'

9. 'Mrs. London and her Little Family of Suburbs taking a Holiday'

strange habits and a stranger appearance.[74] And that is the way Disraeli was now portrayed (see Figure 10, 'The Man in the Street'; Figure 11, 'Fancy Portrait of Dizzy as the Bravo of St. Stephen's'; Figure 12 (page 122 below), 'Trying It On. A Threehatrical Experiment'; Figure 24 (page 131 below), 'Another Assyrian Discovery').[75] Of course, Disraeli's own earlier writings had fixed him in many minds as a Jew, and, as one observer put it, he had deliberately crowned himself with 'a hazy halo of Hebraisms'.[76] But if at one stage in his career Disraeli had gone out of his way to emphasise his Jewish origins and his interest in the Near East, the image he had hoped to impart was that of a polished Anglo-Sephardi elder statesman, a Sidonia or an Alroy. Figure 10, on the other hand, cast him in quite another, certainly less glamorous light. In the eyes of the proprietor of the *Standard*, Disraeli was nothing more than a low, despicable 'Houndsditch Jew'.[77] Figure 11 acknowledged the dashing cloak-and-dagger side of Disraeli's character and his rapier-like sarcastic wit, but, with the three hats, it also reduced him to the level of a street Jew, and that image was synonymous in the popular mind with cunning, deceit and an alien, parasitical presence in England. It was a representation of Disraeli the Jew that dramatically, graphically and instantly made him 'un-English'.

THE MAN IN THE STREET.

APPILY no one in society advocates the opening of Galleries or Museums on a Sunday. That is not good "form." Going to the Zoo is another matter altogether. That belongs to the privileged classes, because it is necessary to have a Fellow's ticket to get in, and that is very different from admission by payment at the door, which would end in our meeting a crowd of nobodies in the Gardens. That would be distinctly a profanation of the Day —and the place. Should money ever be taken, I hope that at least appearances will be saved— that it will be collected in plates, or, better still, in embroidered bags!

10. 'The Man in the Street'

11. 'Fancy Portrait of Dizzy as the Bravo of St. Stephen's' (by courtesy of the National Portrait Gallery, London)

It is surely significant that Disraeli once observed that there was one word that 'baffles discussion more than any other in our language'. That word was 'un-English'.[78] Disraeli, of course, rarely confessed himself baffled by anything, least of all, one would think, the ability, as a novelist and noted epigrammatic wit, to discuss words and their meanings! That Disraeli singled out this word is revealing, indeed, for (unlike 'unconstitutional', his choice of the second most baffling word) 'un-English' was hardly part and parcel of the vocabulary or daily discourse of the world of Victorian politics. But it *was* a word that had serious connotations, for it did not mean 'exotic', or 'flamboyant', or Byronically 'romantic', or even 'unprincipled' or 'devious' – all epithets that had been applied to him throughout his long career, nor did it mean that his statesmanship and vision were so far-reaching that they were difficult for straightforward, plain-thinking Englishmen to decipher. 'Un-English' or 'alien' or 'foreign', as flung at Disraeli in the 1870s, coupled with his Jewish image in cartoons of the period, conveyed a far darker, more sinister meaning. It is little wonder that, despite his reputation as the Sphinx, the man of taciturn and impenetrable demeanor, Disraeli was apparently stung. For the charge of being 'un-English' carried the pointed and specific accusation that he was '*anti*-English'.[79]

'Un-English' also conveyed the charge that he was a crypto-Jew. Like the eponymous hero of his early novel *Vivien Grey*, Disraeli, as Prime Minister, after some 40 years on the public stage, faced a barrage of cries, 'No stranger! No stranger!' and 'seditious stranger'.[80] At least one contemporary interpreted those cries as 'No Jew! No Jew!' and 'Seditious Jew'.[81] Even the hoary image of the wandering Jew was employed. Sometimes the wandering Jew motif was explicit: the anonymous pamphlet *Beaconsfield: A Mock-Heroic Poem and Political Satire* (1878), for example, called Disraeli 'our wandering Jew', 'sprung from a race of migratory Jews'.[82] Sometimes the image was implicit, such as when T. Wemyss Reid, the popular biographer, called Disraeli 'an "outsider" in our social and public affairs ... A stranger and a sojourner in this land of his birth and his adoption, this Egypt of which he has taken possession in the name of his brethren of Judea', or when Lord Bryce commented that Disraeli was 'unlike the Englishmen his lot was cast among' – as if it was just the arbitrary throw of the dice, chance, that saw Disraeli in England![83] Lord Bryce's description is typical of the time: Disraeli, he paradoxically wrote, was 'born in a foreign country' and raised 'amid a people for whose ideas and habits he has no sympathy and little respect'. For J. A. Froude, who was more sympathetic, Disraeli 'was a Jew in his heart ... In his real nature he remained a Jew', for 'he was English only by adoption'. It was a theme Froude chose to hammer home again and again: Disraeli 'was a Hebrew to the heart of him'. 'At heart he was a Hebrew to the end, and of all his triumphs perhaps the most satisfying was the sense that a member of that despised race had made himself master of the fleets and armies of the proudest of Christian nations.'[84] 'For the past six years we have had an Asiatic ruler', declared E. A. Freeman in 1880. 'The word "Jew" seems to be forbidden and I have no wish to insist on it, if it grates on the ear of any man of Hebrew descent who has really turned European. But the point is that Lord Beaconsfield has never turned European, that he remains as purely Asiatic as if he had never left Ur or the Chaldees.'[85] The pamphleteer who condemned the Prime Minister for being a 'sham Christian and a sham Englishman' was simply giving expression to a widely held belief.[86] Even some of his cabinet colleagues referred mockingly to his Jewishness and thought he was not a real 'British minister'.[87]

Radical liberals even saw Disraeli's elevation of Queen Victoria to Empress of India (Figure 12, 'Trying It On. A Threehatrical Experiment'; Figure 13, Tenniel's famous 'New Crowns for Old Ones!') as an 'oriental', specifically Jewish, certainly un-English act.[88] 'Nothing can

12. 'Trying It On. A Threehatrical
Experiment'

13. 'New Crowns for Old Ones!'

be more truly Semetic [*sic*] in its character', wrote T. Wemyss Reid in his *Politicians of To-day* (1880), 'than the instinct which leads Lord Beaconsfield to treat the Queen with that humble and almost abject deference which, during the present century at least, no other English minister has shown towards the occupant of the throne.'[89] In Figure 12 Disraeli is shown as a milliner and the poster on the wall indicates that 'Dizzy's Crown and Coronet Establishment' is Jewish. Its trademark is a Jewish pedlar with hats piled on his head. By piling crowns on Victoria's head, Disraeli is making the British monarch as absurdly foreign, as ridiculously grotesque as the figure in the poster. Tenniel's famous cartoon in *Punch* (Figure 13) also portrays the elevation of Queen Victoria as un-English, this time by casting Disraeli in the role of Aladdin, whose beguiling charm (perhaps aided by some kabbalistic magic, as indicated by the markings on Disraeli's/Aladdin's box and on the hem of his robe) has induced the Queen to surrender her traditional and modest (befitting a liberal democracy) English crown for the far more flashy and ornate Indian one. The expression on Disraeli's face suggests trickery.

In their portrayal of Disraeli as Jew, cartoonists stressed what they took to be typically 'Semitic' features. Above all, that meant his nose, for the 'Semitic' nose, in often grotesquely caricatured form, was a standard marker of Jewishness in Victorian cartoons (Figure 14, 'Moses and Noses'; Figure 15, 'Rattletrap Rhymes').[90] Of course, the nose was a favourite target of political cartoonists then, as it is now, and perhaps one should not make too much of the way Disraeli's nose featured so prominently, literally, in the cartoons of the day. Gladstone's nose, an equally strong one, was also caricatured by the comic journals (Figure 16, 'John Bull In A Fix; Figure 17, 'The Rival Sandwiches'; see also Figure 25 (page 131 below), the frontispiece of Vol. 20 of *Fun*).[91] But two points need to be made. First, although the exaggerated nose was a stock-in-trade of caricaturists whether depicting Gentiles or Jews, for the former there was no sinister connotation, nor sub-text of ethnic slur. The large Gentile nose was used for comic effect, although it might also suggest a predatory or aggressive nature. But for the latter, it always connoted a separate, marked race. It was a badge, an indication of a tribal otherness that separated Jews from the native citizens among whom they dwelt. It marked them as alien. Second, and connected with this, Disraeli's nose was often caricatured to such a grotesque degree that it threatened to become the entire physiognomy, the whole man. (In fact photographs of Disraeli suggest a strong rather than a particularly 'Semitic' nose (Figure 18 (page 125 below).)[92] In this sense,

14. 'Moses and Noses'

15. 'Rattletrap Rhymes'

16. 'John Bull In A Fix'

17. 'The Rival Sandwiches'

18. 'Benjamin Disraeli 1st Earl Beaconsfield, 1804–1881' (by courtesy of the National Portrait Gallery, London)

caricatures of Disraeli confirm Kris's general theory of caricatures: by destroying any natural harmony in the features, they tend to degrade the subject. In effect they de-humanise the individual. Thus *Fun* chose to present Disraeli's nose from every perspective in order to distort it and to make Disraeli appear as grotesque as possible (Figure 19, 'The Last Sensation'; Figure 20, 'Waiting for the Performance'; Figure 24 (page 131 below), 'Another Assyrian Discovery').[93] When *Fun* chose to portray Disraeli as the treasonous Guy Fawkes, it was his nose to which his opponent John Bright was putting the finishing touches, and while the portrayal of Disraeli as a rogue elephant was excellent political capital, giving him an elephantine nose had an extra dimension that gave the cartoon a more complex meaning (Figure 21, 'The Great Guy of the Season'; Figure 22, 'The Great Conservative "Rogue" Elephant').[94]

At this stage it is important to note that cartoons of Disraeli (like most antisemitic literature in mid- and late-Victorian England) were free of any suggestion or even hint of the scientific racism directed in this period against the Irish, who were consistently seen as simian, as bestial monsters or as missing links.[95] Compared to the routine savaging of the Irish in Victorian cartoons, the portrayal of Disraeli (and indeed of Jews generally) might be seen as relatively mild. But if Disraeli, and by extension Anglo-Jewry, were not cast in the role of apes, missing links or the sad products of arrested development or degeneration,

19. 'The Last Sensation'   20. 'Waiting for the Performance'

they were represented in a manner that was equally dangerous, both politically and socially – that of anti-Christians.

In Figure 23 ('England's Pride and Glory') Disraeli, reduced to his essential alien Jewishness as 'Ben JuJu', belligerently turns on the backbone of England, the working man, whom he contemptuously dismisses in the name of his true master, Turkey, as simply 'A lot of Christian rubbish'.[96] The cartoon claims to unmask Disraeli, revealing his foreign policy, and, indeed, his inner motives, for what they were – aggressively anti-English and anti-Christian. The theme is continued in a cartoon (see Figure 2) marking the Liberal attack on Disraeli's administration. Gladstone, as Portia, concedes to Disraeli the right not to dissolve Parliament but in so doing warns him, 'if thou dost shed/ One drop more of Christian blood'. Portia's phrase, coming from Gladstone's lips, draws on the blood-libel imagery of medieval anti-semitism, while that imagery is further conveyed, very powerfully, in the menacing figure of Disraeli as Shylock.[97] The drawn knife ready to take its pound of flesh, the murderous intent, the lust for some warped version of Old Testament revenge, all speak to Disraeli's allegedly real nature. As a Jew he shares with Shylock tribal kinship and a common desire to seek revenge (in Disraeli's case on Eastern Orthodox Christians) and to take his pound of flesh from helpless Christians (his cavalier dismissal of the Bulgarian atrocities and his willingness to risk

21. 'The Great Guy of the Season'   22. 'The Great Conservative "Rogue" Elephant'

23. 'England's Pride
and Glory'

war with Russia – a war which would be fought, it was argued, with
British, Christian blood for Jewish benefit). According to the *Echo*, Lord
Beaconsfield was 'Asiatic' and 'with his strong sympathies for everything Asiatic, would use the blood and treasure of Englishmen' for his
own ends.[98] 'In the mind of Disraeli', declared the *Englishman* in 1876,
'revenge is as strong a passion as it was in Shylock.'[99]

In old age Disraeli's posture was stooped and thus probably bore
some resemblance to the stage Jew.[100] Contemporaries thought so, and
to one:

> Beaconsfield is Shylock entering on the great judgment-scene,
> when triumphing in the consciousness of suppressed power,
> presents us with some prototype (not wishing to be personal),
> as far as external action is concerned, in his [Disraeli's] having
> the same stooping, crouching gait, with the same furtive glances
> of downcast eyes, the same flashes, ever and anon, denoting
> some concealed, fixed purpose.[101]

To the anonymous author of *Peace or War? An Indictment of the
Policy of the Government* (1877), Disraeli was 'our modern Shylock'.[102]

When Disraeli, as Prime Minister, was portrayed as Shylock, it carried a *very* different connotation than it did earlier (Figure 1). Now he is in control of affairs; his hitherto 'suppressed power' is unleashed and his hitherto 'concealed, fixed purpose' now exposed for the horror that it is! In unmasking Disraeli, the cartoon dramatically plays on old fears and draws on old stereotypes to emphasise the purportedly essential, immutable nature of the Jew as an outsider working with a formidable intensity of purpose toward ends antithetical to the health and welfare of the nation as a whole.[103]

When Shylock was used in this way, the effect was both powerful and damaging, for in essence it both represented and condemned Disraeli, the Jew, as the 'other'. It was a representation that was often used in the most vicious manner in cartoons or what might more appropriately be called iconographic prints of the day. In his *Political Prints of the Age of Hogarth*, Herbert Atherton makes a distinction between the iconographic print and the caricature. The latter, he argues, tends to be highly personal or subjective, reflecting the vision and views of the artist (although it may also reflect wider views), while the iconographic print 'satirizes a particular individual or concept by associating him (or it) with appropriate symbols and stereotypes'.[104] The symbols and stereotypes employed to convey Disraeli's Jewishness draw, consciously or unconsciously, on the medieval arsenal of antisemitic mythology, a tribute to their longevity. In 'The Modern Hep! Hep! Hep!', a perceptive analysis of the antisemitism of the 1870s, George Eliot wrote that several 'liberal gentlemen' had, in becoming 'anti-judaic advocates', regressed to 'mediaeval types of thinking'.[105]

The same type of medieval thought and imagery are evident in other cartoons. In Figures 24 and 25 ('Another Assyrian Discovery' and 'Dizzy's Mixture', page 131 below) Disraeli is grotesquely caricatured but, more importantly, he is associated with symbols and stereotypical acts that come straight from medieval antisemitism. In Figure 24 the three-hatted 'High Priest Ben-Dizzy', with eyes up-lifted to his God and with knife raised high, is about to sacrifice England, in an act of ritual murder, on a Near Eastern altar. The specific political event that inspired the cartoon – parliamentary dissolution – is insignificant compared to its conscious symbolic and iconographic choices.[106] Similarly in Figure 25, the medieval blood-libel, the myth that Jews murdered Christians to obtain their blood for ritual purposes, is graphically resurrected. Disraeli, a demented harlequin, is administering a harmful, possibly lethal, portion of his mixture to an alarmed baby (Britannia). The horrified mother, Gladstone, discovers him in the act but since Disraeli is in power it might be too late to save her baby.[107] The symbolism is clear – Disraeli, for evil purposes of his own, is about to drug or destroy the body politic. In this cartoon Disraeli as harlequin is anything but a comic or clownish character. His whole bearing and demeanour are deranged, evil and pathological. It is a classic portrayal of the fears concerning the 'other', and it is worth noting that in some respects it is a satanic portrayal. In medieval art the devil was often depicted playing the comic fool.[108]

Disraeli as an evil, noxious figure was also conveyed in other ways in the cartoons of the day. A bestiary of Gladstone would not have been terribly interesting, but Disraeli was portrayed as various unwholesome, loathsome, unclean creatures: as a serpent in the Garden of Eden (Figure 26); as a toad to Gladstone's bull (Figure 27, 'The Great Conservative Re-Action'); as a dragon (Figure 28 (page 132 below), 'Just Before The Battle').[109]

Much more significant, however, is the frequency with which Disraeli was portrayed as the devil. In the anonymous *Bits of Beaconsfield: A New Series of Disraeli's Curiosities of Literature. Illustrated* (1881), he was Lucifer ejected from heaven (Figure 29, page 133 below).[110] In the pages of *Fun* he was the devil. On numerous occasions, the devil was included in a cartoon of Disraeli.[111] He was also represented as Hecate, the 'queen of witches, and high priestess of the occult' (Figure 30, page 134 below), and as a goat, the devil's close associate (Figures 31 and 32, page 134).[112] It is interesting to note that Disraeli's beard, a goatee, seemed to embarrass *Judy*, which generally merged it so subtly into his necktie that it was lost, and correspondingly to delight *Fun*, which gave it great emphasis. The association of Jews with the devil was a staple of pre-modern antisemitism, and its resurrection and repeated application to the Prime Minister is one of the most striking and appalling elements in the attack on Disraeli's Jewishness.[113] E. A. Freeman boasted to Lord Bryce that he was engaged in a struggle 'against the devil and his angels, Jewish and Turkish', insisting that there could be 'no peace' in England 'with Jews, Turks ... liars, and the whole synagogue of Satan ... [at] Hughenden [Disraeli's country house]'.[114]

Freeman appears to have been swept up in the medieval Christian vision of the Jews as the devil's agents: 'the preservation of the Jews as a separate people, he speculated, apparently in all seriousness, 'might be as an instrument of Satan to buffet all other people'. He also wrote to Bryce about 'the Jews' firm allegiances to the devil'.[115] A contemporary broadside made explicit the link between Disraeli and the devil:

24. 'Another Assyrian Discovery'

25. 'Dizzy's Mixture'

26. 'Disraeli in Garden of Eden:
Disraeli as Serpent'

27. 'The Great Conservative
Re-Action'

And how do you think the devil look'd?
Or black, or cruel, or sinister?
Not at all, not at all, but his shoulder was crook'd
And his head it was bald, and his nose it was hook'd
He look'd like a Cabinet Minister![116]

JUST BEFORE THE BATTLE.

28. 'Just before the Battle'

One can only speculate on how many people who came to the cartoons associating Disraeli with the devil had already been exposed to the image through the literature of the period.

Significantly, the only time Disraeli publicly displayed anger at the imagery employed against him during the Eastern Crisis occurred in July 1878, when Gladstone's alleged description of him as a dangerous and even devilish character provoked an acerbic squabble, during which Disraeli angrily claimed that one of Gladstone's close associates had called him 'Mephistopheles' and that Gladstone had 'sanctioned the propriety of the scarcely complimentary appellation'[117] (Figure 33 (page 135 below), 'The Polite Letter Writer').[118] Catherine, Gladstone's antisemitic wife, safely back home and far away from the London of Disraeli's triumphant return from the Congress of Berlin, employed the foetid imagery of the devil when she wrote: 'I feel as if out of d'Izzy's atmosphere, and the air is so fresh and so sweet.'[119] Gladstone's niece, Lady Lucy Cavendish, also used diabolic imagery to describe Disraeli. She wrote at this time that the Prime Minister looked 'more horribly like a fiend than ever, green, with a glare in his eye'.[120] W. T. Stead was not really stretching for the sensational phrase characteristic of his 'new journalism' when he wrote that the Liberals entered the 1880 general election 'feeling that Lord Beaconsfield was the most authentic

"No doubt you did right to dissemble your love;
But—*why* did you *kick* us downstairs?"

"He falls like Lucifer,
Never to hope again."
Henry viii.

"Hie thee to hell for shame, and leave the world,
Thou cacodæmon! there thy kingdom is."

29. Disraeli as Lucifer
ejected from heaven

incarnation of the Evil One that had ever come within striking range'.[121] He was using imagery distressingly common to the day – imagery applied, I think, to no other statesman. Apparently Disraeli thought so!

Seemingly traditional images can, of course, take on new import. For example, Disraeli had frequently been represented over the course of his long career as a conjurer or wizard, an image that indicated both admiration of his political skill and imagination as well as criticism of his want of that most Victorian characteristic, moral earnestness. Now, in the emotional climate of the Eastern Question, the image of wizard was employed to suggest how Christian England had mysteriously come under the influence of a Jew and offered as an explanation, as Freeman put it, of why the cabinet had caved in to the 'semitic instinct', and so had become 'the Jew Government'.[122] Why had England followed the empty jingoistic rhetoric of a foreign adventurer? One explanation was that Disraeli had bewitched the nation, so mesmerising it that normal political values were now suspended. I am not for a moment suggesting that this was meant literally, but the

30. 'Preparing the Draft'

31. 'Capricornus, the Goat'

32. Disraeli in railway carriage

rhetoric reveals the longevity of folkloric images and an affinity with past imagery as well as a remarkable willingness to incorporate it into the politics of the day.[123] The images of wizard and conjurer take on a special import for they played on misconceptions of Jewish magic. Irrational old fears lingered on in a new form, testimonies to the tenacity of stereotyping (Figure 34, 'The New Alchemy').[124]

The *Spectator* drew its readers' attention to the Prime Minister, 'this great Israelite magician [who] appears and with his wand transforms the whole political horizon', who has 'a half-belief in the cabalistic sorcery, with all its wild spiritual machinery'. It mused: 'What is the strange talisman by which Lord Beaconsfield achieves these wonders – by which he metamorphoses typical Englishmen till they become the most plastic of all materials …?'[125] In Carlyle's jaundiced view, Disraeli was 'a superlative Hebrew conjurer, spellbinding all the great Lords, great parties, great interests of England'.[126] Is England 'bewitched?', asked a broadsheet poem in 1877, 'Has this Jew juggler clean put out her eyes/That she may dance complaisant to his piping?'.[127] Disraeli, the alien Jew, had bewitched and enslaved England

33. 'The Polite Letter Writer'

and diverted her from her traditional course just as, in Anthony Trollope's *The Prime Minister* (1876), Ferdinand Lopez, another mysterious 'evil genius', also of similar Jewish origin, had seduced the gullible Emily away from her true Saxon love, Arthur Fletcher. The image of the pathogenic Jewish sorcerer later found its most extreme expression in Svengali in George Du Maurier's *Trilby*, but already in the 1870s it was present in representations of Disraeli.

My reading of the image of Disraeli as magician and mountebank, not only in the pages of *Punch* and *Fun* and other comic journals but also in pamphlet literature and private correspondence, suggests that far from being an innocent, frivolous or casually satirical rhetorical device, it is one with far more sinister connotations. I certainly agree with Michael Ragussis's important observation that the portrayal of Disraeli as actor, showman, will-o'-the-wisp, chameleon, acrobat and

34. 'The New Alchemy'

circus entertainer must be related to 'the antisemitic stereotype of the crypto-Jew who hid behind the mask of Christianity to subvert the culture of Christian' Europe.[128]

The iconographic prints and cartoons I have been discussing, with their sub-texts of a demented, murderous Prime Minister, a devil and a necromancer, need to be placed in the context of the cartoon conventions of the day.[129] Compared to the eighteenth and early nineteenth centuries, Victorian political cartoons were generally polite. The Tory press, for example, hammered away at Gladstone, caricaturing what it saw as his irrational, emotional, demagogic side. (See, for example, Figure 35, 'Abuse-itis' and Figure 36, 'Policy *Versus* Passion'.)[130] But, however vicious, the press always left him his essential humanity. The same cannot be said for representations of Disraeli, who no doubt would have disagreed heartily with *Fun*'s self-analysis when, in 1880, it made the claim for its political cartoons 'that, if they sting, there is no venom in the wound; that, if they cut, the lash leaves no scar', for 'the fair limits of caricature are never exceeded'.[131]

In a period of intense re-evaluation of the place of both patriotism and liberalism in the national identity, the opposition press chose to represent – and damn – Disraeli as a Jew. There is perhaps nothing particularly surprising about this – any more surprising than that Gladstone would be portrayed as a Scot or, later on, Lloyd George as a Welshman.[132] The question, of course, is what sort of Jew, what ethnic characteristics and generalisations were to be emphasised. It is always hazardous to speculate on the 'perlocutionary act' – the actual impact of communication upon an audience.[133] But, if we place ourselves in, say, the role of a reader of *Fun*, what picture of Disraeli, 'the Jew' would we have? I am suggesting it would hardly be a flattering one. The Disraeli of the cartoons and caricatures I have discussed personifies the Jew as anti-Christ as well as anti-Christian. He is a vengeful schemer, ritual murderer, loathsome and dangerous alien, and traitor to England's moral and political traditions and destiny.[134] The iconography and symbolism employed to convey this message of the pathological Jew, drawing as it did on certain traditions, support the general observation of James Parkes (who pioneered the study of antisemitism in England): 'Because so much [prejudice] ... stems from a bygone age, it helps also to remind us that humanity has a long memory, and that men [even rational Victorians] may be heirs to ancient enmities of whose origins they are themselves unaware.'[135] The cartoons suggest that, at one level, as one anthropologist has written, 'antisemitism, like all aspects of racialism, is a folkloric attitude'.[136]

35. 'Abuse-itis'

36. 'Policy *Versus* Passion'

The literary and pictorial evidence I have presented can hardly be dismissed as the rantings and ravings of a lunatic fringe. *Fun* was an important comic journal with a wide circulation; Bryce, Goldwin Smith, Freeman, O'Connor and others who have been cited in this essay were hardly inconsequential Victorians, just as the *Spectator*, *Nineteenth Century* and *Fortnightly Review*, all of which published articles highly critical of Jews, were hardly trivial journals. I emphasise this point because the significance of antisemitism in modern English history has been questioned in the past decade. David Cannadine has argued that the history of Anglo-Jewry is the 'history of a successful minority'. Ever since 'Anglo-Jewry's return to Britain on the eve of the Restoration, its history has been one of sustained economic progress and successful political assimilation'.[137] Cannadine sees Disraeli as a symbol of this progress and of the pluralistic spirit of the age; unlike America, he stresses, England elected a born-Jew to its top political position. He tends to dismiss English antisemitism as relatively trivial; there is, after all, 'a clear distinction', he rightly points out, 'between the anti-Semitism of the golf club and the gas chamber'.[138]

This interpretation, with its emphasis on the widespread political and social acceptance of Jews, on the triviality of English antisemitism and on the ultimate success of Disraeli is shared by W. D. Rubinstein. In his *History of the Jews in the English-Speaking World: Great Britain* (1996), Rubinstein calls to task the 'younger school' of (mainly twentieth-century) Anglo-Jewish historians, such as David Cesarani and Tony Kushner, who reject the 'triumphalism' of the doyen of Anglo-Jewish historians Cecil Roth and who emphasise the exclusivity of late-Victorian and twentieth-century concepts of 'Englishness' and the attendant distrust and dislike of 'aliens'.[139] Rubinstein indicts this school for competing to uncover 'the most insidious examples of British anti-semitism', for 'systematic exaggeration of both the volume and significance of modern British antisemitism' and for 'insensitivity to ... the explicit and implicit ways in which the British political and cultural system has almost invariably worked to marginalise extremists and anti-semites'. 'The most salient and pertinent fact of the history of the Jewish people in modern Britain', Rubinstein asserts, 'is that, from any comparative perspective, antisemitism was minimal and almost always marginalised to the fringes of society' and lacked 'virtually any element of brutality and tragedy known on the continent'.[140]

In some respects Rubinstein is correct: obviously it is important to balance any analysis of Victorian antisemitism with the strong current of philosemitism that was part of the culture. Without doubt there

was in Victorian society a tradition of fair play, decency and toleration, which, together with constitutional and legal gains, provided, as
Rubinstein says, 'a powerful bulwark against whatever antisemitism
there was in Britain'.[141] Antisemitism in late-Victorian England was,
most happily, different from that in the France of the anti-*Dreyfusards*
and the Germany of Stöcker and the Anti-Semitic League. As Israel
Finestein has pointed out, 'No clerical party arose [in Victorian Britain],
as in France, to disturb Jewish equanimity. No *volk*-type xenophobic
romanticism, as in Germany, stirred their peace of mind.'[142] Any
discussion of English antisemitism that ignores the wider Continental
context runs the danger of being shrill and overwrought – of so accentuating the negative that the positive is all but eliminated.[143]

That said, it must also be stressed that comparisons can be odious:
that English Jews suffered almost no violence and no loss of civil or
political rights hardly invalidates the study of late-Victorian antisemitism.[144] Anglo-Jewry in the 1870s would, I think, have been more
than a little surprised at Rubinstein's analysis, especially his astound-
ing contention that the 'extraordinary success of Disraeli in politics
... can be seen as representing the virtual full acceptance of Anglo-
Jewry in the terms it wished, a legitimate non-conformist minority,
*identical in status and acceptance with Protestant groups, like the Quakers
and Baptists*'.[145] Rightly or wrongly, English Jews in the 1870s saw the
seemingly acceptable public expression of antisemitism as the thin end
of a familar wedge – first names and then sticks and stones leading to
broken bones. In 1880, the educationalist Philip Magnus reviewed for
the *Jewish Chronicle* several recent *Spectator* articles that claimed,
among other things, that 'the Jews in every country form a State within
a State, intent, first of all, on advancing their own interests'. Was
he paranoid to worry that these articles, appearing as they did in a
mainstream, reputable journal, might 'encourage those abroad to
think that there existed a party in England holding views which might
afford some shadow of justification to the social persecutions of the
Jews in Germany'?[146] Was the *Jewish World* making a mountain out of
a mole hill when, reporting on antisemitism in Germany, it nervously
drew attention to 'the malevolent spirit in which Jews are spoken of
[at home] by several of our Liberal and Radical contemporaries' and
predicted 'an impending fanatical attack upon the Jews', driven by
'immediate political enmity and revived theological hatred'?[147] Was
the generally more restrained *Jewish Chronicle* guilty of journalistic
exaggeration in 1878 when it spoke of the 'Jew-revilers' and 'Jew-
assailants' at work in England and reflected on how 'these enemies of

to-day were the friends of yesterday'?[148] Was the *Jewish Chronicle* guilty of irresponsible journalism when it came close to accusing Goldwin Smith of being 'an instigator to murder', so enflaming passions as to incite a possible pogrom, and when it wrote that if English anti-semitism had not yet assumed the force it possessed in Germany, it was 'small thanks to Professor Goldwin Smith and his followers' or to 'the uniform depreciation of all that is Jewish on the part of certain journals which represent the opinions of the Professor and his friends'?[149] Or when, in an editorial entitled 'Epidemic Fanaticism', it denounced Freeman's writings as 'pregnant with fanaticism', serving to pit 'race against race, Aryan against Semite'?[150] Its deep concern is surely under-standable and justified when a journal of the *Spectator*'s standing felt free to imply that the Jews themselves were to blame for antisemitism on the Continent and then went on to state, baldly, that 'in England their conduct in reference to Turkey has undoubtedly modified the opinion of all Liberals, and will affect their future' there.[151] Anglo-Jewry could not take such an ominous forecast lightly. While possibly they derived some comfort from the fact that they were not living in France or Germany, Russia or Rumania, that does not alter the fact that they felt alarmed by the recent 'expressibility' of prejudice in England.[152]

Cartoons and caricatures were an integral and important compo-nent of that 'expressibility'. Gladstone characterised political cartoons as a 'department of warfare' but felt that, compared to the cartoons of the early nineteenth century, they had became much more polite and so were 'always pleasing'.[153] Disraeli would surely have begged to differ, for his Jewish heritage provoked feelings and led to cartoon images that, far from being humorous or 'pleasing', had a great deal of venom to them. In targeting Disraeli they focused and dramatised hitherto partly submerged aggressive feelings and brought private hatreds into the public arena. The symbolism and iconography they employed drew on, and so perpetuated, extremely hostile stereotypes. The antagonistic cartoons of the 'Jew Premier' in fact went well beyond the 'ethnic prejudice', 'xenophobic hostility', 'casual prejudice' and 'peripheral concern' that scholars in the field consider to be features of a less malignant form of antisemitism.[154] They employed imagery to convey what the same scholars regard as essential components of a far more virulent and ominous form of antisemitism, namely 'significant chimerical' or mythic forces, and to suggest that Disraeli's Jewishness was 'a central and life-shaping force, the means by which they [in this case, the cartoonists and possibly their readers] had come to under-stand the world'.[155]

NOTES

1. For the name 'Ben JuJu', see Note 96 below. I include and discuss some of the material in this paper from a different perspective in my essay '"Dizzi-Ben-Dizzi": Disraeli as Alien', *Journal of British Studies*, Vol. 34, No. 3 (July 1995), pp. 375–411. I would like to thank the University of Chicago Press for granting permission to reproduce some of this material.

2. In a work of almost 800 pages Lord Blake, for example, devoted only three short sentences to the antisemitism of this period: Robert Blake, *Disraeli* (New York, 1967), pp. 604–5. Both R. T. Shannon in his *Gladstone and the Bulgarian Agitation, 1876* (London, 1963) and Colin Holmes in his important *Anti-Semitism in British Society, 1876–1939* (London, 1979) and his 'Goldwin Smith (1823–1910): A "Liberal" Antisemite', *Patterns of Prejudice*, Vol. 4, No. 4 (September/October 1972), pp. 25–30, draw attention to the antisemitic strains of the period but do not focus on either the depth of passion levelled against Disraeli or the language of the diatribes. The same applies to recent biographies of Disraeli, among them Sarah Bradford, *Disraeli* (London, 1985), John R. Vincent, *Disraeli* (Oxford, 1990) and John K. Walton, *Disraeli* (London, 1990). Even specialised studies of his Jewishness do not deal with the later period: see Maurice Edelman, 'Disraeli as Jew', *Jewish Chronicle Literary Supplement*, 23 December 1966; P. Rieff, 'Disraeli: The Chosen of History', *Commentary*, Vol. 13, No. 1 (January 1952), pp. 22–3; Isaiah Berlin, 'Benjamin Disraeli, Karl Marx, and the Search for Identity', *Transactions of the Jewish Historical Society of England*, Vol. 22 (1970), pp. 1–20; B. Jaffe, 'A Reassessment of Benjamin Disraeli's Jewish Aspects', ibid., Vol. 27 (1982), pp. 115–23; and P. Smith, 'Disraeli's Politics', *Transactions of the Royal Historical Society*, Vol. 37 (1987), pp. 65–85. An especially sensitive treatment of Disraeli is R. W. Davis, *Disraeli* (London, 1976). See also Ann P. Saab, 'Disraeli, Judaism, and the Eastern Question', *International History Review*, Vol. 10, No. 4 (November 1988), pp. 559–78, which contains a brief but perceptive discussion.

3. Stanley Weintraub, *Disraeli: A Biography* (New York, 1993); David Feldman, *Englishmen and Jews: Social Relations and Political Culture, 1840–1914* (New Haven, CT, 1994), esp. ch. 4, pp. 94–120; Michael Ragussis, *Figures of Conversion: The 'Jewish Question' and English National Identity* (Durham, NC, 1995), esp. chs 5 and 6, pp. 174–290. For a review of this literature see Wohl, 'Will The Real Benjamin Disraeli Please Stand Up? Or The Importance of Being Earnest', *Nineteenth Century Studies*, Vol. 2 (1997), pp. 133–56. For a stimulating analysis of Disraeli's Jewishness (but with a focus earlier than 1874) see Paul Smith, *Disraeli: A Brief Life* (Cambridge, 1996).

4. Indeed, for the first time it became a matter of vital importance to English Jews in general, for their standing as citizens was now closely interwoven with the way Disraeli was portrayed as a Jew in the popular press. The antisemitism directed at Disraeli after 1874 was more virulent and potentially more dangerous than the earlier heckling of the 'old clothes' and 'bacon' variety he encountered during his political apprenticeship. What had hitherto been possibly unthinking and sporadic, now became systematic and sustained and, for a variety of reasons, more threatening to Anglo-Jewry in general. Ragussis puts it very well: 'What began in the 1830s as scattered anti-semitic remarks aimed at him [Disraeli] by the crowds in his early electioneering became in the 1870s a kind of national scrutiny of his Jewishness – a scrutiny that erupted into an anti-Semitic attack led by some of the most prominent intellectuals … of the time and anchored in the fact that Disraeli was a crypto-Jew' (Ragussis, *Figures of Conversion*, p. 175).

5. W. R. W. Stephens, *The Life and Letters of Edward A. Freeman* (London, 1895), 2 vols, and the Bryce Papers, Bodleian Library, Oxford; the Rev. Greville Chester in the *Sheffield Independent*, September 1876, quoted in the *Jewish Chronicle* (JC), 8 September 1876. For epithets with the ring of Shakespeare or Marlow to them, see James Ashworth, *Imperial Ben: A Jew d'Esprit* (London, 1879), pp. 56, 76, 78. In 1868, Salisbury had called Disraeli 'Jew adventurer': see Hatfield Mss 3M/DD, Salisbury to G. M. Sandford, 1 May 1868, cited in Bradford, *Disraeli*, p. 281.

6. Jif, pseud. [Joseph Forster], *Lord Becky's Lies and England's Allies* (London, 1880), pp. 7, 8.

7. For Disraeli as Judas see the poem 'Argyllshire and Achilles', Glynne-Gladstone Mss, 1575; for 'Jewish Dizzy' and the 'Jewish chief' see the poems 'For Gladstone' and 'Gladstone and Achilles' respectively, ibid.; for 'the government of the circumcision' see letter to Gladstone, 8 February 1878, ibid., p. 716; 'Sir Benjamin de Judah' is from *The Lion, the Monkeys, and the Bear: An Apologue on the Eastern Question* (London, 1876), p. 14; for 'Chief Rabbi Benjamin' and 'Jewish brazen coronet' see the poems 'The Rake's Commandments' and 'War', respectively, Glynne-Gladstone Mss, 1575. His support of the Turk against their Christian subject people is a 'Disraelitish' policy, John A. Dowie, *Beaconsfield As He Is* (Sydney, 1878), p. 2, and his 'instincts' and the 'tone' of his government are 'Semitic' (Gladstone marked the paragraph in which the phrase occurred). John Birkbeck, *The Eastern Question: An Appeal to the British Nation* (Settle, 1878), p. 33. In this period the older spelling, 'D'Israeli' is frequently resurrected to emphasise Disraeli's Jewish origins. See, for example, Glynne-Gladstone Mss, 403.

8. John Plumb, in his introduction to Davis's *Disraeli*, p. xii, asserts that 'Disraeli's success took place in an established, deeply status-conscious society, that was by and large unthinkingly anti-Semitic'.

9. George Douglas, Duke of Argyll, *Autobiography and Memoirs*, 2 vols (1906), Vol. 1, p. 280, quoted in Blake, *Disraeli*, p. 9.

10. 'The Political Adventures of Lord Beaconsfield, II', *Fortnightly Review*, Vol. 23 (May 1878), p. 690.

11. Ibid.; 'The Political Adventures of Lord Beaconsfield, I', *Fortnightly Review*, Vol. 23 (April 1878), p. 491. Part III appeared in *Fortnightly Review*, Vol. 23 (June 1878). The articles were reprinted in book form in 1878 and in a publisher's note were called 'a brilliant and incisive analysis'; see *The Political Adventures of Lord Beaconsfield* (New York, 1878). Following the *Dictionary of National Biography, Twentieth Century, 1901–1911* (Oxford, 1920), p. 263, *The Wellesley Index to Victorian Periodical Literature*, Vol. 5, p. 364, attributed the article to Frank Harrison Hill, editor of the *Daily News* from 1869 to 1886.

12. For a revealing discussion of the challenge Jews allegedly represented to the newly defined 'moralised polity' and the nation's 'Christian Morality', see Feldman, *Englishmen and Jews*, pp. 102, 120.

13. Richard Burton, *Lord Beaconsfield: A Sketch* (London, 1882), p. 6.

14. *Beaconsfield: A Mock-Heroic Poem and Political Satire* (London, 1878), p. 23.

15. Caricature has been defined as 'an emblematic drawing': Edward Lucie-Smith, *The Art of Caricature* (London, 1981), p. 9. We should not underestimate the influence of these journals on, or their reflection of, public opinion. In its 14 August 1878 issue, the *Spectator* called *Punch* 'the mirror of the popular mind' and commented 'it teaches us both the strengths and the limitations of popular ridicule'. *Fun* (1861–1900) has been called 'after *Punch*, perhaps the second most important comic periodical in the Victorian period'. J. Don Vann, 'Comic Periodicals' in Don Vann and Rosemary T. VanArsdel (eds), *Victorian Periodicals and Victorian Society* (Toronto, 1994), p. 287.

16. Alvar Ellegard, 'The Readership of the Periodical Press in Mid-Victorian Britain', *Victorian Periodicals Newsletter*, Vol. 3 (September 1971), pp. 13, 20–1, and Alvin Sullivan (ed.), *British Literary Magazines*, Vol. 3, *The Victorian and Edwardian Age, 1837–1913* (London, 1983), p. 505. For Thackeray's jibe see ibid., p. 135. Its publishers insisted that *Fun* 'was outwardly to look as like *Punch* as legally possible'. Francis Burnand, *Records and Reminiscences, Personal and General*, 2 vols (London, 1904), Vol. 1, p. 405.

17. Ernst Kris, *Psychoanalytic Explorations in Art* (New York, 1952), p. 183. 'Adult comic invention' helps the id overcome the super-ego. 'The ego, acting in the service of the pleasure principle' enables us to 'satisfy instinctual demands'. In 'The Principles of Caricature', *The British Journal of Medical Psychology*, Vol. 17, Pts 3 and 4 (1938), p. 338, Kris and Ernst Gombrich argue that 'caricature is a psychological mechanism rather than a form of art' for it employs 'primitive structures' to ridicule and inflict pain on its victims. 'Caricature means freedom, but freedom to be primitive' (p. 341). The 'suggestibility' factor of cartoons is also stressed by Kris: 'In psychological terminology, suggestibility refers to conditions not fully under the control of the adult ego.' Kris, 'The "Danger" of Propaganda' in Lottie M. Newman (ed.), *Selected Papers of Ernst Kris* (New Haven, CT, 1975), p. 412.

18. For the expressibility of prejudice, see Howard J. Ehrlich, *The Social Psychology of Prejudice* (New York, 1973), p. 12. Lawrence Levine puts it well: 'Humor allows us to discuss virtually everything, no matter how taboo. Subjects like incest, sexual performance, prejudice, class feeling, even intense anger toward those on whom we are emotionally or materially dependent, can be expressed openly and freely once they become part of humorous expression.' Review of Mel Watkins, *On the Real Side: Laughing, Lying and Signifying*, *New York Times*, 27 February 1994, book reviews, p. 1.

19. Richard Godfrey, *English Caricature, 1620 to the Present* (London, 1984), p. 7. It is important to note the empowering qualities of ridicule as 'a kind of rhetoric; it prepares the way for action. Before the Jew could be made a scapegoat in Germany, he had first to be made ridiculous.' Robert E. Elliott, *The Power of Satire: Magic, Ritual, Art* (Princeton, NJ, 1960), p. 85.

20. Kris, *Psychoanalytic Explorations*, p. 178. In its grotesque, ludicrous and debunking aspects caricature is 'definitely negative'. See Lawrence Streicher, 'On a Theory of Political Caricature', *Comparative Studies in Society and History*, Vol. 9, No. 4 (July 1967), p. 431. Streicher adds, 'Caricatures are ... stereotypes, which are aimed at dramatizing aggressive tendencies through the definition of targets, the collective integration of private feelings into public sentiments of "self-defence" and the training of ... debunking techniques' (p. 438). For an example of the cartoon literally unmasking, see Forain's vicious 'Allegoire – L'Affaire Dreyfus' for the antisemitic journal *PSST*, portraying a German army officer unmasking Zola to reveal the Jew (or Jew-sympathiser) beneath. In C. R. Ashbee, *Caricature* (New York, 1928), facing p. 95.

21. Kris and Gombrich, 'The Principles of Caricature'. In *Codlingsby* (1847), his satire on Disraeli's *Coningsby* (1844), W. M. Thackeray asserted that 'half the Hebrew's life is a disguise'. Ragussis writes that 'this idea reached its apogee in Trollope's novels, where anti-Semitism takes the form of the constant suspicion of masked Jewish identity'. *Figures of Conversion*, p. 180.

22. Caricatures can unmask by creating an overlay of their own. The created mask of the caricature may represent 'the crude distinctions, the deviations from the norm, which mark a person off from others'. E. Gombrich, 'The Mask and the Face: The Perception of Physiognomic Likeness in Life and Art' in *The Image and the Eye: Further Studies in the Psychology of Pictorial Representation* (Ithaca, NY, 1982), p. 113.

23. For an important study of Victorian interest in *conversos* see M. Ragussis, 'The
     Birth of a Nation in Victorian Culture: The Spanish Inquisition, the Converted
     Daughter, and the "Secret Race"', *Critical Inquiry*, Vol. 20, No. 3 (Spring 1994).
     I am indebted to Prof. Mel Wiebe, Queen's University, Ontario, for bringing
     this article to my attention. Ragussis argues that the image of the *conversos* was
     very much a part of Victorian historical and fictional literature. Enlightened
     liberal England, pluralistic, rational and progressive, defined itself as being against
     the tyranny and fanaticism of the Spanish Inquisition, but, Ragussis cautions,
     Victorian historians and novelists were hardly calling for a truly pluralistic society
     when they portrayed the agony and plight of the *conversos*. For the good Jew was
     one who converted to Christianity, or, at least, one whose daughter did. It was
     possible, while not going so far, of course, as to praise or exonerate the Inquisi-
     tion, nevertheless to argue that the *conversos*, driven by tribal and superstitious
     forces, constituted a 'secret race', one which would never assimilate and which
     harboured ancient sentiments of 'chosen-ness', independence and domination.
     If, on the one hand, *conversos* were pitied as victims of Catholic intolerance, they
     were, on the other, held to be an example of 'Jewish hypocrisy and opportunism'.
     See *Figures of Conversion*, p. 156. Ragussis sees 'certain continuities between
     fifteenth-century Spain and nineteenth-century England' in the way 'the terms
     of inquisitorial Spain' re-emerge in the attack on Disraeli (p. 210).
24. Malcolm MacColl, 'Lord Beaconsfield', *Contemporary Review*, Vol. 39 (June
     1881), p. 1002. What most infuriated MacColl was Disraeli's argument that
     Judaism was but incomplete Christianity. MacColl had served as chaplain in St
     Petersburg and had visited eastern Europe with Liddon (see below).
25. That Disraeli supported Turkish domination of the Balkans at a time when Jews
     in both France (through the Alliance Israélite Universelle, founded in 1860) and
     England (through the Anglo-Jewish Association, founded in 1871) were expos-
     ing the persecution of Jews by the Balkan Christians only seemed to confirm
     these fears. Anglo-Jewry was surprised that its concern about the persecution of
     Jews overseas could be interpreted as a want of patriotism. See Israel Finestein,
     'Jewish Emancipationists and Victorian England: Self-Imposed Limits of Assim-
     ilation' in Jonathan Frankel and Steven Zipperstein (eds), *Assimilation and
     Community: The Jews in Nineteenth-Century Europe* (Cambridge, 1992), p. 42.
26. In a statement that was made public, Gladstone argued: 'I deeply deplore the
     manner in which what I may call Judaic sympathies, beyond as well as within
     the circle of professed Judaism [a reference perhaps to Disraeli among others?],
     are now acting in the question of the East.' In Agatha Ramm (ed.), *The Political
     Correspondence of Mr. Gladstone and Lord Granville, 1876–1886*, 2 vols (Oxford,
     1962), Vol. 1, p. 28. See also John Vincent (ed.), *The Derby Diaries, 1869–1878*,
     Camden Fifth Series, Vol. 4 (London, 1994), 13 October 1876, p. 333. Gladstone
     said that these 'Judaic feelings [were] the deepest, and truest, now his wife has
     gone, in his whole mind'. For Gladstone's use of 'crypto-Jew', see Berlin, 'Disraeli,
     Marx and the Search for Identity', p. 13. Gladstone to Arthur Gordon, September
     1876, quoted in John Morley, *The Life of William Ewart Gladstone*, 3 vols (New
     York, 1904), Vol. 2, p. 552. Gladstone told Halifax that the real motivation
     behind Disraeli's Eastern diplomacy was 'his Judaism'. Richard Millman, *Britain
     and the Eastern Question, 1875–1878* (Oxford, 1979), p. 524, n. 63.
27. Arthur Sketchley, *Mrs. Brown on 'Dizzy'* (London, 1874), p. 55. It is in this con-
     text and in the context of Trollope's Lopez (possibly a 'secret Jew') in *The Prime
     Minister*, rather than George Eliot's sympathetic *Daniel Deronda* (both published
     in 1876), that we should interpret the cartoons of Disraeli. In Trollope's *Is He
     Popenjoy?* (1878), the Dean of Brotherton declares that no good is ever done by
     converting a Jew, clearly a reference to Disraeli, with whom Trollope was

obsessed: see Bryan Cheyette, *Constructions of 'The Jew' in English Literature and Society: Racial Representations, 1875–1945* (Cambridge, 1993), p. 40.

28. For 'perception time', which was quicker for cartoons than for photos, see T. Ryan and C. Schwartz, 'Speed of Perception as a Function of Mode of Representation', *American Journal of Psychology*, Vol. 69 (1956), quoted by Julia Hochberg, 'The Representation of Things and People' in E. Gombrich *et al.* (eds), *Art, Perception, and Reality* (Baltimore, 1972), p. 74.

29. Elliott, *The Power of Satire*, p. 85; Max Beerbohm, *'Punch'*, *More* (London, 1922), pp. 15–16. Gombrich and Kris argue that caricature appeared relatively late in western art because earlier it was feared to have too much power and so to be too dangerous to employ. See Gombrich and Kris, *Caricature* (Harmondsworth, 1940), p. 15.

30. Amy Cruse, *The Victorians and Their Reading* (Boston, 1935), p. 394, quoted in Jerold Savory and Patricia Marks, *The Smiling Muse: Victoriana in the Comic Press* (Philadelphia, 1985), p. 17.

31. *Fun*, Vol. 5 (16 March 1867), p. 9.

32. Ibid., Vol. 31 (18 February 1880), p. 67. The cartoon was reproduced in *One Hundred Cartoons from the Pages of Fun* (London, 1880), p. 99. This cartoon and all those initialled GT are the work of Gordon Thomson, about whom I have been able to discover very little beyond the fact that he exhibited at the Royal Academy in 1878 and that he was a civil servant. See Christopher Wood, *The Dictionary of Victorian Painters* (Woodbridge, Suffolk, 1978), p. 472; Simon Houfe, *The Dictionary of British Book Illustrators and Caricaturists, 1800–1914* (Woodbridge, Suffolk, 1978), p. 478. Remarkably, for so important and prolific a cartoonist, he is not included in Julia Cornelissen and Katherine Rainbirch (eds), *The Illustrators: The British Art of Illustration* (London, 1993). According to the publishers of *Fun*, 'there was a wide difference of opinion' on Thomson's artistry. George and Edward Dalziel, *The Brothers Dalziel: A Record* (London, 1901), p. 308. I would like to thank the staff of the National Art Library at the Victoria and Albert Museum, London, for their assistance.

33. One can understand why the High Church Ritualists, with their friendly attitude towards the Russian Orthodox Church and their bitter opposition to Disraeli's stand on Ritualism (which was shared by Nonconformists, who saw it as unwarrantable state interference in religion), would be highly critical of Disraeli and perhaps, by extension, of Jews, but the strictly theological attitude (as opposed to the broader religious and political attitudes discussed in this essay) of the Nonconformists, who had so recently worked vigorously for Jewish emancipation, is more difficult to explain. Feldman argues that a critical change occurred in Protestant attitudes towards Judaism. From feelings of kinship and empathy towards the people of the Old Testament, several Protestant thinkers now argued that Judaism, as practised in England and elsewhere, was hopelessly mired in superstition, defied reason and was in the grip of the medieval rabbinic mind. Feldman, *Englishmen and Jews*, pp. 48–51. Echoes of old anti-Catholic prejudices can be seen in this emphasis on reason versus superstition, progress versus the domination of priests.

34. 'These monopolist usurers' is how one MP described them. J. G. Tollemache Sinclair, *A Defence of Russia and the Christians of Turkey* (London, 1877), p. 113. Sinclair was MP for Caithness. For the transference of allegiance from the Liberal to the Conservative party during and immediately after the Eastern Question, see Geoffrey Alderman, *Modern British Jewry* (Oxford, 1992), pp. 99ff. The most blatant antisemitic attack on the 'secret Jew' subverting English traditions came from the pen of Trollope, most notably in *The Eustace Diamonds* (1873), *Phineas Redux* (1874), *The Way We Live Now* (1875) and *The Prime*

Minister (1876). 'In novel after novel in the 1870s we find Trollope representing the threat of a Judaized England', Ragussis, *Figures of Conversion*, pp. 238–40.
See also Cheyette, *Constructions of 'The Jew'*, esp. pp. 23–54. For another vicious
attack on the secret Jew, see the work of the MP for Dundee, Edward Jenkins,
Haverholme, or, The Apotheosis of Jingo (London, 1878). The false god Jingo 'came
from the East [and had] a form like a Sphinx and a mould like a Caucasian ...
and his nose was the nose of an Hebrew of the Hebrews'. Jingo was 'the spirit
of a barbarous Asiatic despotism transmigrated from a political body in the east
... and adapting itself cunningly to the circumstances of a free people' (p. 193).
Haverholme is full of veiled references to Disraeli and, in a manner similar to
Trollope, Jenkins sought to unmask the Prime Minister and expose the hidden
Jew. Jingo's 'originally brutal and bloody nature', he wrote, 'was veiled under
constitutional forms and Christian ideals' (p. 194).

35. J. Bryce, *Race Sentiment as a Factor in History* (London, 1915), p. 12. 'The Trinity',
of course, should be substituted for 'the gods of the heathen'.

36. Richard S. Levy, *Antisemitism in the Modern World: An Anthology of Texts*
(Lexington, MA, 1991), pp. 2–3; Gavin Langmuir, *Toward a Definition of Antisemitism* (Berkeley, 1990), pp. 315, 338, 341.

37. For an analysis of the nation-wide protest movement against Disraeli's handling
of the Eastern Crisis, see Ann Pottinger Saab, *Reluctant Icon: Gladstone, Bulgaria,
and the Working Classes, 1856–1878* (Cambridge, MA, 1991). The fullest account
of the diplomacy of the Eastern Question is Richard Millman, *Britain and the
Eastern Question, 1875–1878*. See also Agatha Ramm, *Sir Robert Morier: Envoy
and Ambassador in the Age of Imperialism, 1876–1893* (Oxford, 1973), esp. p. 51,
and R. T. Shannon, *The Age of Disraeli, 1868–1881: The Rise of Tory Democracy*
(New York, 1992), pp. 268–307.

38. Disraeli told the House on 10 July 1876 that he did not believe that the Turks
used torture since they were 'an historical people ... who generally, I believe,
terminate their connection with culprits in a more expeditious manner'. The
Spectator (15 July 1876) rightly predicted that this *'mal-a-propos* levity' would
alienate England – 'England will be all aflame if we are to shield a Power which
restores order by the wholesale use of massacre, outrages, and the sale of
children into slavery' (p. 881). In his *Studies in Contemporary Biography* (London,
1903), p. 32, James Bryce wrote of Disraeli: 'No act of his life ever so much
offended English opinion as the airy fashion in which he tossed aside the news
of the Bulgarian massacres of 1876.' In his revised version of this essay for
Century Magazine, Vol. 23, No. 1 (March 1882), p. 737, he changed 'offended'
to 'repelled' and 'news' to 'tales'. During the summer of 1876, Serbia and
Montenegro declared war on Turkey.

39. Morley, *The Life of William Ewart Gladstone*, Vol. 2, p. 551.

40. W. T. Stead (ed.), *The M.P. for Russia: Reminiscences and Correspondence of Madame
Olga Novikoff*, 2 vols (London, 1909), Vol. 1, p. 293. As Winston Churchill slyly
remarked, Gladstone had the 'gift of rousing moral indignation both in himself
and in the electorate'. Quoted in Peter Stansky, *Gladstone: A Progress in Politics*
(New York, 1979), p. 3. Colin Matthew demonstrates that Gladstone's attitude
towards the Eastern Question was, as one might expect, complex and multi-
layered. He was by no means an out-and-out Russophile. The Eastern Question
divided High Churchmen and destroyed any chance of a concord between the
Anglican and Eastern Orthodox churches. 'The inner force of Gladstone's
pamphlet was always religious, and these failures of ecumenism must be borne
in mind as the more political aspects of the Eastern Question are examined.'
H. C. G. Matthew, *Gladstone, 1875–1898* (Oxford, 1995), p. 13. To this one must
add Gladstone's own evolution: 'Between July and September 1876, Gladstone

experienced a conversion of Evangelical intensity', ibid., p. 30. To Disraeli and the Tories, the agitation whipped up by the 'Bulgarian Atrocities' pamphlet was a classic example of Gladstonian political self-interest masquerading as morality, and of Gladstonian madness. See Disraeli's dark references, a week after the pamphlet appeared, to the world gone mad 'as it does periodically', Disraeli Papers, Hughendon Manor, Box 69, B/XVI/B/1, letter to Montagu Corry, 13 September 1876, and Corry's response that they had entered 'a moment of national madness', Box 69, B/XVI/B/9, 19 September 1876. Thomas Bowles, editor of *Vanity Fair*, 30 September 1876, p. 201, called the agitation led by Gladstone 'lynch law in foreign affairs'. Quoted in John Osborne, 'The Journal *Vanity Fair* in later Victorian Politics', *Journal of Rutgers University Libraries*, Vol. 42, No. 2 (December 1980), p. 83. Bowles was as critical of Disraeli.

41.   For Stead, see Gladstone Papers, Add. Mss, 44303, ccxviiii, letter of 26 August 1876. Stead rushed to congratulate Gladstone on his 'noble pamphlet' and for having 'once more taken your proper place as the spokesman of the national conscience', ibid. In the paper he edited, the *Northern Echo*, Stead rejoiced: 'The pulse of humanity beat as ungovernably in the nation as when Cromwell ruled and Milton sang' (14 September 1876, p. 2). For Morley, see his *Life of William Ewart Gladstone*, Vol. 2, p. 555. While Stead talked in terms of conscience, E. A. Freeman saw the Eastern Question in terms of national sin and penitence. Most of the Liberals, he argued, had repented for their sins (having failed to insist on support for the Eastern Christians at the outset of the crisis), but 'the Conservative party, save for a few righteous men ... refused to repent'. Freeman, 'The Election and the Eastern Question', *Contemporary Review*, Vol. 37 (June 1880), p. 960.

42.   An English Liberal, *The Indignation Meetings of the Liberals and the Conduct of Affairs in the East* (London, 1876), p. 2. Information about the Bulgarian atrocities first reached England on 4 May 1876; by 19 May there was no doubt about the ferocity with which the Turks had suppressed the rebellion and throughout June the papers were full of it. Disraeli Papers, Box 67, B/xvi/A/11a. A. J. P. Taylor goes so far as to say that the 'Bulgarian Horrors of 1876 ... aroused the greatest storm over foreign policy in our history'. The massacres constituted 'the political crime of the century'. Taylor, *The Trouble Makers: Dissent over Foreign Policy, 1792–1939* (London, 1957), p. 74. Interestingly, many who supported Governor Eyre during his trial for having put down the Jamaica Revolt with extreme brutality, and who were, accordingly, associated with 'law and order' within the Empire – Carlyle, Froude, Tennyson, Ruskin – joined the Nonconformist ranks in opposition to Turkey. The Ritualists and Positivists were both pro-Russia. Diplomacy can make for strange bed-fellows. See ibid., pp. 76, 78.

      For the view that both Disraeli and Gladstone had their eyes focused on party politics during the Eastern Crisis, see Marvin Swartz, *The Politics of British Foreign Policy in the Era of Gladstone and Disraeli* (New York, 1985), ch. 2, and Shannon, *The Age of Disraeli*. For a defence of Disraeli's policies see Alfred Austen, *Tory Horrors! Or the Question of the Hour: A Letter to the Right Hon. W. E. Gladstone, MP* (London, 1876). In the opinion of William Smith, editor of the *Quarterly Review* and author of 'The Eastern Question and the Government', *Quarterly Review*, Vol. 42, No. 284 (October 1876), p. 291, Gladstone's view of the Turk was similar to James Mackintosh's characterisation of Henry VIII as one who 'approached as nearly to the ideal standard of perfect wickedness as the infirmities of human nature will allow'.

43.   He was 'prepared for any Ottoman sacrifice consistent with British prestige' is Millman's comment on Disraeli's pragmatism. He concludes that, 'perhaps most fundamentally, a Russian occupation of Constantinople would have been a serious blow to British prestige in the Near East, India, Europe and London'.

Millman, *Britain and the Eastern Question, 1875–1878*, pp. 454–5. Disraeli's bellicose stance has sometimes been called Palmerstonian, but Hugh Cunningham has argued that Palmerston's concept of patriotism and his active policy were associated with the liberties of downtrodden European peoples and so both Disraeli's patriotism and policy were very different. Cunningham, 'The Language of Patriotism', *History Workshop*, No. 12 (1981), pp. 22ff. For Gladstone's less than enthusiastic views on India and his opposition to imperial expansion in general see Matthew, *Gladstone*, pp. 23–4.

44. *Judy*, Vol. 21 (9 May 1877), pp. 14–15.
45. T. Ashcroft, *The Turko-Servian War: Its Prominent Features and Probable Results* (London, 1876), p. 3. Ashcroft denounced Turkey as 'lustful' and 'a cesspool of depravity' (pp. 20–2). He was confident that 'Christianity, with its spirit of liberty, truth, and love, must conquer' (p. 3).
46. Edward Jenkins, *The Shadow on the Cross* (London, 1876), title page.
47. Their diatribes were so openly racist in expression that it is remarkable that Edward Said does not incorporate them in his *Orientalism* (New York, 1978).
48. An English Liberal, *The Indignation Meetings*, Vol. 4, pp. 9–10. Interestingly, to 'An English Liberal', the Russian was a barbarian also, ibid., pp. 14–17. For a typical statement of Turkish decline versus British advance, see E. A. Freeman, 'Medieval and Modern Greece', *Historical Essays* (London, 1879), p. 318. To Freeman the East was 'stationary, arbitrary, polygamous, and Mahometan', *History and Conquests of the Saracens*, p. 4, quoted in Clinton Bennett, *Victorian Images of Islam* (London, 1992), p. 79.
49. *Public Opinion*, 9 September 1876, p. 327.
50. Goldwin Smith, 'England's Abandonment of the Protectorate of Turkey', *Contemporary Review*, Vol. 31 (February 1878), p. 615. For a superb analysis of Smith's antisemitism see Gerald Tulchinsky, 'Goldwin Smith: Victorian Canadian Antisemite' in Alan Davies (ed.), *Antisemitism in Canada: History and Interpretation* (Waterloo, 1992).
51. Baxter Langlet at a protest meeting in Woolwich, *Daily News*, 4 September 1876. In his pamphlet Gladstone called for the expulsion of the Turks 'bag and baggage' from Europe but retreated before considerable public protest, arguing that he had meant the government, not the people themselves. 'What a man is Gladstone!', wrote Disraeli to Monty Corry. 'What a scoundrel! He publishes a pamphlet urging the expulsion on ethnological grounds of the Turks from Europe; an inferior and debased race – but then, becoming alive almost immediately to the folly, he claims he meant only the Turkish ministers.' Disraeli Papers, Hughendon Manor, Box 69, B/XVI/B/1, 13 September 1876. For the way 'bag and baggage' was lifted out of context and divorced from its 'surrounding qualifications', see Matthew, *Gladstone*, p. 28.
52. It is clear that Nonconformist Liberal radicalism did not hesitate to stereotype, damn wholesale or heap contempt on whole cultures. Liberalism was shot through with a keen sense of sin and moral outrage and thus could damn and condemn without a sense of illogic or betrayal of liberal ideology.
53. To E. A. Freeman, Disraeli, like Palmerston before him, was the 'champion of evil' while Gladstone 'stood forth as the champion of good'. Freeman, 'Anthony Trollope', *Macmillan's Magazine*, Vol. 47 (January 1883), p. 240. Freeman regarded the Eastern Question as, in essence, 'Anti-Christ against Christianity'. 'The English People in Relation to the Eastern Question', *Fortnightly Review*, Vol. 29 (February 1877), p. 507.
54. 'English Mahommedans', *Spectator*, 9 September 1876, p. 1122. See also the statement of the Rev. J. Llewelyn Davies: 'It is inevitable that some account should be taken of the fact that the disaffected subjects of Turkey are Christians.

There are many persons in this country – others as well as Jews – to whom this fact is a reason for lending their sympathies to the Turks.' *The Religious Aspect of the Eastern Question*, Eastern Question Association Papers No. 2 (London, 1877), p. 3.

55. Jean-Paul Sartre, *Portrait of the Anti-Semite*, trans. Erik de Maun (London, 1948), pp. 33ff.

56. 'When prejudice is part of a culture, it can shift its direction from one group to another.' Arnold Rose, 'The Roots of Prejudice' in UNESCO, *Race and Science* (New York, 1969), p. 407.

57. *Echo*, 16 August 1879; *Spectator*, 6 November 1880, p. 1404.

58. See Allan Harris Cutler and Helen Elmquist Cutler, *The Jew as Ally of the Muslim: Medieval Roots of Anti-Semitism* (South Bend, IN, 1986).

59. Sinclair, *A Defence of Russia and the Christians of Turkey*, p. 113. Sinclair, MP for Caithness, 1870–85, warned that England would have to turn for war loans to 'these monopolist usurers'. He then informed his readers 'what sort of people the Jews really are' by monochromatically sketching their history from earliest times to the present – a history of nothing but cruelty, blood-lust, usury, deception and the sexual immorality with which an 'out-group' or 'other' is usually stigmatised. 'Can it be wondered then', Sinclair concluded, 'that there is a gulf which can never be bridged between the Jew and Christian.' Having established to his satisfaction that 'Jews are not, and never have been, worthy of our esteem and regard, and that they are the eternal and implacable enemies of the Christian', it followed that 'it would be madness to follow their advice to go to war with Russia, but wisdom always to take the opposite course to that which they recommend' (pp. 124, 131).

60. Smith, *Contemporary Review*, Vol. 31 (February 1878), p. 617.

61. T. P. O'Connor, *Lord Beaconsfield: A Biography* (London, 1905), pp. 654, 611–12.

62. Ibid., p. 612.

63. Ibid., pp. 654, 614. It is revealing that O'Connor confined to a footnote the persecution of Jews by Eastern Christians.

64. E. A. Freeman, 'The Relation of the English People to the War', *Contemporary Review*, Vol. 30 (August 1877), pp. 494–5.

65. E. A. Freeman, *The Ottoman Power in Europe* (London, 1877), pp. xix, xx. 'It is no use mincing matters ... The danger is no imaginary one. Every one must have marked that the one subject on which Lord Beaconsfield ... has been in earnest, has been whatever has touched his own people. A mocker about everything else, he has been thoroughly serious in this' (pp. xviii–xix).
      According to the *Dictionary of National Biography*, Freeman's intemperance on the Eastern Question 'resulted in his not being invited to stand for a constituency in the 1880 General Election' despite the 'services which he rendered' to the Liberals in this period. *Dictionary of National Biography*, Supplement, II, p. 249. Probably it was his infamous 'Perish India' cry rather than his campaign against Disraeli that made him an unattractive candidate. The *Jewish Chronicle*, commenting on Freeman's *Ottoman Power*, pointed out the irony that while 'Gladstone and his followers are probably, unconsciously to themselves, so far carried away by the Christianity which they profess in common with the Bulgarians, as to be ready to sacrifice to it the interests of their own country', they attack the Jews in semi-menacing language, for putting religion over national interest. *Jewish Chronicle*, 10 August 1877, p. 8. The same article drew attention to 'deep-seated and wide-spread ... religious antipathy' in Liberal ranks towards Jews. This antipathy would have assumed a far more outspoken form but 'the religious and moral atmosphere of England is at this moment not favourable to a vigorous life for it'. The phrase 'at this moment' suggests the fears of the Anglo-Jewish community.

66. Quoted in Novikoff, *The MP For Russia*, Vol. I, p. 364. For this quotation and those from Freeman above, see also Feldman, *Englishmen and Jews*, pp. 100, 101.
67. *Church Times*, 25 August 1876.
68. Editorial, *Northern Echo*, 22 September 1876, p. 3.
69. William Crosbie, *The Beaconsfield Policy: An Address* (London, 1879), p. 14, my emphasis. This was an address given to the Victoria Street Chapel Literary Society in Derby and to the Zion Church Young Men's Society in Sheffield, both in December 1878. Crosbie drew the conclusion that Disraeli's quest for Empire was simply 'a vulgar parody of the ancient Jewish dream'.
70. According to John Boyd Kinnear, *The Mind of England on the Eastern Question* (London, 1877), p. 14, 'One voice only in all England, and that the voice of one not an Englishman by blood, was raised ... to plead for their [the Turks'] maintenance in power'. Kinnear was closer to the mark when he argued that only Disraeli spoke in public 'to palliate the Turkish acts [the massacre of Bulgarians]'. According to E. A. Freeman, only Disraeli stood between good men and their consciences and perhaps ultimate salvation; many Conservatives, he argued, 'were quite ready to repent [for their foreign policy], if Lord Beaconsfield would have let them'. Freeman, *Contemporary Review*, Vol. 37 (June 1880), p. 960. For 'Gladstone's personalization of government policy in the 1876–8 period when Disraeli was held largely responsible', see Matthew, *Gladstone*, pp. 54–5. Gladstone did not widen the scope of his attack until 1878. This personification of a complex diplomatic situation is captured in Robert Browning's response to the famous lines:

> We don't want to fight
> But by Jingo if we do
> The head I'd like to punch
> Is Beaconsfield, the Jew.

Quoted in Patrick Waddington, *From 'The Russian Fugitive' to 'The Ballad of Bulgarie': Episodes in English Literary Attitudes to Russia from Wordsworth to Swinburne* (Oxford, 1994), p. 149.
71. Respectively, *Fun*, Vol. 6 (3 September 1864), p. 249; Vol. 4 (1 December 1866), p. 123; Vol. 2 (5 July 1862), p. 155. One could argue that a conspiratorial Dizzy is about to resort to tactics that are hardly cricket – but it is the captain, Derby, who is putting him up to it! Disraeli was also portrayed as a batsman with a remarkably straight bat in the pages of the comic journal *Will-O'-the-Wisp*, Vol. 1 (19 September 1868), p. 17. He is the 'native that cannot be bowled out', the fearless batsman standing up to the formidable bowling of the touring Aborigine team.
72. An exception is the famous Tenniel cartoon of Disraeli as Fagin, teaching his party how to pickpocket the Reform Bill from the Liberals. *Punch*, Vol. 52, No. 9 (November 1867), p. 189.
73. This representation of Disraeli as Jew evoked the old association of Jews and pigs. For a cartoon of Disraeli cuddling a pig, see *Hood's Comic Annual for 1878* (London, 1878), p. 70. This (formerly *Tom Hood's Comic Annual*) was published by *Fun*. The artist is Thomson. Histories of the cartoon generally ignore the portrayal of Disraeli as a Jew. But see Ashbee's comment that Disraeli was depicted, with his 'cynicism and sometimes tawdry grandeur', as 'the Jew boy'. Ashbee, *Caricature*, p. 11. One of the functions of caricature is to emphasise 'the subtle points of difference between the subject and his fellowmen': James Campbell Cory, *The Cartoonist's Art* (Chicago, 1920), p. 12, quoted in Edna Hines, 'Cartoons as a means of Social Control', *Sociology and Social Research*, Vol. 17, No. 5 (May–June 1935), p. 455.

74. Figure 8, 'The Jew', appears in R. Knox, *The Races of Men* (London, 1862), p. 193. Figure 9 is from *Fun*, Vol. 22 (28 August 1875), pp. 90–1. Robert William Buss, *English Graphic Satire* (London, 1974), p. 155, argues that the portrayal of Jews with three hats was inspired by Jonathan Swift's *The Tale of the Tub*, with its satire on the Triple Crown of St Peter. For the association of Disraeli with a Jew wearing two (or three?) hats see *Punch*, Vol. 16 (19 May 1849), p. 211. For other three-hatted Jews in caricature, see M. Dorothy George, *Catalogue of Political and Personal Satires Preserved in the Department of Prints and Drawings of the British Museum* (London, 1954), Vol. 2, *1830–1832*, illusts 16118, p. 290; 16896, p. 563; 17376, p. 730; Eduard Fuchs, *Die Juden in der Karikatur: Ein Beitrag zur Kulturgeschichte* (Munich, 1923), p. 148; G. Croner (ed.), *England: The History of the Anglo-Jewish Community* (Jerusalem, 1978), p. 107. *Punch* often portrayed the two- or three-hatted Jew. See, for example, Vol. 12 (10 April 1847), p. 149, and Vol. 32 (27 June 1857), p. 259. For a particularly vicious portrayal of the three-hatted Jew, see George Du Maurier's cartoon 'A Legend of Camelot', *Punch*, Vol. 50 (24 March 1866), p. 128.
75. 'The Man in the Street' was a regular column in *Funny Folks*. Figure 10 is from No. 78 (3 June 1876), p. 66. Figure 11 is from the archives of the National Portrait Gallery, London, no date. Figure 12, *Fun*, Vol. 23 (1 March 1876), p. 101. Figure 24, *Fun*, Vol. 22 (14 August 1875), p. 69.
76. David Oedipus, pseud., *Benjameni de Israeli: Who is this Uncircumcised Philistine?* (London, 1881), p. 33.
77. *The Englishman*, 19 February 1876, p. 724. This new representation of Disraeli threatened much that he had worked for as both a novelist and politician. 'The Eastern crisis of 1876 not only crystallized the anti-Semitism that had shrouded Disraeli's career from the beginning', Ragussis writes, 'it threatened his attempt, in his writings, to reveal Hebrew culture as the basis of English life, and in his public career, to prove that a person of Jewish ancestry could successfully govern England.' Ragussis, *Figures of Conversion*, p. 210.
78. '... as Disraeli himself observed of the word "unconstitutional", "I never yet have found any definition of what that epithet means, and I believe with the single exception of the word 'Un-English' it baffles discussion more than any other".' Quoted without reference by Robert Blake in his 1992 Romanes Lecture, *Gladstone, Disraeli, and Queen Victoria* (Oxford, 1993), p. 18. For a brief discussion of the use of the phrase 'un-English', see Hugh Cunningham, 'The Conservative Party and Patriotism' in Robert Colls and Philip Dodd (eds), *Englishness: Politics and Culture, 1880–1920* (1986), p. 295. Interestingly, Disraeli himself used the phrase to satirise the electioneering techniques and principles of Rigby in *Coningsby* (New York, Signet Classic edn, 1962), p. 290. See Ragussis, *Figures of Conversion*, p. 187.
79. See, for example, the way W. T. Stead harps on the theme of Disraeli's un- or anti-English character and policies. *Northern Star*, 7 December 1877, p. 2; 18 December 1877, p. 2; 21 December 1877, p. 2; 29 December 1977, p. 2.
80. *Vivien Grey: A Romance of Youth* (London, 1904), pp. 1, 14. For *Vivien Grey* and Disraeli's other early novels as a portrayal of his 'own complex and varied experience as a Jewish patriot in Victorian England', see Montagu F. Modder, 'The Alien Patriot in Disraeli's Novels', *The London Quarterly and Holborn Review*, No. 159 (July 1934), p. 366.
81. MacColl, *Contemporary Review*, Vol. 39 (June 1881), p. 945.
82. *Beaconsfield: A Mock-Heroic Poem*, pp. 6, 24. For the image of the wandering Jew in Victorian England, see Montagu F. Modder, *The Jew in the Literature of England to the End of the Nineteenth Century* (New York, 1960), pp. 352ff. See also George K. Anderson, *The Legend of the Wandering Jew* (Providence, RI, 1965).

The 'Jew might strike his tent tomorrow and not a vestige of him remain among us', wrote *The Times*, 18 April 1853, quoted in Polly Pinsker, 'English Opinion and Jewish Emancipation (1830–1860)', *Jewish Social Studies*, Vol. 14, No. 1 (January 1951), p. 81. Throughout the emancipation struggle and long after, the Jew as doomed wanderer was stressed. See *Jewish Chronicle*, February 1867, p. 5. Eugene Sue's *The Wandering Jew* (1844) was dramatised in England as 'All for Gold'. In his *Good Friday, or The Murder of Jesus Christ by the Jews* (London, 1830), p. 13, William Cobbett stressed how the Jews deserved to wander as perpetual aliens, always 'at the absolute disposal of the sovereign power of the state'. When Disraeli became Prime Minister in 1867, one observer commented that 'the division between him and mere mortals [is] more marked. I would as soon thought of sitting down at table with Hamlet or Lear or the Wandering Jew', Sir John Skelton, *The Table-Talk of Shirley* (London, 1895), p. 257.

The wandering Jew was very much alive as a popular folk legend in the 1870s. In *The Wandering Jew* (London, 1881), p. 159, Moncure Daniel Conway relays an account in *Notes and Queries* (1871) of the author James Pearson meeting an old man on the Lancashire moors and their hearing 'the whistling overhead of a covey of plovers'. The old man then says that that is a bad omen as 'there was a tradition that they [the plovers] contain the souls of those Jews who assisted at the cruxifixion [*sic*], and in consequence were doomed to float in the air forever', and that those who heard the wandering Jews would meet some ill-luck. Pearson then missed his coach and had to continue on foot, whereupon the old man reminded him of the omen.

83. T. Weymss Reid, 'Lord Beaconsfield', *Politicians of To-Day: Series of Personal Sketches*, 2 vols (London, 1880), Vol. I, pp. 38–9. James Bryce, *Century Magazine* (March 1882), p. 733; significantly, Bryce continues by asking how 'did he so fascinate and rule them?' 'However high its [Jewry's] gifts may be, prejudice cannot fail to be excited. The nations will be sure to feel, as they do, that the wanderer comes rather to live upon than with them', Goldwin Smith to Jonas A. Rosenfield, Texas, 12 October 1907, in Arnold Haultain (ed.), *A Selection from Goldwin Smith's Correspondence, 1864–1910* (London, 1913), p. 505.

84. *Pall Mall Gazette*, 19 April 1881; J. A. Froude, 'Lord Beaconsfield' in Stuart J. Reid (ed.), *The Prime Ministers of Queen Victoria* (London, 1890), pp. 85, 170, 261–2. It is interesting that to at least one organ of French opinion Disraeli was, on the contrary, 'English to the very tips of his fingers in his policy, and alien only in his oratory'. *Le Temps*, 15 August 1876, quoted in *Public Opinion*, 9 August 1876, p. 230. Explicit expressions in England of Disraeli's Englishness are rare. For an exception see the obituary in the *Newcastle Express*, which noted that Disraeli, 'with all his faults, was a thorough statesman and a thorough Englishman', *Public Opinion*, 30 April 1881, p. 539. At best all the absurd talk of Disraeli as '"Un-English"', wrote one contemporary, 'makes Mr. Disraeli a sort of Bedouin Sheik who has just stepped out of the desert into our drawing-rooms ... The critic who fancies that a man whose father and grandfather were English citizens cannot be an Englishman because he has a dash of alien blood in his veins, must know little of ethnology.' Shirley, pseud. [John Skelton], 'A Last Word on Disraeli', *Contemporary Review*, Vol. 39 (June 1881), p. 989.

85. E. A. Freeman, *Contemporary Review*, Vol. 37 (June 1880), p. 966. Freeman's awareness of the sensitivities of the age ('the word "Jew" seems to be forbidden') is interesting. The *Jewish Chronicle* campaigned against the way the press customarily referred to the religion of accused criminals who happened to be Jewish. Freeman may have been aware of this or of the *Jewish Chronicle*'s bitter resentment of his and Goldwin Smith's views.

86. 'A Question', a pamphlet in doggerel verse in Gladstone's Hawarden library, Glynne-Gladstone Mss, p. 706.
87. Münster, German ambassador to the Court of St James, to Bismarck, quoted in Millman, *Britain and the Eastern Question*, p. 491, n. 7.
88. For Figure 12, see note 75 above. For Figure 13, see *Punch*, 15 April 1876, p. 147. Tenniel's cartoon of Disraeli lacks the venom and passion of Gordon Thomson's perhaps because he was a Conservative at heart and sympathised with Disraeli's policies. Tenniel told Spielmann: 'As for my political opinions, I have none; at least if I have my own little politics I keep them to myself and profess only those of my paper.' M. H. Spielmann, *The History of Punch* (London, 1895), p. 10, quoted in Houfe, *The Dictionary of British Book Illustrators*, p. 64.
89. Wemyss Reid, *Politicians of To-day*, Vol. 1, p. 48. The elevation of Victoria to Empress of India was to some the fruition of a grand scheme first outlined by Disraeli in *Tancred*, where he had suggested transferring the throne to India. For Freeman, 'The object of Lord Beaconsfield's rule has been to turn the dreams of *Tancred* into realities, and it is wonderful how largely he has succeeded. It is no small feat ... to have turned a European Queen ... into an Asiatic Empress of his own making ... the Empire of India was one form of Asiatic triumph over Europe.' *Contemporary Review*, Vol. 37 (June 1880), p. 966. The other 'triumph' was the continued presence of the Turks in Europe, one that Disraeli was determined to see prevail even if it cost '10,000 or 20,000 murdered Christians'.
90. For Figure 14, see *Fun*, Vol. 5 (6 July 1867), p. 176. For Figure 15, see *Judy*, Vol. 14 (8 April 1874), p. 253. Sander Gilman, *The Jew's Body* (New York, 1991), ch. 7, 'The Jewish Nose', analyses the way antisemites have employed exaggerated representations of the 'semitic' nose. In the late eighteenth century P. Grose, *Rules for Drawing Caricature* (London, 1791), suggested that the Jewish nose should be drawn as a 'parrot's beak'. Quoted in Isaiah Shachar, 'Studies in the Emergence and Dissemination of the Modern Jewish Stereotype in Western Europe' (unpubl. Ph.D. dissertation, University of London, 1967), p. 315. A late-Victorian artist considered that a figure six with a long tail gives the best caricature outline of the Jewish nose. See Joseph Jacobs, *Studies in Jewish Statistics: Social, Vital, and Anthropometric* (1891), p. xvii. For a satire on the 'Oriental-Ikey-Mosaic' nose, see *Funny Folks*, No. 64 (26 February 1876), p. 61.
91. Figure 16 is from *One Hundred Cartoons from the Pages of Fun* (London, 1880), p. 60. The original was published in the issue of 9 May 1877. Figure 17 is from *Fun*, Vol. 31 (7 April 1880), p. 139. For Figure 25, see note 107.
92. Figure 18 is a *carte-de-visite* photograph by Mayall, National Portrait Gallery, London.
93. Figures 19 and 20 are from *One Hundred Cartoons from the Pages of Fun*, pp. 24, 6. The originals were published in the issues of 23 August 1873 and 10 February 1872, respectively. For Figure 24 see note 106.
94. Figures 21 and 22 are from *One Hundred Cartoons from the Pages of Fun*, pp. 92, 48. The originals appeared on 5 November 1879 and 3 May 1876, respectively. Disraeli appears as Guy Fawkes in an 1880 electioneering cartoon, 'Gunpowder Plot: The Arrest of Guy Faux', in the Gladstone collection, Glynne-Gladstone Mss, 1720. In the caption, John Bull, arresting Disraeli, refers to him as 'that ... Jew'. For a German cartoon of the Jew as elephant, see Fuchs, *Die Juden in der Karikatur*, p. 309.
95. L. P. Curtis, *Apes and Angels: The Irishman in Caricature* (Newton Abbot, 1971). Curtis notes that while *Punch* endowed Gladstone with a facial angle of about 86 degrees, it gave Disraeli one of only 78 degrees. It gave Irishmen a facial angle little different from apes – as low as 50 degrees, p. 52.

96. *One Hundred Cartoons from the Pages of Fun*, p. 53. The original appeared in the issue of 27 September 1876. The reference is to the agitation building up over Disraeli's Eastern policy. The caption reads: 'BEN JUJU (who has accepted an engagement as Flunkey to Sir Ottoman Porte, rebukes those who are anxious to see him in his new position) – "Well, you needn't kick up such a row. I was attending on MY master, and such as you must wait. A lot of Christian rubbish!"'

97. Interestingly, Henry Irving's portrayal of Shylock at the Lyceum was sympathetic. For a fascinating discussion of this and interpretations of the *Merchant of Venice* from Shakespeare's day to the present, see John Gross's superb *Shylock: A Legend and its Legacy* (New York, 1992). Irving's Lyceum production opened in November 1879. To Gladstone, the great actor's Shylock was 'Irving's best'. Matthew, *Gladstone*, p. 71. For the persistence of the blood libel in England, see Frank Felsenstein, *Anti-Semitic Stereotypes: A Paradigm of Otherness in English Popular Culture, 1660–1830* (Baltimore, 1995).

98. *Echo*, 25 April 1878.

99. *The Englishman*, 11 November 1876, p. 97.

100. In 'Disraeli: The Chosen of History' Rieff argued that Disraeli's face and posture fascinated contemporaries: 'It was the face and stoop of Irving's Shylock.' *Commentary*, Vol. 13, No. 1 (January 1952), p. 29.

101. George Henry Francis, *The Right Hon. Benjamin Disraeli, MP: A Critical Biography* (London, 1852), p. 115.

102. *Peace or War? An Indictment of the Policy of the Government* (London, 1877), p. 31.

103. In the strip-cartoon, 'The After Life of Shylock', Disraeli-Shylock, in another reworking of medieval antisemitic mythology, kidnaps Portia's son and gets a ransom. His ultimate triumph, made possible with the help of the mysterious and evil 'Chamber of the Upper Ten' (Gladstone made much during the Eastern Question of Disraeli's support among the 'upper ten thousand' – old jingoist aristocrats and city financiers), is to banish Gladstone to 'perpetual opposition'. *Funny Folks*, Vol. 6 (28 February 1880), pp. 69, 274. In November 1867, at the round table discussion at which the weekly main political cartoon in *Punch* was planned, Tom Taylor suggested a cartoon featuring Disraeli carrying a 'Reform baby' and Russell (holding an 'Education baby') saying, 'That nasty Jewboy shan't kidnap you away'. It was objected to, not on the ground that it was antisemitic, but because *Punch* had published too many cartoons featuring babies. Henry Silver, 'Punch Diary, 1857–70', entry for 27 November 1867, C. Smith transcription. I am most grateful to Patrick Lea for both this reference and his typescript of the Smith transcription.

104. Herbert Atherton, *Political Prints of the Age of Hogarth: A Study of Ideological Representations of Politics* (Oxford, 1974), p. 37.

105. George Eliot, 'Hep! Hep! Hep!' in *Impressions of Theophrastus Such* (New York, 1879), pp. 218–19. E. A. Freeman excitedly recalled the medieval cry 'hep-hep-hep' in a letter to Lord Bryce. See Bryce Mss, letter of 26 February 1877.

106. Figure 24 is from *Fun*, Vol. 22 (14 August 1875), p. 69. The £5,000 may refer to the budget surplus, in the face of which Disraeli still retained the unpopular income tax.

107. Figure 25 is from *Fun*, Vol. 20 (July–December 1874), frontispiece. 'Dizzy's Mixture' appears to be more harmful than Godfrey's Cordial, which was an opiate for babies that was held responsible for many infant deaths.

108. Gombrich and Kris, *Caricature*, pp. 7–8.

109. Figure 26 is from *Bits of Beaconsfield: A New Series of Disraeli's Curiosities of Literature Illustrated* (London, 1881). Figure 27 is from *Fun*, Vol. 18 (8 November 1873), p. 193. Figure 28 is from *Fun*, Vol. 19 (7 February 1874), pp. 57–8. Gladstone is, of course, St George. In another *Fun* cartoon celebrating the

victory of 'William the Conqueror' in the 1880 election, the chain mail of a defeated Disraeli makes him look particularly reptilian. Thomson, the cartoonist, could not resist the play on Gladstone's name; however, the analogy makes Disraeli the Anglo-Saxon Harold! *Fun*, Vol. 31 (14 April 1880), p. 149.

110. For Figure 29, see *Bits of Beaconsfield*. It is interesting that he is being rejected with several of his novels. The only concrete reference to his politics is the annexation of Cyprus following the Congress of Berlin. His opponents saw in the annexation both the cynical partition of Turkey and Disraeli's personal vision of imperialism.

111. See, for example, *Fun*, Vol. 27 (2 January 1878), p. 9, and Vol. 26 (13 February 1878), pp. 68–73.

112. Figure 30 is from *Funny Folks*, Vol. 2, No. 61 (5 February 1876), p. 33. Robert E. Bell, *Women of Classical Mythology: A Biographical Dictionary* (Santa Barbara, CA, 1991), p. 219. Hecate was closely linked to Persephone, the Queen of the Underworld. Closely associated with the infernal regions, she had an 'unearthly aspect'. 'At night she sent forth demons ... to prey on and startle the unwary passersby.' Figure 31 is from the signs of the zodiac in Charles Ross, *A Book of Comicalities* (London, 1872), p. 27. Figure 32 is the Tenniel illustration to *Alice Through the Looking-Glass*, reproduced in Rodney K. Engen, *Sir John Tenniel: Alice's White Knight* (Aldershot, 1991), p. 94.

113. The devil image was tapped by Dickens in his portrayal of Fagin. For a convincing analysis of Fagin as devil, see Linda Gertner Zatlin, *The Nineteenth-Century Anglo-Jewish Novel* (Boston, 1981), pp. 124–5. Fagin has red hair, a 'withered old claw' which reminds Bill Sikes of 'being nabbed by the devil' and he is described as 'a hideous phantom, moist from the grave' and a 'merry old gentleman'. From the days of O'Connell's attack and the heated reviews of Disraeli's *George Bentinck*, Disraeli and anti-Christ had been associated with one another, perhaps most outrageously in the comment of the *Spectator* in 1867 on one of Disraeli's proposals in the Parliamentary Reform Bill: 'Had he proposed an addition of eight members instead of seven, the number of the House of Commons would have been the mystic number of the Beast, 666 ... an accidental irony which, considering the man, his antecedents, and his motives, would be nearly perfect.' *Spectator*, 8 May 1867, p. 542.

In *An Answer to Some of the Opinions and Statements respecting the Jews made by B. Disraeli, Esq., MP, in the 24th Chapter of his Biographical Memoir of Lord George Bentinck* (London, 1852), p. 13, Arthur Padley cited 'the most benevolent of Christian writers, St. John', 'Who is a liar but he that denieth that Jesus is the Christ! He is anti-Christ that denieth the Father and the Son.' Padley went on to say, 'so long as Israel is Anti-Christ, suffer him not to sit on the same bench with members of Parliament to make law for a Christian church and a Christian state'. In Maria Edgeworth, *Harrington* (1816), the advice the young Harrington (who has already been terrified by his nurse's stories of a child-eating Jewish pedlar) receives from his father is to avoid all dealings with Jewish money lenders. Dealing with the Jews is, he explains, 'something very like dealing with the devil, my dear ... So Harrington, my boy, I charge you at your peril, whatever else you do, keep out of the hands of the Jews – never go near the Jews, if once they catch hold of you, there's an end of you, my boy.' Quoted in Modder, *The Jew in the Literature of England*, p. 135.

114. Bryce Papers, Ms 6, folio 125, Freeman to Bryce, 22 October 1876; British Library, Add. Mss G. C. Boase, 35,073, folio 61, E. A. Freeman to Boase, 26 March 1877. 'Synagogue of Satan' occurs in Revelations. See Trachtenberg, *The Devil and the Jews*, p. 20. In view of the popularity of *The Merchant of Venice* in nineteenth-century England, it is worth noting that Trachtenberg points out

that there are two references in it to the association of Jews and the Devil: 'Let me say "Amen" betimes lest the devil cross my prayer, for here he comes in the likeness of a Jew' (Vol. II, part i, p. 22) and 'Certainly the Jew is the very devil incarnate' (Vol. II, part ii, p. 27). Bryce Papers, Ms 7, folio 11, Freeman to Bryce, 10 April 1881. To Freeman, Disraeli was the 'Arch-Deceiver', Stead, *The MP for Russia*, Vol. I, p. 371. Freeman regretted the fact that political decorum did not allow him to denounce in public Disraeli's policies as 'Satanic', Freeman, *Contemporary Review*, Vol. 37 (June 1880), p. 963. The American George Mackpeace Towle, in his *Certain Men of Mark: Studies of Living Celebrities* (1880), p. 100, describes Disraeli as 'a political Mephistopheles'. Even the generally reserved J. R. Green, who did not associate himself with the antisemitism of Freeman or Smith, became caught up in the rhetoric of the days. To fight against Russia, he wrote in May 1877, would be to go into war 'on the side of the Devil in the cause of Hell. It will be so terrible to have to wish England beaten.' Leslie Stephen (ed.), *Letters of John Richard Green* (London, 1901), p. 460.

115. W. R. W. Stephens, *The Life and Letters of Edward A. Freeman*, 2 vols (London, 1885), Vol. II, p. 389. Bryce Papers, Ms 6, folio 137, 8 April 1877; folio 125, 22 October 1876.

116. Comus, *The Devil's Visit to Bulgaria and other Lands* (Brighton, 1876), p. 5. A pamphlet published by the Birmingham Liberal Association in 1878 referred to Disraeli as 'Mephistophelian'. J. Cuckson, *Earl Beaconsfield: A Political Sketch* (Birmingham, 1878), p. 18: 'Nearly all our troubles have been hatched in the adventurous and imaginative brains of one man, whose Mephistophelian genius is foreign to the traditions and speech of our political history.' Disraeli's career had been 'un-English from beginning to end'.

117. Gladstone asked Disraeli to document the charge and also the allegation that he verbally abused Disraeli during the Eastern Question, a response that further irked Disraeli, who replied that he was far too busy with matters of state to review the entire record. Gladstone stuck to his guns, saying that he was criticising Disraeli's policies, not his character. He did in fact generally avoid slandering Disraeli's character and would not be drawn into the mud-slinging of the 1870s. For all this, see British Library, Gladstone Papers, Add. Mss, 44,457, folio 168, letters of 30 July 1878. For Gladstone's private reticence on Disraeli see Matthew, *Gladstone*, p. 34. According to the *Saturday Review*, 'As to Lord Beaconsfield, we know that Mephistopheles is the mildest term of reproach which many Dissenting ministers can find for him', *Saturday Review*, Vol. 47, No. 1,212 (18 January 1879), p. 78.

118. *The Hornet*, 7 August 1878, pp. 912–13.

119. Quoted in Georgina Battiscombe, *Mrs. Gladstone: The Portrait of a Marriage* (London, 1956), pp. 158, 174. Her comment recalls the *foetor judaicus* of medieval antisemitism. For its persistence in the nineteenth century, see Felsenstein, *Anti-Semitic Stereotypes*, pp. 257–9.

120. Quoted in Battiscombe, *Mrs. Gladstone*, p. 174. When Disraeli won the election in 1874 Catherine Gladstone wrote to her son, Herbert, 'is it not disgusting, after all Papa's labour and patriotism and years of work to think of handing over his nest-egg to that Jew'.

121. William T. Stead, *Gladstone in Contemporary Caricature* (London, 1898), p. 49.

122. Freeman, *Contemporary Review*, Vol. 30 (August 1877), p. 495; Freeman to Madame Olga Novikoff, 4 March 1877, Stead, *The MP for Russia*, Vol. 1, p. 334. Freeman also thought England was 'Jew-ridden'. Bryce Mss, Ms 6, folio 167. Freeman to Bryce, 5 June 1878.

123. The tenacity of old stereotypical images and the way Victorians drew on them is discussed acutely by Felsenstein in his analysis of Dickens: 'Fagin's "Jewishness"

emanates ... from Dickens's imaginative reinvigoration of attitudes of the endemic anti-Semitic stereotype that for so long had haunted the Christian consciousness.' *Anti-Semitic Stereotypes*, p. 239.

124. Figure 34 is from *One Hundred Cartoons from the Pages of Fun*, p. 49. The original appeared in the issue of 28 June 1876. Once again the specifics that occasioned the cartoon (the issue of state education) are less important than the imagery it employed. For other cartoons of Disraeli as magician or conjurer, see 'The Abode of Mystery', ibid., p. 68 (original appeared in the issue of 23 January 1878); 'The Celebrated Indian Crown Trick or, The Asian Mystery', ibid., p. 55 (original appeared in the issue of 10 January 1877); *Funny Folks*, No. 4 (26 January 1878), pp. 25, 165. For Tenniel's portrayal of Disraeli as alchemist see *Punch*, No. 76 (2 November 1879), p. 235.

125. *Spectator*, 20 July 1878, p. 915; 24 August 1878, p. 1061; 2 November 1878, p. 1357. In its obituary the *Spectator* argued that he 'displayed the genius of a political magician in making English nobles, and English squires, and English merchants prostrate themselves before the image of the policy which he had set up', *Public Opinion*, 30 April 1881, p. 538. In a similar vein the *Spectator* argued: 'The cabinet assuredly has been magnetized ... How this marvellous vision [of an 'Oriental policy'] has been translated from the dreams of the wildest of rodomontade and romance writers into the accepted policy of the stolidest [*sic*] and most practical-minded of all European States, is a question, to our minds, rather for the philosopher of magnetism to determine, than for any strictly political explanation.' *Spectator*, 1 July 1878, p. 883. Similarly, the obituary in the *Sheffield Telegraph* stated: 'The success of Mr. Disraeli would in ancient times have been attributed to supernatural aid', quoted in the *Spectator*, 30 April 1881, p. 539.

126. Quoted in Cecil Roth, *Benjamin Disraeli: Earl of Beaconsfield* (New York, 1952), pp. 84–5. Carlyle also called him 'a cursed old Jew, not worth his weight in cold bacon', ibid., p. 85.

127. *Britain at the Bar: A Scene from the Judgment of Nations, A Domestic Poem* (London, 1877), p. 14. See also O'Connor, *Lord Beaconsfield*, p. 467. In its obituary, the *Birmingham Daily Post* commented on the mystery of Disraeli's power, his possession of an influence, over even those within the party who disliked or distrusted him. Even they 'could neither resist nor explain' that influence, but simply 'obeyed him with a docility which must ever remain one of the mysteries of English politics'. Even 'when the more distrustful broke away, or even passed into open rebellion, he could lure them back again', 20 April 1881. A letter by Horrocks Cocks in the *Nonconformist*, 10 April 1878, argued that 'the Jewish Premier' in his antagonism to Russia was driven as much by 'Semitic' as patriotic urges, for he shared 'all the instincts, passions, prejudices, and antipathies of his race'. Cocks argued that just as Esther had conquered at the court of a real emperor so 'Benjamin – but not by his beauty – has become a great conjurer in the court of a nominal Empress, Victoria'.

128. Ragussis, *Figures of Conversion*, p. 204. In that sense these portrayals echo the rhetoric of Victorian literature on the unmasking of the 'secret Jew' by the Spanish Inquisition.

129. 'Throughout the cartoons of the period [ca. 1870–81] there is no one figure which appears with more persistent regularity than that of Lord Beaconsfield, and with scarcely an exception he is uniformly treated with an air of indulgent contempt. Of course his strongly marked features, the unmistakably Semitic cast of his nose and lips, the closely curled black ringlets clustering above his ears, all offered irresistible temptation to the cartoonist, with the result that throughout the entire series, in whatever guise he is portrayed, the suggestion of charlatan, of necromancer, of mountebank, of one kind or another of the

endless genus fake, is never wholly absent.' Arthur B. Maurice and Frederick T. Cooper, *The History of the Nineteenth Century in Caricature* (London, 1964), p. 246.

130. Figure 35 is from *Judy*, No. 22 (15 May 1878), pp. 314–15. Figure 36 is from *Judy*, No. 20 (7 February 1877), pp. 172–3.

131. *One Hundred Cartoons from the Pages of Fun*, preface. We can only speculate whether Disraeli ever saw any of the *Fun* cartoons. I think Monty Corry would have protected him from them. Disraeli's thick skin and cynicism would doubtless have afforded some protection, and, as he told Sir William Fraser, every politician was now made to appear 'ridiculous'. Wilfrid Meynell, *Benjamin Disraeli: An Unconventional Biography* (London, 1903), pp. 1, 45.

132. For the Conservatives' attempts to tar Gladstone with the brush of being 'un-English', see Cunningham, 'The Conservative Party and Patriotism', pp. 295–6.

133. For 'perlocutionary' acts, see J. L. Austin, *How to Do Things with Words* (Oxford, 1962), esp. 94ff. See also Neil MacCormick's review of Catharine A. MacKinnon's *Only Words* in *The Times Literary Supplement*, No. 4757, 3 June 1994, pp. 3–4, quoting Austin.

134. An analysis of the cartoon literature of the age points decisively to a conclusion identical to that reached by Michael Ragussis after a close examination of the novels of Trollope: 'Disraeli becomes a paradigm by which we can read Jewish identity; every Jew is a crypto-Jew, performing the rite of secret worship, if not to the Jewish God, then to the Jewish race; and every Jew is motivated in the same way, by secret contempt for the people among whom he lives. It is these hidden recesses of the secret Jew's heart that must be revealed to the English nation – especially when such a Jew heads the government – lest England be despoiled like Egypt.' Ragussis, *Figures of Conversion*, p. 260.

135. James Parkes, *Antisemitism* (London, 1963), pp. x–xi, quoted in Venetia Newall, 'The Jew as a Witch Figure', in Newall (ed.), *The Witch Figure: Folklore Essays by a Group of Scholars in England honouring the 75th Birthday of Katharine M. Briggs* (London, 1973), p. 119.

136. Newall, 'The Jew as a Witch Figure', p. 95. Clearly medieval traditions of anti-semitism were still current in Victorian England. Charles Lamb, for example, openly confessed: 'I should not care to be in habits of familiar intercourse with any of that [the Jewish] nation … Old prejudices cling about me. I cannot shake off the story of Hugh of Lincoln … A Hebrew is nowhere congenial to me.' Lamb, 'Jews, Quakers, Scotchmen and other Imperfect Sympathies', *London Magazine*, Vol. 4 (August 1821), p. 152, quoted in Montagu, *The Jew in the Literature of England*, p. 100. The Northampton lace workers in the 1840s incorporated the emotive power of the blood-libel myth in their popular songs. See *Jewish Chronicle*, 22 February 1867, p. 3, and 8 March 1867, p. 3.

137. David Cannadine, 'Cousinhood', *London Review of Books*, 27 July 1989, p. 10. Indeed, so sustained and successful, so smooth and uneventful, that any history of Anglo-Jewry, he argued, runs the danger of becoming 'a bland and lukewarm chronicle'; 'In the context of international Jewry, the history of British Jewry is neither very interesting, nor very exciting. In the context of British history, it is just not all that important', pp. 10, 12.

138. David Cannadine, review of Stanley Weintraub's *Disraeli*, *New York Times*, Book Review Section, 17 October 1993, p. 15; Cannadine, 'Cousinhood', p. 10.

139. See, for example, David Cesarani (ed.), *The Making of Anglo-Jewry* (Oxford, 1990) and Tony Kushner, 'Heritage and Ethnicity: An Introduction' in Kushner (ed.), *The Jewish Heritage in British History: Englishness and Jewishness* (London, 1992), pp. 1–28. W. D. Rubinstein, *A History of the Jews in the English-Speaking World: Great Britain* (London, 1996), pp. 32–3. He also includes in his indictment

the works of Ken Lunn, Geoffrey Alderman, Colin Holmes and Bill Williams. Rubinstein sees Williams's 'The Anti-Semitism of Tolerance' as Orwellian in that it twists even acts 'of friendship or solidarity by Gentiles towards Jews' (p. 32). If Rubinstein had had before him the works of Feldman and Ragussis, he would probably have added the former and certainly the latter to his black list. Although the focus of Rubinstein's attack is scholars working in the twentieth century, his criticisms also have relevance for the nineteenth century.

140. He even likens the new school of Anglo-Jewish historiography to the Monty Python 'Four Yorkshiremen' skit, where each horror of youth is dismissed in turn as luxury, compared to the far more dreadful deprivations another has experienced in his youth! Further: 'Much of the new school has a deliberately adversarial tone and intention about it. While not necessarily ignoring left-wing anti-semitism, it is clearly anti-Tory and anti-British Establishment, assuming, that both will be anti-Semitic almost by definition' (p. 33). Indeed, Rubinstein argues, 'Its interpretations of the Conservative Party and its policies are almost invariably much too harsh and often wildly inaccurate'. He attacks the incorporation of the 'claptrap of post-modernism' and the use of phrases such as 'representation', 'construction' and 'discourse' – an attack, it would seem, on Bryan Cheyette's *Constructions of 'The Jew'*.

141. Rubinstein, *A History of the Jews*, p. 34.

142. Israel Finestein, 'Jewish Emancipationists in Victorian England', p. 43.

143. Rubinstein argues that 'there is little or no attempt to relate levels of anti-semitism intelligently to other social dimensions of society; its existence and ubiquity are accepted virtually as a given'. He believes that philosemitism is minimised and calls for context: 'There is little or no attempt to weigh and assess anti-Semitism, as a prejudice or belief-system ... compared with other ethnic prejudices (especially anti-Catholicism, arguably a far more significant form of bigotry in England than anti-semitism ...)', p. 32.

144. As David Cesarani has written, it would be a 'grave mistake to capitulate' to the easy assumptions and 'prejudicial attitudes' which such comparisons encourage. 'The actuality and horror of Continental antisemitism', he has argued, tend to 'reinforce those prejudices and preconceptions which diminish the Anglo-Jewish experience. Confronted by the absence of pogroms or fatal violence against Jews in Britain when evaluating British antisemitism ... students and teachers [and, we might add, scholars] are easily tempted to respond that this phenomenon fails the "So what?" test. The entire subject can be put down to special pleading, paranoia, or lack of perspective, all persuasive reasons for dismissing it and moving on.' Cesarani, 'The Study of Antisemitism in Britain: Trends and Perspectives' in Michael Brown (ed.), *Approaches to Antisemitism: Context and Curriculum* (New York and Jerusalem, 1994), p. 265.

145. Rubinstein, *A History of the Jews*, p. 87, my emphasis. Goldwin Smith, for one, emphasised that Jews were not 'ordinary Nonconformists'. Smith, 'England's Abandonment of the Protectorate of Turkey', *Contemporary Review*, Vol. 31 (February 1878), p. 617.

146. *Jewish Chronicle*, 3 December 1880, p. 5; *Spectator*, 28 November 1880, quoted in the *Jewish Chronicle*, 3 December 1880, p. 5.

147. *Jewish World*, 19 December 1879, 2 January 1880. Among the reasons for its fear, the paper mentioned the recent publications and public statements of Goldwin Smith, Tollemache Sinclair, the Duke of Argyll, Gladstone and T. P. O'Connor.

148. *Jewish Chronicle*, 22 February 1878, pp. 9, 10.

149. *Jewish Chronicle*, 1 March 1878, pp. 9–10, 7 October 1881, p. 6.

150. *Jewish Chronicle*, 24 August 1877, pp. 9–10.

151. The *Spectator*, 12 October 1878, p. 1259. The *Spectator* also shared Stöcker's view

that Jews were destroying German culture and society. See, for example, the issue of 27 November 1880, p. 1510. For Smith's contention that 'Germans ... can hardly be accused of very shameful bigotry in struggling to keep their father-land to themselves', see his Canadian journal *Bystander*, March 1880, p. 57. German antisemitism, he insisted, 'is not unintelligible; nor a proof of disgrace-ful narrowness of mind. A high degree of liberality – and self-abnegation – must be reached before a nation can see with pleasure an alien race climbing, by superior subtlety and acquisitiveness, over its head in the land which the sweat of its own brow has made fruitful and for which it has poured out its own blood.' *Bystander*, August 1880, p. 445.

152. Todd Endelman has argued that in modern England there was a tension or strain between English liberalism and English culture. On the one hand, 'the liberal political creed', endorsed and protected Jewish identity and Jewish separateness as part of its broader credo of religious toleration and political pluralism. But, on the other hand, English culture (both of the political left and right) was 'ruth-lessly genteel, monolithic, and exclusive and did not acknowledge alternative ways of being English'. Antisemitism took a cultural rather than a political form. Endelman, 'English Jewish History', *Modern Judaism*, Vol. 11 (1991), p. 103, quoted in Cesarani, 'The Study of Antisemitism in Britain', p. 264. Some in the Anglo-Jewish community must have wondered which strain, the cultural or the political, would predominate, especially as cracks were appearing in 'the liberal political creed'.

153. Maurice and Cooper, *The History of the Nineteenth Century in Caricature*, p. 102, no source given.

154. For 'ethnic prejudice, and xenophobic hostility', see Langmuir, *Toward a Definition of Antisemitism*, p. 341. For 'casual prejudice, and peripheral concern' see Levy, *Antisemitism in the Modern World*, p. 2.

155. For the 'significant chimerical' qualities which Gavin Langmuir regards as a crucial feature of 'classic' antisemitism, see *Toward a Definition of Antisemitism*, pp. 315, 338, 341. The phrase about a 'life-shaping force', from Levy, *Anti-semitism in the Modern World*, p. 3, has a special relevance to the glib way in which stereotyping of Anglo-Jewry in general and Disraeli in particular was employed to explain away the complexities of England's foreign policy during the Eastern Question.

If we accept Michael Biddiss's definition of modern racism as being rather more than 'just prejudiced attitudes or discriminatory actions'; that it is the 'relatively systematic attempts at using race as the primary or even sole means of explaining the working of society and politics', then we must say that the antisemitic cartoons of Disraeli represent a form of racism. Biddiss, 'Myths of the Blood', *Patterns of Prejudice*, Vol. 9, No. 5 (September/October, 1975), p. 11.

I would also suggest that the 1870s provide an exception to Rubinstein's generalisation that 'most British "anti-semitism" does not reflect a true "con-struction of reality" in which Jews are seen as a malign, sinister force respon-sible for the world's evils'. Rubinstein, *A History of the Jews*, p. 34. Similarly, two pages earlier, Rubinstein argues that there has been 'little or no attempt to weigh and assess antisemitism' as a 'construction of reality' in which Jews are spontaneously nominated as a source of evil, p. 32.

DISRAELI, THE ROTHSCHILDS AND ANTISEMITISM

R. W. Davis

Benjamin Disraeli was subjected to displays of the most virulent and repulsive antisemitism throughout his career. At the beginning, the displays were cruder and more vulgar. Cries of 'old clothes' greeted him at early election meetings. Roast pork hoisted on a stick was proffered for his delectation. And a donkey was offered to carry him back to Jerusalem.[1]

Later, the attacks were usually more sophisticated, and even more vicious. Toward the end of his career, at the time of his greatest power and success, he suffered the most powerful and concentrated attack to which he had ever been exposed, and was pilloried in Parliament, public meetings, pamphlets and cartoons. One must, it is true, not forget the context. The onslaught on Disraeli and Jews in general had much to do with the fact that they were on the unpopular side of the Bulgarian Atrocities agitation after 1876.[2] British people of a Liberal persuasion and their leader, William Gladstone, concentrated their concern on the suffering of the Bulgarian Christians and thus favoured the latter's Russian allies in the struggle with their Turkish overlords. They could not understand why British Jews, of all people, did not also sympathise with the persecuted underdogs. Jews, for their part, had always found the Turks much to be preferred to the Russians, a position that also matched traditional British foreign policy concerns regarding British interests in India and one that Disraeli's government was to follow in its staunch defence of the integrity of the Turkish empire. This served as the occasion for the noted Liberal historian and Oxford professor E. A. Freeman to ask from a public platform, which he shared with Gladstone, whether 'the Jew in his drunken insolence' would also 'fight to uphold the independence and integrity of Sodom'.[3] He spoke of the Prime Minister. The violence of the attack went beyond anything required by mere policy disputes.

At a time when even the Rothschilds used 'Jew-boy' as a term of derision, it is not always easy to assess the degree of malice in recorded remarks.[4] It is quite striking, however, how often Disraeli's contemporaries, even people who knew him well, went out of their way to identify him as a Jew. It was not a term of endearment. Richard Shannon has remarked on the memory one Conservative MP carried away from the last party meeting Disraeli attended, held in his own house in Curzon Street. 'Beaconsfield stood ..., a lean, dark, feeble figure, against a tinselly background.'[5] He could easily have been conjuring up a picture of an old Jew amongst his wares. One cannot, of course, be certain.

There is, however, nothing equivocal about the evidence presented by hundreds of cartoons. With few, if any, exceptions, when caricaturists exaggerated Disraeli's features, they did so for one purpose, to fix a Jewish identity – if as a shifty commercial Jew, so much the better.[6]

Having been converted to Anglicanism as a youth, Disraeli was not, strictly speaking, a Jew. His friends the Rothschilds quite definitely were, yet they fared much better and suffered relatively little from antisemitism, certainly as compared to Disraeli. True, there are important exceptions, for instance, the well-known pronouncement of the journalist J. A. Hobson, who formulated one of the first and most influential theories of imperialism, about the great agglomerations of finance capital:

> United by the strongest bonds of organization, always in the closest touch with one another, situated in the very heart of the business capital of every State, controlled so far as Europe is concerned chiefly by men of a single and peculiar race, who have behind them many centuries of financial experience, they are in a unique position to manipulate the policy of nations ... Does any one seriously suppose that a great war could be undertaken by any European State, or a great State loan subscribed, if the house of Rothschild and its connexions set their face against it?[7]

Hobson, of course, did not have all the facts and could not have known quite how wrong he was in his suspicions about the Rothschilds and the war he thought they had facilitated against the Boers, which was the source of his venom. But it is strange, to say the least, that he did not think of a number of exceptions to his assertion about the Jewish monopoly of finance capital – in London alone, the Barings, the Grenfells and the English house of Morgan, for example – let alone a Rothschild monopoly. Perhaps Hobson was not even consciously antisemitic. But there can be no doubt that his comment was, conflating as it did an attack on individuals with an attack on a whole people. Wild, reckless and irresponsible, Hobson's assertions contributed to the growth of a wicked myth.

The immediate objects of these charges would not, however, suffer from them. Like earlier exaggerations of Rothschild power – for example, that they had brought down Lord Goderich's government in 1828 – such misconceptions only added to the Rothschild mystique.[8] This mystique of power did not for the most part breed fear and loathing, quite the contrary. In 1848, the former Protectionist Tory leader Lord George Bentinck told another Tory politician and journalist, John Wilson Croker, that 'the Rothschilds all stand high in private character'. He went on to say that the City of London's confidence in Lionel, the then head of the bank and a Liberal candidate for the City, whose 1847 election had been voided by his refusal to swear a Christian oath, was 'such a pronunciation of public opinion' that it was 'like Clare electing O'Connell, Yorkshire Wilberforce'.[9] With the confidence of the largest county, with the largest electorate in Britain, William Wilberforce had become a moral arbiter who, among other achievements, had led the successful effort to put slavery in the British Empire on the path to total abolition. And, with his election to County Clare, Daniel O'Connell, with most of Ireland at his back, had forced the Duke of Wellington's government in 1829 to concede that Catholics as well as Protestants could sit in the British Parliament. Bentinck therefore paid Lionel de Rothschild a high compliment. Lord George also demonstrated his own prescience, for ten years later, during which time Rothschild's electoral support was unswerving, Parliament finally conceded the City the MP of its choice and the right of Jews as well as Christians to sit in the House of Commons.

In 1869, Lord Granville, Gladstone's Foreign Secretary and the Liberal leader in the House of Lords, urged upon Queen Victoria a peerage for Lionel, who, he said, represented 'a class whose influence is great by their wealth, their intelligence, their literary connexions, and their numerous seats in the House of Commons. It may be wise to attach them to the aristocracy rather than to drive them into the democratic camp.'[10] In 1869, even these impressive arguments were not enough to reconcile Victoria to what she called a 'Jew peer'. But in some respects the Queen was even then favourably impressed by the Rothschilds. She was, for example, much struck by the physical beauty of Lionel's children. In April 1856, 122 debutantes were presented at Court. 'Nobody very striking', the Queen remarked, 'excepting Mlle de Rothschild, Baron Lionel's daughter, who is extremely handsome.' The 'Mlle' may suggest that Victoria found the future Baroness Alphonse, who married her cousin, later the head of the French family, somewhat exotic, but there is no doubting her admiration.[11] Ironically, there was nobody more English than this particular Rothschild, Leonora or Laury, as she was known in the family. Five years later her sister Evy found her bearing the abuse of Paris society for wearing deep mourning for the death of the Queen's mother, the Duchess of Kent. Evy wrote home: 'she will be an English woman wherever she is. Quite right!'[12]

The Queen was equally appreciative of Natty, Lionel's eldest son and the future Lord Rothschild. In 1881, she records meeting Disraeli's two executors, Monty Corry and 'Sir Nathaniel de Rothschild a handsome man of about 38 or 40 with a fine type of Jewish countenance'. And in 1885 she made, according to Gladstone's secretary, Eddie Hamilton, 'little or no difficulty' when the Prime Minister recommended Natty (whose name was Nathan, not Nathaniel) for a peerage. Hamilton recorded in his diary: 'Some people are turning up their noses at the Rothschild peerage; but I am very pleased it has been conferred. The stake which the remarkable family hold in this country amply justifies Royal recognition; and it removes the last remnant of religious disqualifications.'[13] As his father had led the last excluded minority into the Commons, Natty led them into the Lords. Doubtless some did turn up their noses, but it was not a posture that was adopted in public. By this time the Rothschilds had sunk deep roots into English soil and were firmly entrenched in English society.

The elder Nathan, founder of the English branch of the Rothschilds, was German-born and German-bred. He was also all business and took no more interest in the nuances and complexities of English society than was absolutely necessary. He was late in moving his town residence from the City to the fashionable West End, and, though he bought the big house that still stands in Gunnersbury Park in 1835, he did not live to take advantage of that ex-urban retreat.

Nathan's wife, Hannah Barent Cohen, who was probably responsible for such westward movement as did occur, was English, and, though she had a head for business for which her husband had profound respect, she was also very sensitive to the demands of society. Nathan had never bothered to assume the Austrian barony his brothers had arranged at the end of the Napoleonic Wars. However, upon his death, Hannah began to call herself Baroness, and very likely it was she who asked her sons to secure royal permission to use the title. From then on mother and sons all affixed the noble 'de' to Rothschild. Such manoeuvring might be called realising on foreign assets. But on the right sort of education, Hannah's English preferences were quite clear. While their father was alive, all four sons – Lionel, Anthony, Nathaniel and Mayer – pursued their university careers in Germany. When Nathan died in 1836, all but Mayer had finished their education and were in the bank. As his father had planned, Mayer spent the autumn of that year in Heidelberg, but the next October he was sent up to Cambridge, first to Magdalene and then to Trinity, where it was apparently easier to escape the compulsory chapel attendance that made life difficult for non-Anglicans at Cambridge. Mayer spent only two years at Cambridge, where in any case as a non-Anglican he could not have taken a degree. They were evidently two very happy years. There are not many details on how he spent his time. There is, however, evidence that he boarded horses, and that is probably the answer to how he employed much of his time, for both Magdalene and Trinity, then and afterward, were socially elite colleges, with a prominent sporting set.[14]

All the brothers were keen hunters. In October 1835, Anthony wrote to Nat (Nathaniel) from Frankfurt, bemoaning the fact that he could not have a few days with the Puckeridge Hunt. As that was impossible, could he please have a brown hunting coat with Puckeridge buttons? In 1842, it was Nat's turn to yearn for the unobtainable. Now a partner in the Paris bank, he wrote to his brothers: 'What magic there is in a pair of leather breeches. I have half a mind to put a pair on and gallop around the Bois de Boulogne – Old Tup [Mayer] would exclaim, Go it you Cockney.'[15] It was an abiding passion, and some years later in middle age, when they were all men of great wealth and position, the four brothers would choose to have Sir Francis Grant paint them together, riding across the Vale of Aylesbury to the Rothschild Staghounds.

But of the four, it was Mayer whose passion was most evident, not to say notorious. In November 1839, shortly after he had come down from Cambridge and was supposed to be hard at work in the bank, his formidable Uncle James, head of the Paris house, wrote wondering why Mayer was not contributing to the constant flow of correspondence among the several family banks. 'Why is it', James enquired, 'that … Mayer does not write? Is he hunting? A young man should and has to work.'[16] Whatever Mayer should have done, he did not have to work, and he did not, at least not in the bank.

It was Mayer who presided over the family's growing country and sporting interests. After a few years of rented accommodations in

Buckinghamshire, in 1842 he bought Mentmore, which became the centre for a variety of the family's activities. In 1841, the Baron's horse (in Buckinghamshire, 'the Baron' always meant Mayer) came third in a steeplechase at Aylesbury. In two events the next year his horses came first. In November 1845, though the brothers had hunted the Vale in select company since 1839, 'was the first public meet of Baron Rothschild's hounds, when a fine stag was uncarted ... on Bierton Hill, Aylesbury. There was a large field.' The Rothschild Staghounds, now open to anyone who paid a subscription, became a popular institution in the county and beyond; Anthony Trollope attended regularly, and the Prince of Wales not infrequently. The stags, which Mayer raised for the purpose at Mentmore, were boxed and carted to whatever starting point had been chosen, whence they led the hunt on a lively chase until they were finally run down by the hounds.

Though certainly not to everyone's taste today, these events did much to raise the Rothschilds' popularity at the time. Mayer's ascent was fast. In 1841, probably because of connections made at Cambridge, he was elected a member of Brooks's, long the club of aristocratic Whigs. In the county, he became High Sheriff in 1847, no longer an office of much power but still a sign of acceptance into the county elite. He amassed the requisite large estate in a remarkably short time. This was partly because of the difficulties of several major landowners in the area, most notably the second Duke of Buckingham, who were forced to sell some or all of their estates. It was also partly because the Vale of Aylesbury contained a large number of relatively small properties, which made it possible to build a large one piecemeal. Mentmore had begun as a small estate, with three or four farms. By the time of Mayer's death in 1874, it had expanded to several thousand acres, presided over by Mentmore Towers, one of the great Victorian country houses, which Mayer commissioned in 1850 from Joseph Paxton, the architect of the Crystal Palace. From this princely establishment, Mayer continued and expanded the country pursuits he loved so well. He became a breeder of fine purebred cattle and of even more famous racehorses, one of which won the Derby.

Though Mayer was the major representative of the family in Buckinghamshire, the Staghounds had been a joint venture of all four Rothschild brothers from the beginning. And, save for Nat, who invested his money in such French assets as Chateau Mouton, all became large landowners in the country. Anthony, who in 1847 received the baronetcy Lionel had spurned, bought the greater part of the Aston Clinton estate, including a large house, in the sale of the Duke of

Buckingham's properties in 1848. Lionel remained content with the Gunnersbury house he had inherited from his mother – a fine house but one with only about 600 acres of land. However, he had been quietly acquiring land in Buckinghamshire all along. In 1872, he presented his eldest son, Natty, Lord Rothschild of Tring as he became in 1885, with Tring Park, just over the Hertfordshire border. A decade later, the estate included just under 10,000 acres of land in Buckinghamshire. Besides this, Alfred, the second son, was provided with an estate at Halton and the youngest son, Leopold, with one at Ascot. Meanwhile, Lionel's son-in-law, Ferdinand, had acquired the former Waddesdon estate of the Duke of Marlborough and had built there his great French chateau, a favourite haunt of the Prince of Wales and now of thousands of visitors who troop through its rooms and park each year.

The first Rothschild to be on intimate terms with the Prince was Natty; they had been college friends at Trinity in the 1860s. Early in the Lent term of 1861 Natty was visiting the rooms of his friend the Duke of St Albans to offer him promotion in the Masonic hierarchy, when the Prince was announced. Natty was asked to stay and 'was addressed by my own name so that I suppose an introduction was considered unnecessary'.[17] There was good reason, apart from his name, why Natty was considered a desirable friend for the Prince. He was at the very centre of the Trinity elite. As Master of the Horse Drag, Natty was a great man, in charge of dragging the scent and thus setting the course for the hunting set. He and the Prince also played cricket together and engaged in horseplay on the river, which ended in dumping St Albans in the water. In short, they did the kinds of things undergraduates are apt to do. What is significant is not that Natty had made the friendship of the Prince. He had not courted it, and though they remained close friends, he never attempted to capitalise on it. His brother-in-law and cousin, Ferdie, who did work hard on a relationship, was latterly much closer to the Prince and part of his somewhat raffish circle, which often gathered at Waddesdon. What was important was what attracted the Prince's advisers in the first place, the position Natty had made for himself at Trinity. He was unlike his beloved Uncle Muffy (Mayer) in that he took his place at the head of the bank. But he was like his uncle in his tastes. The formidable, and even fearsome, banker's club was the Turf. The Rothschilds were both English gentlemen and sportsmen.

If we turn to the caricaturists' treatment of the Rothschilds, we once again find a marked contrast with that accorded Disraeli. The first Rothschild to be portrayed in *Vanity Fair*, a popular periodical of cartoon portraiture, where prominent contemporaries were given a certain immortality, was Mayer in 1871, the year his horse won the Derby. The cartoon is entitled 'The Winner of the Race'. According to the authorities on *Vanity Fair* cartoons, Roy Matthews and Peter Mellini:

> *Vanity Fair* recognized this step with a degree of approval, but not without a condescension which hinted at antisemitism. Ape's caricature of the Baron is not flattering. He has empha- sized his subject's large nose, protruding mouth and lips. The stance is hardly becoming as the Baron leans forward, stiff legged and slightly bent, resting on a cane.[18]

As a matter of fact, Ape (all the *Vanity Fair* artists had *noms de plume*) did not greatly exaggerate Mayer's features, even as portrayed by the fashionable artist George Frederick Watts. Indeed, the nose in the cartoon is rather smaller and sharper. Mayer had a good and kindly face. His sunny nature was celebrated inside the family and outside. All these characteristics, Ape captures. If he did not make Mayer hand- some, it is because he was not. As far as his dress and fashionably slender stick are concerned, he is made to appear like a sporting gentle- man at his ease in the enclosure at Newmarket, which is, in fact, what he was.

Matthews and Mellini are happier with Ape's rendering of Lionel in 1877: 'The heavy eyelids and large nose dominate the face, but the features are softened. He looks like a pleasant elderly man, wise in the ways of the world.' Nevertheless, the two experts conclude that the 'caricature hints at a nineteenth-century stereotyping of Jews'.[19] Ape's rendering of Lionel is certainly more of a caricature than his cartoon of Mayer. Lionel was by anyone's accounting a handsome man, to which a large nose and heavy eyelids are not insurmountable bars. Perhaps this is why Ape took more liberties with him than he did with Mayer. But the face, with a slight smile and twinkling eyes, is one we are clearly meant to like.

By contrast, in many, perhaps most, caricatures of Disraeli, we would not recognise him were it not for other caricatures. Caricatures are, by their nature, exaggerated depictions. But many of the Disraeli caricatures are not merely gross exaggerations – they are simply gross.

The Rothschilds did not suffer that, and Natty's *Vanity Fair* cartoon by Lib in 1888 is hardly a cartoon at all, though it is an amusing rendering. It is called simply 'Natty'. And that is what it is all about. He is portrayed in a shiny top hat and an elegant Chesterfield, with a large red flower in his buttonhole, and leaning on a fine silver-topped ebony stick. As for the face, it is his own.[20]

Miriam Rothschild tells an amusing story about a visit of Edward VII to Natty's house at Tring. One little girl in the town could hardly contain herself in anticipation of the King's visit, but she seemed somewhat crestfallen afterwards. 'Well, what did you think of the King?' she was asked. 'Why', she replied, 'he looked just like Lord Rothschild.' There was a more than passing resemblance. Natty would be caricatured more than once – as a penguin popping up in Antarctica and a knight in a modern Froissart's *Chronicle* – but no caricaturist took undue freedoms with his physiognomy.[21]

Why was it that the Rothschilds received so much better treatment than Disraeli? One seemingly obvious answer is that they were very rich, and he was not. This is true, but the Rothschilds were rich long before they were accepted in society. And it is arguable that in the 1830s Disraeli was more of a figure in society than they were.

Success in London society was not, of course, equivalent to establishing a secure social position, though it might provide an entrée to the aristocratic world, as it did for Disraeli. But the Rothschilds built on more solid foundations. The fact that Mayer was the first to be caricatured in *Vanity Fair* is significant. In the sense of social acceptance, he was ahead of his brothers all along, a country gentleman educated at one of the old universities and an active patron of the sport of kings.

Clearly, the contacts that the Rothschilds established at Cambridge would be important. But perhaps even more important, in what was very much a man's world, they became in every sense of the word, Englishmen. It was a world in which Disraeli was never comfortable and one that he avoided as much as possible. He did not hunt. He did not shoot, the main form of entertainment at the political house parties in the autumn. (Tring was exceptional only in the sense that the sport Lord Rothschild offered his guests was shooting waterfowl rather than pheasants.) He cared nothing for horse racing. He disliked all male social gatherings of any sort.[22] His failure to engage in what is now called 'male bonding' left Disraeli uncomfortably exposed. In male-dominated societies, it is better to be one of the boys. Disraeli forever remained what he had been at school, a bright boy on the outside, an all too easy mark. And antisemitic prejudice aside, this characteristic may help to explain why the Tory rank and file always found him remote – he was.

But there is another reason for the virulence of the abuse Disraeli suffered. He was in the wrong party. At least, he was in the wrong party as far as antisemitism was concerned, and this created a dangerous contradiction in his own position.

It should be stressed that this is a very different question from whether he chose the right party in which to make a political career. If he had succeeded, as he early attempted, in getting the attention of the Whigs or the Radicals of the Lord Durham variety – though a member of the Whig elite, Durham was well to the left of his colleagues in the 1830s on questions of domestic and colonial government – it is unlikely that he would ever have held high office. The Whig-Liberals were never very open to adventurers. The Tories were, of which the career of Disraeli's first patron, Lord Lyndhurst, the son of an American portrait painter, is a good example.

But, if Disraeli chose the right party in which to succeed, he paid dearly for his success. Peel managed for a while to suppress, but never to extirpate, the intolerance of the Tory rank and file. And when Disraeli helped to drive out Peel and the Peelites and himself came forward as a leader, he came face to face with the rancorous rump. The trouble started almost immediately with Lionel de Rothschild's election for the City of London in 1847 and the House's refusal to seat him because he would not take the oath on 'the true faith of a Christian'.

This was an occasion when Rothschild was the object of antisemitic attacks, as he would continue to be, from the organ of the Protectionist Party, *The Morning Post*. But in Rothschild's position, it was easier to take the abuse with equanimity. In July 1849, Lord John Manners, a close friend of Disraeli and a former member of his 'Young England' group, was dining with Mrs Nathan de Rothschild, or 'the Baroness' as she called herself, the mother of Lionel and Mayer. Manners had been made acutely uncomfortable by the latter's laughing remark, 'well I suppose you'll stand against Lionel'. Soon after, Manners had most reluctantly been persuaded by the party to do just that. He recorded in his diary that, on the day of nomination, 'the mob made Rothschild inaudible by applauding, me by groaning'. At the poll, Manners made a respectable showing, but Lionel won an overwhelming victory.

Manners had made little attempt to hide his extreme embarrassment throughout. The editor of the *Disraeli Letters* observes that his discomfort cannot have been lessened by the violent antisemitism of *The Morning Post*, which supported Manners in the election and for which he was then seeking financial support.[23] But what of the man who had just established himself as leader of the Protectionist party

in the House of Commons and who was also busily raising money for
The Morning Post?

Disraeli was, of course, in a cruel dilemma. The Rothschilds knew
that and they were understanding much of the time. From the time
the issue had become a parliamentary one in 1847, Disraeli had been
making the point that the party owed much to Tory friends of the Jews,
such as Lord George Bentinck, Thomas Baring and himself. There
was, however, a very important difference between the Jews' other
Tory champions and himself. Their principles were the principles of
religious liberty, which were traceable to their Whig antecedents.
Disraeli's principle was unique and of his own manufacture. He spurned
arguments of liberty, adopting instead the line that the Jews deserved
special treatment from a Christian state because of the intimate connection between the two religions.

What Louise de Rothschild, the wife of Sir Anthony, called Disraeli's
'strange Tancredian strain' (the argument was first advanced in his
novel *Tancred*) was apparent as well in his life of *Lord George Bentinck*
and in his speeches in Parliament. Some of what he said was very
strange indeed, as, for example, the argument he put in the mouth of
the novel's Jewish heroine, Eva: 'Now tell me: suppose the Jews had
not prevailed upon the Romans to crucify Jesus, what would have
become of the Atonement?' At the end of the long struggle in 1858,
Lionel wrote to his wife of what he saw as one of Disraeli's final shifts:
'you know what a humbug he is.' That was the judgment of a friend.[24]

This is not to deny that Disraeli's statements on the Jewish question, and the several vehicles he employed to make them, constituted
brilliant and necessary political manoeuvring on the part of a man who
aspired to lead the Tory party – not an unworthy ambition nor, on the
whole, a prize he used unworthily. Neither do I mean to question his
courage, for however clever he was in averting it, the danger was great.
And, finally, I do not mean to question his sincerity in the cause, about
which I think there can be no serious doubt.

But the question being addressed is why Disraeli, in contrast to the
Rothschilds, suffered the abuse he did. And part of the answer has to
do with the political party he chose. He himself was acutely aware of
the problem. As he wrote to Prince Metternich in January 1849:
'Surely it is a great anomaly, that a proud aristocracy should find a
chief in one who is not only not an aristocrat, but against whose origin
exist other prejudices, than being merely a man of the people.'[25]

It was indeed an anomaly, one from which he could not escape.
What is more, it was one that was bound to make his motives suspect

to both sides. Liberals doubted his sincerity in the cause of Jewish emancipation; Tories doubted his sincerity in the cause of the Church. It was all too easy to see him as a humbug, a fraud and a cheat. And at the centre of it all was his Jewishness. Of this, he had been reminded since it had first become clear that he was marked for a leading position in the Tory party. On 19 September 1847, *The Satirist* carried a cartoon entitled 'The Modern Moses in the Bulrushes'. Lord Derby, portrayed as Pharaoh's daughter, reaches out to caress the very large head of Disraeli, attached to a very small body cradled in its frail bark, the better to show the dark, sinister scowl on his face.[26] It seems clear that the artist had more in mind than a prince of Egypt raised from the muck and was thinking as well of how Moses had repaid his bene-factors. Disraeli was as sure to attract antisemitism as a lightning rod lightning – and he did.

The Rothschilds, of course, never aspired to high political office, but they did enjoy a good deal of gratifying political success – and they enjoyed it primarily because they were Jews. Disraeli, for his own very good reasons, refused to use liberal arguments for Jewish emancipation. Lionel, as candidate for the City of London, refused to use any other. He called his candidacy for London in 1847 'the effort the electors of London were now making for civil and religious liberty', and they cheered him to the echo. A Dissenter chaired his committee, and Dissenters and Catholics, as well as Jews, flocked to his standard. He was returned with some 6,800 votes, only a couple of hundred behind the Prime Minister, Lord John Russell. In 1849, after he had vacated his seat to submit himself once again to the judgment of the electors of London, he was returned in the by-election with some 6,000 votes to Manners' 2,800. And so it went, for 11 years in all, until he was finally seated in 1858.[27]

Moreover, the position Lionel established in London was a signif-icant part of the reason for the family success in Aylesbury, a large mainly rural borough, which took up most of the southern half of Buckinghamshire. The existing Liberal grandees, Lord Carrington and Acton Tindal, were by no means happy at the arrival of the Rothschilds, especially when the latter allied themselves with the more radical elements in the local party. They would not, Lord Carrington said, 'be the votaries of democracy or Judaism'. His picturesque nickname for the Rothschilds was 'the Red Sea'. Tindal was more direct in his imagery, writing to Sir William Hayter, the Liberal Chief Whip, that he would not 'hand over our party to inevitable *circumcision*'.[28]

No such drastic operation took place, nor did the Red Sea close over the Egyptians, but they did have to give way. The rank and file of the Liberal party in Aylesbury insisted on it. Known as the 'old' Liberal party, and mainly Dissenters, their position had been forged in the religious controversies of the 1820s. Starting as anti-Catholic, they had been weaned away from that position by the determined liberal advocacy of their then MP, Lord Nugent. And, after 1829, when they petitioned for Catholic emancipation, they never looked back. They were still led in the 1850s by one of Nugent's converts, John Gibbs, a Congregationalist and former pawnbroker, who by that time was the proprietor of the *Bucks Advertiser*.

In 1852, Tindal and Carrington attempted to oust the sitting Liberal Member, Richard Bethell, whom the Rothschilds supported, and replace him with Austen Henry Layard. This manoeuvre did not suit the 'old' Liberals in the least, and they got their way. At a meeting of the Liberal electors, it was made clear that they were quite prepared to have Layard, providing that he would promise to vote for the ballot. Carrington had strongly advised against any such pledge, but Layard promised none the less. Acton Tindal thereupon expressed the hope that his personal differences with Bethell would not prevent anyone else from voting for him. Joseph Jones, an Aylesbury solicitor and self-avowed former London Chartist, then moved that Bethell was a fit candidate, which was seconded by Gibbs's son, and carried with enthusiasm.[29]

After this the Rothschild interest in Aylesbury prospered, but it was clearly based on a partnership the success of which depended on agreement on principles. The Rothschilds had the right ones. This was demonstrated again in 1865, when Natty came forward as a candidate, the first member of the family to do so. The Liberal electors put only one question to those who aspired to represent them: what was their stand on the Church-rate question? (Church rates forced non-Anglicans to contribute to the support of the Established Church.) Others waffled, but Natty did not hesitate to pledge himself to support total abolition. In return, the *Bucks Gazette* announced its endorsement of Rothschild alone.[30]

Historians make much of the great electoral power of the British aristocracy, and it is perfectly true that their tenants, whose votes they might influence, and their wealth, which often made them the main support of a constituency party, did give them a powerful position. The Rothschilds enjoyed such a position in Aylesbury, and indeed at least as late as 1970 the Rothschild agent occupied a prominent place on the platform at Liberal meetings. Yet by the middle of the nineteenth century few constituencies existed that could be won or maintained by such methods alone. Political success did not come easily. It required a good deal of courting of the electorate, from the platform and in the long canvasses of the electors. It also required solicitude for the electors' opinions and the flexibility to compromise. Such traits are often forgotten in assessing the success of aristocratic politicians, but they were essential. The Rothschilds' possession of them was one more sign of their membership of the aristocratic club, and they duly took their places in Parliament, Lionel for London, Mayer for Hythe and Natty for Aylesbury.

Aylesbury was also the constituency in which Disraeli always lived; both Bradenham and Hughenden were within its boundaries. There he was relatively safe from antisemitism. Bigotry did not go down well in Aylesbury, and even the Tories found it advisable to pick candidates who were moderates on religious questions; on one occasion they went so far as to pick a Unitarian, which proved more than their own party could swallow.[31] Even Lord Carrington, the Lord Lieutenant, he of the 'Red Sea' quip, behaved well. Indeed, as anyone who has read Disraeli's correspondence knows, he and Carrington appear to have been on cordial terms. They were neighbours who visited back and forth, and the walk over the Chilterns to Wycombe Abbey was one of Disraeli's favourites. In fact, the antisemitic remarks were rather untypical. Natty was also a frequent visitor in the Carrington houses, though that was doubtless mainly because of Carrington's eldest son Charlie, the future Marquis of Lincolnshire, a contemporary at Cambridge who would always be one of Natty's closest friends.

Yet however safe he might be in the shadow of the Chiltern Hills, elsewhere Disraeli was remarkably exposed to the slings and arrows of his enemies. His party was never entirely comfortable with him, nor did he much care for them. They were far too different. One of the main reasons for the coolness was that the Tories distrusted his principles or doubted that he had any, and one of the things that lay at the base of these doubts was the apparent contradictions in his Jewishness – and in their eyes of Jewishness and Conservatism.

The Rothschilds were happy by comparison. Revered in the City of London, the darlings of the hunting field and the racecourse, they had friends at their back wherever they went. And their principles fitted them perfectly. What else should a Jew be but a friend of civil and religious liberty? Some might have raised their eyebrows when upon the death of Cecil Rhodes, Lord Rothschild, his chief trustee, announced that he and his colleagues would spend Rhodes's fortune 'in the interest of, and for the development of the Anglo-Saxon race'.[32] Natty himself clearly did not find anything incongruous about being at the same time an Anglo-Saxon and a Jew, and no one else seems to have been much worried about it either. Another title that he was popularly given was 'King of the Jews'. In other circumstances, this might be considered an antisemitic slur. The Rothschilds never felt it so.

Antisemitism in nineteenth-century England was a complicated phenomenon. It was never – and who would imagine it to be – good or admirable. But just how damaging it was depended very much on individual circumstances. The treatment of Disraeli represented one extreme, though he triumphed over it. The Rothschilds may have represented the other. Their great wealth was undoubtedly an advantage. But more important was the way they used it; they used it to make themselves into English gentlemen. They maintained their Jewish religion and identity with pride, but otherwise they blended into English society, in their case aristocratic English society. Disraeli's situation was unique. That of the Rothschilds was, I suspect, much less so.

Colin Holmes has argued that the great difference between antisemitism in Britain and in other European countries was that in Britain there were structures to challenge, advertise and, thus, contain it.[33] He has in mind mainly the activities of such organisations as the Board of Deputies of British Jews. Their work was undoubtedly important, and it was also in an already established British tradition: the Board's similarity, both in its organisation and its function, to the older Committee of the Protestant Dissenting Deputies of the Three Denominations was too close to have been mere coincidence.

But there was another and greater body that has received less attention. British liberalism was, in large part, born of religious diversity, or more precisely of the struggle of those outside the established Anglican Church to achieve an equality of privilege with those within it. Starting in the second decade of the nineteenth century (with the repeal of the Test and Corporation Acts, which had branded Protestant Dissenters second-class citizens, followed quickly by Catholic emancipation in 1829), the outsiders began to achieve major victories. From the beginning, the Jews were recognised as an integral part of this great campaign for social and civic equality. As William Smith, the leader of the Protestant Dissenters and a doughty champion of religious liberty, assured his fellow Whig, Lord Holland, after the triumph of Catholic emancipation, the Jews too would have their day.[34] As has been seen above, this liberal solidarity (by then in the Liberal party) was marshalled by the Rothschilds to great effect in the 1840s and 1850s. It lasted until religious grievances were largely removed, and thus ceased to dominate politics, in the last two decades of the nineteenth century. At about the same time there began the great immigration of Russian Jews, fleeing persecution in the Russian empire, which some feared would disrupt the comfortable accommodation achieved by Anglo-Jewry. It did not.

By then nineteenth-century Liberalism had done its work. It had given Jews great and small – not only peers of the realm and MPs, but also those of lesser fame, such as the Jewish electors of London – a place in a great British institution, the Liberal party. They fought for it, and it fought for them. In the process they put down roots into British society, roots of a depth and strength that no other European Jews ever achieved. The social and political situation that this created was a largely benign one for Jews. Disraeli battled adversity in his own way, always against the grain, and his achievement was stunning. Other Jews like the Rothschilds had an easier time.

Until relatively recently antisemitism has never been far below the surface in western societies. (In a few it remains close to the surface.) The amount of damage it has done, of course, has varied enormously. Britain's record has clearly been better than most. But whether this fully justifies the optimism in the latest exercise in re-revisionism is questionable. David Feldman had already pointed out the necessity to see apparent antisemitism in the context of the broader society, and W. D. Rubenstein is justified in pressing the point further.[35] But Rubenstein has pushed it rather too far. That antisemitism existed in nineteenth-century Britain is glaringly evident. That anti-Catholicism and anti-Irish prejudice also existed are hardly mitigating circumstances. And philosemitism, the ostensible object of which was to hasten the realisation of Christian revelation, was an ambiguous good, to say the least. Colin Holmes is right, not only that antisemitism was a tangible threat but that the important question is why it never became really dangerous.

As is suggested above, the answer is the one Voltaire gave long ago – albeit with his usual exaggeration and perhaps before its time – that there were too many sects in Britain to be persecuted successfully. Common interests in religious and civic equality mitigated the conflicts between Protestant Dissenters and Roman Catholics, making both more sympathetic to the plight of the Jews. For that matter, it also softened prejudice against the Irish, the popularity of Gladstone's Irish Church measure in 1868–69 providing one example of this. Over the course of the century, institutions that this set of interlocking interests threw up, of which the Liberal party was perhaps the central one, not only promoted those interests directly but also promoted discussion of the issues and their dissemination through the press and other organs of public opinion. The result was gradually to create a social and political culture in which antisemitism found it difficult to thrive. It is perhaps significant that in his own country the poisonous seeds that Hobson broadcast fell on barren soil.

NOTES

1. Stanley Weintraub, *Disraeli: A Biography* (New York, 1993), pp. 161, 197.
2. David Feldman, *Englishmen and Jews: Social Relations and Political Culture, 1840–1914* (New Haven, CT, 1994), esp. ch. 4.
3. Weintraub, *Disraeli*, p. 568.
4. The Rothschild Archive, London, 000/12, Natty Rothschild to his parents, Cambridge, n.d. (1859).
5. Richard Shannon, *The Age of Disraeli, 1868–1881: The Rise of Tory Democracy* (London, 1992), p. 418.
6. For the most extensive consideration of this subject, see Anthony S. Wohl's contribution to this volume, '"Ben JuJu": Representations of Disraeli's Jewishness in the Victorian Political Cartoon'.
7. Harrison M. Wright (ed.), *The 'New Imperialism': Analysis of Late-Nineteenth Century Expansion* (2nd edn, Lexington, MA, 1976), p. 26.
8. R. W. Davis, *The English Rothschilds* (London, 1983), pp. 42–4.
9. Weintraub, *Disraeli*, p. 276.
10. Davis, *Rothschilds*, p. 101.
11. Ibid.
12. Ibid., pp. 123–4.
13. Ibid., p. 196.
14. The Rothschild Archive, 000/109, Trustees of the Baron and Baroness Mayer de Rothschild, Cambridge bills from October 1837 to October 1839.
15. Davis, *Rothschilds*, p. 57.
16. Ibid.
17. Ibid., p. 113.
18. R. T. Matthews and P. Mellini, *In Vanity Fair* (Berkeley, CA, 1982), pp. 160–1.
19. Ibid., pp. 160–2.
20. *Vanity Fair*, 9 June 1888.
21. 'The lord de Rothschild and Sir Acland de Hood', *Froissart's Modern Chronicles, 1903–1906*; 'The whole of British capital having been exported to the South Pole as a result of the Budget Revolution, Lord Rothschild flees from St Swithin's Lane, and succeeds in escaping to Antarctic regions disguised as a penguin', *Westminster Gazette*, 6 December 1909.
22. See, for example, his opinion of large all-male dinners, in M. G. Wiebe *et al.* (eds), *Benjamin Disraeli Letters*, Vol. 5, *1848–1851* (Toronto, 1993), p. 328.
23. Ibid., p. 196, n. 5.

24. Davis, *Rothschilds*, pp. 81–9; R. W. Davis, *Disraeli* (London, 1976), p. 87. Natty, writing to his parents early in 1860, was even more scathing about Disraeli: 'I am not sorry that Dizzy has made so many mistakes, it is the natural consequence of hypocrisy.' The Rothschild Archive, R Fam C/3/90, 23 February 1860.
25. *Disraeli Letters*, Vol. 5, p. 131.
26. M. G. Wiebe *et al.* (eds), *Benjamin Disraeli Letters*, Vol. 4, *1842–1847* (Toronto, 1989), p. 332.
27. Davis, *Rothschilds*, pp. 72–86.
28. Davis, *Disraeli*, pp. 94–5.
29. R. W. Davis, *Political Change and Continuity, 1760–1885: A Buckinghamshire Study* (Newton Abbot, 1972), pp. 162–7.
30. Ibid., p. 197.
31. Ibid., p. 165.
32. Davis, *Rothschilds*, p. 227.
33. Colin Holmes, *Antisemitism in British Society, 1876–1939* (New York, 1979).
34. British Library, London, Add Mss, 51,753, Smith to Holland, n.d. (but late 1829 or early 1830). See also R. K. Webb, 'From Toleration to Religious Liberty' in J. R. Jones (ed.), *Liberty Secured? Britain Before and After 1688* (Stanford, CA, 1992), pp. 156–98; Abraham Gilam, *The Emancipation of the Jews in England, 1830–1860* (New York, 1982).
35. W. D. Rubenstein, *A History of the Jews in the English-Speaking World: Great Britain* (New York, 1996).

'JEW FEELINGS' AND REALPOLITIK: DISRAELI AND THE MAKING OF FOREIGN AND IMPERIAL POLICY

Edgar Feuchtwanger

'Power! It has come to me too late', Benjamin Disraeli was heard to murmur at the height of his success as a maker of foreign policy, after the Congress of Berlin. 'There were days when, on waking, I felt I could move dynasties and governments; but that has passed away.'[1] The management of the Eastern Question in the years from 1875 to 1878, culminating in apparent triumph, had been the only opportunity history had allowed him to prove himself as a major player of international power politics. It occurred – indeed, was in a manner created by him – when he had already achieved, at least in the eyes of his partisans, an equivalent apotheosis in domestic affairs through his electoral triumph of 1874. Yet even at the summit of his career many of his opponents could hardly bear to think of him except as 'the Jew in his drunken insolence'.[2] In the emotionally highly charged clash of opinions about British policy in the Near East, unleashed in the summer of 1876, Disraeli's Jewishness was always no mean factor. Rarely before or since has an issue of foreign policy aroused so much acrimony in British politics. The temperature was further raised as the controversy became absorbed into the ongoing duel between W. E. Gladstone and Disraeli, which only at this point reached a pitch of intense personal hatred.

There had been a time when both men belonged to the same political party, the Tories. Gladstone, five years younger than Disraeli and, unlike his later rival, conventionally educated at Eton and Christ Church, Oxford, had been given the opportunity by Sir Robert Peel to climb 'the greasy pole of office' at an early age. He had, as a result, earned from Thomas Babington Macaulay, the leading Whig historian, the notorious accolade 'the rising hope of stern unbending Tories', which has clung to him ever since.[3] Disraeli, in so many ways an out-sider in the narrow world of nineteenth-century British politics (and not only because of his Jewish origins), did not enter the House of Commons until he was nearly 33 years old and failed to obtain office under Peel. It was only the dramatic split in the Tory party over the repeal of the Corn Laws in 1846, which Disraeli did much to bring about, that catapulted him into the front rank of politics and eventu-ally into the leadership of the Protectionist Tories. Many of them were, and remained almost to the end, reluctant to accept him as leader, and antisemitism was often an element, though by no means the only one, in their enduring distrust of him. Gladstone, on the other hand, as a convinced free trader drifted into coalition with the Whig-Liberals. By 1868, he had become the leader of a fairly coherent Liberal party and Prime Minister for the first time, perhaps the most charismatic leader the Left in Britain has ever had. When in 1874 Disraeli led the Conservative party to its first clear electoral victory since the days of Peel, it not only put an end to Gladstone's first premiership – though not, as it turned out, to his political career – but also established his rival as an equivalent icon on the Right.

History had thus produced a perfect stage setting for the duel between Disraeli and Gladstone over the Eastern Question. This problem had been a major preoccupation for the makers of British foreign policy for most of the nineteenth century. The Ottoman empire was in terminal decline. The Tsarist empire, on the other hand, appeared to be threatening British imperial interests in a line stretching from the Mediterranean and the Levant to India. British policy makers and the wider public were haunted by the spectre of Russia advancing through the Balkans and appearing at Constantinople, thus gaining access to the Mediterranean. Religious and ideological factors added spice to this heady brew. It was over these issues that the Crimean War (1854–56) had been fought. At that time Gladstone was a member of the Govern-ment and supported the war with some reservations. Disraeli, as Leader of the Opposition, was critical of the conduct of policy that had involved Britain in war but for patriotic reasons was bound to support it once it had broken out. The crisis in the Balkans in the 1870s had many features that made it into a re-run of the Crimean War scenario. Disraeli and those who supported his policy still saw the issue in terms of the maintenance of the British national interest against the Russian threat. His opponents, among whom Gladstone soon stood out as the principal figure, regarded any association with Turkish oppression of Christians in the Balkans as immoral. In their eyes the policy of bolstering the disintegrating Ottoman empire had become futile and should be replaced by respect for the emergent nationalities in the Balkans.

The personal duel between Disraeli and Gladstone was thus elevated into a clash of principle, the supremacy of the national interest versus the categorical imperative of morality. As usual, reality was more complex. Disraeli, like all those who exercise power, was never a free agent. Not least among the many difficulties he faced was the fact that his own foreign secretary, the fifteenth earl of Derby, was frequently at odds with his master and resigned at the height of the crisis in 1878. Derby was head of the house of Stanley and almost unbreakable bonds of mutual obligation tied him and the Prime Minister. Disraeli would never have lasted as Tory leader through 20 years of almost constant adversity and defeat, as well as corroding distrust among his own followers, without the backing of Derby's father, the fourteenth earl. The 'Derby–Dizzy' leadership and short-lived cabinets of the 1850s and 1860s owed as much to the fourteenth Earl of Derby as they did to his more famous lieutenant.

In the early stages of this partnership relations between these two very different men, 'the Derby and the Hoax', as the wags had it,[4] were not close, but they were closer between Derby's son, then Lord Stanley, and the fascinating novelist-cum-politician who had risen recently to prominence. Stanley was one of a clutch of young aristo- crats who at various times clustered round Disraeli and whom he favoured with his confidence. It was to Stanley, then aged 25, that Disraeli made, in 1851, the often-quoted and prophetic remarks about restoring the Jews to Palestine:

> money would be forthcoming: the Rothschilds and leading Hebrew capitalists would all help; the Turkish empire was falling into ruin: the Turkish Govt would do anything for money: all that was necessary was to establish colonies, with rights over the soil, and security from ill treatment. The question of nationality might wait until these had taken hold.[5]

Soon Stanley began to distance himself somewhat from Disraeli, at least in public, almost became more of a liberal than a conservative, and at a young age acquired a great reputation among the middle classes, crucial to the election, more so than either his father or Disraeli. These early achievements proved deceptive, for Derby lacked the con- fidence and verve to play the leading role the political world expected of him. The feeling of mutual obligation between him and Disraeli remained. It is therefore not surprising that Derby, who had succeeded to the title on his father's death in 1869, remained Foreign Secretary during the Eastern Crisis long after the differences between him and his master had become obvious. Another reason that Disraeli was reluctant to part with him was that Derby was still regarded, almost in spite of himself, as having strong electoral appeal, particularly in Lancashire, a Tory stronghold, where the main family seat, Knowsley, was located. Derby's continued presence in the cabinet acted as a severe brake on Disraeli's freedom of action.

For Gladstone and his supporters, Disraeli's Jewishness supplied a rationale for a hatred that only became really personal during the Eastern Crisis.

> I have watched very closely his strange and at first sight inexplicable proceedings on this Eastern Question: and I believe their fountain head to be race antipathy, that aversion which the Jews, with a few honourable exceptions, are showing so vindictively towards the Eastern Christians. Though he has been baptized, his Jew feelings are the most radical and the most real, and so far respectable, portion of his profoundly falsified nature.[6]

Two points in particular deserve comment in this passage. Gladstone, as well as Disraeli and most Victorians, was strongly conscious of 'race' and had none of the compunction about using the term, which has become virtually taboo since the Second World War. The various ways in which Victorians used the word defy strict definition. They stretch from a loose sense of ethnicity to a biological determinism that was influenced by Darwin's theories on evolution. There can be no doubt, however, that almost all Victorians considered 'race' a prime mover in history and politics. Disraeli fully, almost obsessively, shared that view. He made Sidonia, the mysterious, all-knowing, all-powerful Jew in *Coningsby* and *Tancred*, half Disraeli and half Rothschild, declare that 'all is race'. The second point deserving comment is the evidence, in these remarks of Gladstone as well as in many other observations of Disraeli's enemies, that they thought him a fundamentally insincere person, a chronic liar, a blatant opportunist. They were, however, sometimes willing to credit him with the one element of sincerity in his character, namely, that on some issues, notably the admission of Jews to Parliament, he had been willing to show his true colours as a

Jew, even when it was politically inconvenient. The corollary of this opinion was that, as Gladstone put it, only his 'Jew feelings' were real.

The antisemitism in Gladstone's hatred of Disraeli at the time of the Near Eastern crisis was relatively muted compared with that of others. The historian E. A. Freeman, an early protagonist in the Bulgarian atrocities campaign, is generally regarded as having plumbed the depths in antisemitic attacks on the Tory Prime Minister. A leading figure among the Oxford liberal intelligentsia, he and others had elaborated a quasi-anthropological, nationalistic view of English history. As a medievalist, Freeman purported to have found a peculiarly Anglo-Saxon capacity for liberty, inherited from 'the free forests of Germany'. It was a race-based view of history, not unlike Disraeli's, but with the Anglo-Saxons instead of the Hebrews as the bearers of salvation. In 1884, Freeman was appointed Regius Professor of Medieval History at Oxford on the recommendation of Gladstone. One of his more moderate effusions appeared in the preface to his book *The Ottoman Power in Europe* (1877):[7]

> If everything rested with Lord Derby, with a man who is steadfastly purposed to employ himself with a vigorous doing of nothing, we should at least have one kind of safety ... but there is another power against which England and Europe ought to be yet more carefully on their guard. It is no use mincing matters. The time has come to speak out plainly. No well disposed person could reproach another either with his nationality or his religion, unless that nationality or religion leads to some direct mischief. No one wishes to place the Jew, whether Jew by birth or by religion, under any disability as compared with the European Christian. But it will not do to have the policy of England, the welfare of Europe, sacrificed to Hebrew sentiment. The danger is no imaginary one. Every one must have marked that the one subject on which Lord Beaconsfield, through his whole career, has been in earnest has been whatever touched his own people. A mocker about everything else, he has been thoroughly serious about this. His national sympathies led him to the most honourable action of his life, when he forsook his party for the sake of his nation, and drew forth the next day from the Standard newspaper the remark that 'no Jew could be a gentleman'. On that day the Jew was a gentleman in the highest sense. He acted as one who could brave much and risk much for real conviction. His zeal for his own

people is really the best feature in Lord Beaconsfield's career. But we cannot sacrifice our people, the people of Aryan and Christian Europe, to the most genuine belief in an Asian mystery. We cannot have England or Europe governed by a Hebrew policy. While Lord Derby simply wishes to do nothing one way or another, Lord Beaconsfield is the active friend of the Turk. The alliance runs through all Europe. Throughout the East, the Turk and the Jew are leagued against the Christian. In theory the Jew under Mahometan rule is condemned to equal degradation with the Christian. In practice the yoke presses much more lightly upon the Jew. As he is never a cultivator of the soil, as he commonly lives in the large towns, the worst forms of Turkish oppression do not touch him. He has also endless ways of making himself useful to the Turk, and oppressive to the Christian. The Jew is the tool of the Turk, and is therefore yet more hated than the Turk. This is the key to the supposed intolerance of Servia with regard to the Jews ... The Servian legislation is not aimed at Jews as Jews ... it is aimed at certain corrupt callings which in point of fact are practised only by Jews ... The union of the Jew and the Turk against the Christian came out in its strongest form when Sultan Mahmoud gave the body of the martyred Patriarch to be dragged by the Jews through the streets of Constantinople. We cannot have the policy of Europe dealt with in like sort. There is all the difference in the world between the degraded Jews of the East and the cultivated and honourable Jews of the West. But blood is stronger than water, and Hebrew rule is sure to lead to a Hebrew policy. Throughout Europe the most fiercely Turkish part of the press is largely in Jewish hands. It may be assumed everywhere, with the smallest class of exceptions, that the Jew is the friend of the Turk and the enemy of the Christian. The outspoken voice of the English people saved us last autumn from a war with Russia on behalf of the Turk. The brags of the Mansion-House were answered by the protest of Saint James's Hall. But we must be on our guard.[8]

Here we have it then: the one sincere feature of Lord Beaconsfield's life is his Jewish feeling, and now that he controls the destiny of England, he is imposing a Hebrew policy on the country. There is one specific element in these attacks on Disraeli that deserves mention. Long-standing antagonism existed between the Tory leader and the

High Church party within the Conservative party. He sometimes referred to them contemptuously as 'the sacerdotal party'.[9] Prominent frondeurs against Disraeli's leadership included High Churchmen, who habitually referred to him as 'the Jew'. Freeman, although in politics a Liberal, was a High Church man. Gladstone was an even more conspicuous example of this combination of Liberalism with High Anglicanism. The most considerable figure among Disraeli's High Church opponents was Lord Salisbury (Lord Robert Cecil before he succeeded to the title in 1868). Salisbury was that rare bird, a Conservative intellectual, and the author of many articles in the *Quarterly*, a Tory periodical that was consistently critical of Disraeli. He was not guilty, however, of employing antisemitism directly as part of his anti-Disraelian invective. Salisbury believed in principled opposition to radicalism and progressivism and was deeply suspicious of Disraeli's progressive conservatism, which became known as Tory Democracy. In 1863, when Disraeli was trying to rally his party against Lord Palmerston, the Prime Minister, with the cry of 'the Church in danger', Salisbury had written to Lord Carnarvon, another High Church man: 'I have long regarded Dizzy's leadership as an irreversible chastisement.' He felt that Disraeli's parade of English churchmanship was a 'senseless affectation of Saxonism'.[10] Salisbury and Carnarvon resigned from the Cabinet in 1867 over the reform bill, in their eyes a disastrous product of Disraelian opportunism.

The 1867 Reform Act at least doubled the number of those entitled to vote and was the decisive breakthrough towards an urban working-class electorate.[11] For some years after 1868, Salisbury was at the centre of anti-Disraeli moves in the Conservative party. High Anglicans like him disliked the blatant 'beating of the Protestant drum' with which Disraeli sought to counter Gladstone's policy of disestablishing the Anglican Church of Ireland in the 1868 election. This exploitation of anti-Catholic sentiment was in striking contrast to the sympathetic treatment of Catholicism in Disraeli's novels of the Young England period. Disraeli again antagonised the High Church in 1874 when, as Prime Minister, he supported the Archbishop of Canterbury's bill to control Ritualism, the romanising tendency in the Church of England, the Public Worship Regulation Bill.[12] Salisbury, having only just buried the hatchet with Disraeli and joined his cabinet as Secretary of State for India, came near to resignation over this. High Anglicans felt a special ecumenical affinity with the Orthodox churches, which made them particularly sensitive to the persecution of Christians within the Ottoman Empire. These factors go some way towards explaining why men like Freeman targeted Disraeli's alleged Judaic feelings when the Eastern Question erupted.

An examination of Disraeli's policy over the Eastern Question cannot give even the slightest substance to these highly coloured, for all their occasional qualifications, entirely antisemitic attacks from which in fact scarcely a single antisemitic stereotype is absent. The main motivation of Disraeli's foreign policy during his last premiership, as in the earlier phases of his career when he had to concern himself with foreign policy as a practising politician, was that he wished to maintain the national interest and the prestige of Britain. In his perception one of the main reasons for his electoral triumph over Gladstone and the Liberals in 1874 was the feeling in the country, especially among the increasingly Conservative middle classes, that Gladstone's government had been weak in its conduct of foreign and imperial affairs. A good deal of the fire that Disraeli had directed against the Liberal government in the last two years of its existence was concentrated on this weakness. In one of his programmatic speeches of 1872 he said that the country had to make a choice between the national and the cosmopolitan principle. He and the Conservatives represented the former, Gladstone and the Liberals the latter.[13]

It seemed therefore essential to Disraeli, a party politician to his fingertips when this was as yet not a well-established characteristic of political leaders, to maintain a clear contrast in his conduct of Tory foreign policy. This strongly influenced his handling of the Near Eastern crisis, from the moment when in May 1876 he launched British policy on a distinct course by refusing to be associated with the Berlin Memorandum, a note of protest to the Ottoman sultan, drafted by Germany, Austria and Russia after the murder of the French and German consuls in Salonika. It influenced the tactics he employed in dealing with the atrocity campaign, all but ignoring it, even if these tactics may not always have been well-advised. He refused to give even the appearance that the policy of HM Government could be in the smallest degree diverted by an emotional upsurge contrary to the best interests of the country. As the crisis progressed in 1877, all the indications were that the atrocity campaign was supported by specific sections of opinion, in the main provincial Nonconformists, but that the majority of opinion, from metropolitan club and down to the working class in the big cities, above all London, supported Disraeli's policy of asserting the national interest and prestige against Russia. Information to this effect reached Disraeli from many sources, including his whips and party agents, and was confirmed in by-elections.

There is no sign whatsoever that Disraeli was influenced by pro-Turkish emotions, whether they stemmed from his Jewishness or from his youthful travels in Turkey. He was not prejudiced one way or the other: 'all the Turks may be in the Propontis, so far as I am concerned', he told Derby.[14] On the other hand he was unimpressed by arguments in favour of the right to independence or autonomy of Balkan nationalities. For all his preoccupation with race, he had little sympathy with the rise of nationalism. He saw the Balkans as an area whose destinies would always be predominantly influenced by great power interests. At various times he toyed with the option of a division of the Ottoman Empire. As the head of a Government that had deliberately resumed the policy of national interest in the tradition of Canning and Palmerston, neglected to its cost by its Liberal predecessor, Disraeli well knew that he could not survive an obvious national humiliation such as a Russian seizure of Constantinople. His attempt to assume for himself and for the Conservative party the role of Palmerston's successors would have ended in failure. He wrote to Derby on 22 May 1877:

> The tactics of the Opposition are clear: they were laid down by Harcourt in the debate. He distinctly laid the ground for an appeal to the people against the Ministry, whose want of foresight and courage will have compelled us to acquiesce either in a ruinous war, or a humiliating peace. Having successfully acted on a nervous and divided Cabinet, and prevented anything from being done, they will now turn round and say, 'This is the way you protect British interests!' They will probably turn us out in the Parliament, or they will force us to a dissolution under the influence of a disastrous defeat abroad.[15]

Disraeli's own policy in strengthening the British hold on Egypt through the purchase of the Suez Canal shares might have lessened the importance of Turkey as a link in the British route to India, but a Russian grip on Constantinople and the Straits would still portend danger. These were the considerations that motivated Disraeli's management of the Near Eastern question and not a 'Hebrew sympathy', as the malign imputations of his enemies would have it. If Disraeli's conduct of affairs sometimes faltered, it was not due to any Jewish emotions, but often to the sentimental and political ties that bound him to a Foreign Secretary whose outlook was so fundamentally at variance with his own and whose competence left much to be desired. Ill health and declining energies further weakened a man to whom power had come too late.

Until 1874, Disraeli's opportunities to make high policy in the international arena were limited. It had been the making of Disraeli's career that the split of 1846 left almost all the ministerial talent in the party with the remaining followers of Peel, thus leaving him a clear field, but the same Tory split condemned him to many years of dispiriting opposition. It was his particular misfortune that Palmerston took over, for a whole decade, the centre ground in British politics. Palmerston's success consisted in combining a conservative position at home with a foreign policy that was vaguely liberal and, at the same time, appealed to the middle classes' sense of national superiority. It was a stance difficult for Disraeli to oppose and eventually, after Palmerston's death, he took over much of it. His pro-active policy on the Eastern Question was designed to confirm him as the inheritor of Palmerston's mantle.

Although it was rare for Disraeli, in the long arid years of opposition, interspersed by brief periods in office, to make major policy, it often fell to him to proclaim the policy of his party or his government on foreign and imperial affairs. He never held the Foreign Office, but when the Tories were about to come into office he was sometimes spoken of as a possible Foreign Secretary. Palmerston, with his reputation as a skilful practitioner of foreign policy, said in 1858, when the Tories were in office, that 'one man only in the ministry, Mr. Disraeli, under-stands anything about foreign policy and he only a little'.[16] Disraeli's speeches on foreign policy were always what one would expect of leading party political and governmental figures. The extravagance that characterises his imaginative writings is mostly absent. Even when it is his task to survey and analyse the international scene with an eye to the future, he becomes entirely the statesman trying to discern the tides of power *sine studio et ira*.

Typical is a speech he made on 9 February 1871, when the defeat of France and the proclamation of the German empire were engaging all minds. Disraeli said:

> This war represents the German revolution, a greater political event than the French Revolution of last century – I don't say a greater, or as great, a social event ... Not a single principle in the management of our foreign affairs, accepted by all statesmen for guidance up to six months ago, any longer exists ... The balance of power has been entirely destroyed, and the

country which suffers most, and feels the effect of this great change most, is England.[17]

He went on to say that the first consequence of the upheaval was Russia's repudiation of the treaty of Paris of 1856. Disraeli thinks the Russian drive to penetrate to the sea understandable. He does not consider the push to Constantinople, initiated by Catherine the Great, legitimate, any more than the French desire to have the Rhine was legitimate. The Crimean War might have been avoided, but it was just, the treaty of Paris was generous, the neutralisation of the Black Sea necessary. He implies criticism of the Gladstone government in saying that to give all this up now would render past sacrifices vain. The calling of a conference was a cynical ploy by Bismarck. Disraeli, having established the weakness of the government's policy in one area, then goes on to another, Anglo-American relations, then over-shadowed by the *Alabama* claims.[18] He repudiates the notion that Anglo-American relations are bad because Tories supported the South in the Civil War. He claims that there is a party in the United States that believes England can be attacked with impunity for political purposes. Disraeli proclaims: 'I have never been alarmist or meddlesome, but I am not prepared to support non-intervention.' The country was in a state of great peril, the object of jealousy, as Venice in the past, but England had not sacrificed power to the accumulation of wealth.

These are the authentic tones of Disraeli, ex-premier and party leader, in which one can already detect the considerations that would guide his conduct when he returned to power. A passage like this also makes it clear that Disraeli did not take a particularly Eastern view of Britain's position, no more so than other contemporary politicians. It was political orthodoxy that the Indian Empire was the most vital prop to British power, the Jewel in the Crown,[19] and that anything that endangered it set alarm bells ringing. In this Disraeli did not differ from other Victorian politicians. He did, however, see more than others that there was an Indian sense of nationality that had to be respected by the British, whether they came as administrators, soldiers or mission-aries. During the Indian mutiny of 1857, when British public opinion became hysterical in demanding revenge for atrocities committed against women and children, Disraeli refused to pander to this senti-ment. He questioned if it was a mere military mutiny, seeing it more as a national revolt.[20] When nearly 20 years later, as Prime Minister, he caused the title of Empress of India to be conferred on Queen Victoria, it was not merely to flatter the monarch, with whom he had built up a close relationship. By such gestures he sought to arouse the imagination and loyalty of an oriental people.

It is hardly surprising that Disraeli was more far-seeing than most of his contemporaries in assessing the implications of the French defeat of 1870. In so far as one can detect any continuous thread in his vision of foreign policy, it is his faith that a good understanding with France should be its cornerstone. Even in this respect he started, as in so many other ways, with an initial inconsistency amounting to an indiscretion. When he was on the verge of diverting his energies from literature to politics in 1832, he was co-author of a pamphlet, *England and France, or a Cure for Ministerial Gallomania*, that attacked, in the wake of the July Revolution of 1830, the Whig government of Lord Grey for its allegedly pro-French policy. This argument did not fit in with Disraeli's current intention of contesting High Wycombe as a Radical in 1832. It may have been part of some financial scheme to free himself from the burden of debt in which he was already enmeshed. Its co-author was Baron Muntz von Haber, son of a Karlsruhe Jewish banker ennobled by the Grand Duke of Baden in 1829, described as 'a mysterious German gentleman of Jewish extraction'.[21] Disraeli was in the phase of his life when he was still adding to the aura of raffishness that he later found so difficult to dispel. In combination with his Jewishness, it fed the distrust that always surrounded him.

After this inauspicious beginning a pro-French attitude became characteristic of him and he always proclaimed it publicly. In the early 1840s, when he was still a comparatively minor political figure, he managed to strike up a relationship with Louis Philippe, though it is unlikely that the French king attached the weight to him that Disraeli professed to have. He came to know Louis Napoleon well during his English exile and sympathised with him as a fellow-romantic. He used these personal ties in the 1850s when Napoleon was the ruler of France and the leader of the opposition, but again it looks as if the Emperor was not too impressed by him. In 1857, Napoleon said to Lord Malmesbury, the Foreign Secretary in the Derby–Dizzy cabinets of 1852 and 1858–59, that Disraeli 'has not the head of a statesman, but that he is, like all literary men, as he has found them, from Chateaubriand to Guizot, ignorant of the world, talking well, but nervous when the moment of action arises'.[22]

A few further examples of Disraeli's foreign policy pronouncements will show that in this area he had usually left the Jewish literary man behind him and had become the responsible parliamentary spokesman. On the Crimean War Disraeli took the line of welcoming all efforts to avoid war by negotiation in 1853; when in 1854 it became clear that the mood was for war, he took the line of 'patriotic opposition'. By 1855, he was arguing for an early conclusion to the war by negotiation, a line that was not popular with many of his own followers. In 1859, the Italian question became an important issue in British politics, with the potential of deciding the fate of the Derby-Disraeli minority ministry. Public opinion veered between sympathy for the Italian cause and suspicion of Napoleon III. Disraeli had little time for Italian nationalism and doubts about Italian liberals, but he divined more accurately than Derby or Malmesbury the motives of Napoleon, in many ways a kindred spirit. When the Austrians clumsily precipitated the war by an ultimatum, it spelt danger for the survival of the Tory government. Derby and Disraeli had to work overtime to assure the public that British diplomacy had not been too pro-Austrian. Disraeli said, on 7 June 1859, just before the government's fall:

> We have adopted the principle of strict and impartial neutral-
> ity; we have endeavoured to act in the spirit of that principle,
> and I treat with utter contempt, because it would be impossible
> to offer a shadow of proof in favour of the monstrous state-
> ment, that in the course we have adopted or the counsels we
> have given, we have ever had either an Austrian or a French
> bias.[23]

Finally in 1864, the Schleswig-Holstein question offered the Conservative opposition a real chance, after years in the doldrums, to attack the Palmerston government effectively. It came at a time when Disraeli himself was politically at a low ebb, perhaps feeling there was not much left for him to do. The obvious line of attack was to accuse the government of empty bluster and mismanagement, while avoiding any suggestion that the Tory party was the war party. Here is a sample of how Disraeli did it, on 29 February 1864:

> When we are asked whether we are advocates of war in favour
> of the integrity and independence of Denmark, my answer is,
> that I cannot say what the policy of England ought to be with
> respect to going to war for the integrity and independence of
> Denmark until I am acquainted with the engagements HMG
> have entered into. But irrespective of that point – which I
> reserve – I assert that if our affairs had been managed with due
> firmness and conciliation, with straightforwardness and with

> common sense, the integrity and independence of Denmark would never have been endangered.[24]

In spite of his legendary skills as a parliamentary tactician Disraeli failed even on this occasion, by 18 votes, to dislodge Palmerston.

Jewishness did not then greatly influence Disraeli when he was acting as a major political figure in domestic or foreign affairs. Nor can too much be made of the theme of the alien patriot. When the political situation at home and abroad seemed to him to demand a low profile, a policy of abstention governed by economy, Disraeli was quite ready to recommend it. His was a many-layered personality, but he had himself so well under control in his later years that his literary imagination was rarely allowed to obtrude on his trade as a politician. His Jewishness was that of the Diaspora Jew, an identity thrust upon him by the hostility of the Gentile world rather than an inward product of faith. His father was a man of the Enlightenment, who found many aspects of the Judaism inherited from his family irritating. It caused him no major pangs of conscience to have his children baptised. Disraeli claims that in his youth he was inculcated with prejudice against Jews.[25] It seems likely that in his family the Jewish connection was viewed rather negatively. His own more positive interest in his Jewishness was kindled by his travels in the Levant in 1830 and became, in conjunction with his romantic self-image, a major component of his outlook. It was a way in which he, as a self-conscious genius, could assert himself against a hostile world. It is difficult to separate Disraeli's Jewishness from two other elements that gave him an alien aspect in the world in which he passed his life: his foreignness in England and his non-aristocratic origins in an aristocratic world. As the gulf widened between him and his Foreign Secretary in 1877, Derby wrote to Salisbury: 'He believes thoroughly in "prestige" as all foreigners do, and thinks it (quite sincerely) in the interests of the country to spend 200 millions on a war if the result was to make foreign States think more highly of us as a military power.'[26] One must infer from this passage that Derby considered Disraeli's reactions those of a foreigner.

In 1878, Salisbury succeeded Derby as Foreign Secretary. Relations between these two had always been cool. Derby was in religion a sceptic, allergic to religious enthusiasm and to all manifestations of clericalism. Salisbury, Lady Derby's stepson, was deeply religious. By this time he was working closely with Disraeli on the Eastern Question and had acquired a high respect for him. But in spite of what Derby says, these alien elements should, no more than his Jewishness, be exaggerated in their influence on Disraeli. He was also a home-counties man, whose experience of abroad was limited and who had mixed all his life with the aristocracy, raffish or otherwise. As the image of the responsible statesman overlaid other facets of his personality, he clearly felt the need to rationalise to the public the more extravagant excursions of his pen. In referring to his *Coningsby-Sybil-Tancred* trilogy in the preface to the collected edition of his novels, published in 1870, he wrote:

> it seemed to me the time had arrived when it became my duty to ... consider the position of the descendants of that race who had been the founders of Christianity. Familiar as we all are now with such themes, the House of Israel being now freed from the barbarism of mediaeval misconception, and judged like other races by their contributions to the existing sum of human welfare, and the general influence of race on human action being universally recognized as the key of history, the difficulty and hazard of touching for the first time on such topics cannot now be easily appreciated.[27]

In spite of this disclaimer, it is hardly surprising that deep suspicion of his Hebrew sentiments remained among his enemies. Had he not described the Jews as the race that, through the medium of Christianity, had civilised and given a mission to the northern races of Europe? Had he not claimed that the great secular event of the French Revolution had amounted to an apostasy by the northern races from their Semitic heritage? Was it not therefore likely that he was using the Anglo-Saxon race for the achievement of his Judaic purpose?

Yet another layer of Disraeli's complex views can be seen on those occasions when he adopted the role of the visionary, as in the famous conversation reported by the young Stanley about resettling the Jews in Palestine, an amazingly prophetic vision of the Zionist enterprise culminating a century later. Then there is his predilection for seeing secret societies at work and his use of private intelligence, especially when obtained through the Rothschild network. Both tendencies can be seen operating on the occasion of the purchase of the Suez Canal shares, as in his exuberant letter to Lady Bradford: 'We have had all the gamblers, capitalists, financiers of the world organised and platooned in bands of plunderers, arrayed against us, and secret emissaries in every corner, and have baffled them all, and have never been suspected.'[28] As for the Rothschild intelligence network, Bismarck also made use of it, through his banker and confidant Bleichröder, to his private and public advantage.[29] Others thought he took too much notice of such sources. For instance, Malmesbury, when Disraeli's colleague as Foreign Secretary, complained to Derby, the Prime Minister, in January 1859: 'Disraeli *never reads a word of my papers* which go round, and knows nothing but what the Jews at Paris and London tell him.'[30] Disraeli himself may not have taken secret societies as seriously as a politician as he seemed to do in his novels and there may well have been an element of tongue-in-cheek in a letter such as that to Lady Bradford about the Suez Canal. His definition of secret societies and conspiracies was often a loose one and could easily include the many revolutionary enterprises of his age. Nor is it to be disputed that conspiratorial societies like the Carbonari in Italy played an important role and that major players like Napoleon III were influenced by such links. The notion of the pervasive influence of Jews, as portrayed in novels like *Tancred*, had great appeal for Disraeli, for his Jewish consciousness as well as for his love of convoluted intrigue. It is not altogether surprising that seekers after Jewish world conspiracies have always found grist to their mill in his writings.

Nevertheless, on a sober assessment one must conclude that Disraeli's Jewishness had virtually no influence on his making of foreign and imperial policy. The antisemitic slanders of his enemies were, like all antisemitism, sheer paranoia. Jewishness may have been important in Disraeli's personality and self-understanding, though it remains difficult to separate it from his sheer love of romance and mystification, but he did not allow it to influence him as a politician. Here he had himself firmly under control. The sphinx-like mask, the elaborate, orotund, sometimes tedious affectation of cynicism, were all part of the system of control. It is a price a man of high imagination and sensitivity has to pay when he becomes a man of affairs, and the price is even higher when he is a Jew.

NOTES

1. W. F. Monypenny and G. E. Buckle, *The Life of Benjamin Disraeli, Earl of Beaconsfield* (new, rev. edn, London, 1929), Vol. 2, p. 639. For the Near Eastern crisis in the mid-1870s and Disraeli's policy, see Richard Millman, *Britain and the Eastern Question, 1875–1878* (Oxford, 1979); R. T. Shannon, *Gladstone and the Bulgarian Agitation* (London, 1963); Ann P. Saab, *Reluctant Icon: Gladstone, Bulgaria and the Working Classes, 1856–1878* (Cambridge, MA, 1991); Marvin Swartz, *The Politics of British Foreign Policy in the Era of Disraeli and Gladstone* (London, 1985).

2. Words used by the historian E. A. Freeman, who also said, when the Queen lunched with Disraeli at Hughenden, that she was 'going ostentatiously to eat with Disraeli in his ghetto', Robert Blake, *Disraeli* (London, 1966), p. 607.

3. Macaulay used this phrase in a review in the Whig *Edinburgh Review* of Gladstone's book *The State in its Relations with the Church*, published in 1838. Gladstone argued the High Tory view of the Established Church, with the implication that full citizenship was confined to members of it.

4. The Derby and the Oaks are the two most important races run during the June meeting at Epsom, the former named after Derby's family. The fourteenth earl was regarded as more interested in the turf than in politics.

5. J. R. Vincent (ed.), *Disraeli, Derby and the Conservative Party: Journals and Memoirs of Edward Henry, Lord Stanley, 1849–1869* (Hassocks, Sussex, 1978), p. 32.

6. W. E. Gladstone to Arthur Gordon, later Lord Stanmore, quoted in Stanley Weintraub, *Disraeli: A Biography* (New York, 1993), p. 577.

7. E. A. Freeman, *The Ottoman Power in Europe* (London, 1877), pp. xviii ff. For Freeman and Anglo-Saxonism, see Paul Smith, *Disraeli: A Brief Life* (Cambridge, 1996), p. 201; also Christopher Harvie, *The Lights of Liberalism: University Liberals and the Challenge of Democracy, 1860–86* (London, 1976), p. 156.

8. Disraeli, or Lord Beaconsfield as he had now become, delivered the customary speech by the Prime Minister at the Lord Mayor's Banquet at the Mansion House on 9 November 1876. A month later, on 8 December, there was a great meeting of the opponents of the government's foreign policy at St James's Hall, Piccadilly, at which Gladstone spoke.

9. For the use of this term by Disraeli, see E. J. Feuchtwanger, *Disraeli, Democracy and the Tory Party* (Oxford, 1968), p. 19, and Blake, *Disraeli*, p. 626.

10. E. D. Steele, *Palmerston and Liberalism, 1855–1865* (Cambridge, 1991), p. 187.

11. For the general election of 1868, see H. J. Hanham, *Elections and Party Management: Politics in the Time of Disraeli and Gladstone* (London, 1959), esp. pp. 91ff. and 284ff.; Richard Shannon, *The Age of Disraeli 1868–1881: The Rise of Tory Democracy* (London, 1992).

12. Smith, *Disraeli: A Brief Life*, p. 174; J. P. Parry, *Democracy and Religion: Gladstone and the Liberal Party, 1867–1875* (Cambridge, 1986), pp. 413–17.

13. See Blake, *Disraeli*, pp. 523–4; Weintraub, *Disraeli*, pp. 504–5.

14. Monypenny and Buckle, *Life of Benjamin Disraeli*, Vol. 2, p. 925, 6 September 1876.

15. Ibid., p. 1012; Swartz, *Politics*, chs 2, 3.

16. Angus Hawkins, *Parliament, Party and the Art of Politics in Britain, 1855–59* (Basingstoke, Hants., 1987), p. 201.

17. *Hansard's Parliamentary Debates*, Third Ser., Vol. 204, col. 81, 9 February 1871.

18. See Kenneth Bourne, *The Foreign Policy of Victorian England, 1830–1902* (Oxford, 1970), p. 95; and *idem, Britain and the Balance of Power in North America, 1815–1908* (Berkeley, 1967), pp. 206–312.

19. The phrase 'jewel in the crown' is Disraeli's, used in his Crystal Palace speech on 24 June 1872, Monypenny and Buckle, *Life of Benjamin Disraeli*, Vol. 2, p. 535. See also P. J. Cain and A. G. Hopkins, *British Imperialism: Innovation and Expansion 1688–1914* (London, 1993), ch. 10; and C. C. Eldridge, *England's Mission: The Imperial Idea in the Age of Gladstone and Disraeli, 1868–80* (London, 1973).

20. Monypenny and Buckle, *Life of Benjamin Disraeli*, Vol. 1, p. 1488.

21. Jane Ridley, *The Young Disraeli* (London, 1995), pp. 111–15; Blake, *Disraeli*, p. 85.

22. Monypenny and Buckle, *Life of Benjamin Disraeli*, Vol. 1, p. 1457.

23. *Hansard*, Vol. 154, col. 135, 7 June 1859. On Disraeli's position during the Crimean War, see Robert Stewart, *The Foundation of the Conservative Party, 1830–1867* (London, 1978), pp. 302ff.

24. *Hansard*, Vol. 173, col. 1266, 29 February 1864.
25. In a letter to his co-religionist Mrs Brydges Willyams, 28 February 1853, Monypenny and Buckle, *Life of Benjamin Disraeli*, Vol. 1, p. 1274; see also Todd M. Endelman, *Radical Assimilation in English Jewish History, 1656–1945* (Bloomington, IN, 1990), pp. 28–31.
26. Lady Gwendolen Cecil, *Life of Robert, Marquis of Salisbury* (London, 1921–32), Vol. 2, p. 171.
27. *Collected Edition of the Novels and Tales*, ten vols (London, 1870–71).
28. Monypenny and Buckle, *Life of Benjamin Disraeli*, Vol. 2, p. 789.
29. See Fritz Stern, *Gold and Iron: Bismarck, Bleichröder and the German Empire* (New York, 1977).
30. Monypenny and Buckle, *Life of Benjamin Disraeli*, Vol. 1, p. 1624.

PART 3:

AFTERLIFE

ONE OF US? CONTESTING DISRAELI'S JEWISHNESS AND ENGLISHNESS IN THE TWENTIETH CENTURY

Tony Kushner

INTRODUCTION

Writing over one hundred years after Disraeli's death, John Walton suggests that 'he remains a figure of compelling interest, to many of today's practising politicians as well as to historians'.[1] One can go even further and point to his iconic status in popular culture: ranging from the pre-First World War custom of wearing a primrose on the anniversary of his death (in some areas of London it was reported that one in two of the population sported the flower)[2], to his appearance in plays, novels and silent and sound films in the inter-war years. Disraeli's image has adorned the figurehead of ships and he was, according to Mass-Observation, the only Victorian politician to be represented in the Blackpool waxworks exhibition in both 1937 and 1960.[3] The left-wing Labour Party leader Michael Foot named his dog after him and, perhaps most bizarrely, the title of one of the seminal rock albums of the 1960s included his name.[4] Indeed, at the end of the twentieth century, interest in Disraeli in academic writing across the humanities, as well as in popular history and cinema, showed little sign of abating.

For the Conservative Party in the twentieth century, the 'myth of Disraeli' proved crucial in appealing to a mass electorate in a rapidly changing economic, social and political world; 'far beyond the grave, Disraeli provided Conservatives with ideas, images and propaganda material, and his name remained a force to conjure with'.[5] As Cecil Roth noted, Primrose Day functioned 'as a sort of Patron Saint's Day of the Conservative Party'.[6] In particular, through a process of ongoing re-fashioning, Disraeli's concept of 'One Nation' became an extremely 'effective myth' in post-1945 Britain, unchallenged in Conservative circles until the emergence of the more divisive, confrontational approach of Margaret Thatcher and her governments from the late 1970s through to the early 1990s.[7] Once established, the Disraeli myth had its own momentum, but it would be misleading to suggest, in hindsight, that its utilisation by his successors in the Tory party was risk free. It was Stanley Baldwin, himself a product of the Primrose League, who established the myth as a working tool of Conservative rhetoric from his first speech as Prime Minister in May 1923. Yet it was, as Philip Williamson suggests, a new tactic and a surprising one for a Conservative leader: 'For many people Disraeli remained an exotic, a political eccentric.'[8] It was in the 1920s particularly that the idea of Disraeli as the ideal Conservative took root and for the remainder of the century, until the Thatcher revolution, it was merely embellished. What is intriguing, however, is that the creation and re-creation of 'St. Dizzy'[9] took place at a time of rampant and escalating anti-alienism, encouraged most notably by those of a Conservative tendency, and that the word Disraeli itself, even when spoken or written in admiration, was almost automatically preceded by that of 'alien'.

It is now largely accepted that throughout his life, responses to Disraeli were conditioned by what Bryan Cheyette has termed a 'semitic discourse'.[10] This discourse continued to shape reactions to Disraeli in the twentieth century. For both Jews and non-Jews, Disraeli became a prism through which group identities were defined. His life and character raised important issues about who did and did not belong within the nation state and about the nature of ethnic particularity. Just as Disraeli has been used to justify a range of Conservative ideologies and policies, so too he became central to the construction of Jewishness for many Jews, both total assimilationists and fervent Zionists, as well as many in between. Moreover, in the process of 'othering', constructions of the 'alien' Disraeli were significant for non-Jews and their sense of identity, ranging from those opposed to antisemitism to those who practised it at an extreme level. By the end of the twentieth century, Disraeli's Jewishness had become an exciting topic in an academic world that was beginning to recognise the importance of racisms as well as take seriously identity politics including issues of gender, ethnicity, religion and sexuality. In the first half of the century, however, the debate about Disraeli's Jewishness, in Britain and beyond, had a much more dramatic impact on the politics and culture of everyday life in what was one of the most dynamic as well as catastrophic periods of Jewish history since the Middle Ages.

1900–1918: OLD BATTLES AND NEW CONTEXTS

T. P. O'Connor, defender of Christians in Ottoman lands and bitter opponent of Disraeli's response to the Bulgarian atrocities in the 1870s, acknowledged in the eighth edition of his vitriolic biography of Lord Beaconsfield (1905) that 'the testimony of London to the dead Minister was sincere, enthusiastic, universal' and that it was rare that 'a statesman is in any country so honoured at a period so soon after his death'. There was, inevitably, a sting in the tail in O'Connor's account of Disraeli's posthumous reputation: 'Not one out of every hundred of the men and women who wore primroses on April 19th could give a lucid account of the real points at issue between Mr Gladstone and Lord Beaconsfield ... over the Eastern question.'[11] Later editions of O'Connor's biography, initially published in 1879, were there to correct such 'ignorance'. Although he updated the text to reflect new research, his vehement antisemitism remained untouched. In particular, O'Connor wanted to challenge the idea that Disraeli returned to Britain as a hero after the Congress of Berlin. As O'Connor infamously put it: 'That day represented the triumph, not of England, not of an English policy, not of an Englishman. It was the triumph of Judea, a Jew.'[12]

O'Connor, in the preface to later editions of his biography, contrasted the 'essentially English' character of Lord Derby (with whom Disraeli had increasingly diverged over foreign policy throughout the 1870s) with that of the 'Eastern showman': 'The somewhat commonplace Englishman, with notions of duty to his country, a horror of bloodshed, the fears of an avenging conscience, had no chance in times of perilous and fateful resolve against the brilliant, callous, self-adoring Oriental.'[13] Similarly, Lord Cromer, reviewing the first volume of Monypenny's biography of Disraeli (1910), presented 'his own picture of Disraeli as a meretricious Oriental charlatan devoid of principle or purpose'.[14]

It is crucial, however, to understand that those who wrote to defend and glorify Disraeli (in fact the dominant tendency) employed a similar 'Oriental/alien' trope to explain the late Prime Minister's 'genius'. In three utterly partisan biographies published between the years 1900 and 1904, Harold Gorst, Wilfred Maynell and Walter Sichel confronted the question of whether Disraeli could have been a true patriot, given his origins. As Sichel, an historical biographer and barrister of German Jewish family background (just one of many Jews following the path of radical assimilation who was to write about Disraeli, beginning with the Danish critic Georg Brandes in 1880), wrote:

> Much has been talked of his alien 'aloofness'. As for alien,
> Mazarin was in this sense an 'alien' ... In the eighteenth century
> a Scotch premier was in England an 'alien'. Augustus partly,
> Napoleon wholly, an 'alien' ... Nobody understood his country-
> men more shrewdly at once and sympathetically than Disraeli.
> His was no sham patriotism, and he loved John Bull fondly,
> even when he poked fun at him.[15]

Nevertheless, Sichel added that there were 'two grains of truth in this
respect. He did regard the world and its history as a fleeting show ...
he understood England, but it took long for his countrymen to understand *him*.' Indeed, it was because Disraeli 'felt that he was not as
others' that he understood his country so well. It was the outsider
Disraeli who 'prevented the raid of alien and disruptive democracy from
making England a home'. Instead he 'naturalised the democratic idea
on the soil of tradition and order; and thereby he cemented the solidarity of the State and the welfare of the nation'. Thus the accusation
that at the Berlin Congress 'as a Semite, he fostered the Moslem,
whom, as a Briton, he should have suppressed', was 'not only untrue,
but inaccurate'.[16]

The poet, essayist and author Wilfred Meynell, in his 1903 study,
confronted the issue of Disraeli's name. O'Connor had made much of
Disraeli's removing the apostrophe in his surname, somewhat disin-
genuously implying that he did so to hide his origins.[17] Meynell claimed
that Disraeli had done so when he stood for Maidstone in 1837, telling
a local newspaper editor: 'Oh, knock out the apostrophe; it looks so
foreign.' But as Meynell added, 'Apostrophe or no apostrophe, the
name could not be other than alien to English ears; and so long as he
lived, Disraeli cannot be said to have been entirely forgiven for it.'
Whereas Sichel problematised the concept of 'alien', Meynell embraced
it in his defence of Disraeli, referring to the 'mere fact that he was an
alien and that throughout his career in the Commons he bore a Jewish
name'. Disraeli, Meynell argued, 'had learned cosmopolitanism from
the vicissitudes of his ancestors'. Those such as Carlyle who ridiculed
Disraeli as the 'superlative Hebrew conjuror' had been proved wrong
by posterity. In contrast to Carlyle, Disraeli stood for tolerance and
understanding, while his lack of English exclusiveness allowed him to
view problems such as the governance of Ireland, relations with
Turkey or the unrest of the labouring classes with greater perception
and goodwill. Scorned and dismissed by his contemporaries, Disraeli
was now 'justified by time'.[18]

The author Harold Gorst (son of Sir John Gorst who had reorgan-
ised the Conservative Party during the 1870s) was also anxious to contrast the rejection, including antisemitism, faced by Disraeli during
his political career with his later vindication: 'It has been left for
posterity to recognize the vast services which Lord Beaconsfield has
rendered to the country by bequesting to future generations a national
policy which has made England's name great among the nations of the
world.' Yet, even in what was the least racialised account of Disraeli's
life published at the turn of the century, Gorst could not resist attribut-
ing the greatness of Disraeli, especially in transforming the Conservative Party into 'Tory Democracy', to his origins. Gorst argued that a
battle against aristocratic elements within the party was needed again
but that 'it would require the genius, the courage, the Jewish imper-
viousness to insult, the eloquence ... of a Disraeli to accomplish again
what he once achieved'.[19] Gorst's conclusion reflected contemporary
political concerns and heralded the tendency of later reflections on
the Earl of Beaconsfield: representations and discussions of Disraeli
became less concerned about the battles of the past and more concerned
about the issues of the present.

In April 1907, members of the Rainbow Circle, 'some of the
most influential and original social and political thinkers and activists
from the liberal and moderate socialist camps', met to hear the MP
J. M. Robertson read a paper on Beaconsfield. As a partisan Liberal,
Robertson almost inevitably emphasised what he saw as the lack of
genuine convictions and the 'sheer calculating self-interest' of Disraeli.
Although there was general agreement with Robertson's conclusion
that 'by the standards of moral character and moral aim, Disraeli had
no aspect of greatness', there were suggestions that his ideas and
achievements still made him relevant to the present day. The minutes
of the meeting concluded, however: 'Some stress was laid upon his
essentially Asiatic temperament, character and outlook', a reflection
no doubt of Robertson's comment that Disraeli's 'talk, like his dress,
was an act of self-obtrusion, a flaunting of his cleverness'.[20]

Those who condemned Disraeli's policies at the height of his
political power could not disentangle his Jewishness from their critique.
This tendency to racialise Disraeli remained irresistible for those who
attacked his alleged political legacy some 30 years later. Robertson,
however, was fighting against the tide in denying contemporary
perceptions, in Britain and elsewhere, of Disraeli's 'greatness'. Indeed,
his international stature had grown to the point where he became a
key figure in a new project: the attempt by national and international

Jewish organisations to improve the image of the Jews in culture and
society, a project in which some non-Jews willingly participated.

Scholarship in literary and cultural studies increasingly recognises
the pervasiveness of antisemitic imagery in the popular culture of
eighteenth- and nineteenth-century Britain and America, countries
previously regarded as inhospitable to what was perceived as purely
continental prejudice.[21] In fiction, drama, ballads, the press and the
new medium of film, the stock antisemitic figure of 'the Jew' – money-
obsessed, foreign, untrustworthy and physically unattractive – continued
into the twentieth century, reinforced by anti-alien agitation against
poor Jews and fear about plutocratic Jewish power.[22] Yet there was also
change and modification, as typified by American theatre and film
representations of the former British Prime Minister in which the
myth of Disraeli became established across the Atlantic.

The British-born actor George Arliss established his reputation
through playing the lead role in Louis Parker's *Disraeli: A Play* for five
seasons. 'This favorable portrait of Disraeli virtually identified Arliss
for decades with the glorified likeness of the famous man.'[23] The play
opened in Montreal in January 1911 and transferred to Chicago. In
his memoirs, Arliss recalled:

> Apart from the Jewish population, I think very few of the
> theatregoers of Chicago knew anything about Disraeli. One
> of the newspaper men assured me that most of the people he
> knew thought it was a tooth powder. Even in Philadelphia
> there was a young lady ... who said she 'didn't know whether
> he was in the New Testament or the Old'.[24]

In a similar vein, Parker remembered that in Chicago 'the title was at
first a little against us. People who saw it on the hoardings asked
whether it was a new breakfast food.' Parker added that it was 'a wholesome correction to a foreigner's conceit to find that the names of his
national heroes are not household words everywhere'.[25]

On the one hand, it is clear that the play struggled initially in Chicago
before becoming a success there, followed by even greater recognition and support in New York and across the country.[26] On the other,
there is an element of the urban folk tale, embellished in order to add
humour to theatrical reminiscences, about Disraeli's name being mis-
taken for tooth powder or breakfast cereal. Louise Mayo, for example,
in her study of nineteenth-century American press and periodicals,
comments that foreign Jewish leaders were

> the sources of far more comments than American Jews ...
> Benjamin Disraeli was a popular topic for articles. Although
> he was a practicing Anglican, the press always considered him
> a Jew ... Disraeli was often cited as indicative of how far Jews
> had come in the present 'enlightened' age.

Mayo adds that 'American articles about him were almost invariably laudatory, particularly stressing his brilliance'.[27]

In an interview with the *Jewish Chronicle* in 1916 when the play first opened in London, Parker provided a somewhat unconvincing account of its origins, stating: 'I presume that every genuine playwright is interested in his material. On looking round I found in the life of Disraeli any amount of theatrical stuff.'[28] In fact, Parker was commissioned to write the play by the theatrical impresario George C. Tylor in 1909. A year later, Arliss recalled, Parker was struggling with the play, complaining that Disraeli's life was not 'dramatic – theatrically. He was in love with his own wife, and nobody else, damn him! He did lots of great things, of course – but no good for the stage.'[29]

Harley Erdman argues that 1910 was a turning point in American theatrical representations of the Jew. It was not that the old stage Jew disappeared, but that he became rarer and less grotesque while 'the exemplary, upstanding Jewish male protaganist' arrived, typified by Parker's *Disraeli* and Augustus Thomas's *As a Man Thinks*, both of which opened in 1911.[30] It was Thomas, a major American dramatist, who publicly opened the debate, in May 1908, on the representation of the Jew in the theatre. Thomas called for a play on the 'philanthropic, far-seeing and above all, sweetly domestic' Jew, or what Louis Harap has described as 'the ideal, middle-class Victorian Jew'.[31] Such calls, which were widely reported and discussed, came alongside attempts by a variety of American Jewish organisations to 'clean' the stage of the 'derogatory characterization of the Jew'.[32]

Louis Parker suggested to the *Jewish Chronicle* that it was 'a domestic play written round the private life of Disraeli' yet in his note to the published edition it was made explicit that it was 'an attempt to show a picture of the days – not so very long ago – in which Disraeli lived, and some of the racial, social, and political prejudices he fought against and conquered'.[33] The play, which focuses on the purchase of the Suez Canal, made little pretence at historical accuracy; it was an opportunity to discuss the hostility Disraeli faced. Sir Michael Probert, 'the short-sighted, anti-Semitic head of the Bank of England',[34] refuses to lend money to Disraeli to purchase the Khedive's shares. Disraeli then turns to Hugh Meyers, a financier, described in the notes for the play as a 'charming man, with only the faintest traces of the Jew', to fund the purchase. Meyers proves the greater patriot than Probert. But if Meyers, the Rothschild figure, is in essence an Englishman, this is not true of Arliss's Disraeli, who, first in theatre and then in film, appeared as an exotic and stereotypically Jewish figure. 'Physically', it has been remarked, Arliss's Disraeli 'could easily pass for a traditional version of Fagin'. Arliss took great trouble to portray Disraeli 'authentically'. He did so by examining contemporary portraits and busts of the man, thereby perpetuating the 'semitic discourse' that was instrumental in shaping artistic representations of the former Prime Minister in the first place. Parker himself played into such constructions, remembering Disraeli's 'oriental cast of features, his dark curl on a serene forehead, his firm jaws, and piercing, penetrating eyes'. Arliss's exaggerated makeup, it has been suggested, 'defined Disraeli's appearance for two generations of Americans'.[35]

While Parker's Disraeli was a scheming Jew, he was one who used his power and intelligence selflessly for the benefit of his country. Thus in a decisive moment in the play, Probert angrily states that he is 'an Englishman; the head of a great national institution. I am not to be ordered about by an – by an alien Jew.' Calmly, Disraeli responds: 'Ah, but the alien Jew happens to be the better citizen.' Eventually, Probert sees the error of his ways and proclaims Disraeli the 'king-maker', to which Meyers quietly adds: 'Better than that. Benjamin Disraeli – the Jew – the Empress-maker.' All eventually are reconciled to the greatness of Disraeli, whose patriotism as well as, it must also be emphasised, his alien status are reinforced by Parker's play.[36] As Harley Erdman puts it, 'Jewish power was performed as actively patriotic, as the play emphasized above all Disraeli's love of country. Any threat of difference was diffused.'[37]

Before examining the impact of the play, it is worth considering Parker's own identity in relation to Disraeli. Whilst Disraeli was a lucrative subject in the cultural field during the twentieth century, it is also the case that many of those responsible for his representations have had, or have developed, a close affinity with the man. Louis Parker admitted that since boyhood he had had 'a real admiration for Disraeli – a sort of hero-worship'. But his attempt to universalise his fascination – 'which Englishmen ... have not?' – hid, perhaps, a deeper personal attraction. Parker's play proclaims that Disraeli 'was greater than Napoleon'.[38] The choice of Napoleon was no accident – it was Parker's middle name. Parker was born in Calvados, France, and admitted that

French influence, 'in spite of all my English years, even now colours my manners, and sometimes my speech'. His father was an American lawyer and when he was a child the family travelled constantly across Europe: 'six months in one place was as much as my father could stand'. In the years before the First World War, Louis Parker attempted to sort out his British citizenship. Even though his reputation as an international playwright was well established, his naturalisation, he found, 'was giving me a good deal of trouble. I had thought I had only to say I wanted to be an Englishman for England to take me to her bosom. Not so. It was a long and tiresome process.'[39] It is not surprising, therefore, that Parker identified so closely with Disraeli, the 'alien patriot'.

Without the endorsement of the Drama League of America, itself a sign that the play and its subject matter were deemed 'worthy' of support, it is possible that Parker's *Disraeli*, one of the most successful American plays of the decade, would have folded in Chicago. Nevertheless, after this initial fillip it struck a chord with American audiences in contrast to its reception when it opened in London in 1916. Harley Erdman has emphasised 'the American nature' of *Disraeli*. He adds: 'Despite its British setting, the play never succeeded in that country, precisely because its audiences would have recognized its simplification and telescoping in ways that clearly lacked verisimilitude.' He also argues that the play had immediate relevance to an American audience during 'an age of high-minded imperialism (when Panama, not Suez, was transparently the canal at issue)'.[40] As we will see, there were contemporary issues which potentially made the play relevant to Britain during the First World War, but the failure to take it to heart in the country where its protagonist was already a folk hero suggests that something else was at work in the American success of *Disraeli*.

In his review of the play, the leading American theatre critic Walter Prichard Eaton stressed how Disraeli had become Prime Minister of England 'in the face of opposition'. Eaton highlighted the triumph of power and will over background – in other words, the story of Disraeli could be universalised to be a metaphor for the American rags-to-riches success story. The play 'enjoyed five full years of excellent business'.[41] However, the theatre critic and British Jewish communal figure M. J. Landa, in his study *The Jew in Drama* (1926), was scathing about Parker's work. In particular, Landa was concerned about its portrayal of Disraeli's Jewishness, limited in effect, he argued, to 'a Jew-badge, no different from the mark of shame of the medieval ages'.[42] Seventy years later, Harley Erdman argued similarly in his study of Jews in the American theatre. Parker's *Disraeli* reflected a tendency to make Jewishness invisible: 'a Jewish character took the lead in a play that was [not] specifically about Jewishness'.[43] To summarise, for an American audience, Parker's portrayal of Disraeli appealed at two levels: first, his success, in spite of his alien outsider status, played into the American myth of the self-made man, and, second, his Jewish identity was never explored, enabling Disraeli's universalisation. As Parker himself admitted: 'I know very little of the interior life of the Jews.'[44]

Disraeli's climb 'to the top of the greasy pole',[45] however remarkable, was hardly a 'rags-to-riches' story. In 1920, George Buckle, summarising 'The Man and His Fame' at the end of his and William Monypenny's six-volume biography, made play of his 'progress from a middle-class Jewish literary home to Downing Street and the Congress Hall of Berlin'. Buckle noted how 'in Disraeli's career there was the realisation in fact of the dream which has floated before the eyes of many an ambitious youth; a clear proof that there is no eminence to which genius, aided by courage, resolution, patience, industry and "happy chance", may not attain in this free country of ours'.[46] But in the 1920s, as earlier, Disraeli's rise to fame was more likely to elicit snide comments about his parvenu status than empathy. As the Conservative politician, Austen Chamberlain remarked after reading Buckle's final volumes, Disraeli had 'the mind of a seer in the body of a mountebank'.[47] Buckle, in his homage to Disraeli and to British toleration, was closer to pinpointing the appeal of the Disraelian myth across the Atlantic. In Britain, it was only a few Disraeli fanatics and, more importantly, sections of the Jewish minority who saw Disraeli in Smilesian terms – his more general appeal, as we shall see, lay elsewhere.

Parker's *Disraeli*, the lead now played by Dennis Eadie, opened in London at the Royalty Theatre in April 1916. It ran for 128 performances over several months – not a total failure, given war-time constraints, but hardly the phenomenal success it had been in the United States.[48] The *Jewish Chronicle* was excited about its prospects, stressing in an editorial its topicality:

> After all, did not Disraeli, generations ago, foresee the Prussian peril? ... Did the great statesman not flutter the political dovecots by bringing the Indian troops to Malta at the critical moment of a certain conflict in the eighties? ... Who was it that stirred the Imperial idea in our fathers' sluggish political mind and by his proclamation of the Queen as Empress of

India brought home to the imagination the grandeur of an Empire which has meant so much to us in the present war? And for what diplomatist did the founder of the German Empire feel such genuine respect or fear?

To the editor, the play was undoubtedly 'quite timely',[49] given that the very loyalty of Jews in Britain was then being brought into question by the war.[50] Elsewhere in the same issue of the paper, its leading commentator, Leopold Greenberg, in an article entitled 'Disloyalty: A Word of Warning', concluded: 'Our enemies are for ever on the prowl ... Nothing is easier when loyalty and disloyalty are being balanced, to weight the scale in the popular mind against the Jew.'[51] It was for this reason that Parker's *Disraeli* was seen as a godsend by the *Jewish Chronicle*. Its editorial stressed that Disraeli's awareness of the danger posed by Germany was 'characteristically Jewish' and, in its interview with Louis Parker, the German was portrayed as an arch antisemite.[52]

However, the connections that the *Jewish Chronicle* highlighted failed to resonate elsewhere. As even it was forced to recognise, the 1870s, in the context of total war, seemed 'as remote and as *passé* as that of the Doges of Venice'.[53] Parker had been ambivalent about staging the play in Britain because he 'felt that the dramatic treatment of an historical character should be quite different in his own country from what it may be abroad'. When it was performed in London he realised that 'the play had not the glamour for an English audience with which the American audience had surrounded it'. The theatre correspondent of *The Times* was both amused and horrified at the historical liberties taken by Parker, mockingly congratulating him 'on his revelation of a Disraeli beyond our wildest dreams'.[54] The London production of the play was viewed as a dramatic fantasy. Indeed, the only real connection to the specific context of the war was made when the proceeds of the performance on 19 April were given to the Primrose League to provide parcels and ambulances for the front.[55]

Yet, although Parker's play was not the landmark in cultural representations of Jews it had been in America, it was still indicative of changes that were taking place in the British theatre with regard to images of the Jew. As the *Jewish Chronicle* wrote:

Jewish plays have become the vogue with Londoners. A fever has broken out, and both Jewish and Christian authors alike have caught the epidemic. But now they are not plagued with an obsession for Jewish villains. Authors are beginning to surround their Jews with dignity. The hooked-nose Jew money-lender has been swept by the board. And now, in the new play of 'Disraeli' ... we have a chance of seeing for the first time on the English stage Mr Israel Zangwill's old dream being realised of a plot being woven round the central figure of a great, historical, noble Jew.[56]

In fact this was not the first time that Disraeli had been put on stage. He had featured as a character in various pre-war music hall performances, where, embellished by 'the excessive appraisement of Hebraic make-up and appurtenances', he joined 'such whimsical oddities as "Jewish" jugglers, acrobats, and minstrels'.[57]

Parker's portrayal of Disraeli was distant from the old 'stage Jew villain', but it was distant as well from the earlier portrayal by John Lawson, a music hall actor of part Jewish origins. Lawson, who was obsessed with introducing Jewish characters into his act, depicted Disraeli in a sketch, taken from a playlet written by Samuel Gordon, a novelist and secretary of the Great Synagogue in London. Significantly, as M. J. Landa noted, Lawson's Disraeli 'was much more Jewish in spirit than the play by Louis N. Parker'.[58] Harley Erdman suggests that plays such as Parker's which 'reform[ed] the Jew to perfection', 'perched on the transitional point between an earlier era of grotesque visibility and a latter one of greater invisibility'.[59] Yet however 'perfect', Parker's Disraeli's could not escape his alien Jewishness. It was, as Landa despaired, 'seemingly, the only part of Disraeli that has not been buried with him, being kept above ground to surmount his tombstone' – an attitude that he described as 'mordant'.[60] Whether hostile or sympathetic, the 'semitic discourse' was too dominant before 1918 to allow an analysis of Disraeli's own construction of his Jewishness and Englishness. It was left to a small group of Jewish intellectuals, many connected to the Jewish Historical Society of England (JHSE), which was established in 1893, and The Maccabaeans, a literary, cultural and intellectual group formed two years earlier,[61] to reclaim both Disraeli's internal sense of Jewishness and also to query the tag of alien that almost inevitably accompanied his representation.

The journalist Lucien Wolf, the first president of the JHSE, 'asserted passionately that the study of history could reinforce Jewish pride and help secure Jewish continuity', and yet was also desperate to 'show the rootedness of Jews in English society, their contribution to English life and their patriotism'.[62] For him and other like-minded writers,

Benjamin Disraeli was clearly a suitable case for treatment. The writer and Jewish nationalist Israel Zangwill, who was also connected to the JHSE, was one of the first to explore Disraeli's complex identity. In his *Dreamers of the Ghetto* (1898), he dismissed Disraeli's attempt 'to be more English than the English' as 'political perseverance' and went on to reveal the mystery of the 'Primrose Sphinx' that is 'the open secret of the Ghetto parvenu'.[63] Wolf, however, a critic of Zionism, was less willing to dismiss Disraeli's Englishness. He was responsible for launching the centenary edition of Disraeli's novels, thus helping to maintain interest in the medium in which Disraeli revealed most about his 'self-fashioning'.[64] It was also on the centenary of Disraeli's birth that Wolf delivered a lecture to the JHSE that was later serialised in *The Times*. In his talk, Wolf demolished the genealogical myths that Disraeli had developed of his family's 'noble' Sephardi origins but at the same time stressed his family's roots in England, making clear the inseparability of Anglo-Jewish historiography from Jewish defence at the turn of the century:

> Lord Beaconsfield was frequently reproached by the more personal of his critics and antagonists as being an alien, without connection of blood with any English family. It is perfectly true that on his father's side his was only the second generation of his family which was English-born, but maternally he came of a family, the Aboab Cardosos, which had been settled in this country since the closing decade of the seventeenth century. In this respect the Disraelis were not more alien than many English families of Huguenot extraction. As for his want of blood relationship with families of English race, that also is an error. It is true that no Anglo-Saxon blood coursed in his veins, but not a little of the blood of his own ascertained fore-fathers was in his time and is still mingled with that of the English landed gentry and peerage.[65]

Adding his own doubts about the relationship 'between the moral character of a man and his often very complex ethnical extraction', Wolf concluded with a classic statement of the assimilationist approach of those connected with the JHSE: 'in Lord Beaconsfield some of the best blood in Jewry – the blood of men and women inured to hardship, a thirst for freedom, and invincibly attached to high ideals – was touched by the sympathetic genius of British traditions and forthwith produced a great Englishman.'[66]

Lucien Wolf's reference to families of Huguenot origin was not accidental. He was writing at the height of the aliens debate, in which many hostile to the entry of Jews from eastern Europe contrasted the suitability of these destitute aliens to 'desirable' and 'deserving' refugees of the past, like the Huguenots.[67] The connection between Disraeli and the aliens debate was made explicit by the prominent Liberal Herbert Samuel. Whereas for most Liberals, Disraeli was still anathema, for Samuel, as for so many British Jews in the twentieth century, the writings of the former Prime Minister were an inspiration in the formation of his own identity, especially in relation to Zionism.[68]

During the second reading of the Aliens Bill in May 1905, Samuel highlighted the achievements of the Jews in the past and present. He admitted that the immigrants had their faults but, echoing a metaphor used by William Hazlitt in support of Jewish emancipation some 75 years earlier, Samuel argued that 'if you give to these broken plants a little soil and water they will soon revive and they will not be the least useful and beautiful in your garden'. He asked the House 'what Disraeli would have thought of the Bill'. Taunting the Conservatives who had introduced the bill, Samuel pointed out their hypocrisy: 'On April 19th you covered his statue with flowers, but the day before that you introduced a Bill which might exclude from this country such families as his.' *Hansard* reported the ministerial cries of 'No! No!' but Samuel continued: 'Indeed, if they were destitute and could not prove that they were able to earn their own living they would be excluded. A progenitor of Lord Beaconsfield was an alien, and there may have been many men who have risen to distinction whose fathers were destitute when they arrived in this country.'[69]

But Samuel's effort to stop the Conservatives' desperate attempt 'to enlist racial intolerance in the support of a declining Government' was futile. Indeed, rather than being embarrassed by the linkage, the Primrose League was at the forefront of the Conservatives' anti-alien campaign. If even Disraeli's Conservative supporters still regarded him as an alien, there was little chance that his memory could be utilised rhetorically to stop the movement against those who were legally as well as culturally defined as such.[70]

1918–1933: THE ALIEN PATRIOT?

Rather than diminishing after passage of the bill, anti-alienism developed its own momentum. Ironically, as under-secretary in the Home

Office in the new Liberal government, Samuel found himself administering legislation he had so bitterly opposed.[71] By the time of the First World War it had led to a policy of almost absolute restrictionism and control of aliens within Britain. After the war, this was consolidated in the Aliens Restriction Act of 1919, which, alongside the growth of conspiratorial antisemitism in respectable sections of British society (as well as in more extremist circles), made life for a range of Jews in Britain distinctly uncomfortable. Moreover, there was great concern within the communal elite about the damage caused to the community by social assimilation and secularisation, both of which were intensified by the war. In such an atmosphere it may seem surprising that both opponents of aliens/Jews *and* communal leaders developed such a close affinity with Disraeli, given his apostate status. Yet the more his death receded, the more relevant Disraeli seemed to different groups trying to make sense of a post-war world that he would hardly have recognised. Increasingly, however, Disraeli's memory became a battleground over constructions of Englishness and Jewishness and more detached from discussion about his life itself.

In 1920, the final volumes of the official biography of Disraeli by Monypenny and Buckle were published. Buckle concluded boldly: 'The fundamental fact about Disraeli was that he was a Jew. He accepted Christianity, but he accepted it as the highest development of Judaism.' Buckle's analysis, whilst no doubt motivated by sincere admiration for Disraeli, was perceptive but also limited by his own racial construction of his subject. In spite of Disraeli's immersion in English history, literature, society and politics, Buckle believed, using the stage metaphor that was so frequently employed to explain Disraeli, that 'he seemed throughout his life never to be quite of the nation which he loved, served, and governed; always to be a little detached when in the act of leading; always to be the spectator, almost the critic, as well as the principal performer'.[72]

But Buckle went further and accepted the alien status of Disraeli, agreeing with Frederick Greenwood, former editor of the *Pall Mall Gazette*, that 'no Englishman could approach Disraeli without some immediate consciousness that he was in the presence of a foreigner'. Buckle was also happy to include Monypenny's notes confronting the racial determinism of Houston Stewart Chamberlain, who insisted that 'will is the distinctive characteristic of the Jewish race'. Monypenny accepted that 'Disraeli had the will of his race in its highest expression; but he also had in a high degree the quality which Houston Chamberlain denies them, imagination'. It was the combination of the two, Monypenny argued, that produced 'a man of genius'.[73]

With such racialisation from even the admirers of Disraeli, the problems of Lucien Wolf and other Jewish writers in establishing Disraeli's Englishness were exposed. As Austen Chamberlain noted after having read the 'very interesting' final volumes of Buckle: '"East is east" [even] through all the generations and Dizzy, tho' an English patriot was not an Englishman.'[74] After his death, the simple parish funeral that Disraeli had requested had infuriated Gladstone: 'As he lived, so he died – all display, without reality or genuineness.'[75] In 1883, after the unveiling of the Beaconsfield statue in Westminster and the inauguration of Primrose Day, Gladstone's private secretary, Eddy Hamilton, wrote in his diary that it was 'marvellously inappropriate and unEnglish!'.[76] No matter how 'English' the associations, whether the primrose or the parish church, a connection to Disraeli rendered them alien. There was change after 1918, however, not in questioning the alien nature of Disraeli, but in perceiving this quality to be dangerous in what was regarded as an exceptional case.

It is true that some were still fighting the battles of the 1870s after the First World War. One was the former editor of *The Times* Wickham Steed who, in a series of articles 'On Jews' in his own *Review of Reviews*, in 1927, spent many pages on 'Disraeli, the outstanding Jew of the nineteenth century'. Disraeli's career was rejected as an exercise in 'Oriental' megalomania: the persistent Jewish ambition 'to direct and control the destinies of Great Britain'. Steed concluded: Disraeli 'never quite lost his proneness to behave with a foreign accent; and is it not to the persistence of their "foreign accent" that the Jews, who are usually unconscious of it, owe so many of the antipathies and misapprehensions which beset their path in the countries of their adoption?'.[77] Four years earlier, M. J. Landa produced a version of Disraeli's novel *Tancred* at the Kingsway Theatre, London, which was panned by the critics. Landa believed that there was 'unmistakable evidence in some of the criticisms of resentment against Disraeli, his wit, and his uncanny prophetic instinct ... and a morbid joy in seizing upon his satire as an opportunity for the taunt that he was un-English'.[78]

Yet change was noticeable in the 1920s, as Wilfred Meynell observed in the second edition of his biography of Disraeli (1927): 'in this interval of nearly twenty-five years a change has come over the public appreciation of Disraeli'. The attacks by Steed and by critics of Landa's play were running against the tide.[79] As Lucien Wolf suggested, in his review of the final volumes of the Monypenny and Buckle biography, 'Mr [G. K.] Chesterton never ceases to wonder how "it was found possible to persuade solid rows of sturdy English squires and English merchants that a swarthy dandy with green trousers and a yellow face, named Benjamin Disraeli, was a great English patriot"'. Yet Wolf added that such views were now 'only lingering vibrations of a mean perversity which long ago spent its main force ... The conversion of Lord Morley [the biographer of Gladstone, who had recently become more sympathetic to Disraeli] is a striking token of this.' Indeed, Wolf noted, there was no better example of the 'sturdy English squire' than Buckle himself. It is significant that the Conservative *Daily Telegraph* would not publish sections of Chesterton's *The New Jerusalem* (1920) because it thought the book was antisemitic and it denied Disraeli's patriotism.[80]

Indeed, what is remarkable in the years after 1918 is how those who were hostile to what they perceived as the malevolent power of Jews were desperately anxious to exempt Disraeli from their strictures. For example, the *Morning Post*, at the forefront of Diehard Toryism, which saw the figure of 'the Jew' behind international Bolshevism, labour unrest and the decline of empire, persistently attacked what it perceived as the oriental/Jewish policy of the secretary of state for India, Edwin Montagu, whilst at the same time praising 'the "great Jew", Disraeli'.[81]

Even more extreme was the analysis of Charles Whibley in *Blackwood's Magazine*, a journal that consistently produced articles and editorials on the 'Jewish menace' after 1918. Disraeli, argued Whibley, was 'a Jew, a sojourner in a strange land, an alien who aspired to the governance of what was to him and to his race a foreign country'. He succeeded because he was a genius, a trait rarely found amongst the Jews. In fact, Disraeli was unique: 'the one single Jew in our annals who has justified the public confidence reposed in him. A Jew by blood ... he was in sympathy and temper wholly English. His patriotism, ever aflame, was the patriotism not of the Ghetto but of Great Britain.' But in every other case, Jews could not understand the word as they had no country of their own. Their loyalty was to wherever they were 'most strongly entrenched'. 'For this reason it would be well if by a common rule Jews were excluded from the privilege of government ... Wherever their influence is felt it is a sinister influence, and hidden underground.' He concluded that Britain could not be loyally governed 'until we exclude Jews from our national councils'.[82]

To many die-hard Conservatives who swallowed the myth of the Jewish world conspiracy, Disraeli was 'a Jew who had triumphed over Jewry' and who had in his writings predicted the 'Jewish Peril'.[83] To Nesta Webster, high priestess of conspiracy hunters, who believed that 'the immense problem of ... Jewish Power' was the most important 'the modern world confronted', the Jews in the arts, science and politics were rarely in the first rank. The exceptions were Heine as poet, Spinoza as philosopher and Disraeli as statesman 'but it would be difficult to prolong the list'.[84] In short, those at the respectable end of right-wing Conservatism, in circles represented by the *Morning Post*, *The Spectator* and *Blackwood's Magazine*, all of which, at least briefly, propagated the *Protocols of the Elders of Zion*, simultaneously praised Disraeli the Jew. As the *Jewish Chronicle* remarked: 'It is discouraging to note that practically the whole of this wicked [post-war antisemitic] propaganda proceeds from those who are political followers of Disraeli. It looks as if in politics, as in religion, the worshippers of the Jew can also be the haters of the Jew.'[85]

W. D. Rubinstein in his analysis of Anglo-Jewry's position in the inter-war period argues that one factor 'making for the diminution of anti-semitism in Britain in this period was the apotheosis of Disraeli'. Yet it was the antisemitism of mainstream newspapers and journals like the *Morning Post* and *The Spectator* that, in spite of their praise of Disraeli, so alarmed British Jewry. Why then were Tory die-hards so anxious to keep Disraeli within the realm of the righteous? One simplistic explanation was that by so doing they could continue to attack Jews in the Lloyd George coalition government (Herbert Samuel, Edwin Montagu and Lord Reading) without risking the charge of anti-semitism. Yet their language in denouncing the 'Asiatic' and 'unpatriotic' policies of these politicians, as well as their constant warnings about the Jewish peril, were so extreme that the desire to appear unprejudiced hardly seems to have caused them concern. Instead, as was the case for more moderate Conservatives in Britain during the 1920s, they needed not just Disraeli, but Disraeli the Jewish alien outsider, to define their own sense of Englishness.

Colin Holmes has suggested that in the marginal world of extreme British antisemitism during the 1920s, 'constant reference was made to certain intellectual sources, including the works of Disraeli'.[86] Disraeli's respectability and Jewishness no doubt gave self-assurance and respectability to those who were frequently dismissed as cranks. To them, however, Disraeli was important for having exposed the 'hidden hand' of world Jewry and was not a figure to be worshipped by 'true' Conservatives. As Nesta Webster warned in 1924: 'Conservatism, which has always stood for [the] great tradition [of preserving the country's priceless national heritage], allows itself to be hypnotized by the memory of Disraeli, and accepts his dictum that "the natural tendency of the Jews is to Conservatism".'[87] Whilst the hold of Disraeli on the

Conservative Party during the 1920s is not in doubt, it was nevertheless far from the case that Jews in general were regarded as desirable
by Conservative politicians and ideologues, both in that decade and
later.

In claiming that the memory of Disraeli acted to combat intolerance, Rubinstein argues that 'no [inter-war] study of Disraeli failed
prominently to highlight his Jewish origins'. What he fails to point
out is that such references came out of a 'semitic discourse' that almost
inevitably stressed Disraeli's alienness. Thus Arthur Bryant, in *The Spirit
of Conservatism* (1929), praised Disraeli above all others for returning
the Conservative Party 'to its true cause' and regaining for it and the
institutions for which it stood 'the affection of the nation'. Whilst
Bryant stressed that 'every Conservative must recall with thankfulness
the love of country which breathes in every page of the speeches and
writings of Burke and Disraeli', he also reminded his readers that
both of these men were 'aliens, the one an Irishman, the other a Jew'.
Disraeli had learned to love England, but it was still 'the land of his
adoption'.[88]

Andrew Roberts has exposed the full depths of Bryant's antisemitism
during the Second World War when the popular writer and broad-
caster came close to being interned by the British government for his
pro-German if not pro-Nazi sentiments.[89] Until 1939, however, Bryant
was a key figure in popular culture, through his books and radio broadcasts, in the construction of Englishness. Again, it is no accident that
Bryant chose Disraeli, the 'alien', to define what it was to be 'English'.
A cultural, more than a biological, racist, Bryant could only define the
'national character' by what it was not. In a series of popular BBC
broadcasts in 1933, Bryant outlined how modern England had been
made of a mixture of 'Celts, Saxons, Danes, Normans and the like'.
Fortunately, however, 'this alien inflow has never been too rapid, and
she [England] has never suffered as other countries have from racial
indigestion'.[90] Anthony Ludovici, who represented the 'extremes of
Englishness', was even more racially explicit than Bryant. Arguing
against immigration and warning against the dangers of 'the mixing
of blood' in *A Defence of Conservatism* (1926), Ludovici nevertheless
praised Disraeli for increasing the power of the crown as well as for
his 'deeply serious regard for the body', as seen, allegedly, in his social
reform legislation.[91]

The theme of Disraeli, the alien reviver of Conservatism, was even
more pronounced in the plethora of biographies published during
the 1920s. The completion of Monypenny and Buckle's *Life* in 1920

provided the foundation for a series of speculative accounts more concerned to explain the force behind his 'genius' than to engage in detailed research. From 1925 to 1927 six major studies of Disraeli appeared, and the Bradenham edition of his novels was launched and completed, causing one Jewish newspaper to quip that 'Mr Baldwin is Prime Minister of England, but Disraeli is Prime Minister of the bookshops'.[92]

In his 1926 biography, Edward Clarke, who had previously applied to replace Monypenny, stressed the antisemitism faced by Disraeli, the 'little Jew boy', at school, hostility that reinforced the feeling that he was 'without a country, without kindred, and without friends'. Disraeli's 'physiognomy', according to Clarke, 'was strictly Jewish'. His attachment to England was clear, but so, argued Clarke, was 'the absolute fearlessness with which he took every opportunity of asserting the claims of his race to which he belonged'. Most striking, given the total lack of evidence, was Clarke's conclusion to the biography: 'The Christian Jew in the last conscious moments of his life on earth was true to the sacred custom of his race, and in their language, made the great avowal, "Hear, O Israel, the Lord thy [sic] God, the Lord is one".'[93] The speculative character of his claim showed Clarke's desperate desire to show the otherness of Disraeli.

A year later, the French Jewish biographer and historian André Maurois also highlighted how Disraeli the schoolboy 'was made to feel that he was not like the others'. Maurois dismissed the 'commonplace amongst summary judges to explain Disraeli by saying, "He is an Oriental"'. Nevertheless, Maurois, despite acknowledging that Disraeli was 'passionately attached to England', suggested that 'he was very, very different from his friends of English blood' even though 'he was much further removed from a Jew of the East than from a man like George Bentinck'.[94] That same year, D. L. Murray, a drama critic and later editor of *The Times Literary Supplement*, whose publisher made much of his part-Jewish origins, went beyond such nuanced differentiation. Murray detected in Disraeli's political pamphlets a 'slight distortion of focus, which gives to the most national sentiments an outlandish flavour'. This was not surprising: 'he was, after all, not of English ancestry. That the conservatism the pamphlets embody is one less of institutions than of ideals is but to say that it is an expression of Hebrew genius.' After Disraeli's death, argued Murray, he began to be treasured, but before his statue 'Englishmen ruminated as before the Pavilion at Brighton or the Pagoda at Kew, wondering by what strange hap they came to be there'.[95]

Maurois stretched the 'alien' building/landscape metaphor even further, highlighting how within the Conservative Party there were 'many who still associated with his name some confused notion of Oriental mystery'. Significantly, he added that this perceived exoticism was not necessarily seen as frightening:

> Just as a beautiful Moorish doorway, brought back stone by stone by some colonist returned home, reconstructed on a trimly mown lawn, and gradually overgrown by ivy and climbing roses, will slowly acquire a grace that is altogether English and blend discreetly with the green harmony of its setting, so too the old Disraeli, laden with British virtues, British whims, British prejudices, had become a natural ornament of Parliament and Society.[96]

Maurois, for all the excesses of his purple prose, was willing to problematise the 'Orientalism' of Disraeli. Yet for other writers in the 1920s, it was his very unEnglishness that made him attractive. As the reviewer of Murray's biography argued in *The Times Literary Supplement*, the mystery of Disraeli, as well as the question of the truth of his principles, could easily be solved: 'it is coming to be seen that [the apparent contradiction in Disraeli] was not insincerity but something else, a thing of which he thought and talked all his life – race. He could not speak the plain truth like an Englishman because he was an Oriental.'[97]

E. T. Raymond took this approach to its most extreme in his *Disraeli: The Alien Patriot* (1925). Disraeli's 'mystery', argued Raymond, was one of his many stage disguises hiding the 'real man'. The 'inner truth' was Disraeli's Jewishness and, in turn, the truth of the Jew was that '[he] may become, in relation to the land of his adoption, a true patriot, but he must always remain, for a multitude of purposes, an alien'. It was, insisted Raymond, 'an injustice to his patriotism to gloss over his alienism'. This was especially so of Disraeli, a man of genius: 'his mind was that of an alien, and his heart was not that of an Englishman. He conquered England, he governed England, he even came to love England. But it was always as a foreigner that he saw England.' Anticipating late twentieth-century studies of Disraeli's identity, Raymond believed that it was in his novels that 'we find the real Disraeli'. In contrast to later work, however, Raymond saw Disraeli's Jewishness as innate and immutable and in no way as a self-construction: 'Whenever he is stirred to sincerities, we find in him the Jew.'[98]

It was, however, the distance that alienness gave him which enabled Disraeli to see so perceptively his adopted country's needs: 'He could see England with the eyes of the foreigner, or even more clearly, since he was free from the distortion of a foreigner's antipathies or idealisations.' It was Disraeli's task, as it was that of the Jewish financier Sidonia in his novels, 'to explain England to an Englishman'. But underlying all his policies, whether domestic or imperial, was the alien Jew. As one sceptical reviewer observed, Raymond was obsessed with Disraeli's 'Jewish blood' – he even explained Disraeli's absence from Balmoral by suggesting 'his race ha[d] generally avoided Scotland'.[99]

Raymond took the concept of the 'alien patriot' to its extreme. Yet unlike many of his contemporaries he was unwilling to swallow the Disraeli myth, noting that 'nothing is more ordinary than to find in Conservative speeches and writings references to the necessity of getting back to or maintaining "Disraelian principles"'. Raymond was 'baffled' by why this was the case: 'Disraeli undoubtedly had principles. But they were by no means generally deducible from his practice, and they have never been the principles of the modern Conservative Party.' Ultimately for Raymond, Disraeli's Jewishness excluded him from Conservative Party tradition, whereas to many of Raymond's contemporaries it was the very alienness of Disraeli that had allowed him to restore the party to its true path.[100]

It was, of course, ironic that the Conservative Party relished the memory of an alien at the same time that its unrelenting anti-alienism both excluded foreign Jews from entry and made it extremely difficult for those already in Britain to gain naturalisation or, indeed, to go about their everyday life without fear of deportation.[101] As was the case before 1914, the Primrose League continued to praise the patriotism of the alien Disraeli whilst simultaneously warning about the potential of 'the Alien to wreck the heritage of the British race'.[102] Clearly the man who, although 'alien by race', became 'the leader of the great Tory Party with the full acceptance of the whole people of this great country and this Empire' was a different kind of Jew from the 'alien Jews' whom the Primrose League warned were spreading revolution and crime in post-war Britain.[103]

What are we to make of this apparent inconsistency in inter-war Conservative rhetoric? Matthew Hendley, in the most detailed analysis of the anti-alienism of the Primrose League, suggests that praising Disraeli and equating him with Conservative Party leader Stanley Baldwin helped deflect 'any criticisms of intolerance': 'How could an organization named for a well-known British political figure of

Jewish heritage ever be unequivocally condemned for anti-alienism?'[104] In fact, Jewish and other opponents of Conservative antisemitism did point out the paradox. Reviewing Raymond's biography, Leopold Greenberg, whilst, as will be shown, sympathetic to the thesis of the book as a whole, was uneasy about the author calling Disraeli, and 'inferentially, all Jews in this country', alien:

> To call us alien, does not ... differentiate those of us who were born abroad from those of us who first saw the light within these realms. The general use of the term, too, would make its application to Jews appear to indicate that they are all subject to the abominable administration of the law affecting aliens by the present Home Secretary [William Joynson-Hicks] and his Ochrana-like police.[105]

The *Daily Mirror* was less gentle in its treatment of post-war Conservative antisemitism. It suggested that the 'dear old lady', Mrs Morning Post, needed a psychoanalyst so she could overcome her medieval nightmare of the Jews. Was Disraeli, asked the *Mirror*, 'a Bolshy' or, for that matter, the founder of Christianity and his disciples? It warned its reader not to ask such questions or they would 'spoil our friend's silly season'.[106]

Rather than a 'balancing process', the ambivalence shown by the Primrose League and others in the Conservative world in constructing the 'good' and the 'bad' alien reflected the complexity of creating a new identity and ideology to fit the dilemmas and challenges of the post-war world. The alien 'insider' and the alien 'outsider' provided parameters within which Englishness, a crucial strand within the rhetoric of Conservatives during the 1920s, and especially their party leader, Stanley Baldwin, could operate.[107] The potential risk of this strategy was shown by Baldwin himself, who, while identifying closely and consistently with Disraeli through good times and bad in the inter-war period, rarely or never referred to Disraeli's Jewishness explicitly.[108]

For non-Jews, especially Conservatives, after 1918 Disraeli was thus a touchstone of national as well as political identity. Partially in response, but for other reasons as well, he came to play an even more important role within the Jewish world. With the growth of political antisemitism everywhere and the challenge of assimilation in an increasingly secular and nationalistic atmosphere, the figure of Disraeli loomed large both in images presented to non-Jews and in debates within Jewish circles.

The use of Disraeli as a Jewish super-hero was not without its problems. His apostate status and belief in Christianity as the completion of Judaism made him, to say the least, suspect to many orthodox Jews. The following passage reveals the position of Revd A. A. Green, a prominent figure in British Jewish communal and religious politics:

> from every point of view, [Green] deemed it a mistake to refer to [Disraeli] as a Jew ... So far as the volition of the great statesman was concerned he was not a Jew, and never should be claimed as such by Jews ... Judaism was a religion, and a Jew was a man who professed and believed in that religion. He deplored the fact that when great men had either renounced their Judaism or, by reason of the apostasy of their predecessors, had never known what it meant nor had felt its call, their accidental Jewish origin should be raked up and the skeletons of their ancestors exhumed and rattled before them as something of which Jews ought to be proud.[109]

Yet for many Jews, especially in the tense atmosphere generated by the growth of conspiratorial antisemitism after 1918, the cult of Disraeli proved to be irresistible. With so much attention devoted to the alleged revolutionary and subversive tendencies of Jews, it was not surprising that Disraeli, whose star was so clearly in the ascendant, should be highlighted as an example of the conservative, patriotic nature of Jewish politicians. At the forefront of such tendencies in Britain was the *Jewish Guardian*, a weekly established in 1919 by communal notables to distance the community from Zionist politics and the accusation of Bolshevism.

As Stuart Cohen has suggested, the *Jewish Guardian*, which survived until 1931, did not have a particularly promising future when it was launched. It could easily have become limited 'to a series of attacks on the "chauvinistic" aspects of political Zionism or to a turgid repetition of the [anti-Zionist League of British Jews'] litanies'. Instead, as Cohen adds, 'it soon developed into a medium of Anglo-Jewish opinion which invited views from various quarters and addressed itself to a wide spectrum of subjects'.[110] Indeed, another author has quipped (in a sideswipe at the intellectual limitations of British Jewry) that it was a 'weekly paper of impressive quality. It floundered perhaps because its quality was too impressive for it to be able to attract more than a minute circulation.'[111]

Its editor was Laurie Magnus (1872–1933), a talented literary critic and journalist who cherished the memory and legacy of the Victorian age.[112] Firmly in the Conservative camp, Magnus was deeply distressed by the antisemitism of journals and newspapers with which he himself had enjoyed close relations before the war. In its first years of existence in particular, the paper reminded publications like the *Morning Post* and *The Spectator* that their 'enemies' – politicians like Edwin Montagu and Herbert Samuel – shared the same religious origins as their hero Disraeli. To object to the Jewishness of these men was 'false to Christian teaching, to British justice, and to the principles of the Conservative party'.[113] Later, in the mid-1920s, when anti-alienism was becoming an obsessive theme in Conservative rhetoric, the *Jewish Guardian* defended the potential patriotism of east European Jews: 'D'Israeli, Goschen, Herschell, Mond were foreign names and the year 1881 [when mass immigration from the east was commonly dated] did not mark a terminus in Jewish virtue.'[114] Most of all, however, the *Jewish Guardian* wished to offer an alternative to the widespread linkage of 'Marxism, Bolshevism and Judaism' and replace them with 'three equal names of one good' – 'Disraelism, Conservatism and Judaism'.[115] If, as Magnus rightly claimed, Disraeli was 'described by his Jewish characteristics in every volume of Victorian reminiscences', it was logical for the Jewish community to accept 'the cumulative evidence of history, biography and reminiscence to the essentially Jewish genius which inspired his national and Imperial policy'.[116]

The *Jewish Guardian*, whose contributors included Lucien Wolf, Sir Philip Magnus, Israel Zangwill and the young Cecil Roth, regularly celebrated Disraeli and his Jewish connections, however obscure they might be. Outside the Jewish intellectual elite, what would later be labelled 'ethnic cheerleading' in relation to Disraeli – rejecting him was like 'throwing *leonem ad Christianos*' – extended into broad sections of the Jewish world.[117]

Minerva College in Leicester was a boarding school for Jewish girls notable for its largely benevolent eccentricity, appalling food and erratic education. It aimed to 'finish off' its charges for marriage, preserving them in religious orthodoxy and protecting them from any temptations of the flesh. (Its senior teacher, Miss Whaplate, warned her girls always to carry a hat-pin to repel white slavers: 'She claimed to know a family where a girl had been innocently shopping in Selfridges, apparently a hotbed of such activity, with her mother, when she received a stab in the thigh from a syringe, only to wake up in South America'.) In this somewhat bizarre milieu, an attempt was made to mimic the ethos of the old public schools, with the girls divided into two houses: Disraeli and Rothschild.[118] One 'old girl', Caryl Brahms, later one of the leading female comic writers of her generation, got her revenge, in a skit on Victorian pomposity that poked fun at Disraeli's great moments at Berlin ('Let's sign the thing in Munich' – 'Don't, Mr Disraeli') and in winning control of the Suez Canal ('Shall we let in an Italian? ... Don't ...'). As Brahms remembers, the very thought of Minerva brought her 'out in a rash. On the rare occasions when my work takes me to Leicester, I grip my driving wheel and feel terribly sick until I'm out of it.'[119] In Gloucester and then Sussex, Mr Charles Lyon-Maris ran a similarly idiosyncratic boarding institution, Beaconsfield School, which catered 'for the sons of modern British Jewry'.[120]

Whether girls from the house of Disraeli ever married boys from Beaconsfield School is unknown, but such naming shows the esteem in which Disraeli was held by British Jews in the inter-war period. Sir Robert Waley Cohen, president of the United Synagogue, put forward Disraeli, 'remarkably imbued with the Jewish spirit', as an example to all Jews in Britain. Whilst

> [h]e did not suggest that they could all be Disraelis ... let them at least realise what their Judaism could do for England, and how, by neglect or indifference, they would be false not merely to the cause of Judaism for which their ancestors had suffered so tragically through the ages, but also to the British nation to which they belonged, and which gave them religious freedom that they might fulfil their task in their midst.

That the lay leader of mainstream orthodoxy invoked Disraeli in an address aimed at the 'Jewish duty to maintain an active virile Jewish life' whilst admonishing Jewish parents 'to see that their children were brought up with a knowledge of their wonderful history and were imbued with the ideals of their Judaism' was an indication of how easily Disraeli was readmitted into the fold. Indeed, for Waley Cohen, it was only as a result of a silly accident, 'in consequence of some stupid quarrel between his father and his congregation', that Disraeli was not brought up Jewish – a detail of no major consequence.[121] For others, such as Laurie Magnus, however, the issue was of much greater significance and the complexities of Disraeli's identity were of critical importance: 'They drive us back on to the rock bottom of first principles ... What is a Jew?'[122]

To the *Jewish Guardian* this question was 'more than a debating society point; it goes to the root of the question, which has become a very life question in these days: Do we mean by a Jew an adherant to

Judaism, or a descendant of the race, which adherance to Judaism has preserved?'[123] The advantage of discussing such issues of identity through the case study of Disraeli was that his unimpeachable reputation and status allowed him to become in effect neutral territory on which forms of Jewishness could be projected which would normally have been beyond bounds. Debates about his Jewishness could thus hide behind statements that he was 'one of those exceptional cases calling for peculiar treatment'.[124] Yet if Disraeli was 'an extreme case', the possibility of his continued attachment to Judaism, argued the *Jewish Guardian*, could not 'be dismissed as absurd'.[125] Indeed, the weekly managed to convince itself increasingly over its 12-year life that in almost all respects Disraeli should be acknowledged as a Jew.

In its first issue the *Jewish Guardian* declared that it aimed to preserve 'the root-distinction between religion and nationality so as to guard Judaism as the *differentia* of the Jew'.[126] Yet in spite of the clarity of its mission statement, in practice, the newspaper and its circle of contributors articulated a far more complex form of Jewish identity, of which its editor was representative. Described by G. K. Chesterton as a 'semi-detached Jew', no doubt because he failed to meet the antisemite's stereotypes, Magnus was in fact, as his friend Claude Montefiore remarked, 'deeply interested in Jewish affairs and Judaism'. Magnus regularly attended synagogue but his identity was in no way confined to the religious sphere or to any particular form of observance: 'As a Jew, he did not find any expression of the Jewish heart or mind alien to himself. As a Jew, his religious faith had room for kindly and even affectionate regard for all manifestations of Judaism.'[127]

Montefiore was somewhat dismissive of the wider significance of Laurie Magnus's Jewishness which, the co-founder of Liberal Judaism argued, 'was somewhat special, and peculiar to himself'.[128] Yet a different perspective emerges when the overall achievements of the *Jewish Guardian* are taken into account. Rather than becoming a stale relic of uncompromising assimilationist opposition to political Zionism, it provided a secular forum for Jews of various outlooks to write about religion, politics and most crucially culture. Jewish literature and history were prominent in its pages, forcing the *Jewish Chronicle* to take a less philistine approach to such matters in order to fend off its rival.[129] Nor were its pages of interest only to the Jewish elite. It took the side of poor alien Jews suffering from the anti-alienism of the British state and criticised the refusal of some Jewish communal bodies to support them.[130] Thus from its narrow and unpromising beginning, the *Jewish Guardian* in its relatively short history became perhaps the highest quality weekly Jewish newspaper produced in the English language during the twentieth century. Throughout its life, it returned again and again to Disraeli to probe the boundaries of Jewishness in the modern world.

As Magnus observed in 1920, Disraeli was not a promising example: 'By every test of law and religion, Benjamin Disraeli was not a Jew. He was baptized in 1817, at the early age of twelve years old, and thus became a member of the Church of England ... and he never by any indication reverted from his acceptance of the Christian faith.' Yet the matter could not rest there. Although Magnus rejected the view of Zionist 'hotheads' that 'it is "Jewishness" which counts, or at any rate, which counts first, and before Judaism', he did not want to let go of Disraeli. Initially he argued that Disraeli's Jewishness would not go away because the non-Jewish world would not let it: 'Disraeli was a non-Jew by all the evidence of the text-books; but by the evidence of Bismarck and Mr Buckle, representing history and biography, he is a Jew to the world for ever. We have to reckon with this fact, and which, therefore, can never be argued away.'[131]

In 1924, the historian Cyril Picciotto pleaded for a reassessment of Disraeli's Jewishness, suggesting that 'Disraeli occupied a definite place in Jewish history'.[132] The biographies of the mid-1920s and the increasing attention given to Disraeli's novels empowered Magnus and contributors to the *Jewish Guardian* to reclaim Disraeli, not simply as, in their words, a '*Hatikvah* [Zionist] Jew' but also as a '*Shema* [religious] Jew'. By 1927 Magnus boldly stated that 'we are content to be inconsistent in claiming Disraeli, the great exception to Victorian standards and yet the great representative of the era, as, typically, a Jew', or as one of the newspaper's contributors put it even more strikingly, as 'a Jew of the purest water'.[133]

According to this stance, in spite of his childhood conversion, Disraeli could be praised for contributing to British politics and culture, while managing to keep pride in his Jewishness. Isaac D'Israeli's decision to convert his children could be defended in a period before full emancipation and the fiction of his Jewish faith could be maintained if one accepted the fantastic death-bed scene that Sir Edward Clarke imagined.[134] Even the chief rabbi, Joseph Hertz, believed, against all evidence, that he had 'an intimate knowledge of Jewish customs and characteristics and a poetic appreciation of Jewish ceremonies'.[135] It was left to Revd A. A. Green, minister of the prestigious Hampstead Synagogue, to state categorically that in no way could Disraeli be regarded as a Jew. Anxious about the impact of assimilation – he was a leading figure in the Jewish Memorial Council, set up after 1918 to reinvigorate Jewish religious observance in Britain – Green 'thought it right to say just this in these days, when men who had no interest in the tenets and practice of Judaism, who set at nought all that it held sacred, were hailed as Jews either out of inexcusable vanity or for still more unpardonable reasons of utilitarian interests'.[136] Curiously, it was Disraeli's Englishness, rather than his Jewishness, that generated more heat amongst Jews.

The publication of E. T. Raymond's *The Alien Patriot* caused some distress amongst British Jews. Mr Alfred Emanuel wrote to *The Times* 'amazed at the title'. 'Disraeli was an Englishman born and the son of a well-known English man of letters.'[137] One Jewish commentator noted that he had 'heard Mr Raymond's book denounced as anti-Semitic, because it insists upon Disraeli having been a Jew and not an Englishman'.[138] Yet Leopold Greenberg, who 'made the *Jewish Chronicle* into a firm and influential champion of Zionism' in the 1920s,[139] saw nothing objectionable in 'styling Disraeli as an alien, because he was a Jew'. At one level Greenberg welcomed the opportunity to

> glory in the fact that it was a Jew ... who played the part he did in the affairs of this great country. What possibly could be higher praise for the Jew and his capacities? What could redound more to the credit, the honour, and the glory of our race than for the world to be told that a Jew performed the part Disraeli did in shaping the destinies of one of the greatest nations in modern times?

But more important was the message it sent out to Jews about 'the futility of deeming themselves Englishmen, Germans, Americans, Russians or what not, merely because of their residence, shorter or longer, among the people of those lands'. Raymond's study showed 'that we Jews are a people apart, because we are racially apart; our history has been different from and our destiny will not be the same as the peoples among whom we dwell'. Disraeli was a superb test case, argued Greenberg, because, in spite of his supreme cleverness, his attempt 'to assimilate himself to English and the English ... failed completely ... A donkey will not become a horse, however long he lives in a stable.'[140]

Zionists and non-Zionists alike praised Disraeli for his *Jewish* contribution to British life, whether as outsider or insider. Disraeli's Jewishness, for so long denigrated by non-Jews, was, during the 1920s, reclaimed and re-examined in the light of contemporary concerns about the nature of belonging and its potential price. Disraeli became not just a hero but also a role model for a wide range of Jews trying to make sense of their place in a world that offered no easy options between ethnic and national identity. The Zionist Henry Mond, the second Lord Melchett, believed that Zionism was compatible with a commitment to British imperialism and that it was no accident that it was 'Disraeli, the Jewish Prime Minister of England, who brought the Empire into being and laid the Imperial Crown at the foot of the throne of England'.[141] His identification with Disraeli followed a family tradition of sorts. His great-grandmother had allegedly sent his father to England from Cassel in the belief that if Disraeli could become Prime Minister, 'Ludwig too should be an Englishman'. His father, Alfred Mond, also drew inspiration from the example of Disraeli when he was attacked in politics as an alien Jew.[142]

The Mond family were hardly alone amongst Jews in their identification with Disraeli. Indeed, as before 1914, Jews, or those of part-Jewish origin, were prominent in preserving his memory. Mention has already been made of the French writer André Maurois, whose account, the first to probe Disraeli's private life, was probably the most commercially successful of Disraeli biographies in the twentieth century. Isaiah Berlin commented that the book revealed 'more about [Maurois] than about the subject' but failed to explore the importance of Disraeli to this prolific and complex individual.[143] When Maurois wrote that as a child Disraeli was 'made to feel that he was not like the others', he could have been relating his own experiences growing up as Emile Herzog in 'a staunchly patriotic home' in Alsace. As Cecil Roth noted: 'Himself a convinced assimilationist [Maurois supported the Vichy regime before fleeing to the United States], he nevertheless remained interested in problems of Jewish identity.'[144] Significantly, another assimilated Jew from the same region, Joseph Reinach, who was prominent in pre-1914 French politics, also had 'a great admiration for Benjamin Disraeli, the man whom he considered as a model for Jews participating in public life'. Not surprisingly, given Maurois' assimilationism, his analysis of Disraeli's Jewishness was far less immutable – it was a handicap but also a source of strength, something that marked him out but did not in any way hinder his attachment to England, a view also shared by Reinach.[145] Similarly D. L. Murray, who, unlike Maurois, did not hide his Jewish roots, believed that Disraeli, in spite of his 'ineradicable exoticism', was 'securely planted' in England.[146] Lastly, mention should also be made of the role of Philip Guedalla in the Disraeli revival of the 1920s and its Jewish input. Like Maurois, Guedalla was a prolific man of letters with a particular interest in Disraeli. In contrast, however, Guedalla was a leading Zionist and Jewish communal activist. Guedalla was editor of the series in which Murray's biography appeared and was responsible for the high-quality, 12-volume Bradenham edition of Disraeli's novels, which was completed in 1927. For intellectual Jews in inter-war Europe, whatever their outlook, Disraeli was a touchstone of their place in the modern world, a figure from the recent past whose success and achievements offered reassurance for the future.[147]

Even more striking and, perhaps, bizarre was Disraeli's importance to the group of immigrant Jews across the Atlantic, who, in the words of Neal Gabler, were 'inventing Hollywood'.[148] Gabler's analogy that 'like Disraeli, another Jew who felt alienated from and patronized by a class-conscious society, the Hollywood Jews would cope through "a sustained attempt to live a fiction, and to cast its spell over the minds of others"', probably would not have occurred to Isaiah Berlin, the author of the quotation within a quotation.[149] Disraeli, of course, with his Sephardi aristocratic pretensions, would have utterly failed to identify with these *nouveaux riches* Jews of east European origin even had such an imaginary meeting across time and place been possible. Nevertheless, it is clear that they, or at least two of their leading lights, Harry and Jack Warner, identified so much with his story that they used it for one of their first historical blockbuster talking pictures.

Disraeli (1929) followed on the North American success that Louis Parker's play had enjoyed before the war. There was a direct connection for the film was based on Parker's play and also starred the now veteran actor George Arliss. In fact, there were two earlier silent versions: the first scripted by Parker himself and released in 1917, and the second, drawing on the play and starring Arliss, released in 1921. As Lester Friedman suggests, 'the most popular historical Jew of the silent period is the nineteenth century's most famous politician, Benjamin Disraeli'.[150]

It has been suggested that the 1929 film's conclusion, 'that the outsider has more loyalty and love for his country than the native Englishman', gave it 'dramatic tension'.[151] Its attack on an exclusive Englishness probably accounted for its greater success in the United States than in Britain, where it was rejected as historically inaccurate.[152] But the triumph of the outsider over racial prejudice, at a time of rampant American xenophobia and antisemitism, was certainly a theme that appealed to the Warner brothers, especially the more thoughtful and sensitive Harry. In this respect, *Disraeli* was the first of a series of Warner Brothers' films about 'the contributions and victimization of Jews', including *The Life of Emile Zola* (1937).[153]

Disraeli went further, however, than simply representing the brothers' 'vague underdog liberalism' and, as the only one of their inter-war films that was explicit in revealing the Jewishness of the victim, reflected their own crisis of identity. As Gabler puts it: 'The Warners, split as they were between Harry and Jack, between obligation and aspirations, between the old and the new, between Judaism and America, were actually a kind of paradigm of the tensions of assimilation generally.'[154] Making a film about Disraeli appealed to them because of who he was and what he had achieved. But it was also important to them through the respectability it brought by buying into the 'theatrical quality' of a serious and well-received Broadway play at a time when Hollywood was being accused of low morality.[155] In many respects, however, the Warner Brothers' film marked the end of the post-1918 infatuation with Disraeli's alien patriotism. Thereafter, until well after 1945, the liberal democratic world attempted to put the genie of his Jewishness back in the bottle.

DISRAELI'S JEWISHNESS IN THE NAZI ERA

It is no accident that the Warner Brothers' other major treatment of antisemitism, *The Life of Emile Zola*, a study of the Dreyfus affair, makes only the most passing reference to the accused's Jewishness. It has been suggested that what is most revealing about the film is the 'Warner Brothers' total evasion of the anti-Semitic sentiments that motivated the Dreyfus case. Nowhere is this mentioned. Dreyfus is simply presented as an innocent victim, a wronged man. Given that the year was 1937 ... the implications are clear and avoidance questionable.'[156]

The avoidance is indeed blatant but it needs to be contextualised rather than condemned. In the late 1930s and during the Second World War, Warner Brothers, like other Jewish film companies, responded to the growth of antisemitism at home and abroad largely through the tactic of universalisation. Jewish particularity, even in the form of victim-hood, was to be avoided lest it gave ammunition to the enemies of the Jews.[157]

From the late nineteenth century, extreme antisemites, as we have seen, had distorted Disraeli's writings to 'prove' the existence of a world Jewish conspiracy. During the Nazi era, however, Disraeli increasingly appeared in their paranoid world as a key player in implementing

Jewish control. During the 1920s authors like Hilaire Belloc saw the rise of Disraeli as evidence of the increasing political power of Jews across Europe after the French revolution. Belloc, however, was an isolated voice at the time in believing that Disraeli's Jewishness disqualified him from leading Great Britain.[158] Arnold Leese, leader of the Imperial Fascist League, a tiny but virulently antisemitic organisation that prided itself on having 'absolutely no connection with the pro-Jewish so-called "Fascism" of Sir Oswald Mosley', was thus anxious to expose 'a great fraud, part of an age-long world campaign of Jewish fraud ... that Disraeli was a great man'.[159]

To Leese, 'the foul campaign for Jewish World Supremacy' had succeeded in Judaising the Nordic/Aryan mind in Britain and America, explaining why 'we British people still tolerate Democratic Politicians, the Jews in our midst – and Disraeli-boosting propaganda'. In fact, Disraeli was working for the Jews, not Britain, and was in essence an agent of the Rothschilds, 'who governed Europe'. In particular, Disraeli was responsible for deflecting the Conservatives away from their true path: he 'knew that no country can do without a true aristocracy; by instilling the Liberal Jewish Poison into the Tory Party he gave it that mortal wound which destroyed it long after his death'.[160]

Leese, a believer in Jewish ritual murder and an early advocate of extermination, can easily be regarded as a lunatic, even within the crazy world of extremist antisemitism in Britain.[161] He dismissed, for example, the Primrose League because 'it was started by a Jew', Sir Henry Drummond Wolff, whom he suspected was a Rothschild agent. In reality the founder, whose father, Joseph Wolff, was a Christian missionary, orientalist and traveller (who had converted first to Roman Catholicism and then to Protestantism but always maintained a strong sense of his Jewishness), was extremely ill at ease with both his Jewish and German origins.[162] The grandson of Sir Henry, who carried the same name, was even more self-hating and became part of the small coterie of pro-Nazi British antisemites in the late 1930s and during the Second World War. Even so, he was rejected by those, like Leese, who saw Jews everywhere: 'I always had an idea that old man Wolff, in spite of the Drummond, was a Jew.'[163]

As they numbered in the hundreds rather than in the thousands, it would seem surprising that individuals such as Leese had such a profound influence on the representation of Disraeli. Yet alongside his more popular rival fascist leader in Britain, Oswald Mosley, he raised for the British state, as well as for the organised Jewish community, the spectre of violent antisemitism, which was then sweeping the continent. From 1933 to 1945 the dominant response in Britain and the USA to organised domestic antisemitism was a policy of appeasement – nothing should be done to encourage the general population to focus on the Jews, even as victims. In both countries fear of antisemitism at home was a major reason behind restrictionist policies towards Jewish refugees during the 1930s and the failure to focus on the plight of the Jews during the war. On a popular cultural level official and self-censorship of films and plays ensured that references to Jewishness would be at best muted and at worst totally eliminated.[164]

Aside from Arnold Leese, the idea that Disraeli's career represented a Jewish takeover of Britain had few subscribers. The propaganda of the British Union of Fascists (BUF) occasionally denounced 'Jewish' influence on the Conservative Party, especially in relation to female support for the Primrose League. Nora Elam, a leading BUF activist, denounced the use women had made of their enfranchisement since 1918: 'once more [they have] allied themselves with the very Parties in the State which had treated them with such unprecedented contempt. They once again wear the primrose in memory of the Jew Disraeli.'[165] Anthony Ludovici, who had been ambivalent about Disraeli during the 1920s, writing under the pseudonym 'Cobbett' in 1938 simply portrayed him as a malign and sinister influence.[166] In the USA Father Coughlin's 'Social Justice' movement followed Leese and, closer to home, Henry Ford viewed Disraeli as a tool of the Rothschilds in their conspiracy to achieve global power.[167] But it was the historians and propagandists within the Third Reich who were most obsessed with Disraeli's Jewishness.

Disraeli had a particular significance for those scholars who willingly prostituted their talents to further the policies of the racial state. Professor Rudolf Crämer of the University of Königsberg had, as early as 1937, been keen to advance the idea of an Anglo-American plutocracy in which, of course, the Jews were a powerful force.[168] When Britain declared war on Germany in September 1939, this theme was given a powerful boost: Britain had betrayed its racial destiny and had let itself be undermined by the Jews. In the years 1940 and 1941 in particular, Nazi antisemitic propaganda melded with anti-British racism – for Goebbels, the British were 'the Jews among the Aryans'.[169] The 1940 film *Die Rothschilds* concluded with the statement: 'As this film was being completed, the last descendants of the Rothschilds fled Europe as refugees. The fight against their accomplices, the British plutocracy, continues.'[170] The film was an answer to Twentieth Century's *The House of Rothschild* (1934). *The House of Rothschild*, like *Disraeli*, starred

George Arliss as well as other members of the cast of the earlier film and similarly attacked antisemitism, ultimately showing the Jew to be the better citizen – Jewish influence is shown to be a force for the good.[171] In contrast, in *Die Rothschilds* Jewish power is subversive and self-serving.

Historians in the Third Reich such as Claus Kruger (writing under the pseudonym Peter Aldag) and Rudolf Crämer used the work of British writers on Disraeli from the 1920s such as E. T. Raymond to stress the essential alienness and also the power of the Jew. The concept of the 'alien patriot', although utilised and abused in a totally different manner, was essential to historians in the Third Reich, especially Crämer in his biography of Disraeli published in 1941, in showing how Jews had subverted English national identity by weakening its racial foundations. Jewish power could only be welded to the nation at a cost; Britain was now paying dearly for it in the war against the Nazis; the Jews and the British had become inseparable.[172] Yet even in Nazi Germany, Disraeli's Jewishness was contested. The Jewish linguistics scholar Victor Klemperer read *Tancred* in 1942 to those in hiding with him. Klemperer clearly took pride in Disraeli's Jewish roots and the reading represented an act of cultural resistance at a time of immense personal danger to the diarist and his circle.[173]

In contrast to such defiance, the response to Nazi propaganda amongst the western democracies was defensive. In Britain in the 1930s and during the Second World War, the Board of Deputies of British Jews and other Jewish organisations circulated literally millions of leaflets and booklets attempting to refute antisemitic allegations made at home and abroad. Disraeli, when he did feature, was mentioned mainly for his literary contributions – to emphasise the role of Jews in politics was to risk the allegation of Jewish power unless it was apologetically to point out that Jews supported all the mainstream parties.[174]

There were a few isolated attempts during the 1930s to utilise the example of Disraeli to show the dangers of antisemitism at home and abroad. In 1934 the writer Hector Bolitho edited a volume containing biographies of 12 prominent modern Jews, including Disraeli. It had no political significance, argued Bolitho, other than to show 'how the Jew struggles towards honourable citizenship when the laws of the country allow him his self-respect, his freedom, and equal opportunity with his Christian contemporaries'. As with the Disraeli biographies of the 1920s, Bolitho's volume was double-edged. His subjects were exceptional Jews. As for the average Jews, centuries of oppression had 'undermined the qualities in [their] character'. Indeed, on the continent, Bolitho had 'met the Jews who have incensed modern Germany'. Bolitho portrayed Disraeli as having triumphed over the hostility to his Jewishness, but still saw his attempts to identify with England as premeditated and contrived: underneath there still remained 'a semitic instinct'.[175] Elswyth Thane's play, *Young Mr Disraeli*, first produced at the Kingsway Theatre, London, in 1934, was even more explicit about the antisemitism faced by Disraeli in politics and society. Ultimately the play was a love story in which Disraeli and Mrs Lewis overcome the prejudices of her circle against 'the man you call *Jew*!'. Yet it was an isolated example during the 1930s of a cultural production in Britain that made reference to contemporaries' hostility to Disraeli's Jewishness and even then made no direct comparisons to events in Germany.[176]

Formal and informal censorship in Britain during the 1930s reduced cinematic references to prejudice and limited them to that located in the past. Gaumont British managed to get *Jew Süss* passed for release in 1934, which featured German antisemitism in the eighteenth century, because, as Jeffrey Richards argues, 'a historical setting made the message palatable'. By the latter part of the decade, films made on either side of the Atlantic that dealt with modern persecution down-played or totally ignored the Jewishness of the victims.[177] Moreover, with the outbreak of hostilities, the fear of the British government and its state apparatus that the conflict would be perceived as a 'Jews' War' led to paranoia about antisemitism on the home front. In September 1939, a senior Foreign Office official warned of giving Goebbels any 'opportunity of talking once again about the influence of international Jewry in this country'.[178] In early 1941 another Foreign Office official objected to a broadcast which referred to refugee Jews as it was wrong 'to emphasise the mainly Jewish character of our refugee population' as there was 'so much antisemitic feeling in the world'.[179] Most notori-ously later that year the Ministry of Information instructed explicitly that propaganda 'must deal with indisputably innocent people. Not with violent political opponents. And not with Jews.'[180] It is thus not surprising that *The Prime Minister*, released in March 1941, which out-lined the whole of Disraeli's career, should fail to mention once his Jewishness.

Kevin Gough-Yates has suggested that 'only in Britain could a film on the life of Benjamin Disraeli ... be made without a mention, and barely a hint, of his Jewish background'.[181] Whilst the tendency to universalise in liberal British culture has been particularly profound, it was, as we have seen, far from the case with references to Disraeli before the 1930s: the refusal to acknowledge his Jewishness relates specifically to the context of the war against the Nazis. Even then, the Jewish particularity as exemplified in the Warner Brothers' *Disraeli* had been largely abandoned across the Atlantic: such universalising was hardly specific to Britain. Indeed, *The Prime Minister*, whilst essentially a British production, was released by Warner Brothers, anxious, if nothing else, 'to fulfil their quota obligations' – the requirement that American companies make a certain number of films within Britain.[182]

Along with another American-financed film, *The Young Mr Pitt* (1942), *The Prime Minister*, it has been suggested by Sue Harper, 'displayed an extraordinary consonance with M[inistry] o[f] I[nformation] views'. She adds that they should therefore be categorised as 'official histories'. For the Ministry of Information, history 'was a priority' in 1940 and 1941. On the one hand, it was to bolster British national identity, a theme that the art historian Sir Kenneth Clark, the director of its Film Division, particularly emphasised.[183] On the other, it could be used to re-present recent history in the light of the past, particularly in the case of Pitt and Disraeli, to restore the reputation of the Conservatives, which the failure of appeasement had so tarnished – a pragmatic necessity now that Churchill was Prime Minister.

The Prime Minister was unsubtle in its historical parallels. Disraeli is the arch anti-appeaser, his success at Berlin contrasting explicitly with Chamberlain's failure at Munich, which Caryl Brahms had made blatant a few months earlier in her historical parody, *Don't, Mr Disraeli*. Nigel Mace has argued that the 'almost intangible exorcism of Munich makes it clear [in the film] that, while new spirits were being conjured, the old devil of Chamberlain was also being cast out'.[184] The boldness of this confrontation with the recent past stands in contrast to the film's silences on other contemporary matters. As the *Jewish Chronicle*, commented: 'It is ... greatly to be regretted that from the start to finish there is no mention of the Jewish origins of Disraeli and no hint that the reason for his early difficulties in being accepted in Parliamentary society were largely due to his Jewishness.'[185] It is also significant that *The Prime Minister* has subsequently been critiqued within film studies for its patriarchal nature and not for its 'colour blind' approach to Disraeli's origins.[186]

Ironically, in his memoirs, Sir John Gielgud, who played Disraeli in *The Prime Minister*, perceived it as a 'Jewish' role: 'Possibly because I have a big nose, some people think that I have Jewish blood and am perfect for Jewish parts.' The Ministry of Information was very keen for Gielgud to take the part, but because of his reputation as an actor, and not, at least consciously, because of his appearance. As Gielgud acknowledged, it was one of his least successful roles and the film as a whole, whilst treated respectfully by the press, was not a commercial success. Significantly, Gielgud's Disraeli was seen by British officials as too intellectual and therefore dangerously effeminate – if Disraeli was a latter-day Churchill, his 'manliness' should not have been questionable. Ironically, although the film eschewed mention of Disraeli's Jewishness, it inadvertently played into the discourse of the effeminate and subversive Jew against which, as George Mosse argued, the ideal of masculinity was constructed in modern western culture. Gielgud's Disraeli was much closer in his facial expressions to his Shylock, whom he had played two years earlier in an unsympathetic stage portrayal ('I tried to play him as a little monster, shabby and dirty, with a foreign accent'). If Gielgud's representation of Disraeli was Churchillian, his body language was closer to the effeminate and emasculated Jew rather than to the virile British bulldog: it now appears, in his biographer's words, as 'an embarrassing performance'.[187]

Moreover, there was one passing reference to Disraeli in the film that explicitly placed him as racially 'other'. Apart from being represented throughout the film as a 'self-made man', he is accused by Gladstone of cultivating through his premiership an 'Oriental mystery'. Through his dress and mannerisms, Gielgud's Disraeli confirms such an allegation, in spite of his obvious patriotism.[188] Thus the power of the discourse that made Disraeli 'alien' proved irresistible, even when there was a countering force to place him at the bedrock of British tradition.

The same was true at Hughenden Manor, Disraeli's country home in Buckinghamshire, which shortly before the war had been acquired by the National Trust and become part of the nation's heritage industry. Disraeli's purchase of the Hughenden estate prompted George Buckle to reflect on his identity in the third (and his first) volume of *The Life*:

> It must have been a proud moment for Disraeli when the purchase was completed, and he was lord of Hughenden. Hebrew as he was by origin, and with a deep feeling of race, he was also in a very real sense a patriotic Englishman. Indeed, it is one of the most pleasing characteristics of the Jews that, without in any way losing their distinctive nationality, the *best of them* [my italics] are able to associate themselves intimately with the peoples who treat them well.[189]

On the eve of the Second World War, *The Times* went even further in contrasting the alien outsider with the English countryside: 'It was a decidedly exotic plant that was bedded out in 1847 among the primroses of the Chiltern Hills; but the success of the acclimatization did equal credit to the adaptability of an ancient race and the nourishing riches of the English soil.' It was fitting, argued *The Times*, that Hughenden should become a monument 'both to the hospitality that England showed to a brilliant stranger, and to the response made by the child of a long Hebrew lineage in placing himself among the greatest of English patriots and public servants'.[190]

Thus, Disraeli's non-Jewish admirers, in describing his purchase of Hughenden, represented him either as one of those exceptional Jews who could 'associate themselves intimately' with the English or as simply 'a brilliant stranger'. The labours of Lucien Wolf and other Jewish scholars to stress both his rootedness in England and his positive Jewish identity had, still, by 1939, been in vain. As one disgruntled Jewish reader of *The Times* complained: 'Although Disraeli was an Englishman of the second generation on his father's side and of the fourth on his mother's', he remained at best the alien patriot.[191] The tendency to downplay Jewishness in liberal democratic culture in the 1930s and particularly during the Second World War left him with only a residue of oriental otherness. Rather than countering antisemitism in the inter-war years and the Second World War, representations of Disraeli served to emphasise what was perceived as the *undesirable* alienness of non-exceptional Jews. As George Orwell wrote at the end of the war, whilst not exempting the Left, it was those of Disraeli's own party who were particularly prone to prejudice: 'antisemitism comes more naturally to people of Conservative tendency, who suspect Jews of weakening natural morale and diluting national culture.'[192]

Various surveys were carried out in Britain between 1938 and 1951 by the social anthropological organisation Mass-Observation on attitudes towards Jews. Respondents were asked about famous Jews, but Disraeli was never referred to, unlike Einstein, Heine, Mendelsohn and others who were admired by the general population.[193] Indeed, only one respondent, in a 1946 survey, referred explicitly to Disraeli, and she was amongst the small minority who held distinctly negative views of the Jews ('a perfect nuisance wherever they go and wherever they settle'). Reflecting on what sources had influenced her attitude, she highlighted the New Testament and history books (in which she 'hated Disraeli').[194] Far more typical was the response of another female contributor to the 1946 survey: 'I think probably it boils down to this – Jews are foreigners, and distant foreigners at that.'[195] After 1918, representations of Disraeli, both before and during the Nazi era, which had attempted to portray him sympathetically not only failed to break down prejudices, but reinforced the 'otherness' of Jews. At the same time, ironically, they made it extremely difficult to confront his Jewishness head on.

1945 TO THE PRESENT: FROM ALIEN TO MULTI-CULTURAL HERO

In 1951, the Oxford Jewish historian Cecil Roth explained his purpose in writing a new biography of Disraeli: 'Its object is to sketch his personality, to indicate the Jewish element in his background, and to elucidate how far, if at all, this affected his career, his outlook and his policies.' Roth's *Benjamin Disraeli* was almost the antithesis of *The Prime Minister*. Roth, like the *Jewish Guardian*, to which he had been a contributor, concluded that there 'does not seem to be much doubt that to the end of his days he remained Jewish in sentiment'. He also followed the paper's lead in suggesting that 'if we are searching in Disraeli's political career for traces and effects of his Jewish background, it is to ... his social legislation that our attention should perhaps be directed, rather than to some vague Oriental coloratura'. It was here, argued Roth, offering a Jewish spin on the Disraeli myth, 'we find expressed that Jewish craving for social justice which is one of the heritages of the Bible, and that Jewish sympathy for the underdog which is one of the results of his history'.[196]

Roth has been described as 'the pivotal figure in Anglo-Jewish historical studies from the 1930s to the 1960s'. He was, argues David Cesarani, 'constantly engaged in writing history as communal defence. During the 1930s and 1940s he produced a stream of apologetic works demonstrating the Jewish contribution to English arts and science, politics and the economy, and the defence of the country.'[197] Roth's *Benjamin Disraeli* generally fits into this pattern although it also reflected, to a lesser extent, an engagement with the European Jewish catastrophe in the war that was at odds with his overall Whiggish approach.

Roth was anxious to continue the apologetic fight pursued by his friend and historical predecessor Lucien Wolf to highlight Disraeli's Englishness. Commenting that 'Disraeli was characterized even by some of his admirers as an "alien" patriot [and] by his detractors as an utter foreigner', Roth argued that even if three of his four grand-parents were Italians 'that did not make him a foreigner, any more than the foreign descent of Defoe, Churchill, Gibbon or for that matter George III made them any less English'; indeed, Roth added, 'it may have made them somewhat more so'. The exoticism and exhibitionism Disraeli demonstrated at the beginning of his career 'had nothing to do with his "alien" origin, and were poles removed from his father's excessive unostentation'. Similarly, in commenting on the Eastern Question, Roth was adamant that Disraeli's Jewishness was irrelevant to his policies: 'right or wrong, [it] was the traditional policy of England', and to argue that it was influenced by Jewish sympathies was 'wholly preposterous'.[198]

There was, however, a sombre note in Roth's conclusion. While emphasising the genius of Disraeli, he also expressed a sense of irreparable loss: 'The end came on April 19th: exactly a year after he had resigned office, and by a way of coincidence on a date that has been constantly fraught with disaster in Jewish history, from the storming of Cordova in 1013 to the Battle of the Warsaw Ghetto in 1943.'[199] Whereas in 1928, the *Jewish Guardian* had challenged Roth's contribution to the weekly – an unrelentingly bleak 'tale of woe' concerning the day of his death – by referring to a subsequent positive image of Disraeli, in the years after the Second World War such an optimistic reading would be hard if not impossible to sustain.[200] Indeed, Roth, whilst emphasising the 'living force' of Disraeli and the 'extra-ordinary career' of the 'Jewish boy who without forgetting his origins became Prime Minister of England', did not end solely on a note of triumphalism. He pointed out the bitter irony that the monument to Disraeli in Westminster Abbey was placed 'among the clutter of memorials which now so disfigure the glorious Church to whose con-struction ... certain thirteenth-century Jews were forced to contribute handsomely'. It might be argued that it was himself whom Roth had in mind when he suggested that Disraeli's 'Semitic features, fixed in marble, sardonically survey the unending procession of English history of which he had become part'.[201]

One reviewer accused Roth of delving into 'controversies [about the patriotism and contested Englishness of Disraeli] which raged so many years ago',[202] yet others revealed a continuity in attitudes that help to explain the defensive tradition of which his *Benjamin Disraeli* was part. With regard to the Eastern Question, Walter Hall argued in the *American Historical Review* that Roth could not, on the one hand, dismiss as 'preposterous the accusation that Disraeli's Jewish blood had anything to do with his pro-Turkish policy' and, on the other, argue that the 'same blood' gave him a unique perspective on inter-national matters. Robert Livingston Scuyler of Columbia University argued, following the biographers of the 1920s, that Disraeli 'was the most dramatic and exciting of Prime Ministers mainly because he was so un-English'.[203] But the dominant note was that Disraeli's Jewishness, contrary to Roth's analysis, did not matter at all: 'today it seems rather unconvincing, despite a decade of Nazism'.[204] To John West of the University of Southern California, Roth was simply providing 'another expression of exuberant Jewish nationalism' and evidence of 'a con-genital Jewish hope for supremacy'.[205]

For several decades after 1945, literary and historical studies of Disraeli were hindered by two discourses that typified responses to Roth's biography. The first was a liberal universalism that failed to confront either ethnic particularity or manifestations of ethno-centricism. It was heightened by an embarrassment about referring to Disraeli's racial ideology in the light of Nazism. Anticipating this problem, Roth typically was defensive, arguing that 'Disraeli's concep-tion of "race" was as unsound scientifically and historically as that of the Nazis ... [He] was among the spiritual ancestors of the Nazi brand of anti-Semitism in our own day.' Writing a decade later, Paul Bloomfield, in an otherwise perceptive overview of Disraeli's novels, referred to Disraeli's faith: 'what he [Disraeli] rather misleadingly called "race" ... By race he meant good breeding, but by Jewish race (*which is not a true category* [my italics]) he meant something more esoteric.' That Bloomfield had to qualify his reference was an indica-tion that in the early 1960s it was still common to believe that 'race' was a biological fact rather than a social construct.[206] Robert Blake, in his still standard biography, first published in 1966, was equally ill at ease when dealing with both Disraeli's Jewishness and his racial theories as propounded in his novels (which he discussed, in any case, only briefly in a book of over 700 pages). With regard to the latter, Blake reassured his 1960s audience that Disraeli's contemporaries 'would not have regarded it as the nonsense we consider it today' (it should be added that his book was published at the same time that Britain was exclud-ing New Commonwealth migrants purely on grounds of colour).[207]

The second limitation in studying Disraeli was the persistence of a 'semitic discourse' that insisted on his oriental nature. In 1947, the novelist Anthony Powell referred to Disraeli's 'Asiatic delight in luxurial description' and a few years later D. L. Hobman argued that he 'owed many traits of character to his racial descent. His awareness of it kindled his imagination; it may have caused the Oriental flamboyance which made him conspicuous in political and literary circles.' [208] Muriel Masefield's major study of Disraeli's novels, published in 1953, linked Disraeli's 'race' thinking to that of the Nazis and then queried his Englishness. Masefield suggested that *Tancred* 'expressed the inner mind of Disraeli and some of his abiding convictions'. It provided, she argued, 'the best example of the oriental culture and imagery in which Disraeli's mind was steeped'.[209] In 1939, when Hughenden Manor passed into the hands of the National Trust, *The Times* suggested that Disraeli could not resist his 'Oriental instincts', which 'kept cropping up' – as in the form of the peacocks on its terraces. Masefield played with the two images associated with Disraeli in the public's memory – peacocks and primroses – reminding her readers that when Queen Victoria sent a wreath of the latter 'To many people this seemed an incongruity; they would have expected him to prefer a more gaudy flower'.[210] Masefield believed that Disraeli's attachment to the primrose was in fact sincere, but so was his desire to have peacocks. The two 'symbolise[d] a dual nature' – Disraeli in her analysis was still the alien patriot.[211]

There were alternative voices in the 1950s and 1960s. From the Second World War, Hannah Arendt, a refugee from Nazism who had eventually found safety in the United States, developed an increasing interest in Disraeli's place as a Jew in British society. She first touched upon the theme in her essay 'The Jew as Pariah: A Hidden Tradition' (1944), in which she commented on the tendency of privileged, assimilated Jews to stress their linkage to the Hebrew prophets in their attempt to prove their descent from 'an especially exalted people'. In contrast, a smaller number, like Disraeli, 'sought to validate their people by endowing it with some extraordinary, mystic power'.[212] Arendt was particularly anxious to develop the idea of the 'conscious pariah', such as the French Jew Bernard Lazare, whom she contrasted with the parvenu Jew who simply tried to get on in the non-Jewish world. In the words of Hanna Fenichel Pitkin: 'What Arendt, following Lazare, means by becoming a conscious pariah is rejecting pariah status on principle, consciously and openly, as unjust, and opposing it actively in solidarity with others.'[213]

Arendt herself 'chose the role of "conscious pariah"',[214] but it would be misleading from this to see a direct personal identification with Disraeli. Instead, he was for her a fascinating test case of her theories of Jewish assimilation and identity at a point, as Pitkin suggests, when she was 'open[ing] up theoretical difficulties without resolving them'.

In her wartime and immediate post-war essays, 'even the distinction between pariah and conscious pariah is not yet stable in Arendt's thinking'.[215] In her classic *Origins of Totalitarianism* (1951), Arendt devoted a whole section to Disraeli in the chapter 'The Jews and Society' where she developed her concepts further. Disraeli was 'the only great man whom the elaborate self-deception of the "exception Jews" ever produced', but Arendt was repelled by his 'unbelievable naïveté', which made him articulate his fantasy of the world being Jewish. She was aware of the use later antisemites made of his Jewish conspiracies and also his 'consistency' as a race fanatic. But she also mitigated his 'pariahdom' by suggesting that 'it remains true that he was the only Jew of his kind and his century who tried as well as he knew to represent the Jewish people politically'. Moreover, 'although Benjamin Disraeli was still one of those Jews who were admitted to society because they were exceptions', Arendt argued that 'his secularized self-representation as a "chosen man of the chosen race" foreshadowed and outlined the lines along which Jewish self-interpretation was to take place'.[216]

In Arendt's account, Disraeli's Jewishness was perceived as an elaborate and a unique self-construct: 'It seems that every commonplace idea gets one chance in at least one individual to attain what used to be called historical greatness.' It is an indication of the power of the existing literature on Disraeli, however, that she drew upon sources, Jewish and non-Jewish, that provided an essentialised reading of his status as Jew, including the crude work of E. T. Raymond, *Disraeli, The Alien Patriot*. Indeed, her label for Disraeli, 'The Potent Wizard', came from an extremely racialised portrait of Disraeli drawn by Sir John Skelton in 1867.[217] In stark contrast to *The Prime Minister*, Arendt's Disraeli overstated his Jewishness and failed to confront the multi-layered nature of his identity.

Writing independently of Arendt, and a year after the publication of *Origins of Totalitarianism*, Philip Rieff, an American Jewish academic, published a similarly perceptive study in *Commentary*, which had already established itself as the major forum for Jewish intellectual debate in the United States. The Jewishness of Rieff's Disraeli was not imposed by the 'hostile consciousness of others', as Sartre had argued in, among others, a series of articles in *Commentary*, but was his own construction. His 'exaggerated Jewishness', suggested Rieff, was 'a pleasure, a revenge, a resource ... the centre of his strength'. In an approach not totally dissimilar to Arendt, but with perhaps greater nuance, Rieff concluded: 'Like many more modern Jewish intellectuals, Disraeli wrote partly to protect himself against the completest assimilation: the loss of his own consciousness as a Jew.' His sense of chosenness 'gave him the necessary aggressive mystique he needed to survive in English politics, a unique achievement for a man in his position, unrepeated in England since'. Rieff acknowledged that 'much of what England heard from Disraeli [was] outside the limits of [his] essay' but argued that his task was 'to follow the voice to its origins, that is, to Disraeli as Jew'.[218] Such a statement was extravagant, but as with Arendt, Rieff was writing against a background where Disraeli's Jewishness was either essentialised or universalised – both the refugee German Jewish and the American Jewish writer wanted it taken seriously in its own right.

In spite of the efforts of Arendt and Rieff in the early 1950s, there was little serious academic debate about Disraeli's Jewishness in North America for several decades (although he continued to appeal to popular American audiences, as in the television drama *The Invisible Mr Disraeli*).[219] Similarly, across the Atlantic, apart from Roth, there were few others in the British Jewish world who were interested in Disraeli's Jewishness and their significance should not be overstated. *The Jewish Monthly*, the journal of the Anglo-Jewish Association, was in some respects the intellectual successor to the *Jewish Guardian*. In 1952, Dennis Sandelson argued in this journal that Disraeli's 'life and thought are explicable only in terms of his essential Jewishness'.[220] Whilst not immune from the tendency to fail to problematise Disraeli's 'oriental' nature (it is far from clear, for example, whether Sandelson's analysis refers to Disraeli's self-construction), these authors helped keep alive the possibility of taking seriously Disraeli's construction of his own identity.

At a popular level, this can be seen in the novels of the Labour politician and British Jewish communal figure Maurice Edelman. Clearly identifying closely with his fellow politician-writer, Edelman wrote a series of highly successful novels, best described as romantic potboilers, beginning with *Disraeli in Love* (1972). Disraeli's love interests were a constant feature in popular portrayals of his life story: romance, it might be suggested, highlighting his perceived heroic nature. Edelman was, through endless love scenes, the first to eroticise such encounters but he was at pains also to show the power of the anti-semitic sentiment Disraeli was forced to endure in his early career.[221] Earlier, Edelman had written a more serious article on Disraeli's Jewishness in response to Robert Blake's biography. Blake, argued Edelman, had presented Disraeli as 'a man and a politician' but what was still needed (clearly ignoring Roth's work) was a biography of 'Disraeli the Jew'. 'Mr Blake touches on Disraeli's genealogy and his espousal of the cause of Jewish emancipation, but he does not examine in any detail the quality which I regard as essential in Disraeli – his Jewish affiliations and sympathies and his mould of thought.' At his best, argued Edelman, 'Disraeli was concerned with the basic and universal expressions of the Hebraic spirit – law and justice, compassion and the practice of charity, and an unquenchable faith in Divine inspiration'. Like Roth and some of the writers of the 1920s, Edelman, as a somewhat marginal British Jew, was desperately attempting to provide a Jewish twist to the Disraeli myth.[222]

Towards the late 1960s, however, a shift occurred in the study of Disraeli's Jewishness that moved it beyond the three until then dominant approaches: the essentialising tendencies of those who regarded him as the 'alien Jew', the absence of reference to his Jewishness as in Blake's biography, and the defensiveness of much British Jewish writing on the subject. Instead it moved back to the more sophisticated approach developed fleetingly by the *Jewish Guardian* circle in the 1920s and more thoroughly by Arendt and Rieff in the post-war years. Providing a far more sophisticated framework than Roth, the British-born Israeli literary scholar Harold Fisch in a 1967 essay highlighted what he termed 'the unconscious dimension of Disraeli's Jewishness', drawing together through his writings and political career, 'the imaginative *correlative* of Disraeli's public life'. What made Fisch's analysis more persuasive than his predecessors was his connection between Disraeli's 'particular Hebraic drives and compulsions' and those of John Milton and Matthew Arnold – as a result, his identity was contextualised outside a specific Jewish sphere, even if the author did not fully avoid, through his use of psychoanalytic language, the essentialising focus of those who previously had highlighted Disraeli's Jewishness.[223]

Similarly, Isaiah Berlin's presidential address to the Jewish Historical Society of England, in the same year, 1967, presented Disraeli as caught in a complex struggle for identity in which his own 'position was thoroughly ambivalent': 'The Eastern melodies were called into being in response to the need to construct a *persona*, an inner image of himself with which he could establish for himself a place in the world, and play a part in history and in society.'[224] Other Jewish scholars in the United States and Israel added to these early attempts to reveal the processes by which Disraeli constructed his identity, in particular in relation to his early novels, Daniel Schwarz, and in the field of history, Benjamin Jaffe and Todd Endelman.[225]

In 1981, Thom Braun, editor of the Penguin edition of *Sybil*, in a study of Disraeli's novels, deliberately avoided confronting his 'idiosyncratic ideas on Christianity and Judaism', which he had earlier argued, in relation to the character Sidonia's 'long speech on the Jews' seemed 'peripheral'.[226] By the end of the century, such a dismissive approach would have been unthinkable. Work stressing the importance of Disraeli's Jewishness had entered the 'mainstream' of popular and academic studies of Disraeli.[227] The last section of this essay will analyse briefly why this shift took place and what dilemmas remain in approaching Disraeli's Jewishness at the dawn of a new century and nearly 200 years after his birth.

TOWARDS A CONCLUSION?

The late twentieth century in western society has seen, on the one hand, the increasing recognition of racisms of the past, most notably in relation to the horrors of Nazism and less profoundly with regard to slavery and imperialism, and, on the other, the persistence of racism in the form of violence and discrimination experienced particularly by those of colour. Sometimes acceptance of past hostility has been used to confront contemporary problems but it has equally been a way of avoiding such linkages, especially when, as in the case of Anglo-American society, racism has, until recent years, been identified as someone else's problem, most obviously that of the Germans or continental Europe as a whole. Whilst in liberal democracies such as Britain and the United States there has been, in the last quarter of the twentieth century, the raising of the idea that such countries have their own traditions of intolerance, it is still far from widely accepted. Indeed, the prominence and success of national Holocaust museums and exhibitions in the capitals of both countries contrasts starkly with the absence of memorialisation relating to racism 'at home'. The impact and legacy of American slavery, for example, is still contested in a country that permitted institutionalised racial segregation in the South until the 1960s. Moreover, in the British case, minority groups who have raised the possibility of racism in the past have faced responses that they have exaggerated the problem or that they should keep silent in gratitude for their contemporary toleration.[228]

In the case of Disraeli, there is a consensus that he faced antisemitic hostility, especially early and late in his political career, but far less agreement about how powerful a force it was in British society as a whole during these years.[229] Greater awareness of the problems faced by Disraeli in this respect have come out of a recognition of the damage caused by different forms of racism as well as the willingness, based on increasing confidence, of Jewish scholars in Britain to highlight past prejudice without the fear of appearing disloyal. The Jewish Historical Society of England, whose leading lights from Lucien Wolf in the 1890s through to Cecil Roth in the 1960s presented a defensive portrayal of Disraeli, became an important forum, from Isaiah Berlin's 1967 lecture onwards, in which Disraeli's Jewishness could be considered more openly and critically.[230]

But it also needs to be recognised that, just as scholars during the 1920s who emphasised the idea of an 'alien patriot' in a decade of rampant anti-alienism, some of those who have in the last decade of the twentieth century identified with Disraeli and acknowledged the anti-semitism faced by him have themselves been linked to contemporary anti-alien politics. These include the historian John Vincent, part of a group of 'New Right' commentators who, it has been argued, 'have reinforced racist analysis, myths and stereotypes and undermined anti-racism',[231] and the Conservative politician Michael Portillo, who was a leading xenophobe in the Thatcher and Major years in one of the most intolerant periods of twentieth-century British politics and yet a man who has proclaimed Disraeli 'An Icon for the Tories'.[232] Moreover, there has been a tendency, even in the most sympathetic recent British biographies of Disraeli, to assume, or to at least raise the possibility, that somehow the victim was to blame for his own misfortune: 'The question is whether anti-Semitism stood in his way, or whether his character and conduct created anti-Semitism.'[233] We need to remember as the Christian scholar and activist James Parkes put it, antisemitism was created by non-Jews and was in essence a 'problem for non-Jews'.[234]

Nor is discussion of the antisemitism faced by Disraeli irrelevant to the place of Jews and others in contemporary politics in Britain and beyond. In an analysis of 'new minority ethnic groups in British politics', Harry Golbourne has argued that he takes no account of the activities of 'new white minority ethnic groups' because persons from these groups, such as Michael Portillo or Michael Howard, 'have been able to participate in national politics with little or no attention to their ethnic origins', while this is 'an option that is unavailable to individuals from nearly all African Caribbean and Asian groups'.[235] Similarly, the political writer Simon Hoggart, when confronted with a contemporary antisemitic parliamentary sketch of Disraeli from 1871, commented that he would 'doubt if any paper would publish them today'.[236] Yet in 1997 there was a widespread and hardly disguised antisemitic whispering campaign against Michael Howard (a second-generation

British Jew, whose father immigrated before the Second World War
from Rumania) and his candidature to become Conservative leader.[237]
Similarly, Michael Portillo, son of a Spanish Republican refugee, con-
fided that he knew 'he would never become Conservative leader
because of his surname'. Having attempted to deal with his origins by
suppressing them through an exaggerated sense of English nationalism
in the 1980s and most of the 1990s, Portillo 'came out' as 'half-Spanish'
at the Conservative Party conference in 2000, referring to himself as
Miguel, denouncing 'little Englandism' and no doubt attempting to
copy Disraeli's tactics in embracing his otherness rather than distancing himself from his origins.[238] The problems faced by Howard and
Portillo, certainly at the top reaches of British politics, indicate the
limitations of Golbourne's analysis – ethnic groups constructed as
'white' are still not full members of the club. One commentator, in
response to the Tory antisemitism faced by Michael Howard, pondered
'what Disraeli would have thought', to which one can only respond that
he would have been anything but surprised. Disraeli, shortly before
his death, referred to 'you English' and Paul Smith in his majesterial
overview of his life concludes that his was 'never a complete settle-
ment' in England.[239]

In contrast to the general failure to connect the prejudice faced by
Disraeli with contemporary concerns, there have been some explicit
attempts to employ him in anti-racism campaigning. In Britain, the
Commission for Racial Equality used Disraeli, alongside Oscar Wilde
(Irish), Brunel (of French parents), Olaudah Equiano (the eighteenth-
century African British writer and former slave), Prince Kumar Shri
Ranjitsinji (the Indian-born cricketer who played for England), Princess
Noor Inayat Khan (who served as a secret agent in France during the
Second World War) and an unknown black trumpeter from 1511
heralding the birth of a son to Henry VIII, in a poster campaign highlighting the contribution of and prejudices faced by ethnic minorities
in British history. The exhibition, book and posters of 'Roots of the
Future' (1996 onwards) were designed to show 'ethnic diversity in the
making of Britain'. Success, loyalty and talent are emphasised in an
attempt to fulfil the commission's mission of 'uniting Britain'.[240] In
many respects the campaign echoes the 'ethnic cheerleading' approach
of the Jewish Historical Society of England, which also celebrated
Disraeli, in its first 80 years. There are dilemmas, however: Disraeli
sits uneasily next to the black Africans whom he denigrated as coming
from an inferior and inherently backward race. Arendt rightly exempts
Disraeli from responsibility for Nazi racialism, but she was surely wrong

to say that his racist fanaticism and imperialism had no contemporary relevance: 'He was lucky enough to do his dreaming and acting in a time when ... his superstitious belief in blood and race ... carried no suspicion of possible massacres, whether in Africa, Asia or Europe proper.'[241] In light of the slavery and genocidal imperialism that took place in Disraeli's own lifetime, Arendt's perspective was both insensitive and ill-informed in the extreme. In short, there are huge dangers if Disraeli is to be used as a multi-cultural hero – a categorisation which would require a denial of the racism of the past, from which he cannot be exempted (even if it provided the one way by which he could find a place at the top in a party run by those of nobility of birth).[242]

Similarly, Disraeli's Jewishness has become vogue in the late twentieth century when identity politics, especially those relating to ethnicity, have come to the fore, matched by the growth of interdisciplinary studies in which literature and history are no longer seen as incompatible bedfellows. There is the potential now that – in absolute contrast to the essentialised construction of Disraeli's alien Jewishness that dominated responses to him throughout his career and thereafter until the Nazi era (and the Jewish apologetics that developed in reply), through to the universalisation that was in the ascendancy from the 1940s through to the 1980s – Disraeli will become a plaything of crude postmodernism where ethnicity is simply one more identity to be adopted or discarded as seen fit.

Disraeli's own and unique construction of Jewishness was not simply imposed upon him, but he would never have been able to escape the label of 'the Jew' had he desired to do so. Yet his Jewishness is perhaps now in danger of being overstated at the cost of many other features that made up this remarkable figure, returning, ironically, to the belief at the turn of the last century that, at bottom, Disraeli was, as the writer and political campaigner Wilfred Scawen Blunt put it in 1903, 'a very complete farceur ... [who never] for an instant took himself seriously as a *British* statesman ... [although] his *Semitic* politics were genuine enough'.[243]

Disraeli will undoubtedly continue to be a source of fascination and there will be many who will, in a world far removed from Victorian Britain, still identify with him. In the process, they will highlight the constantly unstable and dynamic categories of 'Jew' and 'non-Jew'. It would be naïve, however, to expect to resolve the importance of his Jewishness. Moreover, confrontations with his identity will no doubt continue to be relevant, as they were throughout the twentieth century, to contemporary ideological and political concerns – Englishness, in particular, as we have seen, has been frequently imagined and constructed in relation to the 'alien patriot' and especially with regard to who 'belongs' and on what terms. In turn, Jews from a wide spectrum have confronted their own identity through the prism of Disraeli and have been prominent in creating representations of him in a wide range of media.

David Feldman has written with regard to the 1870s: 'The critique of Disraeli and the Jews underlines both the centrality of contending conceptions of national identity in English political culture and also their pivotal significance in the politics of Jewish integration.'[244] The same can be argued in regard to the period since Disraeli's death and to many other national and global contexts. A man whose portrait can appear simultaneously on an anti-racist poster and a National Trust tea towel raises the unanswerable question posed by Disraeli himself: 'What is He?' – to which, it might be added, and who are we?[245]

NOTES

I should like to thank Todd Endelman, Nadia Valman and Greg Walker for extremely helpful comments on earlier drafts of this article. Thanks also to James Jordan for locating obscure television and film references.

1. John K. Walton, *Disraeli* (London, 1990), p. 1.
2. T. P. O'Connor, *Lord Beaconsfield: A Biography* (London, 8th edn, 1905), p. xi. Originally published by William Mullan & Son in 1879.
3. See the exhibition in the lower deck of the *Cutty Sark* in dry dock in Greenwich; Tom Harrisson, *Britain Revisited* (London, 1961), pp. 158–60.
4. John Vincent, *Disraeli* (Oxford, 1990), p. 57. The album by Cream, 'Disraeli Gears', was released in 1967. For the story behind its name see John Platt, *Disraeli Gears* (New York, 1998), pp. 90–1.
5. Walton, *Disraeli*, p. 67. See also Frank O'Gorman, *British Conservative Thought from Burke to Thatcher* (London, 1986), p. 30, and Paul Smith, *Disraeli* (Cambridge, 1996), pp. 213–20.
6. Cecil Roth, *Benjamin Disraeli: Earl of Beaconsfield* (New York, 1952), p. 173.
7. Philip Norton and Arthur Aughey, *Conservatives and Conservatism* (London, 1981), p. 78. Walton, *Disraeli*, p. 66, suggests that references to Disraeli were absent from Thatcher and her supporters but Smith, *Disraeli*, p. 214, gives counter-examples proving the flexibility and durability of the myth of Disraeli.
8. Philip Williamson, *Stanley Baldwin: Conservative Leadership and National Values* (Cambridge, 1999), p. 179.
9. The phrase is Roth's in his *Benjamin Disraeli*, p. 174.
10. Bryan Cheyette, *Constructions of 'The Jew' in English Literature and Society: Racial Representations, 1875–1945* (Cambridge, 1993).
11. O'Connor, *Lord Beaconsfield*, pp. xii–xiii.
12. O'Connor, *Lord Beaconsfield*, p. 672. The most detailed analysis of O'Connor's rhetoric against Disraeli is to be found in Michael Ragussis, *Figures of Conversion:*

        'The Jewish Question' and English National Identity (Durham, NC, 1995), pp.
        200–6.
13.   O'Connor, *Lord Beaconsfield*, pp. xvii–xviii.
14.   Robert Blake, *Disraeli* (London, 1969 (orig. 1966)), p. 761.
15.   Walter Sichel, *Disraeli: A Study in Personality and Ideas* (London, 1904), p. 320.
        For his family origins see *The Times*, 9 August 1933, and A. C. Bradley's intro-
        duction to Edith Sichel, *New and Old* (London, 1917), p. 1. More generally
        see Todd Endelman, *Radical Assimilation in English Jewish History, 1656–1945*
        (Bloomington and Indianapolis, 1990). On Brandes and other assimilated Jews
        writing about Disraeli see Abraham Gilam, 'Disraeli in Jewish Historiography',
        Midstream, Vol. 26, No. 3 (March 1980), pp. 24–5.
16.   Ibid., pp. 223, 320, 322.
17.   O'Connor, *Lord Beaconsfield*, p. 5.
18.   Wilfred Meynell, *The Man Disraeli: A Revised Edition of Benjamin Disraeli: An
        Unconventional Biography* (London, 1927 (orig. 1903)), pp. 71–2, 232–5.
19.   Harold Gorst, *The Earl of Beaconsfield* (London, 1900), pp. 225–8.
20.   Minutes of the 115th Meeting of the Rainbow Circle, 12 April 1897, in Michael
        Freeden (ed.), *Minutes of the Rainbow Circle, 1894–1924*, Camden 4th Ser., Vol.
        38 (London, 1989), pp. 160–1.
21.   On England see Frank Felsenstein, *Anti-Semitic Stereotypes: A Paradigm of Other-
        ness in English Popular Culture* (Baltimore, 1995); James Shapiro, *Shakespeare
        and the Jews* (New York, 1996); Ragussis, *Figures of Conversion*, and Don Herzog,
        Poisoning the Minds of the Lower Orders (Princeton, 1998). For America see Louise
        Mayo, *The Ambivalent Image: Nineteenth-Century America's Perception of the Jew*
        (Cranbury, NJ, 1988); David Gerber (ed.), *Anti-Semitism in American History*
        (Urbana, 1986); Michael Dobkowski, *The Tarnished Dream: the Basis of American
        Anti-Semitism* (Westport, CT, 1979); Leonard Dinnerstein, *Antisemitism in
        America* (New York, 1994).
22.   Colin Holmes, *Anti-Semitism in British Society, 1876–1939* (London, 1979);
        Dobkowski, *The Tarnished Dream*; Dinnerstein, *Antisemitism in America*.
23.   Louis Harap, *Dramatic Encounters: The Jewish Presence in Twentieth-Century
        American Drama, Poetry, and Humor and the Black–Jewish Literary Relationship*
        (New York, 1987), p. 77.
24.   George Arliss, *Up the Years from Bloomsbury: An Autobiography* (New York, 1927),
        pp. 242, 245.
25.   Louis N. Parker, *Several of My Lives* (London, 1928), p. 234.
26.   Arliss, *Up the Years*, p. 263, concludes that 'To pursue "Disraeli" through all its
        travels would be to write a guide book to the United States'.
27.   Louise Mayo, *The Ambivalent Image*, p. 106.
28.   *Jewish Chronicle*, 7 April 1916.
29.   Parker, *Several of My Lives*, p. 202; Arliss, *Up the Years*, p. 238.
30.   Harley Erdman, *Staging the Jew: The Performance of An American Ethnicity, 1860–
        1920* (New Brunswick, NJ: Rutgers, 1997), p. 145.
31.   Louis Harap, *Dramatic Encounters*, pp. 75–6.
32.   Erdman, *Staging the Jew*, p. 150.
33.   *Jewish Chronicle*, 7 April 1916; Louis N. Parker, *Disraeli: A Play* (New York, 1911),
        p. 11.
34.   The description is by Gerald Bordman, *American Theatre: A Chronicle of Comedy
        and Drama, 1869–1914* (New York, 1994), p. 693.
35.   Parker, *Disraeli*, p. 57, on Meyers and *Jewish Chronicle*, 7 April 1916, on his
        memory of Disraeli's appearance; Arliss, *Up the Years*, pp. 240–1; Patricia Erens,
        The Jew in American Cinema (Bloomington, IN, 1984), p. 158; Bordman, *American
        Theatre*, p. 694, on the lasting impact of Arliss's Disraeli.

36. Parker, *Disraeli: A Play*, pp. 104–5, 108, 114.
37. Erdman, *Staging the Jew*, p. 147.
38. *Jewish Chronicle*, 7 April 1916.
39. Parker, *Several of My Lives*, pp. 6, 25, 250.
40. Erdman, *Staging the Jew*, pp. 147, 198 n. 5. See also Bordman, *American Theatre*, p. 693, for a somewhat more hesitant acceptance of the play's Americanness.
41. Bordman, *American Theatre*, p. 694.
42. M. J. Landa, *The Jew in Drama* (London, 1926), pp. 244–5.
43. Erdman, *Staging the Jew*, p. 149.
44. Quoted in *Jewish Chronicle*, 7 April 1916.
45. Sir William Fraser, *Disraeli and His Day* (1891), p. 52, quoted by Blake, *Disraeli*, p. 487.
46. George Buckle, *The Life of Benjamin Disraeli: Earl of Beaconsfield*, Vol. 6, *1876–1881* (London, 1920), pp. 632, 633.
47. Chamberlain to Hilda, 2 July 1920, in Robert Self (ed.), *The Austen Chamberlain Diary Letters: The Correspondence of Sir Austen Chamberlain with His Sisters Hilda and Ida, 1916–1937*, Camden 5th Ser., Vol. 5 (Cambridge, 1995), p. 136.
48. Parker, *Several of My Lives*, p. 258. See also *The Times*, 5 April, 17 July 1916.
49. Editorial: 'Disraeli', *Jewish Chronicle*, 7 April 1916.
50. See David Cesarani, 'An Embattled Minority: The Jews in Britain During the First World War' in Tony Kushner and Ken Lunn (eds), *The Politics of Marginality: Race, the Radical Right and Minorities in Twentieth Century Britain* (London, 1990), pp. 61–81; Mark Levene, 'Going Against the Grain: Two Jewish Memoirs of War and Anti-War, 1914–1918', *Jewish History and Culture*, Vol. 2, No. 2 (Winter 1999), pp. 66–95, esp. 66–76.
51. Writing under the pseudonym of Mentor: 'In the Communal Armchair', *Jewish Chronicle*, 7 April 1916. More generally for the paper and Greenberg during the war see David Cesarani, *The Jewish Chronicle and Anglo-Jewry, 1841–1991* (Cambridge, 1994), pp. 114–21.
52. *Jewish Chronicle*, 7 April 1916.
53. Ibid.
54. Parker, *Several of My Lives*, pp. 250, 258; *The Times*, 5 April 1916: 'A Stage Disraeli'.
55. *The Times*, 14 April 1916.
56. *Jewish Chronicle*, 7 April 1916.
57. Landa, *The Jew in Drama*, p. 279.
58. Ibid., pp. 278–9.
59. Erdman, *Staging the Jew*, p. 149.
60. Landa, *The Jew in Drama*, pp. 244–5.
61. For the origins of The Maccabaeans, see Cesarani, *The Jewish Chronicle*, p. 90. For the interest of its members in Disraeli see MS 126/2 and 3, University of Southampton archive.
62. David Cesarani, 'Dual of Heritage or Duel of Heritages? Englishness and Jewishness in the Heritage Industry' in Tony Kushner (ed.), *The Jewish Heritage in British History: Englishness and Jewishness* (London, 1992), p. 34.
63. 'The Primrose Sphinx' in Israel Zangwill, *Dreamers of the Ghetto* (Leipzig, 1898), pp. 158–63, esp. 161. See Gilam, 'Disraeli in Jewish Historiography', p. 26, on Zangwill's interest in Disraeli.
64. Only two volumes of this series were published, but for their significance see Daniel Schwarz, *Disraeli's Fiction* (London, 1979), p. 154, n. 4, and Cecil Roth, 'Lucien Wolf 1857–1930: A Memoir' in *idem* (ed.), *Essays in Jewish History* (London, 1934), pp. 7, 29. Wolf, suggested Roth, 'always keenly regretted that he had not been chosen to write the "Official" life of the Earl of Beaconsfield'

(p. 29); Charles Richmond and Paul Smith (eds), *The Self-Fashioning of Disraeli, 1818–1851* (Cambridge, 1998).

65. Lucien Wolf, 'The Disraeli Family', *Transactions of the Jewish Historical Society of England*, Vol. 5 (1902–1905), p. 218, and also *The Times*, 20 December 1904 and following.

66. Ibid.

67. See, for example, Bernard Gainer, *The Alien Invasion: The Origin of the Aliens Act of 1905* (London, 1972), pp. 154, 163.

68. Bernard Wasserstein, *Herbert Samuel: A Political Life* (Oxford, 1992), p. 204, refers to the influence of *Tancred*, which Samuel was reading and re-reading at the time of the aliens debate.

69. Samuel in *Hansard* (HC) 4th ser., Vol. 145, col. 731, 2 May 1905. Hazlitt argued in a piece published posthumously in *The Tatler* (March 1831): 'You tear people up by the roots and trample on them like noxious weeds, and then make an outcry that they do not take root in the soil like wholesome plants.' See M. C. N. Salbstein, *The Emancipation of the Jews in Britain: The Question of the Admission of the Jews to Parliament, 1828–1860* (East Brunwick, NJ, 1982), pp. 65–6. I am grateful to Nadia Valman for drawing my attention to this connection.

70. See the *Primrose League Gazette*, 1902–1905; Matthew Hendley, 'Defending Hearth and Home? The Primrose League and the Rhetoric of Domesticated Xenophobia, 1912–1932', paper delivered to the 68th Anglo-American Conference of Historians, London, July 1999, published in revised form in *Albion*, Vol. 33, No. 2 (Summer 2001), pp. 243–69.

71. In a speech to The Maccabaeans, 'Herbert Samuel attempted the rather delicate task of apologizing to an audience of Jews for the painful task of controlling the administration of the Aliens Act which he [had] assumed. He made no attempt to disguise his dislike of the Act itself, and … did not defend its administration.' Reported in *The Tribune*, 5 March 1906.

72. Buckle, *Life of Benjamin Disraeli*, Vol. 6, p. 635. For a more sophisticated analysis of Disraeli's outsider status see Smith, *Disraeli*, pp. 221–2.

73. Buckle, *Life of Benjamin Disraeli*, Vol. 6, pp. 635, 641–2; Houston Stewart Chamberlain, *Foundations of the Nineteenth Century* (London, 1910 (orig. in German, 1899)), Vol. 1, p. 271: 'In days when so much nonsense is talked concerning this question, let Disraeli teach us that the whole significance of Judaism lies in its purity of race.'

74. Austen Chamberlain to his sister Hilda, 2 July 1920, in Self, *The Austen Chamberlain Diary Letters*, p. 136.

75. Richard Shannon, *Gladstone: Heroic Minister, 1865–1898* (London, 1999), p. 275. See also the comments in the 'Disraeli' room in Hughenden Manor.

76. Quoted by Smith, *Disraeli*, pp. 213–14.

77. Wickham Steed, 'On Jews III: The Gospel According to Marx', *Review of Reviews*, Vol. 75 (15 August–15 September 1927), p. 119; ibid., 'On Jews II: The Disraeli Tradition' (15 July–15 August 1927), pp. 17, 27.

78. Landa, *The Jew in Drama*, p. 245.

79. Meynell, *The Man Disraeli*, 'Postscript 1927', p. xi.

80. Lucien Wolf, 'The Life of Disraeli', *Jewish Guardian*, 2 July 1920. On the Chesterbelloc circle and Disraeli see Bryan Cheyette, *Constructions of 'the Jew'*, p. 203, in relation to G. K. Chesterton's *The New Jerusalem* (1920).

81. As reported in the *Jewish Guardian*, 9 January 1920, 'The Morning Post and the Jews'. See also *idem*, 16 July 1920, 'Danger!', and more generally Keith Wilson, '"The Protocols of the Elders of Zion" and "The Morning Post" 1919–1920', *Patterns of Prejudice*, Vol. 19, No. 3 (1985), pp. 5–14, and David Cesarani,

'Anti-Zionist Politics and Political Anti-Semitism in Britain 1920–24', *Patterns of Prejudice*, Vol. 23, No. 1 (1989).

82. Charles Whibley, 'Benjamin Disraeli', *Blackwood's Magazine*, Vol. 207, No. 1,258 (August 1920), pp. 236–47.

83. Ibid.; 'Disraeli on the Secret Societies and the Jews', *The Spectator*, 5 June 1920.

84. Nesta Webster, *Secret Societies and Subversive Movements* (London, 1924), pp. 369, 396.

85. Editorial: 'Anti-Jewish Attacks', *Jewish Chronicle*, 6 August 1920.

86. Colin Holmes, *Anti-Semitism in British Society, 1876–1939* (London, 1979), p. 158.

87. Webster, *Secret Societies*, p. 398.

88. Arthur Bryant, *The Spirit of Conservatism* (London, 1929), pp. 38–9, 78. Andrew Roberts, *Eminent Churchillians* (London, 1995), p. 289, does not really get to grips with what he calls the 'patronising' references to Disraeli's alien patriotism. Whilst Roberts is the first to expose fully the deep-seated antisemitism and racism of Bryant, he does not acknowledge the centrality of Disraeli in the formation of Bryant's identity.

89. Roberts, *Eminent Churchillians*, ch. 6.

90. Arthur Bryant, *The National Character* (London, 1934), pp. 6, 24.

91. Anthony Ludovici, *A Defence of Conservatism: A Further Text-Book for Tories* (London, 1926), pp. 59, 66, 188; Dan Stone, 'The Extremes of Englishness: The "Exceptional" Ideology of Anthony Ludovici', *Journal of Political Ideologies*, Vol. 4, No. 2 (1999), pp. 119–218.

92. 'The Book World', *Jewish Guardian*, 11 November 1927.

93. Sir Edward Clarke, *Benjamin Disraeli: The Romance of a Great Career, 1804–1881* (London, 1926), pp. 4, 39, 122–3, 297. Clarke, in fact, misquoted the first line of the Shema.

94. André Maurois, *Disraeli: A Picture of the Victorian Age* (London, 1942 (orig. in English, 1927)), pp. 9, 178.

95. D. L. Murray, *Disraeli* (London, 1927), pp. 70, 287. Murray was editor of *The Times Literary Supplement* from 1938 to 1944. See his obituary in *The Times*, 31 August 1962. Aside from the reference in the publicity material, little is known of his Jewish connections.

96. Maurois, *Disraeli*, pp. 251–2.

97. 'The Problem of Disraeli', *The Times Literary Supplement*, 3 March 1927.

98. E. T. Raymond, *Disraeli: The Alien Patriot* (London, 1925), pp. 2–5, 7, 9. Although such descriptions of Disraeli echo his own description of Sidonia, 'His religion walled him out from the pursuits of a citizen ... independent of creed, independent of country', Disraeli was insistent that Sidonia was 'An Englishman, and taught from his cradle to be proud of being an Englishman'. See Disraeli, *Coningsby* (London, 1989 (orig. 1844)), pp. 237, 239.

99. Ibid., pp. 48, 119; 'A Study of Disraeli', *The Times Literary Supplement*, 5 November 1925.

100. Raymond, *Disraeli*, pp. 297–8. See p. 5 for his argument that Disraeli could never be a true patriot and that the Conservative Party was in denial of this 'fact'.

101. David Cesarani, 'Anti-Alienism in England after the First World War', *Immigrants & Minorities*, Vol. 6, No. 1 (March 1987), pp. 5–29; Tony Kushner and Katharine Knox, *Refugees in an Age of Genocide: Global, National and Local Perspectives During the Twentieth Century* (London, 1999), ch. 3.

102. Dowager Countess of Jersey, 'A Call to Women', *Primrose League Gazette*, Vol. 41, No. 11 (November 1924), quoted by Matthew Hendley, 'Defending Hearth and Home? The Primrose League and the Rhetoric of Domesticated Xenophobia, 1912–1932', 68th Anglo-American Conference of Historians, London, July 1999.

103. *Primrose League Gazette*, Vol. 39, No. 5 (May 1931), quoted by Hendley (see note 102).

104. Hendley, 'Defending Hearth and Home?'.

105. 'Mentor' (Leopold Greenberg), *Jewish Chronicle*, 20 November 1925, 'The Alien Patriot'. See David Cesarani, 'Joynson-Hicks and the Radical Right in England after the First World War', in Tony Kushner and Kenneth Lunn (eds), *Traditions of Intolerance* (Manchester, 1989), pp. 118–39.

106. *Daily Mirror*, 21 July 1920, leading note.

107. Paul Rich, *Prospero's Return? Historical Essays on Race, Culture and British Society* (London, 1994), pp. 30–3.

108. See, for example, Stanley Baldwin, *On England and Other Addresses* (London, 1926), p. 205; *Jewish Chronicle*, 15 May 1936, for a recent Baldwin speech praising 'that great man'. Baldwin added, as he had so many times: 'I have tried to mould my policy, my speeches, and the policy of my party on the principles of Disraeli.'

109. Debate in Hampstead Literary Society, January 1924, reported in *Jewish Guardian*, 1 February 1924.

110. Stuart Cohen, *English Zionists and British Jews: The Communal Politics of Anglo-Jewry, 1895–1920* (Princeton, 1982), p. 309.

111. Chaim Bermant, *The Cousinhood: The Anglo-Jewish Gentry* (London, 1971), p. 278. See also Cesarani, *The Jewish Chronicle*, pp. 139–40, who deals with the relationship and rivalry between the two major Jewish weeklies during the 1920s.

112. The longest treatment of this neglected figure is by his daughter. See Ruth Sebag-Montefiore, *A Family Patchwork: Five Generations of an Anglo-Jewish Family* (London, 1987), ch. 6.

113. Editorial, *Jewish Guardian*, 9 January 1920.

114. 'A Home Office Problem', *Jewish Guardian*, 5 December 1924.

115. 'The Conservative Mind', *Jewish Guardian*, 5 September 1924.

116. 'Jews and Conservatism', *Jewish Guardian*, 7 November 1924.

117. 'Was Disraeli a Jew?', *Jewish Guardian*, 8 February 1924.

118. Zoe Josephs, *Minerva or Fried Fish in a Sponge Bag* (Warley, West Midlands, 1993), pp. 22, 69.

119. Caryl Brahms and S. J. Simon, *Don't, Mr Disraeli* (London, 1940); Josephs, *Minerva*, p. 69.

120. See, for example, the advertisement in *Jewish Year Book 1945–6* (London, 1947), p. 468.

121. 'Jews as British Citizens', presidential address by Sir Robert Waley Cohen to Birmingham Jewish Literary Association, reported in *Jewish Chronicle*, 23 October 1925.

122. 'Disraeli and Palestine', *Jewish Guardian*, 9 July 1920.

123. 'Was Disraeli a Jew?', *Jewish Guardian*, 8 February 1924.

124. Bernard Hyman, 'Was Disraeli a Jew?', *Jewish Guardian*, 22 February 1924.

125. Editorial: 'Family Affairs', *Jewish Guardian*, 1 May 1925.

126. Founding editorial, *Jewish Guardian*, 3 October 1919.

127. Anonymous obituary and additional reflections by Claude Montefiore, *Jewish Chronicle*, 5 May 1933; Sebag-Montefiore, *A Family Portrait*, p. 48.

128. *Jewish Chronicle*, 5 May 1933.

129. Cesarani, *Jewish Chronicle*, p. 140.

130. The paper was requested and supplied to a group of stranded Ukrainian Jewish trans-migrants stuck during the mid-1920s near the railway town of Eastleigh in Hampshire. See Kushner and Knox, *Refugees in an Age of Genocide*, pp. 93, 95.

131. 'Disraeli and Palestine', *Jewish Guardian*, 9 July 1920.

132. See *Jewish Guardian*, 1 February and 4 April 1924.

133. 'Disraeli Again', *Jewish Guardian*, 11 March 1927; I. M. Trachtenberg, 'Benjamin Disraeli and Other Apostates', *idem*, 25 March 1927.

134. *Jewish Guardian*, 2 July and 8 October 1926.

135. *Jewish Guardian*, 4 April 1924. See also J. Hertz, *A Book of Jewish Thoughts* (New York, 1926), p. 201.

136. *Jewish Guardian*, 1 February 1924; Alexander Rosenzweig, *The Jewish Memorial Council: A History 1919–1999* (London, 1998), pp. 34, 74.

137. *The Times*, 2 November 1925.

138. 'Mentor' in *Jewish Chronicle*, 20 November 1925.

139. Cesarani, *The Jewish Chronicle*, p. 130.

140. Mentor, 'The Alien Patriot', *Jewish Chronicle*, 20 November 1925.

141. Lord Melchett, *Thy Neighbour* (London, 1936), p. 221.

142. Hector Bolitho, 'Ludwig Mond', in *idem* (ed.), *Twelve Jews* (London, 1934), p. 159; Jean Goodman, *The Mond Legacy: A Family Saga* (London, 1982), p. 16; Hector Bolitho, *Alfred Mond: First Lord Mond* (London, 1933), p. 73, who suggests that when Mond despaired of getting on in British politics 'there was always the example of Disraeli to comfort him'.

143. Isaiah Berlin, 'Benjamin Disraeli, Karl Marx and the Search for Identity', *Transactions of the Jewish Historical Society of England*, Vol. 22 (1968–69), p. 7.

144. Maurois, *Disraeli*, p. 9; 'André Maurois' in *Encyclopedia Judaica*, Vol. 11 (Jerusalem, 1971), pp. 1134–5; André Maurois, *Mémoires* (New York, 1942).

145. Michael Marrus, *The Politics of Assimilation: A Study of the French Jewish Community at the Time of the Dreyfus Affair* (Oxford, 1971), pp. 138–41, who quotes Reinach on Disraeli: 'He never ceased in his heart to be a Jew, an Italian, and an Oriental; and there never was a more stubborn Englishman' (p. 140); Maurois, *Disraeli*, pp. 44, 178.

146. Murray, *Disraeli*, pp. 70–1.

147. *Jewish Guardian*, 9 December 1927. For a brief snapshot of Guedalla see Rubinstein, *A History of the Jews*, pp. 126, 249.

148. Neal Gabler, *An Empire of Their Own: How the Jews Invented Hollywood* (London, 1988).

149. Ibid., p. 6; Berlin, 'Benjamin Disraeli', p. 14.

150. Lester Friedman, *Hollywood's Image of the Jew* (New York, 1982), pp. 11–12.

151. Patricia Erens, *The Jew in American Cinema* (Bloomington, 1984), p. 158.

152. See the correspondence in *The Times*, 11, 12, 13, 15 and 20 March 1930; *Jewish Guardian*, 17 March 1930.

153. Gabler, *An Empire of Their Own*, p. 195.

154. Ibid., pp. 150, 195.

155. Donald Crafton, *History of the American Cinema*, Vol. 4, *The Talkies: American Cinema's Transition to Sound, 1926–1931* (New York, 1997), pp. 327, 352.

156. Erens, *The Jew in American Cinema*, pp. 161–2.

157. K. R. M. Short, 'Hollywood Fights Anti-Semitism, 1940–1945' in *idem* (ed.), *Film and Radio Propaganda in World War II* (London, 1983), pp. 149–60; Ilan Avisar, *Screening the Holocaust: Cinema's Images of the Unimaginable* (Bloomington, 1988), pp. 94–6.

158. Hilaire Belloc, *The Jews* (London, 1922), p. 47. Laurie Magnus in the *Jewish Guardian*, 31 March 1922, referred to 'the evil tendency of this vicious book' but concluded that 'Mr Belloc is not a very important person'.

159. Arnold Leese, *Disraeli the Destroyer* (London, 1934), pp. 2, 8.

160. Ibid., pp. 2, 5, 6.

161. Holmes, *Anti-Semitism*, ch. 10.

162. Paul Emden, *The Jews of Britain: A Series of Biographies* (London, 1943), pp. 351–5, for Joseph and Drummond Wolff.

163. Charles Gray, 1940, quoted by Richard Griffiths, *Patriotism Perverted: Captain Ramsay, the Right Club and British Anti-Semitism, 1939–40* (London, 1998), p. 211; Roberts, *Eminent Churchillians*, pp. 300–1, 310–11, for Drummond Wolff.

164. Tony Kushner, *The Holocaust and the Liberal Imagination: A Social and Cultural History* (Oxford, 1994), Parts I and II; Jeffrey Richards, 'The British Board of Film Censors and Content Control in the 1930s: Foreign Affairs', *Historical Journal of Film, Radio and Television*, Vol. 2, No. 1 (1982), pp. 40–2; Short, 'Hollywood Fights Anti-Semitism', pp. 146–72. For theatre, see Nicholas de Jongh, *Politics, Prudery and Perversions: The Censorship of the English Stage, 1901–1968* (London, 2000).

165. Nora Elam, 'Women and the Vote', *Action*, No. 6 (26 March 1936).

166. 'Cobbett', *Jews, and the Jews in England* (London, 1938), pp. 63, 102–3.

167. Nathan Belth, *A Promise to Keep: A Narrative of the American Encounter with Anti-Semitism* (New York, 1979), p. 136; *The International Jew*, Vol. 2, *Jewish Activities in the United States* (London, 1921), ch. 37, 'Disraeli'.

168. Max Weinreich, *Hitler's Professors: The Part of Scholarship in Germany's Crimes Against the Jewish People* (New York, 1946), p. 160.

169. Erwin Leiser, *Nazi Cinema* (London, 1968), p. 78; David Welch, *Propaganda and the German Cinema: 1933–1945* (Oxford, 1983), pp. 257–95. More generally see Gerwin Strobl, *The Germanic Isle: Nazi Perceptions of Britain* (Cambridge, 2000), esp. pp. 54–6.

170. Dorethea Hollstein, *Antisemitische Filmpropaganda: Die Darstellung des Juden in nationalsozialistischen Spielfilm* (Munich, 1971), pp. 65–76.

171. Erens, *The Jew in American Cinema*, pp. 159–61.

172. Peter Aldag, *Juden beherrschen England* (Berlin, 1940), pp. 119–30; Rudolph Crämer, *Benjamin Disraeli* (Hamburg, 1941), esp. pp. 8–9. Distorting the reality, Crämer argued that before the 1920s biographers and others in Britain had ignored Disraeli's alien-Jewishness.

173. Victor Klemperer, *Ich will Zeugnis ablegen bis zum Letzen: Tagebucher, 1942–1945* (Berlin, 1996), diary entries, 24 March 1942 (p. 52), 27 March 1942 (p. 57) and 2 April 1942 (p. 59). As a linguist, Klemperer was concerned that the copy of *Tancred* was a translation circulated by an organisation approved by the Third Reich. For Klemperer's identification with Disraeli see his diary entry, 3 October 1943 (p. 440).

174. Sidney Salomon, *The Jews of Britain* (London, 1938), p. 114 (although on p. 14 Salomon did mention Disraeli, but only to highlight Jews as loyal citizens and conservatives – a similar tactic was employed by Cecil Roth, *The Jewish Contribution to Civilisation* (London, 1938), pp. 281–2); Louis Golding, *The Jewish Problem* (Harmondsworth, 1938), p. 80; Board of Deputies of British Jews, *Speaker's Notes* (London, 1937?), p. 3.

175. Introduction in Bolitho, *Twelve Jews*, pp. 9–10; John Hayward, 'Benjamin Disraeli: Earl of Beaconsfield' in *idem*, pp. 49, 53.

176. Elswyth Thane, *Young Mr Disraeli: A Play in Three Acts* (London, 1935), pp. 43, 65, 80, 92.

177. Jeffrey Richards, 'The British Board of Film Censors and Content Control in the 1930s: Foreign Affairs', pp. 40–1; Short, 'Hollywood Fights Anti-Semitism', pp. 149–50.

178. Sargent minute, 29 September 1939, Public Record Office (PRO) FO 371/23105 C16788.

179. Latham minute, 22 January 1941, PRO FO 371/29173 W821.

180. 'Plan to Combat the Apathetic Outlook of "What Have *I* Got to Lose Even If Germany Wins"', 25 July 1941, PRO INF/251 Pt 4.

181. Kevin Gough-Yates, 'Jews and Exiles in British Cinema', *Leo Baeck Institute Yearbook*, Vol. 37 (1992), p. 540. Gough-Yates mistakenly dates 'The Prime Minister' to 1940.

182. James Chapman, *The British At War: Cinema, State and Propaganda, 1939–1945* (London, 1998), p. 236.

183. Sue Harper, *Picturing the Past: The Rise and Fall of the British Costume Film* (London, 1994), pp. 88, 79; James Chapman, 'Film and the Second World War' in Justine Ashby and Andrew Higson (eds), *British Cinema, Past and Present* (London, 2000), pp. 198–9.

184. Brahms, *Don't, Mr Disraeli*, p. 78; Nigel Mace, 'British Historical Epics in the Second World War' in Philip Taylor (ed.), *Britain and the Cinema in the Second World War* (London, 1988), pp. 116–17.

185. 'Disraeli: John Gielgud as The Prime Minister', *Jewish Chronicle*, 7 March 1941.

186. See various essays in Taylor, *Britain and the Cinema*. Only Gough-Yates, 'Jews and Exiles', p. 540, highlights the absence.

187. John Gielgud, *An Actor and His Time* (London, 1979), p. 199; Harper, *Picturing the Past*, pp. 79, 89; Jonathan Croall, *Gielgud: A Theatrical Life, 1904–2000* (London, 2000), pp. 293–4; George Mosse, *The Image of Man: The Creation of Modern Masculinity* (New York, 1996) but see the important critique by Daniel Boyarin, *Unheroic Conduct: The Rise of Heterosexuality and the Invention of the Jewish Man* (Berkeley, 1997), pp. 3–4, who argues that 'there is something correct – although severely misvalued – in the persistent European representation of the Jewish man as a sort of woman. More than just an antisemitic stereotype, the Jewish ideal male as counterly to "manliness" is an assertive historical product of Jewish culture.' See also Nadia Valman's contribution to this volume. On Shylock, gender and circumcision fears, see Shapiro, *Shakespeare and the Jews*, esp. ch. 4, 'The Pound of Flesh'.

188. 'The Prime Minister' (Warner Brothers, dir. Thorold Dickinson, 1941); Gough-Yates, 'Jews and Exiles', p. 540, gives a somewhat inaccurate description. Anthony Aldgate and Jeffrey Richards, *Britain Can Take It: The British Cinema in the Second World War* (Oxford, 1986), p. 140, comment that Disraeli 'had bested Bismarck at the Congress of Berlin and had the additional aggravation value of being Jewish' but do not acknowledge or analyse why that value was not exploited.

189. Buckle, *Life of Benjamin Disraeli*, p. 153.

190. 'Hughenden', *The Times*, 19 April 1939.

191. Unpublished essay by the Belgian Jew Alexandre Behr sent to *Jewish Chronicle*, 24 April 1939, in AJ 110/13 Folder 1, University of Southampton archive.

192. In S. Orwell and I. Angus (eds), *The Collected Essays, Journalism and Letters of George Orwell*, Vol. 3 (London, 1968), pp. 375–6. A Mass-Observation survey in 1946 added weight to Orwell's analysis, suggesting that a sample of 74 detailed responses showed 'Conservatives to be more prone to anti-Jewish feeling than Labour people'. Mass-Observation archive (M-O A), File Report 241, University of Sussex.

193. M-O A, DR 'DG', October 1940.

194. 'ER', M-O A, DR, July 1946.

195. M-O A, DR 'U', July 1946.

196. Roth, *Benjamin Disraeli*, pp. v, 67, 118–19.

197. Cesarani, 'Dual Heritage or Duel of Heritages?', p. 36. More generally see Lloyd Gartner, 'Cecil Roth, Historian of Anglo-Jewry' in Dov Noy and Issacher Ben-Ami (eds), *Studies in the Cultural Life of the Jews in England* (Jerusalem, 1975), pp. 69–86, and Geoffrey Alderman, 'The Young Cecil Roth, 1899–1924', *Transactions of the Jewish Historical Society of England*, Vol. 34 (1994–96), pp. 1–16.

198. Roth, *Benjamin Disraeli*, pp. 86–7, 145, 152.

199. Ibid., p. 170. See similarly Roth in *Jewish Guardian*, 13 April 1928.

200. 'Notes of the Week: April Nineteenth', *Jewish Guardian*, 13 April 1928.

201. Roth, *Benjamin Disraeli*, pp. 172, 174.

202. Gerhardt Neumann in *St Louis Post-Dispatch*, 4 September 1952.

203. Reviews in Cecil Roth papers, AJ 151/ADD 8, University of Southampton archive.

204. Neumann in *St Louis Post-Dispatch*, 4 September 1952.

205. In *World Affairs Interpreter* in Roth papers, AJ 151/ADD 8.

206. Roth, *Benjamin Disraeli*, p. 67; Paul Bloomfield, *Disraeli* (London, 1961), pp. 6–7.

207. Blake, *Disraeli*, pp. 3–7, 202.

208. Anthony Powell, *Novels of High Society from the Victorian Age* (London, 1947), p. vii; D. L. Hobman, 'Disraeli and the Welfare State', *The Jewish Monthly*, Vol. 5, No. 2 (May 1951), p. 81.

209. Muriel Masefield, *Peacocks and Primroses: A Survey of Disraeli's Novels* (London, 1953), pp. 225, 240–1.

210. *The Times*, 19 April 1939; Masefield, *Peacocks and Primroses*, p. 316.

211. Masefield, *Peacocks and Primroses*, p. 317.

212. Hannah Arendt, 'The Jew as Pariah: A Hidden Tradition', *Jewish Social Studies*, Vol. 6, No. 2 (April 1944), pp. 99–122, reprinted in Ron Feldman (ed.), *The Jew as Pariah: Jewish Identity and Politics in the Modern Age* (New York, 1978), p. 74.

213. Hannah Fenichel Pitkin, *The Attack of the Blob: Hannah Arendt's Concept of the Social* (Chicago, 1998), p. 64.

214. Feldman, 'Introduction' in *The Jew as Pariah*, p. 18.

215. Pitkin, *The Attack of the Blob*, p. 68.

216. Hannah Arendt, *The Origins of Totalitarianism* (London, 1967 edn), pp. 68–83, esp. 68, 70, 78, 83.

217. Ibid., pp. 68, 72.

218. Philip Rieff, 'Disraeli: The Chosen of History', *Commentary*, Vol. 13, No. 1 (January 1952), pp. 22, 26, 28, 32, 33. Sartre's *Reflexions sur la Question Juive* had been largely serialised by *Commentary* between April and July 1948.

219. 'The Invisible Mr Disraeli' (1963), part of George Schaefer's Showcase Theatre and starring Trevor Howard as Disraeli.

220. Dennis Sandelson, 'Benjamin Disraeli – Some Literary and Domestic Aspects', *The Jewish Monthly*, Vol. 6, No. 1 (April 1952), p. 13.

221. Maurice Edelman, *Disraeli in Love* (Glasgow, 1972) and subsequently reprinted in 'Book Club' versions.

222. Maurice Edelman, 'Disraeli as a Jew', *Jewish Chronicle*, 23 December 1966.

223. Harold Fisch, 'Disraeli's Hebraic Compulsions', in H. Zimmels, J. Rabbinowitz and I. Finestein (eds), *Essays Presented to Chief Rabbi Israel Brodie on the Occasion of his Seventieth Birthday* (London, 1967), pp. 81–94, esp. 81–3.

224. Berlin, 'Benjamin Disraeli', pp. 8, 11.

225. Schwarz, *Disraeli's Fiction*; Benjamin Jaffe, 'A Reassessment of Benjamin Disraeli's Jewish Aspects', *Transactions of the Jewish Historical Society of England*, Vol. 27 (1978–80), pp. 115–23; Todd Endelman, 'Disraeli's Jewishness Reconsidered', *Modern Judaism*, Vol. 5 (1985), pp. 109–23.

226. Thom Braun, *Disraeli the Novelist* (London, 1981), pp. 83, 118.

227. See comments in the introduction to this volume.

228. See Panikos Panayi, 'Anti-Immigrant Violence in Nineteenth- and Twentieth-Century Britain in *idem* (ed.), *Racial Violence in Britain in the Nineteenth and Twentieth Centuries* (London, 1996 edn), pp. 1–25.

229. Contrast Smith, *Disraeli*, p. 46, drawing on Blake, which minimises British anti-semitism, with the approach of Ragussis, *Figures of Conversion*, ch. 6.

230. Berlin, 'Benjamin Disraeli'; Jaffe, 'A Reassessment'.

231. Paul Gordon and David Rosenberg, *Daily Racism: The Press and Black People in Britain* (London, 1989), pp. 24–5. See, for example, Vincent's contributions to *The Sun*, 6 September 1984, 13 October 1985, 22 February 1986 and 28 October 1986. Smith, *Disraeli*, pp. 214–15, for caustic comment on Vincent's attempt to turn Disraeli into a proto-Thatcherite.

232. Michael Portillo, 'An Icon for the Tories', *Daily Telegraph*, 21 August 1997; Dennis Kavanagh and Anthony Seldon (eds), *The Major Effect* (Basingstoke, Hants, 1994).

233. Vincent, *Disraeli*, p. 13; Blake, *Disraeli*, p. 10.

234. Robert Everett, *Christianity without Antisemitism: James Parkes and the Jewish-Christian Encounter* (Oxford, 1993).

235. Harry Golbourne, 'The Participation of New Minority Ethnic Groups in British Politics', in Tessa Blackstone, Bhikhu Parekh and Peter Sanders (eds), *Race Relations in Britain: A Developing Agenda* (London, 1998), p. 181.

236. Simon Hoggart, 'Irascible Outbursts from the Commons' Silent Member', *Guardian*, 30 September 2000. In similar fashion, the right-wing commentator A. N. Wilson denied that the opposition to the Labour politician Peter Mandelson could have any antisemitic impetus – 'a far cry from the time of Disraeli' – in *Evening Standard*, 29 January 2001.

237. Alasdair Palmer, 'The Genteel Art of Tory Anti-Semitism', *Sunday Telegraph*, 18 May 1997.

238. See Andrew Rawnsley and Gaby Hinscliff in *Observer*, 8 October 2000, and Michael White, 'Contrite Portillo Talks of Change', *Guardian*, 4 October 2000. Portillo also 'confessed' to an earlier 'phase' of homosexuality.

239. Palmer, 'The Genteel Art'; Smith, *Disraeli*, p. 221.

240. *Roots of the Future* (London, 1996); posters available from the Commission for Racial Equality.

241. Arendt, *The Origins*, p. 75.

242. Douglas Lorimer, *Colour, Class and the Victorians: English Attitudes to the Negro in the Mid-Nineteenth Century* (London, 1978), p. 120, on Disraeli's dismissal of slavery abolitionists.

243. William Scawen Blunt, 30 September 1903, in response to reading Meynell's biography of Disraeli. See *idem*, *My Diaries: Being a Personal Narrative of Events, 1888–1914* (London, 1932 edn), pp. 485–6. See also comment on Blunt's analysis in Rieff, 'Disraeli', p. 26, and Smith, *Disraeli*, p. 3.

224. David Feldman, *Englishmen and Jews: Social Relations and Political Culture, 1840–1914* (New Haven and London, 1994), p. 120.

245. Tea towel, with Disraeli surrounded by primroses, available from the National Trust shop, Hughenden Manor; Disraeli's pamphlet *What Is He?* was published in 1833.

INDEX

Abbott, G. F. 12
Aguilar, Grace 35, 75, 77
'alien patriot' 193, 221–3, 229–30, 235, 240–3, 251
Aliens Bill (1905) 214
Aliens Restriction Act (1919) 215
Alliance Israélite Universelle 6
anti-alienism 214–15, 222–3, 225
anti-racism 249–50
antisemitism 8–9, 106–7, 129, 224; cartoons and 141 (*see also* Disraeli: cartoon portrayals of); liberalism and 176–7; in modern Britain 248–9; responses to 232–6; Victorian 10–14, 110–17, 139–41, 176–8
Arendt, Hannah 9, 14; Disraeli's Jewishness 23–4, 243–5, 249–50
Arliss, George 206–8, 231, 235
Arnold, Matthew 56

Balfour Declaration 4
Belloc, Hilaire 233
'Ben Juju' 105, 127
Berlin, Isaiah 9, 24, 246
Blake, Robert 8, 10–12, 14, 23, 242–3, 245
Board of Deputies of British Jews 176
Bolitho, Hector 235–6
Brahms, Caryl 225–6
Broad Stone of Honour, The 85–6, 87
Bryant, Arthur 219
Bryce, James 121, 130, 139
Buckle, G. E. 7–8, 210, 215–17, 219–20, 238
Bulgarian atrocities 10, 111–12, 113–14, 162

caricatures, significance of 107–8, 109, 129
Carlyle, Thomas 83–4, 85–6, 93
cartoons 137, 141, 163; significance of 107–8, 109, 129; of Rothschild family 168–70; Victorian 137; *see also* Disraeli: cartoon portrayals of
Century Magazine 1
Cheyette, Bryan 9, 56, 59, 202
chivalry 85–6, 92
Christianity, muscular 86, 92
Clarke, Edward 220
Cobbett, William 85–6
Coningsby 49, 51–4, 63–4, 67–71, 76, 89, 194

Contarini Fleming 42, 43–4, 47

Derby, Lord 13–14, 182–3, 193, 203
Digby, Kenelm Henry 85–6
Disraeli, Benjamin 1–3, 23, 201–2;
    antisemitism 10–15, 105–8, 110–11, 162–3, 172–3, 217–20, 232–5;
    as 'Zionist' 4–5, 182, 194, 214;
    assimilationists' views of 212–14, 239;
    beliefs on Judaism 43–4, 49–50, 53, 56–7, 172, 183, 193–5;
    biographical works on 7–15, 23–5, 105–9, 115–16, 203–5, 210, 215–22, 228–31, 235, 240–7;
    cartoon portrayals of 109–10, 117–37, 163, 169–70;
    dandyism 58, 76, 191;
    dramatic portrayals of 13, 14, 206–11, 216, 231–2, 236–8;
    early political career 181, 189, 191–2;
    Eastern Question and 111–16, 132, 181–5, 187–9;
    family origins 25–7;
    foreign policy and 187–93;
    'Hebraic' policies 6, 7, 116–17, 185;
    heroines 64–6;
    High Anglicanism and 186–7;
    identity construction 243–7, 250–1;
    Jewish emancipation and 6, 71, 78–82, 85–6;
    Jewish history 69–71;
    masculinity and 87–94, 238;
    mythologised 201–2, 210, 215, 223–5;
    novels 41–59, 73–5, 190–2 (*see also* writings);
    perceived as alien 203–5, 213, 219–20, 229, 238–9;
    perceived Jewishness of 7–10, 59, 105–8, 121–3, 193–5, 216, 228–32;
    portrayal as alien 203–5, 213, 219–20, 229, 238–9;
    portrayal as devil 130–3, 141;
    portrayal as Shylock 109–10, 116, 127–9, 238;
    portrayal as sorcerer 133–6;
    positive views on 216–19, 222–7, 229–31, 249–50;
    race 23–4, 92–4, 242–3;
    relations with Gladstone 132, 183;